Sustainable Innovation

The most important theme of the discourse on sustainable development and sustainability challenges concerns the relationship between innovation and sustainability. This book represents a realistic critical overview of the state of affairs of sustainable innovations, offering an accessible and comprehensive diagnostic point of reference for both the academic and practitioner worlds. In order for sustainable innovation to truly become mainstream practice in business it is necessary to find out how organizations can strategically and efficiently accommodate sustainability and innovation in such a manner that they accomplish value capturing (for firms, stakeholders, and for society), not merely creating a return on the social responsibility agenda. Addressing this challenge, the book draws together research from a range of perspectives in order to understand the potential shifts and barriers, benefits, and outcomes from all angles: inception, strategic process, and impact for companies and society. The book also delivers insights of (open) innovation in public sector organizations, which is not so much a process of invention as it is one of adoption and diffusion. It examines how the environmental pillar of the triple bottom line in private firms is often a by-product of thinking about the economic pillar, where cost reductions may be achieved through process innovation in terms of eliminating waste and reducing energy consumption. The impact of open innovation on process innovation, and sustainable process innovation in particular, is an underexplored area but is examined in this book. It also considers the role of the individual entrepreneur in bringing about sustainable innovation; entrepreneurs, their small- and medium-sized enterprises (SMEs), as well as the innovation ecosystems they build play a significant role in generating sustainable innovations where these smaller organizations are much more flexible than large organizations in targeting societal needs and challenges. The readership will incorporate PhD students and postgraduate researchers, as well as practitioners from organizational advisory fields.

Cosmina L. Voinea is assistant professor of Strategy and International Business at the Faculty of Management at the Open University of the Netherlands.

Nadine Roijakkers is full professor of Open Innovation at the Faculty of Management and general director at the Expertise Centre for Education at the Open University of the Netherlands.

Ward Ooms is assistant professor of Innovation Management at the Faculty of Management at the Open University of the Netherlands.

Routledge Studies in Innovation, Organizations and Technology

Research, Innovation and Entrepreneurship in Saudi Arabia
Vision 2030
Edited by Muhammad Khurram Khan and Muhammad Babar Khan

Developing Digital Governance
South Korea as a Global Digital Government Leader
Choong-sik Chung

Digital Business Models
Perspectives on Monetisation
Adam Jabłoński and Marek Jabłoński

Developing Capacity for Innovation in Complex Systems
Strategy, Organisation and Leadership
Christer Vindeløv-Lidzélius

How is Digitalization Affecting Agri-food?
New Business Models, Strategies and Organizational Forms
Edited by Maria Carmela Annosi and Federica Brunetta

Social Innovation of New Ventures
Achieving Social Inclusion and Sustainability in Emerging Economies and Developing Countries
Marcela Ramírez-Pasillas, Vanessa Ratten and Hans Lundberg

Sustainable Innovation
Strategy, Process and Impact
Edited by Cosmina L. Voinea, Nadine Roijakkers and Ward Ooms

For more information about this series, please visit: www.routledge.com/Routledge-Studies-in-Innovation-Organizations-and-Technology/book-series/RIOT

Sustainable Innovation
Strategy, Process and Impact

Edited by
Cosmina L. Voinea,
Nadine Roijakkers and Ward Ooms

LONDON AND NEW YORK

First published 2021
by Routledge
2 Park Square, Milton Park, Abingdon, Oxon OX14 4RN

and by Routledge
52 Vanderbilt Avenue, New York, NY 10017

Routledge is an imprint of the Taylor & Francis Group, an informa business

© 2021 selection and editorial matter, Cosmina L. Voinea, Nadine Roijakkers and Ward Ooms; individual chapters, the contributors

The right of Cosmina L. Voinea, Nadine Roijakkers and Ward Ooms to be identified as the author of the editorial material, and of the authors for their individual chapters, has been asserted in accordance with sections 77 and 78 of the Copyright, Designs and Patents Act 1988.

All rights reserved. No part of this book may be reprinted or reproduced or utilised in any form or by any electronic, mechanical, or other means, now known or hereafter invented, including photocopying and recording, or in any information storage or retrieval system, without permission in writing from the publishers.

Trademark notice: Product or corporate names may be trademarks or registered trademarks, and are used only for identification and explanation without intent to infringe.

British Library Cataloguing-in-Publication Data
A catalogue record for this book is available from the British Library

Library of Congress Cataloging-in-Publication Data
A catalog record has been requested for this book

ISBN: 978-0-367-28073-4 (hbk)
ISBN: 978-0-367-69386-2 (pbk)
ISBN: 978-0-429-29950-6 (ebk)

Typeset in Bembo
by codeMantra

Contents

List of illustrations	xv
List of contributors	xvii

EDITORIAL   1

1 Be authentic, follow through, and think holistically: Editorial thoughts on the virtuous circle that is sustainable innovation   3

1.1 *Mainstreaming sustainable innovation: A multifarious perspective 3*
1.2 *The strategy perspective 5*
1.3 *The network perspective 7*
1.4 *The process perspective 9*
1.5 *The impact perspective 11*
1.6 *Concluding editorial thoughts 15*

THEMATIC SECTION ONE
The strategy perspective   17

2 Business model innovation for sustainability: The role of stakeholder interaction and managerial cognitive change   19

2.1 *Introduction 19*
2.2 *Theoretical background 20*
    2.2.1 Core concepts of this study 20
        2.2.1.1 Sustainable business model innovation 20
        2.2.1.2 Stakeholder interaction 21
        2.2.1.3 Managerial cognition 21
    2.2.2 Identifying the research gap 22

vi *Contents*

2.3 *Research design 23*
2.3.1 Case selection 24
2.3.2 Data acquisition and analysis 24
2.4 *Findings 26*
2.4.1 A stakeholder-induced managerial cognitive change 26
2.4.1.1 NP case 27
2.4.1.2 D-Grade case 27
2.4.1.3 WeGo case 28
2.4.2 Three shaping processes 28
2.4.2.1 Market approach shaping 31
2.4.2.2 Product and/or service offering shaping 31
2.4.2.3 Credibility shaping 32
2.5 *Discussion 32*
2.5.1 The role of manager–stakeholder interaction in enabling managerial cognitive change 32
2.5.2 Three shaping processes and related types of managerial cognition 34
2.5.3 Limitations and further research 35
2.6 *Conclusions 36*

3 Sustainable innovation for the business model of nonprofit organizations

39

3.1 *Introduction 39*
3.2 *Literature review 40*
3.2.1 Sustainable business model in general 40
3.2.2 Sustainable business model of NPOs 41
3.2.3 Analyzing a sustainable NPO business model 42
3.2.4 NPO sustainable innovation and its connection to a NPO's sustainable business model 44
3.3 *Methodology 44*
3.4 *Case studies 46*
3.4.1 World Wide Fund for Nature (WWF) 46
3.4.2 Women's International League for Peace and Freedom (WILPF) 47
3.4.3 Oxfam 48
3.5 *Findings and research propositions 49*
3.6 *Conclusion 51*

4 Beyond the Business Model Canvas: Towards a framework of success factors in sustainability startups – an Austrian perspective

53

4.1 *Introduction 53*
4.2 *Literature review 54*
4.2.1 Defining sustainability 54

Contents   vii

4.2.2 Sustainability and economics 55
4.2.3 Business modelling for sustainability 56
4.2.4 Startup success and entrepreneurial cognition 57
4.3 *Methodology 58*
4.3.1 Sample of sustainability startup cases 60
4.3.1.1 Vresh 60
4.3.1.2 Brotsüchtig 60
4.3.1.3 Die Fairmittlerei 61
4.3.1.4 Blün 61
4.4 *Results – framework development 62*
4.4.1 Consciousness 62
4.4.2 Meaning 63
4.4.3 Proactive attitude 64
4.4.4 Responsibility 65
4.4.5 Pioneering role 66
4.4.6 Authenticity 67
4.4.7 Transparency 68
4.5 *Discussion 71*
4.6 *Conclusion 73*
4.6.1 Limitations and suggestions for further research 74

THEMATIC SECTION TWO
The network perspective   77

5 **Buyer-supplier collaboration for eco-innovations in a**
   circular economy: A network theory approach   79
5.1 *Introduction 79*
5.2 *Literature review 80*
5.2.1 Eco-innovations and the circular economy 80
5.2.2 Supplier collaboration for innovation 81
5.2.3 From supply chains to supply networks 82
5.2.4 Network theory 84
5.3 *Theoretical background and hypotheses development 84*
5.3.1 Power and innovation 84
5.3.2 Traditional measures of power in networks 85
5.3.3 Power in reference to others 86
5.3.4 Strong ties and incremental innovation 87
5.3.5 Weak ties and radical innovation 88
5.3.6 Innovation determined by spatial-linked
       collaboration 89
5.4 *Effect of buyer-supply network collaboration on innovation 90*
5.5 *Conclusions 91*
5.6 *Limitations 92*

viii *Contents*

6 Open innovation and sustainability: on potential roles of open innovation ecosystems for a sustainability transition

93

6.1 The role of different ecosystems in sustainability transitions 93

6.2 Sustainability transitions 95

6.3 Ecosystem types and their characteristics 97

    6.3.1 Business ecosystem 98

    6.3.2 Innovation ecosystem 98

    6.3.3 Knowledge ecosystem 100

    6.3.4 Entrepreneurial ecosystem 100

6.4 Connecting different dimensions of ecosystems 102

6.5 Focus points for investigating combined roles of ecosystem types in a sustainability transition 103

6.6 Discussion 106

7 Sustainable innovation: drivers, barriers, and actors under an open innovation lens

109

7.1 Introduction 109

7.2 Sustainable innovation and open innovation: Definitions and peculiarities 110

    7.2.1 Sustainable innovation 110

    7.2.2 Open innovation 117

7.3 Open sustainable innovation: Evidence from the literature 118

7.4 Discussion of findings and implications for theory and practice 120

THEMATIC SECTION THREE
The process perspective

123

8 The role of research centers in developing radical innovation for sustainability

125

8.1 Introduction 125

8.2 Theoretical framework 126

    8.2.1 Sustainability-oriented innovation 126

    8.2.2 The role of incremental and radical innovation in sustainability 127

    8.2.3 Knowledge needed for the development of sustainability-oriented radical innovation 129

    8.2.4 The role of collaboration for radical innovation for sustainability 130

        8.2.4.1 R&D collaboration for radical innovation for sustainability 131

        8.2.4.2 The role of research centers for sustainable radical innovation 132

Contents ix

8.2.5 Key enablers of firms seeking to develop radical
    sustainable innovation in research centers 133
    8.2.5.1 Establishing phase – steering enablers 133
    8.2.5.2 Performance phase – knowledge-transfer enablers 137
    8.2.5.3 End phase – forwarding enablers 139
8.3 Concluding remarks 140

9 Making innovation sustainable: Lessons from an internal innovation idea challenge   142

9.1 Introduction 142
9.2 Theoretical background 143
    9.2.1 Sustainable innovation using open innovation 143
    9.2.2 Strong leadership for change 144
    9.2.3 Systematic knowledge management: Idea Suggestion
    Platform 145
    9.2.4 Change Agents as facilitators 146
9.3 Research method 147
    9.3.1 Data collection 147
9.4 Case analysis 148
    9.4.1 Research setting 148
      9.4.1.1 Introduction of the case firm 148
      9.4.1.2 Reigniting innovation 149
    9.4.2 Strengthening sustainability through collective intelligence 149
      9.4.2.1 What is the bottom-up innovation program? 149
      9.4.2.2 Process of the Idea Suggestion Platform 151
    9.4.3 Why is the ISP working well? 153
      9.4.3.1 Forming a consensus of sustainable innovation 154
      9.4.3.2 Beyond the scope of the idea proposal 156
      9.4.3.3 Change Agent for ISP 156
    9.4.4 Current status of the Idea Suggestion Platform 157
      9.4.4.1 Current status 157
      9.4.4.2 From the improvement of the inconvenience to the
      opportunity of the new business 157
      9.4.4.3 Lessening the burden on innovators for sustainable innovation 158
    9.4.5 Challenges of the Idea Suggestion Platform 159
      9.4.5.1 NIH syndrome in the execution of ideas 159
      9.4.5.2 Different evaluation results among the idea reviewers 159
      9.4.5.3 Thinking about continuing ideas 160
9.5 Conclusions 160

10 Shaping sustainable innovation based on cultural values   162

10.1 Introduction 162
10.2 Organizational culture and business ideas for innovation 163
    10.2.1 GABV: Business idea and guiding principles 164
      10.2.1.1 Meaning 164

x *Contents*

        10.2.1.2 Uniqueness 165
        10.2.1.3 Values and guiding principles 166
        10.2.1.4 Positioning 167

10.3 Cultural change for sustainable innovation 168

    10.3.1 GABV: innovation based on dialogue, learning, and development 170

10.4 Leadership for sustainable innovation 173

    10.4.1 GABV: leadership and innovation 174

10.5 Managing sustainable innovational values 175

    10.5.1 Managing cultural values and innovation 175
    10.5.2 Values-based Strategy Map 177
        10.5.2.1 Strategic objective: Business development 177
        10.5.2.2 Change process and target: To attract more members to the movement 178
        10.5.2.3 Strategic objective: Profile development 178
        10.5.2.4 Change process and target: To raise visibility through advocacy and communication 179
        10.5.2.5 Strategic objective: Partnership development 179
        10.5.2.6 Change processes and target: Partnerships and the #BankingOnValues movement 179
        10.5.2.7 Strategic objective: Network and service development 180
        10.5.2.8 Change processes and targets: To help members and strengthen networking 180
        10.5.2.9 Strategic objective: Overall development 180
        10.5.2.10 Change processes and targets: Measuring impact and providing capital solutions 181
        10.5.2.11 Results 181

10.6 Conclusion 181

THEMATIC SECTION FOUR
The impact perspective   183

11 The role of sustainable innovation in building resilience   185

11.1 Sustainable innovation (SI) within the concept of climate change resilience 185

11.2 Vulnerability 186

    11.2.1 Vulnerability: A conceptual framework 186
        11.2.1.1 Reducing vulnerability in urban centers and cities 188
    11.2.2 Urban vulnerability as an impact 188
    11.2.3 Inherent urban vulnerability 190

11.3 Challenges involved in developing vulnerability indicators 192

11.4 Conclusion 193

12 Strategic or symbolic?: A descriptive analysis of the application of social impact measurement in Dutch charity organizations 195

12.1 Introduction 195

12.2 Measuring impact 196

  12.2.1 Defining impact 196

    12.2.1.1 Long-term results and logic models 197

    12.2.1.2 Evaluation 198

  12.2.2 Learning and accountability 199

    12.2.2.1 Organizational learning 200

    12.2.2.2 Accountability 201

    12.2.2.3 Institutional pressure 202

  12.2.3 A typology on the application of social impact measurement 203

    12.2.3.1 Type 1: Symbolic logic model 203

    12.2.3.2 Type 2: Coherent logic model 204

    12.2.3.3 Type 3: Learning organization 204

12.3 Data 204

  12.3.1 Survey 204

  12.3.2 Sample 205

12.4 Results 207

  12.4.1 Main findings 207

  12.4.2 Typology per size and sector 209

  12.4.3 Evaluation and impact practices 209

12.5 Conclusion 211

13 Impact of sustainable innovation on organizational performance 213

13.1 Introduction 213

13.2 Defining sustainable innovation 215

  13.2.1 Innovation compass and innovation spaces 215

  13.2.2 Incremental and radical innovation 216

  13.2.3 Proposed definition of sustainable innovation 217

13.3 Sustainability performance construct 218

  13.3.1 Context 219

  13.3.2 Values 220

  13.3.3 Organizational culture 220

  13.3.4 Strategies 220

  13.3.5 Business models 221

13.4 Sustainable innovation analysis framework 222

  13.4.1 Single value creation–regime-oriented strategies 224

  13.4.2 Single value creation–transition-oriented strategies 225

xii *Contents*

13.4.3 Multiple value creation–transition-oriented strategies 225
13.4.4 Multiple value creation–regime-oriented strategies 225
13.4.5 Business model innovation 226

13.5 Conclusion 227

14 Sustainable innovation and intellectual property rights: friends, foes or perfect strangers?   229

14.1 Introduction 229
14.2 Sustainable innovation and IPRs: What are the options? 231
14.2.1 Archetypes of sustainable innovation 231
14.2.2 IPRs applicable to sustainable innovation 232
14.3 Motives (not) to file IPRs for sustainable innovation 234
14.3.1 Patents 234
14.3.2 Trademarks 234
14.3.3 Design rights 235
14.4 Conclusions: Towards a research agenda on IPRs for sustainable innovation 236

15 Challenges in measuring sustainable innovations performance: Perspectives from the agriculture plantations industry   239

15.1 Introduction 239
15.2 Sustainable innovations 241
15.3 Sustainable innovation performance and measurement 242
15.4 Sustainable innovations in the plantation agriculture sector 244
15.4.1 Tea industry in Sri Lanka 244
15.4.2 Strip-spreading of tea bushes (SSTB) 245
15.4.3 Herbicide-free integrated weed management (HFIWM) 245
15.5 Challenges in the measurement of sustainable innovations 247
15.5.1 Determination of the dimension of sustainability performance to be measured 248
15.5.2 Measurement of the sustainability performance under different dimensions 249
15.5.3 Establishment of accurate measurement methods which are easy to communicate 249
15.5.4 Determination of the system boundary for the measurement of sustainability performance 249
15.5.5 Determination of the time horizon for the measurement of sustainability performance 250
15.5.6 Variability in the sustainability performance on the nature of the biological assets 250

Contents xiii

15.5.7 Variability of the sustainability performance on the innovation process 251

15.5.8 Variability of the sustainability performance on uncontrollable factors 251

15.6 Possible solutions 251

15.6.1 Determination of the dimension of sustainability performance to be measured and measurement of the sustainability performance under different dimensions 252

15.6.2 Establishment of accurate measurement methods which are easy to communicate 252

15.6.3 Determination of the system boundary for the measurement of sustainability performance 252

15.6.4 Determination of the time horizon for the measurement of sustainability performance 253

15.6.5 Variability in the sustainability performance based on the nature of the biological assets 253

15.6.6 Variability of the sustainability performance on the innovation process 253

15.6.7 Variability of the sustainability performance on the uncontrollable factors 253

15.7 Conclusions 254

References	257
Index	295

Illustrations

Figures

1.1	A holistic perspective on sustainable innovation: Strategy, network, process, and impact	15
3.1	NPO business model framework for NPOs with multiple income streams (Sanderse et al., 2020)	43
4.1	Beyond the Business Model Canvas – proposed framework of soft success factors in sustainability startups (the author, 2019)	72
5.1	The supply network from the perspective of the focal firm (Kemppainen & Vepsäläinen 2003)	83
5.2	Representation of weak ties between nodes A and B	88
5.3	Conceptual model for studying eco-innovation outputs	91
7.1	The OSI framework (author, 2020)	121
8.1	Firm enablers for managing radical innovation for sustainability in research centers (authors, 2020)	134
9.1	Services and solutions of firm A (authors, 2020)	150
9.2	The four-step process of the ISP (authors, 2020)	151
10.1	Business idea for innovation (Boonstra, 2019)	164
10.2	Business idea GABV (GABV, 2019c)	165
10.3	GABV cultural values and principles (GABV, 2019c)	166
10.4	Approaches to cultural change in organizations (Boonstra, 2019)	169
10.5	Choosing and combining change strategies (authors, 2020)	171
10.6	Perspectives on leadership (Boonstra, 2013)	173
10.7	GABV's managing sustainable innovational values (GABV, 2019c)	176
10.8	GABV's values-based Strategy Map (GABV, 2019c)	178
11.1	Climate *vulnerability* (IPCC, 2014)	187
11.2	Lineages of urban innovation in vulnerability research	189
11.3	Vulnerability	190
11.4	Social safety nets	191
12.1	Steps in the logic model or results chain	197

xvi *Illustrations*

12.2	Number of charities per type	207
13.1	Incremental versus radical innovation (Bessant, 2018)	216
13.2	Sustainability performance construct (Dommerholt, 2019)	219
13.3	The sustainable innovation analysis framework (SIAF) (Dommerholt, 2019)	223

Tables

1.1	Summary of chapters in the *strategy* section	6
1.2	Summary of chapters in the *network* section	8
1.3	Summary of chapters in the *process* section	10
1.4	Summary of chapters in the *impact* section	12
2.1	Description of cases and changes in the value proposition	24
2.2	Overview of interviewees and archival data sources	26
2.3	Three shaping processes and its stakeholder-integrating activities	29
3.1	Comparing perspectives on sustainability	41
5.1	Types of innovation required across the circular value chain	81
6.1	Relation between ecosystem types and network collaborations	102
7.1	Definitions of sustainable innovation	112
7.2	The two-level taxonomy of sustainable innovation	115
8.1	Distinction between incremental and radical innovation	128
9.1	Interview participants	147
9.2	The case firm overview	148
10.1	GABV communities of practice	172
12.1	Number of responding charities, categorized by industry and size	206
12.2	Indicators used for typology	208
12.3	Impact types per sector	208
12.4	Impact type per size (budget per year)	210
12.5	Evaluation practices per typology	210
14.1	Archetypes of sustainable innovation and applicable IPRs	233
14.2	Motives for (sustainable) innovators to apply or not to apply for the patents, trademarks, and design rights	236
15.1	Challenges in measuring sustainable innovation performance (Gunarathne, 2019)	243
15.2	An overview of the two sustainable innovations in the tea industry	246
15.3	Contribution of the sustainable innovations to SDGs	247
15.4	Sustainable innovation performance measurement challenges and possible solutions	254

Contributors

Joon Mo Ahn Graduate School of Management of Technology, Sogang University, Seoul, South Korea

John Bessant University of Exeter, United Kingdom

Barbara Bigliardi Universita di Parma, Parma, Italy

Jaap Boonstra Esade Business School, Barcelona, Spain

Bart Bossink Science Business and Innovation, Faculty of Science, VU Amsterdam, the Netherlands

João Brillo Ibmec Business School, Rio de Janeiro, Brazil

Carolina Castaldi Department of Human Geography and Planning, Utrecht University

Dieudonnee Cobben Faculty of Management, Open University of the Netherlands, the Netherlands

Frank de Langen Faculty of Management, Open University of the Netherlands, the Netherlands

Ard-Pieter de Man School of Business and Economics & Amsterdam Business Research Institute, VU Amsterdam, the Netherlands

Egbert Dommerholt International Business School of the Hanze University of Applied Sciences, Groningen, the Netherlands

Serena Filippelli Universita di Parma, Parma, Italy

Maria A. Franco Department of Engineering and Information Technology, Bern University of Applied Sciences Biel, Switzerland

Francesco Galati Universita di Parma, Parma, Italy

AD Nuwan Gunarathne University of Sri Jayewardenepura, Sri Lanka and Griffith University, Australia

xviii *Contributors*

Frank Hubers Faculty of Management, Open University of the Netherlands, the Netherlands

Matthew Kensen World Maritime University, Malmö, Sweden

Jong Rak Kim Graduate School of Management of Technology, Sogang University, Seoul, South Korea

Dries Maes Economics, Science and Innovation, Flanders Government, Belgium

Ward Ooms Faculty of Management, Open University of the Netherlands, the Netherlands

Inge Oskam Circular Design and Entrepreneurship, Amsterdam University of Applied Sciences, the Netherlands

Dan F. Orcherton CCADIMO (Corp, Inc.). (Climate Change Adaptation, Mitigation and International Development, Corp. Inc.) Prince George, B.C-Canada.

Mahendra Peiris Postgraduate Institute of Agriculture, University of Peradeniya, Sri Lanka and Maskeliya Plantations PLC, Sri Lanka

Francisca Perez Salgado Faculty of Management, Open University of the Netherlands, the Netherlands

Carly Relou Erasmus University, Rotterdam, the Netherlands

Nadine Roijakkers Faculty of Management, Open University of the Netherlands, the Netherlands

Judith Sanderse Faculty of Management, Open University of the Netherlands, the Netherlands

Mariusz Soltanifar International Business School of the Hanze University of Applied Sciences, Groningen, and the Open University, the Netherlands

Marianne Steinmo Nord University Business School, Mo i Rana, Norway

Cosmina L. Voinea Faculty of Management, Open University of the Netherlands, the Netherlands

Lisa Winkler De | Re | Sa, Design Research Salzburg, at Salzburg University of Applied Sciences, Austria

Editorial

1 Be authentic, follow through, and think holistically

Editorial thoughts on the virtuous circle that is sustainable innovation

Cosmina L. Voinea, Nadine Roijakkers, and Ward Ooms

1.1 Mainstreaming sustainable innovation: A multifarious perspective

The view that firms should aspire to obtain 'triple wins', in terms of a triple bottom line (integrating social, environmental, and economic goals; Elkington, 1994), rather than merely aspire to generate profits, has existed for well over two decades. This view took shape as sustainability and gradually grew to be on the agenda of not only environmentalists but also politicians and policy makers, via the Brundtland report (1987), generally known by its name *Our Common Future*, and management scientists and business leaders alike. In fact, such views have even become stronger in recent years, as doing business responsibly and to the benefit of the firm, society, and environment at the same time is more and more regarded as a moral obligation of firms (Longoni & Cagliano, 2018).

This development at large has led to the proliferation of concepts that are conceived to help firms improve their triple bottom line. Studies on eco-innovation have focused on the environmental impact of innovation (e.g. Carrillo-Hermosilla, Del Río, & Könnölä, 2010), and thus part of the triple bottom line. These studies discuss how innovation may lead to more eco-efficiency of processes and products, or even create wholly new systems that are more effective in meeting the requirements of the environment or even contribute to it. Other studies have focused on the social impact of organizations, via the concept of social innovation, which has sparked research interest in four intellectual communities after 2002 and each with their distinct foci (Van der Have & Rubalcaba, 2016). A common denominator across research on social innovation is its impact – at some level of analysis – on social problems.

Yet despite the considerable research attention at least two higher level problems persist with regard to the study of sustainable innovation. First, from a research point of view there should be more attention on how firms may reconcile and truly simultaneously cater to the needs of their triple goals. Eco-innovation and social innovation research are both open to the understanding of system-level impacts of innovation (e.g. Carrillo-Hermosilla

4 *Cosmina L. Voinea et al.*

et al., 2010; Van der Have & Rubalcaba, 2016), yet by nature and terminology they are narrowly focused on either the environmental bottom line or the social bottom line nonetheless. Relatively little research has been conducted to understand how these two goals may jointly be integrated with traditional economic goals. Sustainable innovation for the triple bottom line should be understood at this system level, which is not surprisingly dubbed 'edge of chaos' by some (Seebode, Jeanrenaud, & Bessant, 2012). Second, what also clearly follows from research on sustainable innovation is that academia may be expecting more from business (sustainable innovation as moral obligation) than business is currently able to deliver. That is, empirical research goes to show that doing business to attain triple wins is certainly not commonplace among firms, and that many firms still focus on compliance or – at best – eco-efficiency (e.g. Longoni & Cagliano, 2018; Seebode et al., 2012).

Complex sustainability challenges have become motives to innovate, reasons for novel innovation trajectories, which could enhance firms' competitiveness while contributing to sustainable development. Multifarious sustainability issues have thus proven stimulating not for research alone, but across the world, as sustainability challenges are being transformed into opportunities and are sparking fundamental interest in the business community. Yet we established that despite its promise for academia and business, sustainable innovation is not straightforward or commonplace. These observations give rise to the study of the interconnected nature of firms' innovation undercurrents and sustainability.

In order for sustainable innovation to truly become mainstream practice in business, we need to find out how organizations can strategically and efficiently accommodate sustainability and innovation, preferably in such a manner that they accomplish value capturing (for firms, stakeholders, and society) rather than merely create a return on the social responsibility agenda. The aim of this book is both to advance our conceptual understanding of sustainable innovation and to conduct in-depth empirical research into the complex concept of sustainable innovation from four perspectives. We take multiple perspectives in order to understand sustainable innovation's potential shifts and barriers, its benefits, and outcomes from all angles. The first theme in this book takes a *strategic perspective*. It considers the inception of sustainable innovation and presents a set of studies about the business models for sustainable innovation. These studies are reported in Chapter 2 (Oskam, de Man, and Bossink), Chapter 3 (de Langen, Sanderse, and Perez Salgado), and Chapter 4 (Winkler). We summarize the chapters' aims, methodology, and main findings in Table 1.1. Second, we take a *network perspective* on the way firms and other organizations coordinate their efforts for sustainable innovation by using networks. The studies included in this thematic section are Chapter 5 (Franco), Chapter 6 (Cobben, Maes, and Roijakkers), and Chapter 7 (Bigliardi, Filippelli, and Galati). We list the aims, methodology, and main findings of these studies in Table 1.2. Third, we take an inside look in organizations that engage in sustainable innovation, adopting a *process perspective* on sustainable innovation. The chapters that make up the third thematic section are Chapter 8 (Steinmo), Chapter 9 (Ahn and Kim), and Chapter 10 (Boonstra and Brillo). Table 1.3 presents the aims, methodology, and main findings of these studies. Fourth and final, the chapters in the last thematic section in this book address the important issue of (measuring) impact of sustainable innovation. This area of research is particularly underdeveloped as it stands, yet the research book offers five enticing conceptual chapters and chapters with original empirics: Chapter 11 (Kensen and Orcherton), Chapter 12 (Relou and Hubers), Chapter 13 (Dommerholt, Soltanifar, and Bessant), Chapter 14 (Castaldi), and Chapter 15 (Gunarathne and Peiris). The studies are outlined in Table 1.4.

We proceed this editorial by outlining each perspective covered in the thematic sections of this research book on sustainable innovation. Furthermore, we present a brief research agenda and managerial implications for each of the thematic sections.

1.2 The strategy perspective

Strategy is the starting point of organizational behaviour and structure and as such strategic goals with respect to sustainability can form the basis for choices, for example, when it comes to the business model. Following this line of reasoning, creating value for society and the environment at large needs to be an integral part of the way an organization conducts its business, innovates, and captures value from it. In the introduction, we have identified that the latter is not yet commonplace in most organizations. As such, the first thematic section of our book addresses topics within the strategy perspective on sustainable innovation.

The strategy chapters of our book are all empirical in nature and offer a multiple case study view on sustainable innovation. The chapter by Oskam, de Man, and Bossink studies business model innovation in Dutch firms and concludes that business model innovation within organizations is stimulated by interactions with stakeholders. The view that interactions with external parties open up new ways of thinking and can thus feed strategy from the outside-in is very consistent with more recent views on strategy including contributions to the field of open strategy. Furthermore, this chapter adds to the idea that sustainable innovation needs to be approached in a holistic way including input from like-minded external partners. The study by de Langen, Sanders, and Perez Salgado examines sustainable business models within the context of non-profit organizations and finds that social and eco-innovation can lead to changes and improvements in business models over time, thus outlining clear strategic benefits from focusing on sustainability. Winkler studies start-ups in Austria and points out that soft factors, such as the traits of the entrepreneur, are important to consider when studying the success of start-ups with a drive to create societal and environmental value. In congruence with Voinea, Logger, Rauf, and Roijakkers (2019) this chapter shows

6 *Cosmina L. Voinea et al.*

Table 1.1 Summary of chapters in the *strategy* section

Authors	Research goal(s)	Research design and empirical setting	Main findings
Inge Oskam, Ard-Pieter de Man, and Bart Bossink	• Interaction between managers and stakeholders is often considered to limit business model innovation. • This study seeks to show how interaction with stakeholders may also lead to managerial cognitive change, and thereby stimulate business model innovation.	Multiple case study of the introduction of emerging sustainable technologies via business model innovation in three Dutch firms.	• Interaction with stakeholders is shown to be able to benefit business model innovation via three shaping processes: market approach shaping, product/service offering shaping, and credibility shaping. • The impact of new or latent stakeholders is greater than that of existing stakeholders.
Frank de Langen, Judith Sanderse, and Francisca Perez Salgado	• Identifying the components of a sustainable business model for non-profit organizations (NPOs). • Defining sustainable innovation in a context of NPOs. • Understanding the links between sustainable innovation and sustainable business models.	Multiple case study of three large NPOs.	• NPO's sustainable business model is composed of financial, societal, and environmental aspects in the key programs of their value proposition and sometimes even in their mission. • Sustainable innovation in NPOs is described as the intentional sustainable changes that improve the economic, social, and environmental values of the NPO. • NPOs use sustainable innovation as a means to reconsider and improve their business model over time.

Editorial thoughts on the virtuous circle   7

Authors	Research goal(s)	Research design and empirical setting	Main findings
Lisa Winkler	• Identifying the soft success factors (i.e. culture, internal dynamics, characteristics of the entrepreneur) of a sustainability-driven start-up. • Setting up a framework (for exploration, categorisation, and structuring) of said factors to be used by researchers and practitioners.	Multiple case study of Austrian start-ups in fashion, food, social services, and agriculture.	• Complementing existing tools for sustainable business modelling this chapter proposes a categorization of soft success factors of sustainability-driven start-ups including: (1) Mindset, (2) Commitment, (3) Execution, which is subdivided into Consciousness, Meaning, Proactive Attitude, Responsibility, Pioneering Role, Authenticity, and Transparency.

that lessons from large organizations cannot simply be transferred to start-ups and small firms. In small firms, the founding entrepreneur and his/her vision, personality, attitude, and behaviour (outlining the importance of individual-level analysis) are much more influential in strategy formation than is the case in larger organizations. As such, the author calls for the adaptation of existing sustainable business modelling tools to include these insights. Furthermore, the chapter points at the importance of authenticity in pursuing social and eco-innovation goals for sustainable business model success.

1.3 The network perspective

In the introduction to this editorial we highlighted that pure sustainable innovation takes place at the systemic level. This implies that sustainable innovation may at times shake up or even replace existing "technical, organizational and socio-economic structures" (Seebode et al., 2012, p. 199). No single organization or firm will have the leverage to effectuate such changes, which is why the second thematic section in this research book is concerned with a network-level perspective on sustainable innovation. This theme is tightly connected to the strategic theme where it was already highlighted that while strategic views of sustainable innovation may lead to collaboration with external parties (execution of strategy), external parties and their input may also be an important source of strategic repositioning choices.

8 *Cosmina L. Voinea et al.*

We include a set of conceptual chapters on network theory, ecosystems, and open innovation. The study by Franco theorizes about network effects on eco-innovation, and calls for future research to empirically validate suggestions about such effects. This important research builds on well-known studies of the role of strategic suppliers and their important contributions to the focal organization's innovation strategies. The ecosystems literature is heavily informed by network theory as well, and the chapter by Cobben, Maes, and Roijakkers conceptualizes the roles of different types of ecosystems in realizing sustainability transitions (see also Ooms, Caniëls, Roijakkers, & Cobben, 2020). Here, the link with strategy is similarly clear in the sense that different strategic goals with respect to social and eco-innovation may call for the use of different ecosystem types. Again, future research may seek to investigate ecosystems' role in sustainable innovation. Finally, the impact of open innovation on sustainable innovation is somewhat underexplored. A notable exception is Kennedy, Whiteman, and Van den Ende's (2017) work

Table 1.2 Summary of chapters in the *network* section

Authors	Research goal(s)	Research design and empirical setting	Main findings
Maria A. Franco	• Investigating how collaboration for innovation is more likely to materialize in a buyer-supplier network. • Illustrating how buyer-supplier networks may be conducive to the development of eco-innovations.	Conceptual study developing propositions derived from network theory about network effects on eco-innovation.	• Theory development that can be used for empirical validation of relationships between network power (in different forms), strong ties, weak ties, and geographical proximity on the one hand, and eco-innovation on the other hand.
Dieudonnee Cobben, Dries Maes, and Nadine Roijakkers	• Exploring the potential roles that different ecosystem types (business, innovation, knowledge, and entrepreneurial ecosystems) may take to enable sustainability transitions.	Conceptual study that conceptualizes the potential of different ecosystem types to contribute to sustainable transition by linking the two bodies of literature.	• The findings shed light on the importance for firms and policymakers to combine different ecosystem types to stimulate socio-technological niche-innovations to grow into new dominant regimes or to influence the development directions of the existing regime.

Authors	Research goal(s)	Research design and empirical setting	Main findings
Barbara Bigliardi, Serena Filippelli, and Francesco Galati	• Illustrating the state of the art in literature linking sustainable innovation and open innovation. • Identifying the main drivers, barriers, and actors involved in sustainable innovation when examined through an open innovation lens.	Conceptual study of the literature on the sustainable innovation and open innovation.	• The chapter proposes the Open Sustainable Innovation (OSI) framework where findings from the sustainable innovation literature and the open innovation literature regarding drivers and barriers of OSI and the main actors involved are integrated.

on the role of open innovation in sustainable innovation. Even more recently, in a special issue of R&D Management, the guest editors explore the ways in which open innovation can be leveraged to improve society and call on open innovation researchers to further explore the phenomenon (Ahn, Roijakkers, Fini, & Mortara, 2019). In this book, Bigliardi, Filippelli, and Galati build on this earlier work and identify the main drivers, barriers, and actors involved in sustainable innovation from an open innovation perspective. Their Open Sustainable Innovation framework offers managers grips to design open innovation initiatives aimed to lead to sustainable innovation. From this theme it becomes clear that taking a holistic view on sustainable innovation and including relevant external parties as well as a clear link to strategic goals related to social and eco-innovation are paramount (in line with Rauf, Voinea, Bin Azam Hashmi, & Fratostiteanu, 2020).

1.4 The process perspective

When it comes to the execution of strategy, in our introduction we have pointed out that while striving for the creation of social and environmental value may in fact increase firms' innovativeness and competitiveness, to date, large numbers of organizations tend to engage in sustainability superficially at best. As is the case in many other areas of business, however, becoming successful at sustainable innovation requires thoroughness in managing and organizing the creation of social and environmental value as an integral part of doing business and embedding it within the organizational mindset, culture, and processes. The third thematic section of our book, examining the organizational processes behind engaging in sustainable innovation, covers a variety of methodological approaches such as action research and case study research.

10 *Cosmina L. Voinea et al.*

Steinmo examines the important role of research centres in developing radical innovation for sustainability and calls out to managers by pointing out specific activities to be undertaken towards this end in different phases of research centre development. Ahn and Kim, in congruence with some of the authors in the network section of the book, take an open innovation approach to sustainable innovation and purport that leadership aimed at making sustainable innovation an integral part of an organizations' culture and mindset is crucial to success. Furthermore, they bring forward the idea that input for sustainable innovation can be found anywhere within the organizational boundaries as well as beyond. Tools to support idea generation processes need to be implemented and effectively used. Boonstra and Brillo similarly point at the importance of establishing a supportive culture for sustainable innovation. These authors also argue that leaders should stimulate that authentic organizational values and qualities underlie sustainable innovation efforts and that parties with similar values both within the organization (at all levels) and the wider environment are identified and involved in efforts to improve society and the environment. They offer managers a practical methodology for managing sustainable innovation based on authentic values.

Table 1.3 Summary of chapters in the *process* section

Authors	Research goal(s)	Research design and empirical setting	Main findings
Marianne Steinmo	• Understanding the role of research centres in developing radical innovation for sustainability. • Conceptualizing firm enablers for managing innovation development during three phases of a research centre's development.	Conceptual study on radical innovation targeted at sustainability and taking place in research centres.	• The identification of several important activities for research centres and the associated firms to undertake in three phases of research centre development: the establishment phase, the performance phase, and the end phase. • Actionable suggestion for managers at firms or research centres.
Joon Mo Ahn and Jong Rak Kim	• Exploring how open innovation processes can be used for implementing sustainable innovation within companies.	Single, in-depth case study research design. Case firm is an ITC company situated in South Korea.	• Top management's use of open innovation tools and their commitment to create a shared mindset within their organization is crucial for making innovation within the firm sustainable.

Editorial thoughts on the virtuous circle 11

Authors	Research goal(s)	Research design and empirical setting	Main findings
Jaap Boonstra and João Brillo	• Exploring the relations between sustainable innovation, organizational culture, and leadership. • Developing a methodology to manage sustainable innovational values.	Action research involving a network of organizations in the global banking industry.	• Sustainable innovation is concerned with building on the individual character of the organization, putting core qualities in action, and about differentiation. • Cultural changes for sustainable innovation can be undertaken from any role or position, not just top management. • Leadership for sustainable innovation is about actively involving other members within the organization as well as external parties with a similar mindset. • The proposed methodology of "Managing by Sustainable Innovational Values" can aid organizations in aligning sustainable innovation with internal values and initiatives.

1.5 The impact perspective

The last thematic section of this research book deals with the question of how to measure the impact of sustainable innovation or closing the loop of cause and effect. This is perhaps one of the most fundamental questions, as strategy can only be improved based on accurate measurement of effects where actions can be formulated to do better in the future. When focusing on creating social and environmental value adds to organizations' innovativeness and competitiveness, we are in need of accurate ways of measuring these effects that go beyond traditional indicators for measuring innovative performance. This measurement challenge thus opens up opportunities for businesses and researchers, yet it also constitutes a complex question to answer. At first glance, it may seem obvious how to measure and study the impact of sustainable innovation at least for some of the pillars in the triple bottom line, from both the researcher and practitioner point of view. The ultimate economic impact of innovation is usually assessed by looking at indicators

12 *Cosmina L. Voinea et al.*

such as profitability, sales growth, and market share, and there are a plethora of indicators to measure innovation itself (Dziallas & Blind, 2019). Beyond the economic pillar, the literature on the environmental and social pillars also offers tools to evaluate innovations' environmental or social impact (Seebode et al., 2012). The main gap in our understanding is therefore in (1) choosing from the plethora of indicators to measure impact and (2) mostly in taking the holistic perspective on impact and understanding the interrelationships between different kinds of impacts and also potential trade-offs organizations may have to make in creating triple wins.

The mostly conceptual chapters in this book do not offer a ready-made solution to the problem of understanding and measuring the impact of sustainable innovation. Yet, they do call attention to several fruitful avenues for further research into this issue, and offer managers advice as well as real-life examples of best practices in measuring sustainable innovation's impact. First, several chapters consider the potential of existing ways to capture value from innovation to contribute to a triple bottom line, such as intellectual property rights in Castaldi, or consider novel and less obvious indicators from adjacent fields of research that may complement existing indicators (e.g. Kensen & Orcherton and Gunarathne & Peiris, this book). We gather from these

Table 1.4 Summary of chapters in the *impact* section

Authors	Research goal(s)	Research design and empirical setting	Main findings
Mathew Kensen and Dan F. Orcherton	• Understanding societal level and stakeholder impacts of sustainable innovation. • Understanding urban climate resilience in a context of climate change in Small Island Developing States (SIDS).	Literature review of vulnerability, its assessment, and measurement in the context of urban environments and in connection with urban climate resilience.	• Vulnerability indicators to measure vulnerability to natural, technological, and climatic hazards. • Call for research to also develop social vulnerability indicators. • It is challenging to develop vulnerability indicators that are applicable and operable and at the right scale to consider issues that suit a specific study areas or specific social, cultural, or institutional contexts such as those of SIDS.

Editorial thoughts on the virtuous circle 13

Authors	Research goal(s)	Research design and empirical setting	Main findings
Carly Relou and Frank Hubers	• Proposing a typology of practices of impact measurement. • Differentiating between charities merely using impact measurement symbolically and charities actively adopting it to develop, adjust, and refine a strategy to reach long-term objectives.	Exploratory survey data about impact measurement in Dutch charities.	• There are both charities that use impact measurement symbolically and without clear links to long-term strategy, as well as charities that use impact measurement departing from a coherent logic and linked to their long-term strategy. • Large organizations are more likely to use impact measurement strategically.
Egbert Dommerholt, Mariusz Soltanifar, and John Bessant	• Defining sustainable innovation. • Applying the sustainable innovation framework to answer the question of whether creating societal value is a randomised, unpredictable process.	Conceptual study of the literature on sustainable innovation.	• Societal value derived from sustainable innovations is highest when these innovations stimulate the economic transition towards a circular economy and multiple value creation. • The above-mentioned transition requires radical innovations, predominantly business model innovations.
Carolina Castaldi	• Shedding light on the appropriation strategies of companies engaged in sustainable innovation, predominantly intellectual property rights (IPR).	Conceptual study exploring a new research field.	• Deduction of new research themes including reforming IPR systems to fix distortions; sustainable innovation cases for collecting best practices and bottlenecks in leveraging

(Continued)

14 Cosmina L. Voinea et al.

Authors	Research goal(s)	Research design and empirical setting	Main findings
	• Linking IPR types to archetypes of sustainable innovation. • Developing a corresponding research agenda.		IPR; how IPR can facilitate the mainstreaming of sustainable innovation; to broaden the geographical scope of appropriation research; and ideas on conceptual studies.
AD Nuwan Gunarathne and Mahendra Peiris	• Discussing the challenges in measuring sustainable innovation performance at the firm level. • Offering solutions to these challenges.	Conceptual study drawing on illustrative case examples from the Sri Lankan plantation agriculture industry.	• An overview of general and industry-specific challenges to the measurement of sustainable innovation performance. • When thinking about solutions to these challenges it is of eminent importance to take into account the requirements of information users of sustainable innovation performance.

chapters' findings that (1) further research is warranted to study the potential of existing appropriation mechanisms to capture value that goes beyond the economic value these mechanisms were designed to capture and (2) a further exploration is warranted to see what impact measures other fields of research may stand to offer. Second, two chapters investigate why some organizations are (more) successful at creating impact in the three pillars of the triple bottom line than others, thereby offering an understanding of the links between strategy and impact (Relou & Hubers and Dommerholt, Soltanifar, & Bessant, this book). In this sense, Relou and Hubers strongly link to other thematic chapters where there is a clear call for authenticity when pursuing sustainable innovation and where it is pointed out that creating value for society and the environment needs to be embedded in all aspects of the organization. Furthermore, Dommerholt, Soltanifar, and Bessant relate to Steinmo and business model innovation chapters in suggesting the importance of radical changes to business models being necessary for solving sustainability challenges. More research is required to understand the antecedents of impactful sustainable innovation. Third, specific chapters offer useful typologies to differentiate between practices of impact measurement used in organizations today (e.g. Relou & Hubbers, this book). It is worthwhile to investigate what combinations of practices for impact measurement actually coincide with sustainable innovation with systemic impact.

1.6 Concluding editorial thoughts

This edited book offers a cross section of both the conceptual work and empirical research that is currently being conducted in the field of sustainable innovation. Apart from conveying current insights, the chapters offer research suggestions for bringing forward our knowledge of the strategy, network, process, and impact perspectives of sustainable innovation (depicted in Figure 1.1). All chapters put forward a piece of the puzzle portraying the ultimate message of this book: Social innovation and eco-innovation need to be approached in a holistic manner. Sustainable innovation cannot simply be a superficial goal that organizations pursue; it needs to be their authentic way of setting up their business and relating to and collaborating with

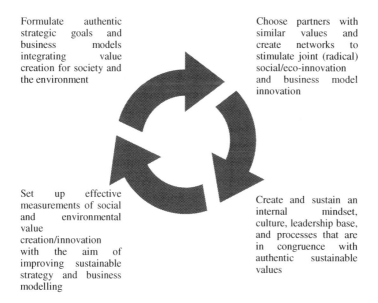

Figure 1.1 A holistic perspective on sustainable innovation: Strategy, network, process, and impact.

external parties in the outside world. When pursued, sustainable innovation needs to be part of the organization's and its people's DNA, being an integral part of mindset, leadership, strategy, culture, structure, and processes. When pursued in such a holistic and authentic way, it will drive innovation and competitiveness.

Thematic section one

The strategy perspective

2 Business model innovation for sustainability

The role of stakeholder interaction and managerial cognitive change

Inge Oskam, Ard-Pieter de Man, and Bart Bossink

2.1 Introduction

In order for a company to create a viable business case for sustainability, it may need to make substantial changes to its business model (Boons & Lüdeke-Freund, 2013; Schaltegger, Lüdeke-Freund, & Hansen, 2012). The literature indicates that stakeholders play an important role in business model innovation (Boons & Lüdeke-Freund, 2013; Doganova & Eyquem-Renault, 2009; Stubbs & Cocklin, 2008; Zott, Amit, & Massa, 2011). Although stakeholder interaction is considered a proactive strategy that can radically change a business logic (Dmitriev, Simmons, Truong, Palmer, & Schneckenberg, 2014; Schaltegger et al., 2012), it remains unclear exactly how interaction with stakeholders influences business model innovation (Aspara, Lamberg, Laukia, & Tikkanen, 2011; Della Corte & Del Gaudio, 2014; Spieth, Schneckenberg, & Matzler, 2016).

Building on recent insights about the role of managerial cognitive change in business model innovation (Cavalcante, Kesting, & Ulhøi, 2011; Spieth et al., 2016; Tikkanen, Lamberg, Parvinen, & Kallunki, 2005), we propose that stakeholders affect managerial cognition and hence business model innovation. Following Barr, Stimpert, and Huff (1992), we define managerial cognitive change as an adjustment of the manager's 'mental models', 'cognitive maps', or 'beliefs'. Most extant research has studied how stakeholders reinforce existing managerial cognitions and hence constrain business model innovation (for example, Aspara et al., 2011; Saebi, 2015; Tikkanen et al., 2005). The way in which manager–stakeholder interaction may also trigger managerial cognitive change, and thus stimulate business model innovation, has been understudied (Aspara et al., 2011; Spieth et al., 2016). This possible effect is especially relevant when developing business models for sustainability, as these confront managers with new technological possibilities and require the involvement of various (new) stakeholder groups. Through three case studies of business model innovations for sustainability, we aim to gain insights into stakeholder-induced managerial cognitive change in business model innovation for sustainability and identify processes that trigger and support this managerial cognitive change.

20 *Inge Oskam et al.*

This chapter proceeds with a review of the existing literature on the connection between the three elements of our study: business model innovation, stakeholder interaction, and managerial cognition. We then analyse three empirical cases of business model innovation for sustainability, focusing on stakeholder-induced changes in managers' cognitions. Our findings propose that stakeholders affect managerial cognitive change, and subsequently business model innovation, via three shaping processes.

2.2 Theoretical background

2.2.1 Core concepts of this study

We start this section by defining sustainable business model innovation and then explore the role of stakeholder interaction and the role of managerial cognition in business model innovation. We then review the literature on the connection between the role of stakeholders, managerial cognitive change and business model innovation in order to identify the research gap.

2.2.1.1 Sustainable business model innovation

Scholars are increasingly regarding the successful implementation of sustainable innovations as a business model challenge (Boons & Lüdeke-Freund, 2013; Boons, Montalvo, Quist, & Wagner, 2013; Schaltegger et al., 2012). For the purposes of this chapter, we regard a business model as a conceptual representation of a business comprising a value proposition offering products and/or services to customers and describing how this value is created and delivered, including the value capture mechanisms it employs (Teece, 2010). However, business models are rarely perfect from the start. Instead, they develop over time (Spieth, Schneckenberg, & Ricart, 2014), often following an iterative process (Dmitriev et al., 2014). The outcome of this innovation process involves changing one or several components of the business model (Cavalcante et al., 2011; Schaltegger et al., 2012; Spieth et al., 2016). When this process leads to a completely new value proposition, this can be considered a business model innovation (Schaltegger et al., 2012), providing customers and end users with product or service offerings that were not previously available (Mitchell & Coles, 2003). This business model innovation process can be defined as 'the search for new business logics of the firm and new ways to create and capture value for its stakeholders' (Casadesus-Masanell & Zhu, 2013, p. 464), and is especially relevant for a firm's strategy when commercialising new ideas such as technological innovations for sustainability (Chesbrough, 2010; Evans et al., 2017; Spieth et al., 2014). In contrast with generic business models, a sustainable business model not only creates economic value for customers and end users, but also considers the needs of a broader variety of stakeholders, including stakeholders with soc(iet)al and environmental wishes and demands (for example, Evans et al., 2017; Schaltegger, Hansen, &

Lüdeke-Freund, 2016; Stubbs & Cocklin, 2008). Such a model captures 'economic value while maintaining or regenerating natural, social, and economic capital beyond its organizational boundaries' (Schaltegger et al., 2016, p. 6).

2.2.1.2 Stakeholder interaction

Stakeholders are an important trigger for business model innovation for sustainability (Evans et al., 2017; Oskam, Bossink, & de Man, 2018; Schaltegger et al., 2012; Stubbs & Cocklin, 2008). Following Freeman (1984), we define stakeholders as those groups that 'can affect or are affected by' a manager's decisions or actions (Freeman, 1984, p. 46). We use this broad view on stakeholders as it explicitly includes 'latent' stakeholders, given that 'the potential relationship can be as relevant as the actual one' (Mitchell, Agle, & Wood, 1997, p. 859). A firm's stakeholders include classic primary stakeholder groups such as employees, customers, suppliers, and financiers (Clarkson, 1995; Freeman, 1984). In the case of sustainable innovations, a broader range of more or less latent stakeholders is considered critical (Buysse & Verbeke, 2003; Schlange, 2009) and may include stakeholder groups such as academia, industry bodies, regulators and policy-makers, environmental non-governmental organisations, local communities, the media, and nature (Azzone, Brophy, Noci, Welford, & Young, 1997; Evans et al., 2017; Stubbs & Cocklin, 2008). Which of these latent stakeholders are perceived as salient depends on the type of sustainable innovation and on the context in which the firm operates (Buysse & Verbeke, 2003) and changes over time (Dentchev & Heene, 2004; Mitchell et al., 1997). According to Mitchell et al. (1997), the degree of stakeholder salience is determined by the impact of three attributes: power, urgency and legitimacy. Schlange (2009) proposed that, in the case of sustainable innovations, these attributes should be changed to philosophy, impact and legitimacy. Dependent on the perceived salience, a latent stakeholder may become an active partner; managers should thus observe and adapt to changes in stakeholder importance (Dentchev & Heene, 2004). A firm's business model is about how these stakeholders and managers interact and create value (Freeman, 2010b), stressing the reciprocal relationships between managers and stakeholders. Especially for commercialising sustainable and technological innovations, stakeholder interaction in the business model innovation process is considered a proactive strategy that may radically change the business logic and help reconceptualise value (Dmitriev et al., 2014; Evans et al., 2017; Schaltegger et al., 2012).

2.2.1.3 Managerial cognition

The role of managerial cognition in business model innovation is of particular interest when managers are confronted with new information and new technological possibilities (Foss & Saebi, 2017; Spieth et al., 2016) as, in that case, 'managers must expand their perspectives to find an appropriate business model in order to be able to capture value from that technology' (Teece, 2010, p. 355). One characteristic of business models is that, in the minds of managers, they can be manipulated (Baden-Fuller & Mangematin, 2013; Doz & Kosonen, 2010; Hadida & Paris, 2014). Consequently, managerial cognition should play a central role in understanding business model innovation (Foss & Saebi, 2017; Martins, Rindova, & Greenbaum, 2015). However, research into the conditions under which it has either an impeding or a stimulating effect remains in a developmental stage (for example, Baden-Fuller & Mangematin, 2013; Hadida & Paris, 2014; Nadkarni & Barr, 2008). The literature argues that cognitive blindness may impede business model innovation when managers are not receptive to other ways of thinking about their business model (Baden-Fuller & Mangematin, 2013). However, other authors have proposed that externally induced changes in managerial cognition can stimulate business model innovation (Cavalcante et al., 2011; Chesbrough, 2010; Hadida & Paris, 2014; Martins et al., 2015; Nadkarni & Barr, 2008; Spieth et al., 2016). It is clearly important to analyse managerial cognition in order to gain a better understanding of its effect on business model innovation.

2.2.2 Identifying the research gap

In short, even though the literature agrees on the importance of both stakeholders and managerial cognition in business model innovation, only a few authors have considered these three elements together. There is little clarity regarding how stakeholders can change managerial cognition in a way that leads to business model innovation. Further research is needed to identify nuanced insights regarding when, how and why stakeholders induce managerial cognitive change that leads to business model innovation. For example, Aspara et al. (2011) were explicit about the connection between these three elements, finding that the understandings of the role of the firm that are shared by the manager and its stakeholders have a considerable influence on business model innovation. However, Saebi (2015) stated that external drivers for change are no guarantee that business model innovation can occur, because managerial cognition may stand in the way. 'On a cognitive level, management might be unable or unwilling to perceive the need for change' (Saebi, 2015, p. 159).

This view of managerial cognition as being limited in how it allows manager–stakeholder interaction to influence business model innovation is further explored in the literature. Porac, Ventresca and Mishina (2002) proposed a distinction among four types of managerial cognition that may influence a firm's actions related to business model innovation: industry or corporate recipe, reputational rankings, boundary beliefs, and product ontologies. Aspara et al. (2011) and Tikkanen et al. (2005) used this operationalisation of managerial cognition to explore how managerial cognition may limit business model innovation. They found that the stronger the 'industry recipe', the more uniform the business model will be across competing firms and the narrower the alternatives for change. Regarding existing 'reputational rankings', decisions related to business model innovation reinforce existing rather than prospective reputational rankings, leading to more uniform business models. 'Boundary beliefs' about who the firm can pursue as a customer or serve as a supplier tend to constrain the firm's marketing efforts. Finally, cognitions of current 'product ontologies' constrain the redesign of product/service offerings (Aspara et al., 2011; Porac et al., 2002; Tikkanen et al., 2005). These four types of managerial cognition are a useful operationalisation to research the effects of managerial cognitive processes (Porac et al., 2002) on new business modelling (Aspara et al., 2011; Tikkanen et al., 2005). However, these have focused exclusively on how stakeholders constrain business model innovation.

Other research has also dealt only marginally with the question of how manager–stakeholder interaction may trigger cognitive change and spur business model innovation, despite the fact that an outside perspective may play an important role in business model innovation by increasing an organisation's strategic sensitivity (Doz & Kosonen, 2010). The literature only shows that managerial cognition changes through negotiating with stakeholders (Aspara et al., 2011), and by experimenting in emerging markets, which brings a different set of stakeholders (Chesbrough, 2010). The business model literature also has a tendency to lump all stakeholders together (Evans et al., 2017; Schaltegger et al., 2016) and to assume that the set of stakeholders a firm faces is static, whereas, in practice, they may change.

In summary, existing contributions make it clear that a promising avenue for further research lies in the study of (1) managerial cognitions as an ingredient of business model innovation, (2) the role of stakeholders in changing these cognitions, and (3) the influence of managerial cognitive change on business modelling. How exactly managers' interaction with stakeholders contributes to managerial cognitive change, and thus influences business model innovation, remains unclear (Aspara et al., 2011; Spieth et al., 2016). Our research aims to take a step towards answering this question.

2.3 Research design

The objective of this study is to gain insight into how managers' interactions with stakeholders contribute to managerial cognitive change that induces business model innovation for sustainability and unravel its constituent processes. We use a qualitative research approach to provide in-depth insights into this phenomenon – an insight that can potentially be generalised to theory (Eisenhardt, 1989; Yin, 2017). The research design consists of multiple case studies and is a first step towards developing insights that are analytically valid for comparable cases (Eisenhardt & Graebner, 2007; Yin, 2017).

24 *Inge Oskam et al.*

2.3.1 Case selection

We build on three cases following a replication logic that enables within-case and cross-case analysis, as well as pattern matching (Eisenhardt, 1989). We have selected three cases in which a manager interacts with stakeholders and, based on that interaction, develops a new understanding of the role of his/her business and consequently decides to adapt the appropriate business model. The cases are comparable because each case concerns an emerging sustainable technology that has been successfully introduced by a firm into the market by innovating its business model, including the value proposition (Schaltegger et al., 2012). Table 2.1 provides a description of the cases and shows that, in each case, the change of the value proposition includes a change of both the product/service offering and the target group. The cases are recent Dutch examples of environmental or social sustainable innovations.

2.3.2 Data acquisition and analysis

The main data sources for this study consist of semi-structured interviews and archival data sources (see Table 2.2). Interviews were conducted with

Table 2.1 Description of cases and changes in the value proposition

Characteristics	Case study		
Innovation	Bio-based and soil-degradable products for landscaping	Bio-based and compostable products for horticulture	Car sharing service for consumer market
Business idea	2009	2004	2011
Market launch	2011	2009	2014
Initial value proposition	Product system (sustainable tree anchoring system), aimed at direct customers (gardener)	Single product (biodegradable pot), aimed at direct customers (grower)	Product-service system (smart box and car sharing platform), aimed at consumer market (car owners)
New value proposition	Service plus accompanying products (advice/training and bio-based product portfolio), aimed at decision makers (municipalities)	Combination of products (e.g., pack consisting of tray, bio-pot, aquapad, and sheet), aimed at end customers (retailer)	Service plus technology (fleet management solution, incl. smartbox, and software tools), aimed at business-to-business market (fleet owners/managers)

the managers who are directly responsible for the sustainable innovation and commercialisation trajectory and with key partners involved. These interviews covered all of the main players, as our studies concern small firms. The interviews pertained to the inter-firm-level value creation processes and focused on changes in the managers' understanding of the role of the firm in its business, and the influence of manager–stakeholder interactions therein, as well as on forthcoming strategic actions. All interviews were recorded and transcribed verbatim. For the preparation of the interviews and for triangulation purposes, we gathered and studied archival data sources, consisting of internal and external data sources covering a prolonged period prior to and after the innovation of the business model. The archival data were especially helpful in validating the changes in managerial cognition and business model that were found in the interview data through expression of the role and offering by the firm prior and after the changes had occurred. Those changes are documented in archival data of the companies involved (for example, in company reports, websites, presentations and press releases) but there is also recognition of these changes by the media (in magazine articles and media coverage, for instance) and the market (such as in case study reports). Therefore, the role of the secondary data is, on one hand, to document the business model changes, but on the other hand to act as an independent source that confirms changes in the business model are recognised in the outside world.

The analytical process consisted of three stages, constituting open coding, axial coding, and selective coding (Strauss & Corbin, 1990). Software for qualitative data analysis (Atlas.ti) was used to manage the volume and variation of the data and to make data displays. In the first stage, open codes were created for changes in the manager's understanding of the business in each case and the interactions with stakeholders that contributed to this change. In line with Aspara et al. (2011), Barr et al. (1992), Martins et al. (2015), and Tripsas and Gavetti (2000), we looked for instances in our data where managers explicitly mentioned that stakeholder interaction had changed their understanding of the role their business plays, stimulating them to look for new value propositions. Additionally, text segments related to value creation activities, both prior to and after the innovation of the business model occurred, were coded in both interviews and secondary data sources. In the second stage, a process of sorting and grouping took place, identifying sequences and differences between value creation activities and types of stakeholders involved, before and after the manager's change of business understanding occurred. In this stage, categories were created by reducing, comparing and clustering the more than 100 open codes that were initially found and by looking at similarities and differences among cases through a process of cross-case pattern matching. In the third and final stage, we explored the relationships between the categories and defined concepts around the central research question. An overview of the final coding scheme is provided in the Appendix.

26 *Inge Oskam et al.*

Table 2.2 Overview of interviewees and archival data sources

Characteristics	Case study		
	Natural Plastics (NP)	*D-Grade*	*WeGo*
Interviews			
Nr. of interviews	5	3	4
Manager case	Manager/ entrepreneur (2x)	Marketing & sales manager (2x)	Manager/ entrepreneur (2x)
Key partners and their roles	Launching customer (co-creator and sales partner), consultant (consultant), partner (co-developer and reseller)	Knowledge provider (research and development partner, representing three launching customers)	Launching customer (co-creator), partner (co-developer, reseller, and financier)
Year conducted	2015	2015	2016
Archival data			
Nr. of archival data	29	30	23
Company data	1 website, 3 videos, 3 presentations, 4 company documents	2 websites, 6 press releases, 1 presentation, 2 company documents	1 website, 1 company blog, 2 company documents
External data	14 news items on external websites, 4 magazine articles,	10 news items on external websites, 5 magazine articles, 1 presentation, 1 case study report	12 news items on external websites, 6 magazine articles, 1 case study report
Other		2 memos of company visit and informal interview with manager	
Period covered	2010–2015	2007–2015	2012–2016

2.4 Findings

2.4.1 A stakeholder-induced managerial cognitive change

For each case, we describe the initial business model for sustainability, focusing on the value proposition and its dominant logic, and explain the change that occurred in the manager's cognition and the stakeholder interactions that led to this change.

2.4.1.1 NP case

Natural Plastics was initiated by a civil contractor who saw how plastics used around roads pollute the soil. He developed a system for underground tree anchoring made of soil-degradable bio-based plastic. After a successful pilot period, the system was introduced to direct customers (gardeners and contractors), with the dominant logic in business model being that a sound, sustainable product sells itself. Although the system was received as 'a bio-based economy best-practice', the distribution channel and gardeners appeared reluctant to adopt the solution, even though it did not involve any extra costs.

Increased interaction with potential direct customers did not mitigate this reluctance. A consultant from an intermediary organisation that guided the manager during the commercialisation stage encouraged the manager to rethink the role the firm should play in the market. The manager realised he had to reframe the value of the system he was offering and needed to target municipal decision makers instead of direct customers. Through interaction with academic researchers and a new product partner, the manager's understanding of the firm's role changed from that of supplier towards that of a change agent in the bio-based economy, giving presentations and offering advice to municipalities centred on a variety of bio-based solutions for landscaping. About this change the manager said:

> We came to the conclusion that when you're just selling products, when your product is just standing somewhere [one-off], you are nowhere. You have to turn it into a concept ... You have to get into the heads of the municipal purchasers and in their perception of the environment.

2.4.1.2 D-Grade case

Desch Plantpak, a producer of thermoform pots, containers, and trays for the horticultural market, introduced a sustainable product line made of 100% biodegradable and renewable material called D-Grade. Initially, the value proposition (products that can be disposed of through composting) was aimed at professional horticulturalists. The dominant logic was that this line could be commercialised with the same business model as that for traditional products and the product's sustainable quality would compensate for the somewhat higher price. Although the D-Grade line was received well by market parties, the higher price proved to be a stumbling block with potential direct customers (such as growers).

Following numerous encounters with reluctant direct customers, the manager developed a new line of thinking. He stated:

> We approached the growers, and they all reacted enthusiastically, but eventually they didn't want it because it was too expensive. We then came up with the idea that we shouldn't be approaching the grower; we should go to the grower's customer [the retailers] and they will increase the demand.

28 *Inge Oskam et al.*

This changed perception spurred the manager to start enticing the retailers to prescribe the bio-pot to the growers. Following interactions with retailers, the manager realised that they were not interested in a single bio-pot and instead sought a solution into which this product is integrated. A new employee, hired to approach retailers, decided to express the value-added feature by collaborating with partners with complementary goods, offering total solutions that made the price of its components less relevant.

2.4.1.3 WeGo case

We Go started its business by offering an automated peer-to-peer car-sharing service that allowed car owners to rent their unused cars to people in their neighbourhood. A unique part of the offering was the installation of a 'smart box' – a technical solution that enabled renters to lock and unlock the car with a smartphone, eliminating the logistical problem of exchanging keys. During a pilot period in an Amsterdam neighbourhood, interaction with users revealed that the lack of physical contact between owner and renter made the smart box vulnerable to malicious intent.

A new manager, intentionally hired by WeGo to bring in fresh insights, realised that although the smart box was technologically superior, it was not particularly suited for open communities:

> In a closed community where people are friends of each other, or colleagues working for the same firm, it is completely different. That's why we started looking where to find that [closed community] and realised: shouldn't we go to business-to-business?

We Go decided to target their service at business markets, changing the firm's role fundamentally. WeGo's role changed from that of a technology provider and open community builder towards that of a business partner, enabling organisations to realise the same mobility performance for their closed community with fewer vehicles while saving on costs and reducing CO_2 emissions. This change in the manager's understanding of the business was triggered by a combination of different manager–stakeholder interactions, including interactions with users, but also with product partners and financiers.

2.4.2 *Three shaping processes*

Based on cross-case analysis of patterns in manager–stakeholder interactions, we observed that managerial cognitive change is triggered and supported by three 'shaping' processes that contribute to the actual innovation of the business model for sustainability: market approach shaping, product and/or service offering shaping, and credibility shaping. Table 2.3 presents an overview of the managerial activities and the stakeholder groups involved in the three shaping processes. Quotes provide examples of the managerial activities.

Table 2.3 Three shaping processes and its stakeholder-integrating activities

Shaping process and dominant change	Activities	Stakeholders	Examples from the case studies
Market approach shaping From *technology push* to *market pull*	Creating awareness for environmental and social issues	Both existing and new stakeholders (direct/end customers, environmental NGOs, governmental agencies, researchers)	A political party invited WeGo to give a presentation to create enthusiasm among politicians for car-sharing solutions and to show what role the government could play (from archival data WeGo). 'Natural Plastics started giving training seminars and presentations about biodegradable plastics and how that could be a sustainable solution for trees.' (NP case, product partner)
	Enticing end customers or decision makers to prescribe	New stakeholders (end customers, governmental agencies)	'What he did was involve the whole market in his product instead of approaching them one-by-one. What happened is that the product started showing up in specifications.' (NP case, consultant)
	Focused market development with allies with additional networks	Predominantly new stakeholders (new employees, product partners, service providers, financiers, channel)	'What are firms that fit our philosophy, and have also impact on the market? Who, let's say, can realise volume? And you have to make a choice in that, upfront.' (D-Grade case, manager) 'The good thing is that next to being an investor, they also have an enormous commercial network for us.' (WeGo Case, entrepreneur)
Product and/or service offering shaping From *delivering functionality* to *creating total solutions*	Understanding needs and motives of end customers and decision makers	New stakeholders (end customers, product partners, service providers, financiers)	'Those applications are not finished and WeGo is not able to finish that themselves. They need a market for that. And our salesmen know exactly what our clients are looking for.' (WeGo, partner) 'Of course I am influenced by the things I hear from them [financier]' (WeGo case, manager)

(Continued)

Shaping process and dominant change	Activities	Stakeholders	Examples from the case studies
	Creating superior offerings with horizontal and/or vertical complementarities	Predominantly new stakeholders (end customers, product partners, service providers, suppliers)	Through stakeholder interaction the entrepreneur understood they needed to collaborate to create a superior offering: 'We started working with other companies... so you can apply the whole spectrum of products around these trees, give advice.' (NP case, manager)
	Focusing on the effect of the solution	Predominantly new stakeholders (end customers, product partners, service providers, suppliers)	When talking to one of the first potential end customers, it was understood that 'They do not only sell a pot, they want to establish something ready-to-use ... We are just one component in that, so we have to search for partners.' (D-Grade, manager)
Credibility shaping From *providing evidence* to *gaining legitimacy*	Endorsement by reputable key customers	Both existing and new stakeholders (direct customers, end customers, channel, researchers)	'This client acts as a sort of ambassador for us. Because he has the connection with retail, we don't have to go to retail ourselves. He just makes sure that new points of reference keep coming.' (D-Grade case, manager)
	Endorsement by influencers (e.g., awards)	Predominantly new stakeholders (media, consultants, independent bodies)	'Our first contacts were environmentally-conscious civil servants ... These civil servants work as an ambassador for your system.' (NP case, manager)
	Building extra-business relationships	Predominantly new stakeholders (independent bodies, consultants, financiers)	'We came into contact with a partner that wanted to invest in us ... When you have the back-up of such a partner, then your entry [i.e., with potential customers] is very different.' (WeGo case, manager)

2.4.2.1 Market approach shaping

The first process, 'market approach shaping', relates to a redefinition of the market interface and go-to-market strategy through managerial interaction with both existing and new stakeholders. This shaping process contributes to a change in managerial understanding of the situation the business is in, from primarily being focused on technology-push toward being actively concentrated on creating market-pull. Several activities are found to contribute to this process, each involving different stakeholder groups (see also Table 2.3).

First, the case studies show that creation of awareness of environmental and social issues is vital for market approach shaping. This is especially apparent in the NP case, in which, instead of approaching potential customers one-by-one, the manager started providing training sessions and presentations to civil servants to pitch NP's new sustainable approach. Second, we saw a shift from trying to attract direct customers to enticing the customers of these customers (that is, end customers) to prescribe the sustainable product to the direct customers. For example, the NP case did this by convincing decision makers at municipalities that the new sustainable product contributes to reaching CO_2 emissions reduction goals. Third, we traced a focused market development activity that includes partnering with key market players with additional networks. In the D-Grade case, demand for the offering is created by approaching influential retailers whose vision fits the offering's philosophy. In the WeGo and D-Grade cases, collaboration with reputable complementary partners with large commercial networks enabled cross-selling activities. In the NP case, the manager joined forces with a company with a geographically complementary network.

2.4.2.2 Product and/or service offering shaping

The second process is 'product and/or service offering shaping'. Central in this shaping process is managerial interaction with (potential) end customers and complementary partners. Through this interaction, the offering is (re) shaped to realise and/or improve customer value creation. In the shaping process, the understanding of the role of the business changes from delivering functionality-oriented products and/or services toward creating total solutions that combine several of these products/services into one concept. Product and/or service offering shaping can comprise three activities each involving different stakeholder groups (see also Table 2.3).

First, managerial interaction with potential end customers is important in order to gain a deep understanding of underlying needs and problems. The WeGo case shows how intensive collaboration with a key customer increases awareness of requirements and desired service levels. In the D-Grade case, by interacting with retailers, the manager realised that the market is not interested in single products but rather desires total solutions into which this product is integrated. Second, in all cases, a superior offering is created

32 *Inge Oskam et al.*

by providing complementarities. Collaboration is set up with partners offering complementary services and products of similar quality and reputation, thereby creating offerings that have a synergetic effect and providing the convenience of one-stop shopping (horizontal complementarities). Vertical complementarities are also found. For example, in the WeGo case, the offering is extended with planning and monitoring software and services through partnering. Third, the cases demonstrate that, for creating customer value, the end effect of the offering is more important than just cost issues. Managerial interaction with end customers is an important driver here.

2.4.2.3 Credibility shaping

The third type of shaping emerging from the data is 'credibility shaping', which we define as employing and expanding the firm's network to enhance the credibility of the value proposition. The managerial understanding of the business triggered by this shaping process has changed, from proving the functionality and sustainability of the innovation towards gaining legitimacy for the innovation. Each of the three activities that are relevant for credibility shaping involves different stakeholder groups (see also Table 2.3).

First, the case studies demonstrate that endorsement by reputable key (end) customers is vital for credibility shaping. Key customers act as ambassadors of the sustainable innovation and provide firms with new leads. In the D-Grade case, key customers were actively selected for this purpose based on their sustainability approach and market impact. In the NP case, municipalities created positive exposure and endorsed the solutions, recommending them to colleagues from neighbouring municipalities. Second, we found that endorsement by partners and influencers (such as independent bodies) were equally important. In all cases, the reputation of partners opened doors to new customers. In the NP and WeGo cases, awards from independent bodies further increased the credibility of the offerings. Third, building extra-business relationships with parties such as consultants, financiers, and academic researchers proved to be beneficial in all three cases, leading to stronger legitimacy through relationships with influential and renowned actors in the field.

2.5 Discussion

2.5.1 The role of manager–stakeholder interaction in enabling managerial cognitive change

Our findings indicate that, in each case, a manager's changed understanding of the value potential of his/her firm's offering preceded a change of the business model. This change in understanding can be considered a change in managerial cognition (Aspara et al., 2011; Barr et al., 1992; Martins et al., 2015; Tripsas & Gavetti, 2000). The case studies reveal that this cognitive change is instigated by managerial interaction with stakeholders.

First, the stakeholder set may include customers, suppliers, employees, financiers, academics, governmental organisations, product partners and independent bodies (such as environmental NGOs, intermediary organisations, consultants, and certifiers). Our findings confirm the view that many different stakeholder groups may be relevant (for example, Azzone et al., 1997; Evans et al., 2017; Stubbs & Cocklin, 2008). We add what kind of stakeholders, in particular, contribute to managerial cognitive change in the case of business model innovation for sustainability. Table 2.2 shows in more detail which stakeholder types may be involved in each shaping process and indicates how these stakeholders contribute, for example, through a role as influencer, decision maker, or endorser. In our cases, interactions with end customers appear to be the most important among these factors, as end customers contribute to all three shaping processes and related cognitive changes. End customers appear to be more perceptive to the sustainability of a product/service offering and are able to express the desired effect of a sustainable solution. Therefore, they can play a major role in the decision making around adopting sustainable innovations. Other notable stakeholder groups are governmental agencies, product partners, and independent bodies, which contribute to market approach shaping, product and/or service offering shaping, and credibility shaping, respectively. Our case studies show that interactions with these stakeholder groups provide new perspectives on the value potential of the sustainable innovation and help to find and effectuate the right business model for the sustainable innovation. In addition to these stakeholder groups, new employees played a major role in the WeGo and D-grade cases, as did interaction with a consultant of an intermediary organisation in the NP case.

A second observation is that it is primarily managerial interaction with new stakeholders – as in new-to-the-firm – that influences the direction of change in the managers' cognition and, consequently, the innovation of the business model. In all cases, the number of quotes indicating that a manager's understanding of the business was induced by new stakeholders exceeded the number of quotes related to existing stakeholders. The interactions with new stakeholders emphasise the importance of taking an outside-in perspective to stimulate business model innovation (Doz & Kosonen, 2010). Our findings show that, in the case of business model innovation for sustainability, new stakeholders, or 'latent' stakeholders in the view of Mitchell et al. (1997), may be more important than existing ones.

This implies an interesting avenue for further research. The literature on business model innovation points towards the idea that managers' interaction with stakeholders may drive innovation in business models through managerial cognitive change (Doz & Kosonen, 2010). However, as we have shown in Section 2.1, the literature mainly studies how stakeholders constrain managerial cognitive change (for example, Aspara et al., 2011; Tikkanen et al., 2005). Our cases find the opposite, which leads to the question of how these findings relate to each other. One possible explanation may be that interaction with existing stakeholders reinforces existing managerial cognitions and

34 *Inge Oskam et al.*

hence leads to the maintenance of an existing business model. New or latent stakeholders may have the opposite effect. They appear to be more important for the development of new business models for sustainable innovations than for generic business models. This raises questions around how latent stakeholders can be identified and involved to spur sustainable business model innovation. Latent stakeholders may be difficult to identify. They may also be less amenable to participate in the process of sustainable business model innovation, because they perceive this as being less relevant to them. Therefore, we suggest the following research agenda. First, the identification of latent stakeholders needs more scholarly attention. Future empirical analysis could study how managers can identify and select latent stakeholders of sustainable innovations, for example, by building on the stakeholder attributes philosophy, impact, and legitimacy, as proposed by Schlange (2009). Further research could also study which stakeholder groups may be relevant for different types of business models for sustainability. Second, further research is necessary to explore how deliberate interaction with these stakeholders may be activated and managed in a way that contributes to managerial cognitive change and advances the sustainable business model innovation process. For example, future research could study how a process of stakeholder motivation that includes attention to the distribution of value among the stakeholders (Dentchev & Heene, 2004) can drive active involvement of latent stakeholders in the process.

2.5.2 Three shaping processes and related types of managerial cognition

We find that the influence of stakeholders on managers' understanding about their businesses runs via three shaping processes, which can be related to the four types of restricting managerial cognitions: industry recipe, boundary beliefs, reputational rankings, and product ontologies (Aspara et al., 2011; Tikkanen et al., 2005). Overcoming restrictions related to three of these types enables managers to innovate their business model for sustainability. We found boundary beliefs to be important in market approach shaping, as changes occur in who the manager thought they could pursue as a customer (Tikkanen et al., 2005). Our case studies indicate that stretching these boundaries – for example, from direct customer to end customer and other decision makers – was indispensable for finding the right business model for the sustainable innovations. Product ontologies appeared to be related to product/service offering shaping as the manager's belief related to a superior offering for the target group changed in all cases from the original functionality-oriented offering towards a total solution that unburdens the customer, as the mere sustainability of the solution was not enough for adoption by the market. Reputational rankings also played a significant role in all shaping processes in the cases; for example, in relation to the reputation of the partners, the managers' chose to collaborate with reputable product partners and customers that fit the sustainability philosophy of the firm and independent bodies that are able to legitimise the sustainability of the solution. However, in our cases we did not find a relation of shaping processes to industry recipe, perhaps because the cases concern an emerging sustainable technology and a sector-logic has yet to emerge.

The strategic relevance of the shaping processes for changing these cognitions can be explored further in the future. A relevant question could be whether the relative strength of the described shaping processes and the four managerial cognitions is a predictor of the outcome of the sustainable business model innovation process. Hence, our concepts may enable us to get a better understanding about why some manager–stakeholder interactions ultimately lead to sustainable business model innovation in one situation, whereas similar interactions do not lead to sustainable business model innovation in another.

Based on an analysis of the relationships among the concepts, we further propose that market approach shaping, product and/or service offering shaping, and credibility shaping are interrelated. We found that the processes are not sequential and linear, but actually run in parallel and are iterative. They mutually contribute to the change in a manager's cognition and, subsequently, for business model innovation for sustainability. This parallel and iterative aspect may be caused by the possibility that interaction with some stakeholders contributes to more than one shaping process, as well as that each shaping process delivers different information to the manager. First, this indicates that some stakeholders may play multiple roles. Second, insights gained in one shaping process may not necessarily align with insights gained in another. They need to be reconciled in order to build a coherent business model for sustainability, which requires another iteration with the respective stakeholders. Further research could provide a fine-grained perspective on this iterative process and could explore the different roles that each stakeholder group may play in inducing cognitive change and finding a viable sustainable business model.

Even though the shaping processes are found to be iterative in our cases, all three cases indicate a priority for market approach shaping. This may be related to the observation that the stakeholder-induced managerial cognitive changes we identified in our case studies all started by (re)considering what the main beneficiaries of the value potential of the sustainable technology were. The starting point may be different in other cases, which may lead to another order of the shaping processes. Further research could explore the conditions that determine which shaping process is dominant in which situation.

2.5.3 Limitations and further research

The setup of this study has certain limitations, which also provide opportunities for research. First, the empirical part of our study was restricted to three cases involving relatively small firms. The analytical generalisability of the results to firms with other characteristics could benefit from research among larger firms, from other sectors, and with other types of sustainable business models. Second, we only examined the influence of stakeholders on managers as if this is a one-directional process. It is likely that the cognitive beliefs of stakeholders are also influenced by managers or by being exposed to the new sustainable technologies and the new business models for sustainability. In that situation, there would not only be an influence of stakeholders on a manager's cognitive beliefs but also vice versa. Third, and relatedly, the present study focused on a change in managerial cognition by stakeholder interaction triggering and supporting business model innovation and omitted other strategic actions and influences. Future research could concentrate on how a change in managerial cognition relates to other causes of business model innovation for sustainability.

2.6 Conclusions

Although research assigns a central role to both stakeholder interaction and managerial cognition in business model innovation for sustainability, the connection between the two has not been studied. This chapter aims to respond to the call to search for processes that may trigger and support this managerial cognitive change. We propose that managerial cognitive change is triggered by manager–stakeholder interaction, in which latent stakeholders have a relatively prominent role, and is supported by three stakeholder-driven shaping processes (market approach shaping, product and/or service offering shaping, and credibility shaping), adding to a further understanding of business model innovation dynamics for sustainability, and specifically the role of manager–stakeholder interactions therein.

Business model innovation for sustainability 37

Appendix
Coding scheme

Examples of open codes	1st order codes	2nd order codes	Categories
Broadcasting	Creating publicity and visibility	Technology push (prior to change)	
Participating in fairs			
Persuading potential direct customers	Persuading direct customers		
Market exploration	Expanding the network with potential customers		
Active networking			
Changing the target group	Changing the go-to-market strategy		Market approach shaping
Changing the message			
Shift to end clients and influencers	Creating awareness for environmental and social issues	Market pull (after change)	
Understanding drivers of influencers			
Listening to end clients	Enticing end customers or decision makers to prescribe		
Message shift towards emotion			
Hiring new manager	Focussed market development with allies with additional networks		
Gaining market access			
Organising the value network			
Providing value for the chain providing functional value	Seeking value for the whole value chain	Delivering functionality (prior to change)	
Providing ecological value	Focusing on total cost of ownership		
Acceptance added value versus costs			

(*Continued*)

38 *Inge Oskam et al.*

Examples of open codes	1st order codes	2nd order codes	Categories
Changing the product/ service offering with partners	Changing what the firm has to offer		Product and/ or service offering shaping
Listening to needs of end customers	Understanding needs and motives of end customers and decision makers	Providing solutions (after change)	
Co-creation with customers			
Creating added value for end customers	Creating superior offerings through collaboration		
Meeting complementors Providing complementary products	Focussing on effect of end solution		
Adding services			
Providing convenience			
Unburdening the client			
Making price less relevant			
Technology testing with R&D partner	Proving functionality Proving sustainability	Providing evidence (prior to change)	
Field testing with chain			
Acceptance testing with launching customer certification for sustainability			
Quantifying CO_2 reduction			
Collaboration for enhancing credibility and legitimacy	Changing how the firm builds credibility		Credibility shaping
Endorsement by key customers	Endorsement by reputable key customers	Gaining legitimacy (after change)	
High reputation			
Reselling by partner	Endorsement by influencers		
Legitimisation by independent bodies	Building extra-business relationships		
Acquainted through awards			
Endorsement by the channel			
Using experience of partners with other markets			

3 Sustainable innovation for the business model of nonprofit organizations

Frank de Langen, Judith Sanderse, and Francisca Perez Salgado

3.1 Introduction

Research in sustainable business model (SBM) is growing and is expected to supersede the business model research (Geissdoerfer, Vladimirova, & Evans, 2018). The sustainable business model concept is evolving (Dentchev et al., 2018) with one approach focusing on the triple bottom line while the other approach focusing on sustainable innovation (Wadin & Ahlgren, 2019). The research presented in this chapter touches on both streams.

Sustainability is an ambiguous concept as there are different interpretations (Gatto, 1995). Sustainability can mean financial viability in the long term. Weerawardena, McDonald, and Mort (2010, p. 346) argue that NPOs *"cannot rely on profit, and lack the taxing authority of the government sector"* so they have to rely on other business models to sustain their existence. Reficco, Layrisse, and Barrios (2020, p. 2) notice that *"Experimenting with business models has proven to be a particularly fruitful path for not-for-profit organizations."* So sustainable business models in this sense take the perspective of organizational financial continuation.

The most cited definition of sustainable development at present is the one from the 'Our Common Future' report (Brundtland, 1987), namely *"… development that meets the needs of the present without compromising the ability of future generations to meet their own needs."* This encompasses environmental, social and economic aspects. In 2015 the United Nations tried to make sustainability more concrete, by describing the sustainable development goals (SDGs), of which SDG 9 focuses on sustainable and innovative enterprises and infrastructure (United Nations, 2020).

So, the use of the concept sustainability by nonprofit organizations (NPO) can be confusing. According to Daub, Scherrer, and Verkuil (2014) little research has been conducted with regard to other aspects of sustainability of NPOs and sustainable innovation in NPOs (Adams, Jeanrenaud, Bessant, Denyer, & Overy, 2016). In the nonprofit literature, sustainable innovation is seen as enabling the NPO to create a greater impact (McDonald, 2007). Yet, both Geissdoerfer et al. (2018) and Weerawardena and Mort (2012) show that there is no common definition of sustainable innovation. Yet, given the importance of the NPOs, both in size as in importance with respect to the

40 *Frank de Langen et al.*

creation of social value, it is important to bridge this gap. This chapter will address the question of what sustainability and sustainable innovation means for the business model of nonprofit organizations. And how, for NPOs, sustainable innovation is related to sustainable business models. A definition of sustainable NPO business models is given and related to methods for analyzing the NPO's sustainable business models and investigate sustainable innovation. By using three case studies, the business models will be described and the sustainable innovations will be determined, answering the following questions:

- How can a sustainable nonprofit organizational business model be described?
- How can sustainable innovation be described for nonprofit organizations?
- For nonprofit organizations, how is sustainable innovation related to the organization's sustainable business model?

3.2 Literature review

3.2.1 Sustainable business model in general

At a general level, a business model is a description of an organization and how that organization functions in achieving its goals such as social good, growth, profitability (Massa, Tucci, & Afuah, 2017). It is a simplified representation of the components of an organization and the interaction between these components (Geissdoerfer, Savaget, & Evans, 2017). There is no definitive definition of a sustainable business model; the theory is still developing. Dentchev et al. (2018) argue that sustainable business model research fundamentally focuses on the why and how organizations respond to sustainability issues. To do so, the organizations change their existing business model or develop new models. Organizations adjust their business model, in a way that it supports sustainable goals, other organizations change their value offer in a way that sustainability becomes part of it.

Sustainable business models differ from traditional business models in at least three fundamental ways (Geissdoerfer et al., 2018). First, they assume a view of business as an engine of societal progress. Second, they include a broader notion of value beyond economic to encompass social and environmental values. Third, they undertake and offer a multi-stakeholder perspective, as well as, a system perspective on value creation (Massa et al., 2017).

Sustainable business models are helpful tools for

> describing, analyzing, managing and communicating (i) a company's sustainable value proposition to its customers, and all other stakeholders, (ii) how it creates and delivers this value, (iii) and how it captures economic value while maintaining or regenerating natural, social, and economic capital beyond its organizational boundaries.
>
> (Schaltegger, Hansen, & Lüdeke-Freund, 2016, p. 6)

As Schaltegger et al. (2016) use 'company' as the object of the sustainable business model, it still is to be determined if this concept can be used to analyze sustainability in the context of NPOs.

3.2.2 Sustainable business model of NPOs

There are different perspectives on sustainability with regard to NPOs and what it means in practice (Hailey, 2014). These perspectives are confronted with those on for-profit organizations in Table 3.1.

A sustainable NPO is defined as an organization that is able to fulfill its commitments to its clients, its donors, and the community in which it operates. Hence, the civil society can place their trust in that commitment (Weerawardena et al., 2010). Hailey (2014) adds that sustainable NPOs are able to respond strategically and effectively to external changes by adapting their mission, accessing new sources of income and adapting their system and processes to meet the new challenges. Sustainable NPOs incorporate ecological and social aspects in their structure, process and activities (Daub et al., 2014). Ceptureanu et al. (2017) point out that any analysis of sustainability needs to not only acknowledge the diversity of these perspectives, but also recognize that each perspective complements the other and should not be viewed in isolation. Hence, for a NPO to have a sustainable business model it will need

Table 3.1 Comparing perspectives on sustainability

Perspectives on sustainability for NPOs	The perspectives seen from for-profit viewpoint
Financial sustainability, meaning being able to survive so that it can serve its constituency (Weerawardena et al., 2010) or long-term economic growth of the NPO (Ceptureanu, Ceptureanu, Orzan, & Marin, 2017).	Financial viability is taken as granted in the case of the for-profit-organizations.
Program or intervention sustainability, meaning that the quality of a particular program or service is maintained after the targeted intervention has ended (Ceptureanu et al., 2017; Hailey, 2014).	—
Organizational sustainability focuses and assesses those organizational characteristics which are critical for NPOs (Stopper, Kossik, & Gastermann, 2016)	Similar (see Stopper et al., 2016)
Environmental sustainability and social sustainability (Hailey, 2014).	Sustainable products and services (Geissdoerfer et al., 2018) Social or sustainable entrepreneurship (Schaltegger et al., 2016)

42   *Frank de Langen et al.*

to focus on all the above mentioned aspects of sustainability, being financial, organizational, social and environmental, to ensure its long-term survival.

This is the view taken in this research. The value component of nonprofit organizations includes value creation for its beneficiaries, donors and society at large. From the foregoing argument it is clear that sustainability involves the interaction between different elements, but this does not tell us how one can assess a NPO's sustainable business model.

3.2.3 Analyzing a sustainable NPO business model

The Doughnut Economy developed by Raworth (2018) is a tool which can be used to analyze the state of sustainability on a regional, national and international level. Raworth (2018) distinguishes between the social and environmental aspects of sustainability. She argues that there are essential human conditions that have to be met and that no one should fall below these 'social foundations of well-being', such as access to clean water, education, food, as well as energy, gender equality and democracy. On the other hand, to realize these social foundations, resources are required, the sustainable utilization of which must be within an upper limit, called the ecological ceiling. Stopper et al. (2016) have translated the concept into an ecological sustainable approach for small and medium-sized manufacturing enterprises using the prevalent EU social standards. They are providing a checklist according to Raworth's principles and parameters for companies to analyze and measure their sustainability. However, this method is only applied to for-profit organizations.

A relevant dimension concerning NPO sustainability is the actual operational aspects of the organization and its impact on the social and environmental surrounding. For example, the activities of humanitarian NPOs in saving people can harm the environment, for instance, refugee camps that degrade the surrounding natural resources such as forests (IUCN, 2019).

There are different methods which can be used to analyze the sustainability of NPOs. The Business Model Canvas by Osterwalder and Pigneur (2010) is a tool widely used within the academic sustainability business model literature (Dentchev et al., 2018). However, researchers have commented that this framework provides insufficient insights on how exactly organizations achieve environmental and social sustainability (Brehmer, Podoynitsyna, & Langerak, 2018). Ceptureanu et al. (2017) warn that as NPO's activities are multidimensional: they cannot be captured by a single method of measurement. Adams et al. (2016) have highlighted that many sustainable business models continue to be developed based on the neoclassical economic worldview that emphasize profit more heavily than other sustainability components. This has led to derivatives based on Osterwalder and Pigneur's Business Model Canvas (2010).

The Sustainable Business Model Framework (Joyce & Paquin, 2016) adds two elements – environmental and social – to provide insight on how exactly organizations achieve environmental and social sustainability. The Social Enterprise Model Canvas of Sparviero (2019) gives extra attention to social value in an organization's business model. The sustainable business model archetypes framework by Ritala, Huotari, Bocken, Albareda, and Puumalainen (2018) incorporates inclusive value creation, collaboration and Bottom of the Pyramid segments, and takes an inclusive approach to innovation. Even though these various sustainability business model frameworks have been developed with elements which go beyond profit-only and inclusion of sustainability aspects of an organization, none are focused on NPOs. As the focus of this study is on sustainable business model for nonprofit organizations, any analytical model requires recognition of the NPO worldview as research has shown differences between NPOs and non-NPOs. Hence, the direct application of business tools developed for organizations besides NPOs needs to be evaluated for being fit to the nonprofit context.

The NPO business model framework (Sanderse, de Langen, & Perez Salgado, 2020, Figure 3.1) is one such model. The framework is divided into two layers, the programmatic and the operational (fundraising/marketing & financial), in order to distinguish the different strategies and components that nonprofits use in serving their 'programmatic' customers (beneficiaries) and their 'financial' customers (donors). However, even though this framework reflects an NPO business model and shows its financial and organizational as well as its social and/or environmental sustainability, this framework does not specially capture the social and environmental sustainability aspects of

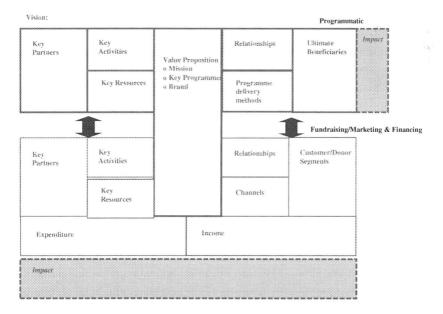

Figure 3.1 NPO business model framework for NPOs with multiple income streams (Sanderse et al., 2020).

44 *Frank de Langen et al.*

the operations of the organizations itself. To enable this, we need to also look at other sustainability models that do not specially focus on business models.

3.2.4 NPO sustainable innovation and its connection to a NPO's sustainable business model

For NPOs to be successful or just to survive they need to innovate throughout their lifetime (Jaskyte, 2004). Sustainable innovation is innovation that improves the ecological, economic and social performance of an organization (Carrillo-Hermosilla, Del Río, & Könnölä, 2010). Adams et al. (2016) go further and describe it as making intentional changes to the organization's philosophy and values, as well as to its products, processes or practices to serve the specific purpose of creating and realizing social and environmental value in addition to economic returns. This moves the concept closer to the values of nonprofit organizations. The changes in the external environment, a sense that the existing ways of working are not solving problems and the need to be sustainable has led NPOs to develop multiple innovative strategies (Lindgardt & Shaffer, 2012). Weerawardena and Mort (2012) found that NPOs pursue incremental and radical innovation for achieving greater impact with their work. Interestingly large NPOs tend to undertake more radical innovation due to their strong financial resource base and their well-established brands (Weerawardena & Mort, 2012). These innovative strategies can be realized through business model innovation or product or service innovation (Lindgardt & Shaffer, 2012). For some NPOs business model innovation means redefining their mission or approach to their mission, with the aim of achieving greater impact (Lindgardt & Shaffer, 2012), while for others, sustainable business model innovation is a break from the current practice, large or small, that leads to positive effect (Sahni, Lanzerotti, Bliss, & Pike, 2017). Research has shown that successful NPOs use innovation to have impact (McDonald, 2007; Sahni et al., 2017). McDonald (2007) calls this mission-driven innovation. As innovativeness is defined as the organization's ability to offer new products and services and to keep abreast of advances in technologies and practices (McDonald, 2007). This is closely related to an organization's sustainable business model.

Hence, sustainable innovation within the NPO context can be seen from different angles. The literature review provided the description of how sustainable NPO business model and how sustainable innovation can be described for NPOs. This leads us to the analyzing and measuring of NPOs sustainable business model and how sustainable innovation has been applied in practices by NPOs.

3.3 Methodology

The research is conducted in several stages. The first stage is a literature review of nonprofit sustainability, sustainable business models, sustainable

NPO innovation and frameworks for analyzing an organization's sustainable business model. The literature review provided the theoretical answers to the research questions as well as a framework that can be used to analyze a NPO's sustainable business model. In the second stage, documentary research of three NPOs is undertaken to analyze their sustainable business model using the NPO business model framework (Sanderse et al., under review). The NPO business model framework was chosen as it was specifically designed for NPOs and takes sustainable business model elements into account. The framework provides a visualization of the organization's business model and enables analyses of a NPO's sustainable business model. In addition, it shows the sustainable innovation undertaken by the organization over time resulting in the greater sustainability of the business model. By visualizing and comparing the NPO's business model at the time of its establishment and in 2019 allows us to describe the NPO's sustainable business model and sustainable innovations undertaken over time.

To provide empirical data for answering the research questions, we conducted case studies using documentary research. Documents and research papers of the selected NPOs were studied to enable the researchers to identify the sustainable business model and the sustainable innovations developed. The researchers have selected three NPOs for the following reasons and criteria:

- The researchers were able to collect sufficient documentation on the NPOs to enable them to draw the business models of these NPOs at time of their creation and the present time. This allows for a comparison over time.
- Materials on various innovations undertaken by these NPOs could be collected and analyzed. This ensured that in addition to the theoretical explanation one could see that real-world examples and empirical date were gathered.
- Existence of the organization for over 50 years, proving the financial (long-term) sustainability of the organization. For this study, the selected NPOs were all established between 1915 and 1961.
- Long-term existence requires innovation (Jaskyte, 2004; Lindgardt & Shaffer, 2012). The selected NPOs being over 50 years old enables us to analyze the sustainable innovation of their sustainable business model.
- At least one NPO needs, at the time of its establishment, to have focused almost exclusively on the social elements of the sustainable business model, while another NPO's focus should almost exclusively have been on the environmental elements of the sustainable business model. This is due to the fact that the researchers are not aware of any long existing NPOs that focused on both the social and the environmental elements of a sustainable business model.

To achieve reliable metrics an analytical tool to analyze the data was used.

46 *Frank de Langen et al.*

3.4 Case studies

In this section a single case analysis is given of each of the case studies.

3.4.1 *World Wide Fund for Nature (WWF)*

Established in 1961, the World Wild Fund for Nature (WWF) is the world's largest environmental organization (Schwarzenbach, 2011). The organization is active in over 100 countries in the world and in 2018/2019 had an annual income of Euro 778 million (WWF, 2020). It was originally founded to save the world's wildlife.

At its establishment, WWF was known as World Wildlife Fund, as the value proposition of its business model focused mainly on conservation of iconic wildlife species such as lions and tigers. It was established to raise funds for conservation projects carried out by International Union for the Conservation of Nature (IUCN) and other environmental organizations in order to prevent the irreversible loss of species (Schwarzenbach, 2011). In 1973, they changed their business model from a sole focus on protection of specific wildlife species to the creation of protected areas. Later they moved to a more holistic approach combining efforts at larger spatial scales (landscape, regional and global) and wider drivers of change (WWF-US, 2019). In addition, they also started fundraising for and implementing their own projects. Currently, WWF focuses on nine broad issues (Forests, Oceans, Wildlife, Food, Climate & Energy, Freshwater, Finance, Markets and Governance) and 35 priority places (WWF, 2019).

Mission statement:

The mission of World Wildlife Fund is to conserve nature and reduce the most pressing threats to the diversity of life on Earth. Our vision is to build a future in which people live in harmony with nature.

We seek to save a planet, a world of life. Reconciling the needs of human beings and the needs of others that share the Earth, we seek to practice conservation that is humane in the broadest sense. We seek to instill in people everywhere a discriminating, yet unabashed, reverence for nature and to balance that reverence with a profound belief in human possibilities. From the smallest community to the largest multinational organization, we seek to inspire others who can advance the cause of conservation.

We seek to be the voice for those creatures who have no voice. We speak for their future. We seek to apply the wealth of our talents, knowledge, and passion to making the world wealthier in life, in spirit, and in living wonder of nature.

(https://help.worldwildlife.org/hc/en-us/articles/360007905494-WWF-s-Mission-Vision)

An example of WWF's sustainable product innovation is the Forest Stewardship Council (FSC). WWF was one of the founding members of this market-based approach to reduce loss of biodiversity-rich tropical forests through certification of better forest management practices. This not only recognizes economic and ecological but also social factors, such as indigenous peoples' rights and local community and workers' rights. FSC and Marine Stewardship Council (MSC) were developed in partnerships with industry groups, social and environmental NGOs and the public. FSC together with MSC are recognized as some of the most significant sustainability certification systems for natural resources (Adams et al., 2016). Both of these initiatives contribute to key forest and marine goals of WWF and hence towards the social and environmental values of the organization.

3.4.2 Women's International League for Peace and Freedom (WILPF)

Established in 1915, Women's International League for Peace and Freedom (WILPF) is the world's oldest international women's peace organization (Confortini, 2011). In 2018 it had an annual income of more than EUR 4 million (WILPF, 2019a). The organization is operational on a global scale with 47 offices and groups (WILPF, 2019b). The founders of the organization initially met with a view to contributing to ending the First World War.

With its focus on peace and freedom (Women's International League for Peace and Freedom, 1983) the organization touches on social parameters, such as gender equality, social equity, political voice, peace and justice and income and work. These factors show the complexity of seemingly simple targets. The underlying factors can have inverse effects on each other and the higher goals of the organization. At several points during WILPF's long history (1919, 1946, 1968), the members wondered at the purpose or the organization's ability to fulfill its mission or the vision of its founders. In all instances this led to a period of organizational reflection and adjustment of the organization's programs and activities (Confortini, 2011).

WILPF is mostly run by volunteers. Its operational costs were covered by individual membership fees. According to their Annual Report 2018 the current income is generated as follows: *"Main donors are governments and private foundations. Other income sources are the United Nations, partners and major donors, private donations, membership contributions, merchandising, bequests and legacies, and miscellaneous income sources"* (WILPF, 2019a, p. 31).

The first mention of the organization's work on environmental aspects occurred in 1955 (Bussy & Tims, 1980) and has since then addressed environmental issues, due to link between environmental destruction and increased conflicts, especially, armed conflicts, showing a shift in the value offerings, beneficiaries and so the business model framework.

48   *Frank de Langen et al.*

Interestingly, for WILPF the contribution of the organization's innovative work was recognized in 1931 and 1946 as two of its founding members received the Nobel Peace Prize for their and the organization's innovative work in the field of women's right and peace. Even with such recognition in the early history of the organization it has had to realign its focus and business model several times through its history due to the changes to the external environment.

Mission Statement:
WILPF members create the peaceful transformation they wish to see in the world by making connections that:

- *Provide continuity with the past so that knowledge of historical events and patterns informs current activities for change*
- *Create analysis and action that reflect and reinforce each other*
- *Link and challenge root causes of oppression, especially racism, sexism, heterosexism, militarism, economic disparity, and political disempowerment*
- *Build and strengthen relationships and movements for justice, peace, and radical democracy*

(https://wilpfus.org/story/vision–and–mission)

3.4.3 Oxfam

Oxfam is a humanitarian organization which started in 1942 as Oxford Committee for Famine Relief. It is now an international development NPO and is one of the main proponents of the rights-based approach to development, in particular in the context of collaboration with business (Pesqueira & Glasbergen, 2013). Oxfam is a global organization and works in 67 countries, with an annual income of more than EURO 1 billion in 2018/2019 (Oxfam, 2019).

With Oxfam one can see several changes in its business model and mission innovation over time. In 1942, the group campaigned for food supplies to be sent through an allied naval blockade to starving women and children in enemy-occupied Greece during the Second World War. After the war, Oxfam continued its work, sending materials and financial aid to groups helping poor people throughout Europe. As the situation in Europe improved, Oxfam's attention shifted to the needs of people in developing countries (Oxfam, 2019a). Although Oxfam's initial concern was the provision of food to relieve famine, over the years the organization has developed strategies to combat the causes of famine.

Oxfam developed a new sustainable business model innovation by introducing their physical and online shops which are a new funding mechanism of its charity work (Bond, 2016).

Another business model change is the acceptance that a major cause of the famines is climate change. Oxfam has combined advocacy for climate action

> Mission statement:
> Our purpose is to help create lasting solutions to the injustice of poverty. We are part of a global movement for change, empowering people to create a future that is secure, just and free from poverty. And we are building this positive future now.
> (https://www.oxfam.org/en/what-we-do/about/what-we-believe)

with provision of humanitarian assistance to people affected by climate related emergencies, and efforts to build communities' resilience to changing climate (Oxfam, 2019b). The importance Oxfam sees in changing targets is stressed by the fact that they created a fund to test new and/or complementary business models (Sahni et al., 2017).

3.5 Findings and research propositions

In the three case studies presented in this chapter, our analyses confirmed that the societal value of the NPO is mentioned in the organizations' mission and is part of the organizations' value proposition. Comparative analysis of the NPOs business model at the time of their establishment and that in 2019 shows that the societal value of the NPOs was important both at the time of establishment and at the current time. For the NPOs the income of the organization is mainly geared towards enabling the NPO to implement its program and activities to be able to reach the organization's mission.

This leads to proposition 1: The most important part of the value proposition of a NPO business model framework is its social value.

Proposition 2 is that the original nine building block business model canvas with its for-profit focus is not suitable for describing the sustainable business model of a NPO. Due to the complexity of the NPOs and the fact that NPOs have different forms of value – economic, social and/or environmental – the depiction and analysis of the sustainable business model of analyzed NPOs required a specific business model framework focused on NPOs. The nine building block business model canvas can be used to analyze the NPO's sustainable business model at the time of their establishment as the case study of NPOs had more than a single mission and limited programmatic activities and funding sources. With growing complexity due to a more holistic approach to programmatic activities the proposed business model framework is better attuned to NPOs.

In addition, the nine building block business model canvas was not able to articulate the different roles played by the same key NPO players or stakeholders, within different components of the NPO's sustainable business model. For example, for the NPOs governments are represented in different roles in the NPO's sustainable business model components: key partners, donors and program delivery methods, which can be visualized in the NPO business model framework.

50   *Frank de Langen et al.*

The case study findings showed that all three NPOs conducted intentional changes by various forms of sustainable innovation throughout its lifetime. This shows that the organizations innovate to improve their value, as shown by comparing the organization's sustainable business model at establishment to their 2019 sustainable business model. This could be termed mission innovation. WILPF did change its mission several times, and WWF conducted intentional organizational changes to improve the value proposition and the programmatic impact of the organization. The Oxfam case study confirmed the same.

WWF and Oxfam have also clearly documented cases of sustainable product innovation which is another form of sustainable innovation. The three case studies have undergone various forms of incremental as well as radical innovation during their lifetimes.

Based on the case studies in the research, we suggest proposition (3) that NPOs conduct various forms of sustainable innovation.

Sustainable innovation in the context of nonprofit organizations means intentional changes that improves the economic, social and environmental value of the organization (proposition 4).

It does need to be recognized that the NPO can experience tensions between the different values. Similar to the case of WWF, tensions can be experienced between achieving the ecological values and the social values. For example, establishing protected areas for species conservation does create tensions with the social parameters regarding rights of communities within or on the boundaries of these areas. This was most highlighted by a series of exposés by Buzzfeed in 2019 of human rights abuses by park guards in Central Africa, India and Nepal. Even though the organizations experience tensions between the different values, the case literature and case studies show that when the NPO conducts a sustainable innovation this was done as an intentional change to improve the economic, social and/or environmental value of the organization.

The findings from the three case studies lead to proposition 5: NPOs can only have a long-term sustainable business model when they apply at least one form of sustainable innovation.

The proposition: The sustainable business model of the three NPOs changed during the 50 plus year of the organizations' existence. Therefore, one can conclude that all three have a long-term sustainable business model. One can also see that the NPOs undertook one or more forms of sustainable innovation that resulted in a change in their sustainable business model. Therefore, an additional conclusion can be that for a NPO to have a long-term sustainable business model they need to apply at least one form of sustainable innovation. This is in line with the opinion of Jaskyte (2014) and McDonald (2007). However, the case studies did not confirm that a sustainable business model can 'only' come about due to sustainable innovation. The wording 'only' seems to be a too strong statement to prove based on three case studies. Therefore, the wording of the proposition is changed to: At least one form of sustainable innovation contributes to a NPO sustainable business model. And with this new wording the proposition is accepted.

3.6 Conclusion

This chapter has addressed what a sustainable business model and sustainable innovation means in the NPO context. From the literature we synthesized a concept and framework for analyzing the sustainable business model and sustainable innovation of NPOs. The researchers tested these concepts and frameworks on three selected NPOs, to assess its usability in a real-world setting. The literature review showed that for NPOs to have a sustainable business model it needs to focus on financial, social and environmental sustainability, to ensure its long-term survival. One way of achieving this is sustainable innovation. This can be done via sustainable business model innovation, or sustainable product innovation, but mostly for NPOs it is via the former. With the three NPOs presented we looked at how this played out in existing, long-standing, NPOs. These analyses lead to the suggestion of five propositions, which should be tested in an advanced empirical study.

Research question 1: How can a sustainable nonprofit business model be described?

The description is based on the literature review and the results from the case studies. A sustainable nonprofit business model focuses on the financial, social and environmental aspects of the organizations. The literature indicates that this definition has changed over time with initially the focus of sustainability for NPOs being long-term financial survival. The literature review showed that not all authors use the same definition as there are different opinions and views on what sustainability entails. However, the case studies show that due to the interrelation of the issues and the need to address them, NPOs see a sustainable business model composing of financial, societal and environmental aspects in the key programs of their value proposition and sometimes even in their mission.

The research showed the importance of the societal value of the sustainable business model for NPOs. And that due to the complexity and the holistic approach required for the NPO to achieve its mission, the NPO business model framework was required to analyze the NPO's sustainable business model.

Research question 2: How can sustainable innovation be described for nonprofit organizations?

With the findings of the literature review and propositions 3 and 4, sustainable innovation is described as the intentional sustainable changes that improve the economic, social and environmental values of the NPO.

Research question 3: For nonprofit organizations, how is sustainable innovation related to the organization's sustainable business model?

The results highlight that the NPOs have significantly changed their sustainable business model during their lifetime. Comparison of both the sustainable business model and the sustainable innovation developments of

NPOs shows that NPOs moved towards a holistic concept of sustainable business models. This is increasing complexity of the organizations and leading to sustainable innovation within the organizations. The NPOs were established for a single purpose focused on either tackling a humanitarian or development or environmental issue with their conception of sustainability being to ensure sufficient resources to undertake their mission. This single focus approach has broadened over the course of the organization's life to a more holistic approach that recognizes the interplay between development and environment. The literature mentioned that for NPOs to be financially viable over the long-term they need to adjust to their external environment by adapting their business model and being innovative (McDonald, 2007; Weerawardena et al., 2010). The NPOs highlighted in this chapter show that each has done so by conducting one or various forms of sustainable innovation and hence as a consequence adjusting their sustainable business models. Hence sustainable innovation is closely linked to a NPO's sustainable business model.

4 Beyond the Business Model Canvas

Towards a framework of success factors in sustainability startups – an Austrian perspective

Lisa Winkler

4.1 Introduction

Tfhe call for sustainability is ubiquitous these days in the public discourse; it has become a buzzword (over-) used by media, policy makers and business practitioners, claiming to create "innovation" for "sustainability". But there is still uncertainty left about the exact meaning of this term that seems to "mean different things to different people" (White, 2013). In the face of threat by climate change, it is primarily used in the sense of ecological sustainability. Yet, that covers only one part of today's most commonly accepted definitions of sustainability – the Triple Bottom Line, a term coined by John Elkington in the 1990s. According to his definition, sustainability, in the context of business and economics, takes into account the three pillars of "people, planet, profits", i.e. creating value for society, environment and lastly, the company itself (Elkington, 1994).

In this chapter, we present an Austrian perspective on true innovation for sustainability, taking a step towards creating a comprehensive framework to systematically analyze and understand success factors of startup companies that have set complex sustainability as standard and prerequisite for their respective business practice. The core of our research goes way deeper than e.g. one of today's most popular tools for business modelling, the Business Model Canvas by Osterwalder and Pigneur (2010). We lay our focus on organizational aspects and internal dynamics, the "human side" of a business, instead of on the company itself as an entity of value creation. Organizational culture and entrepreneurs' individual characteristics and motivations are to this day notoriously under-researched aspects of new venture success (especially in a sustainability context) and cannot be grasped by quantitative methods and tools currently in use for business modelling for sustainability (among others: Triple Layer Business Model Canvas (Joyce & Paquin, 2016), Value Mapping Tool (Bocken, Short, Rana, & Evans, 2013) or Ecologies of Business Models Experimentation Map (Bocken, Boons, & Baldassarre, 2019)).

54   *Lisa Winkler*

To address our research objective in the most holistic way possible, literature from various fields (including psychology, philosophy and alternative socioeconomic concepts) is being reviewed, focusing on topics of sustainability in economics, business models for sustainability and entrepreneurial cognition. We work towards bridging the gap between the individual level of an entrepreneur's vision and ideology and the corporate level of sustainability put into action in business practice and organizational culture.

Building on this theoretical foundation, empirical field research is carried out in cooperation with best-practice case companies to investigate the aspects of (1) Reason & Vision (see e.g. DeMol, 2019; Shepherd & Patzelt, 2018), (2) Business Opportunity (see e.g. Ardichvili, Cardozo, & Ray, 2003; Bocken et al., 2019; Bocken, Short et al., 2014), (3) Action & Communication (see e.g. Felber, 2014, 2016; Klotz, Hmieleski, Bradley, & Busenitz, 2014; Shepherd & Patzelt, 2018) and (4) Resilience (see e.g. Mitchell, Mitchell, & Smith, 2004; Shepherd & Patzelt, 2018). With the help of four innovative sustainability businesses from the sectors Fashion, Food, Social Service and Agriculture, we explore what we call "*soft* success factors" in the following.

This chapter aims to answer the questions: (1) What are success factors to a sustainability startup, specifically the non-quantifiable factors like organizational culture, internal dynamics, entrepreneurial qualities and individual characteristics? (2) How can those factors be systematically explored, categorized and structured in a framework, to be applied subsequently by scholars, startup entrepreneurs and future founders?

The intended contribution to existing research is threefold: (1) Opening up new vistas on startup success in a sustainability context, (2) creating a first framework of these factors as a tool to enable systematic reflection on existing business endeavours and (3) presenting founders, teachers and counsellors with aspects to take into consideration at the start of a sustainability business.

4.2 Literature review

Literature on sustainability in economics, business models for sustainability and entrepreneurial cognition is reviewed to shed light on how these areas have been dealt with separately. The struggle of finding a unifying definition of sustainability is discussed, as well as economic concepts and business models for sustainability, and startup success factors linked to aspects of entrepreneurial cognition. This creates a basis for systematic reflection with startup representatives to investigate the topics in a real-world context.

4.2.1 *Defining sustainability*

The terms "sustainability" and "sustainable", although widespread and commonly used these days by politics, business, media and in daily conversation do not have a single clear definition – they "mean different things to different people" (White, 2013). The World Commission on Environment and

Development published a first attempt of a precise definition in their report, Our Common Future (1987) (also called the "Brundtland Report"):

> "In essence, sustainable development is a process of change in which the exploitation of resources, the direction of investments, the orientation of technological development; and institutional change are all in harmony and enhance both current and future potential to meet human needs and aspirations.
>
> (WCED, 1987)

Yet, terms like "resources", "harmony" or "needs" are vague and can differ greatly in meaning, depending on context or audience and are not measurable for economic applications. Extensive work has since been done regarding the conception of sustainability, e.g. the differentiation in "strong sustainability" focusing on ecological aspects, and "weak sustainability" focusing on human well-being (cf. Jamieson, 1998). A commonly accepted way of defining sustainability in a business context is through the so-called Triple Bottom Line, coined by John Elkington. Earlier, the author had already described a "win-win-win situation" for companies, their customers and the environment (Elkington, 1994), also often formulated as 3P – "people, planet, profits", putting a company's pursuit of profit in the last place.

To pursue a common goal of acting sustainably, e.g. in a startup team, it might not be necessary (or possible) to construct one apt sentence to define the term, but the important factor for a business to succeed is a shared set of values (DeMol, 2019). Terms linked to sustainability, visualized in word tag clouds, can be useful to achieve a shared vision, approaching the sustainability discourse as a case of "I know it when I see it" (White, 2013). Theory and practice of sustainability are subject to constant change: Competition in markets, societal values, a growing global demand for transparency, life-cycle technologies, corporate partnerships, etc. (Elkington, 2013). Therefore, the whole discourse remains active and cannot be put to an end once and for all. In all startup teams examined in the context of this chapter, a common vision is pursued, leading to success (DeMol, 2019), but individual ideas of and reflections on sustainability can coexist, as an open discourse is encouraged within each company.

4.2.2 Sustainability and economics

The Austrian Federal Ministry of Agriculture, Forestry, Environment and Water Management, or "Lebensministerium" – "Ministry of Life" (since January 2020: Federal Ministry of Agriculture, Regions and Tourism), published a dossier in 2012, dealing with alternative concepts for economy and society (Zukunftsdossier alternative Wirtschafts- und Gesellschaftskonzepte. BMLFUW 2012) as part of the ongoing project Growth in Transition. This paper gives an overview of well researched ideas for alternatives to the

56 *Lisa Winkler*

present economic systems, among others the Steady State Economy, describing a globally sustainable economic development on a physically acceptable level (Daly, 1973) or Post-Growth Economy (theorizing an economy without growth within the natural boundaries of our planet's finite resources (Jackson, 2009; Paech, 2012). Creating "shared value" – economic value that also creates value for society (Porter & Kramer, 2011) – is the central principle of the so-called Economy for the Common Good. Austrian author Christian Felber took a pioneering role in designing a more humane, social, ecologic and democratic economic system. Economy for the Common Good is a holistic approach "thinking together" economics, ethics based on Christian social doctrine, democracy, gender and ecology (Felber, 2016).

Benefitting the common good is in fact inherent to the word "economics", stemming from Greek "oikonomia" (the art of housekeeping – money as means to an end), as described by Aristotle, in contrast to "chrematistike" (the art of acquiring money) (Aristotle, Pol., 1258 b 34–35). Today's approaches to the basics of business modelling, taking as popular example the Business Model Canvas by Osterwalder and Pigneur (2010), can be viewed as inherently chrematistic in Aristotle's words, treating the creation of value for the common good as something additional and rather new ("shared value"). Change towards sustainable business models is about the implementation of alternative paradigms other than the neoclassical economic worldview on the organizational level – the culture, structure and routines within a company, shaping the way of doing business towards sustainable development (Boons & Lüdeke-Freund, 2013). Economy for the Common Good is a process in which every private person, small or big business, organization or community can participate (Felber, 2016). Its significance lies in the commitment to a set of principles rather than the membership in an association. The case companies in part 3 pursue value creation for the common good through innovative approaches to sustainability instead of it being but an added value (De Chernatony, Harris, & Dall'Olmo Riley, 2000).

4.2.3 Business modelling for sustainability

Similar to the vague nature of the term sustainability, there are various definitions of a "business model", "business model innovation" or "sustainable business models" (Evans et al., 2017). A commonly accepted definition of "business model" refers to how a firm creates, delivers and captures value (Magretta, 2002; Osterwalder, Pigneur, & Tucci, 2005). An entire branch of research has emerged around sustainable business models (SBM's). SBM innovation is about creating superior value for customers and firms, maximizing social profit by addressing societal and environmental needs (Bocken et al., 2019; Boons & Lüdeke-Freund, 2013). Several factors are important for a unified perspective on SBMs: the significance of economic, social and environmental benefit; consideration of entire value networks and mutual satisfaction of numerous stakeholders; developing or transforming business models into product-service-systems as an opportunity for innovation through life-cycle thinking and effective supply chain management (Evans et al., 2017). Building on and interconnecting with academic literature, tools have been developed for a systemic sustainable business modelling practice, among others the Triple Layer Business Model Canvas (Joyce & Paquin, 2016), the Value Mapping Tool (Bocken et al., 2013) or the Ecology of Business Models Experimentation Map (Bocken et al., 2019). "The literature and practice of innovations for sustainability is vast but fragmented," state Bocken et al., since there are various conceptual approaches contributing to SBM innovation. However, they rarely get taken out of the academic context and into the practice of evaluating or transforming existing business endeavours or founding new ones. Parallelly, industrial practice seems to be ahead of academia in some cases, exploring and developing novel business models that have not yet been described (Bocken et al., 2014). A first categorization of eight sustainable business model archetypes was made by Bocken et al. in 2014, drawing influence from conceptual literature and economic practice. The actual adoption of these models was explored (Ritala, Huotari, Bocken, Albareda, & Puumalainen, 2018), leading to a refinement into nine archetypes, three each focussing on either the environmental, social or economic pillar of sustainability (Bocken et al., 2019). A map of these archetypes had been used in our own empirical research, supporting the entrepreneurs in explaining their respective business models. However, it was never just one type that applied to the company's practice, as each of them already takes quite holistic approaches on sustainability.

4.2.4 Startup success and entrepreneurial cognition

What comes first – the idea or the entrepreneur? Business idea and model are crucial to the success of a nascent startup company and also numerous other factors linked to the people who are founding it. Previous research on companies, individual entrepreneurs and teams has tried to identify factors for startup success (or failure). Among others, the following aspects have been examined: Team efforts leading to success by conjoining prior individual experience with a shared passion and strategic vision, having entrepreneurs' different skills complement each other (DeMol, 2019; Klotz et al., 2014), and also multiplying the social capital brought in by team members' respective networks of trust and knowledge outside the company (Klotz et al., 2014). It also proves important to have a realistic but optimistic perception of risk in the market (consequently showing the importance of risk management) (Van Gelderen, Thurik, & Bosma, 2005), as well as reflection and learning experience from previous venture failure (Mitchell et al., 2004). Starting a business full-time (as opposed to part-time) tends to lead to success as there are less distractions; and for ventures in the manufacturing sector, the likelihood to be successful in the long run is greater once they have gotten started with the required high amounts of knowledge and capital (Van Gelderen et al., 2005).

58 *Lisa Winkler*

Individual entrepreneurs' characteristics, thinking and actions have been subject to discussions and research. Successful businesspeople are often seen as having the "entrepreneurial gene", although entrepreneurship is a behavioural set of activities rather than an innate personality trait, as "what differentiates entrepreneurs from non-entrepreneurs is that entrepreneurs create organizations, while non-entrepreneurs do not." (Gartner, 1988). The decision making associated with entrepreneurial action is a process high in uncertainty, complexity, time pressure, emotionality and identity investment (Shepherd & Patzelt, 2018). Therefore it makes sense to apply a "cognitive lens" (Shepherd & Patzelt, 2018) to understand aspects of knowledge, motivation and emotion in individuals' entrepreneurial processes.

Founding a business calls for the ability to identify of an opportunity (Ardichvili et al., 2003) and take action on it. There are two dimensions to the identification process: The objective reality of one's environment and an individual's subjective interpretation of this environment and their role in it. Higher levels of prior knowledge facilitate opportunity recognition in general, different types of knowledge facilitate the recognition of different opportunities. Awareness about the ecological environment, specific cultures or societal problems helps recognize chances for sustainable action, e.g. protecting or maintaining the environment or benefitting disadvantaged people. Expertise in particular areas (through work, education or personal/social experience) supports opportunity recognition linked to one's individual focus and capabilities (Shepherd & Patzelt, 2018).

Individual motivation is needed to focus attention in order to be able to spot an opportunity. This can occur either in the shape of a threat to the environment (motivation to act is raised, if one's psychological or physical well-being becomes increasingly threatened) or altruism (through empathy and sympathy). Entrepreneurs with strong environmental values tend to draw attention to a specific harm to nature (or its prevention), influencing their decision making. To actively seek, assess and seize sustainability opportunities, it is important for an entrepreneur to utilize and conjoin prior environmental/communal and entrepreneurial knowledge (Shepherd & Patzelt, 2018).

On an emotional level, values and passions influence the recognition and exploitation of (sustainable) opportunities: The more obsessively passionate an entrepreneur is (i.e. the higher their internal compulsion to pursue an activity), the more likely they are to seize an opportunity (Shepherd & Patzelt, 2018).

4.3 Methodology

Success factors of startup companies with sustainability as a crucial point in their business model are explored in this chapter. The definition of success varies, depending on the respective interpretation of "sustainability". We investigate factors that cannot sufficiently be analyzed with current tools for business modelling and analysis, focusing on the organizational side of a business (including entrepreneurs' individual characteristics or corporate culture). These "*soft* success factors", aim to look beyond the business model canvas or lean startup approach and their quantitatively measurable features. Four business cases were scrutinized through exploratory interviews, leading to the creation of a framework of success factors in sustainability startups. To address the research objective, this instrumental multiple-case study methodology was chosen to investigate "a contemporary phenomenon within its real-life context" (Baxter & Jack, 2008; Yin, 2003). Two research questions were formulated in the previous stage:

1   What are success factors to a sustainability startup, specifically the non-quantifiable factors like organizational culture, internal dynamics, entrepreneurial qualities and individual characteristics?
2   How can those factors be systematically explored, categorized and structured in a framework that can be applied by scholars, startup entrepreneurs and future founders?

Four illustrative cases of Austrian sustainability startups in different sectors are presented in 3.1: Vresh (Fashion), Brotsüchtig (Food), Die Fairmittlerei (Social service provider/NGO) and Blün (Agriculture). The founders of each company were invited to a retrospective dialogue about their process of starting and running a business for sustainability. Public data and general information about the company had been collected beforehand to address aspects on a deeper level during the conversation.

Additionally, the founders were asked to describe their business model with the help of nine archetypes (adapted from Bocken et al., 2019). To abide by quality criteria for qualitative research in our case studies (Baxter & Jack, 2008), interviews were conducted in German with the help of a literature-based compendium of questions. A content analysis was carried out afterwards to summarize and structure the findings. The coding guidelines constitute as starting point for identification, categorization and denomination of the soft success factors described in the final framework. As the aim during the interview was to maintain the atmosphere of a dialogue rather than an interrogation, the order of questions was changed slightly, questions were added (arising from context) or omitted, if they had been dealt with sufficiently within the scope of another aspect. At Vresh and Die Fairmittlerei, the two team members we talked to are graduates of Design & Product Management at Salzburg University of Applied Sciences; therefore, their motivation to participate was very high and provided an opportunity for unusual insight and data access. In the cases of Vresh, Brotsüchtig and Blün, the author was given a tour of the company's location after the interview. As the cases were remarkably revelatory and provided unique insights (Baxter & Jack, 2008; Yin, 2003), a limited number of cases allowed for the development of a comprehensive framework. Multiple inputs helped create a rich picture of business practice, innovation processes and organizational culture within the companies.

60 Lisa Winkler

4.3.1 Sample of sustainability startup cases

The analysis of the following four cases served as the main base for our proposed framework of success factors, adding real-world context to existing literature.

4.3.1.1 Vresh

Type of company:	Limited liability company
Industry:	Textile retail & wholesale
Year of foundation:	2016 (Ltd.), 2012 (fashion brand)
Employees:	Two full-time, one freelance, two interns
Mission:	Attributing more value to textiles through own action and awareness creation.
Business model:	Closing resource loops, Adopt a stewardship role, Encourage sufficiency, Scale-up solutions

Clothing and merchandise company is based in Linz, Upper Austria, run by founder and managing partner Klaus Buchroithner. Upon taking over the family-owned skate shop, Klaus created Vresh in 2012 as a skateboard fashion project, gaining independence from big established brands and supporting local team riders and artists. When this had grown to sell a thousand items per year, he switched to fair and sustainably produced textiles – the independent Vresh Ltd. was founded in 2016. By now, the complete production chain is based in Europe and integrates small family businesses in Portugal and Poland, guaranteeing them independence from the price depression exerted by international textile corporations. High-quality clothes made from recycled and organic fibres come in timeless aesthetics and are marketed and sold via sales partners, online and in an own retail store. Additionally, a B2B branch dubbed DasMerch has emerged to become the only provider of EU-made, recycled merchandise textiles, cooperating with brands, companies or associations that decide to switch to sustainable products.

4.3.1.2 Brotsüchtig

Type of company:	Limited liability company
Industry:	Bakery trade
Year of foundation:	2016 (2018 opening of second shop)
Employees:	20
Mission:	Positive social value creation by manufacturing bread traditionally & uncompromisingly.
Business model:	Maximize material and energy efficiency, Adopt a stewardship role, Encourage sufficiency, Inclusive value creation

Organic bakery "Brotsüchtig" (addicted to bread) is based in Linz, Upper Austria, founded in 2016 by Stefan Faschinger and Oliver Raferzeder. The

Beyond the Business Model Canvas 61

founders' initial aim was to create a business for sustainability, only then deciding on the bakery trade because of personal competencies, interest and background. They manufacture breads and pastries, using traditional sourdough recipes, processing organic resources only, without wheat flour or additives. All ingredients are locally sourced, maintaining close personal relations with suppliers and collaborating with them along the entire value chain, e.g. in range planning. Products are sold via selected sales partners around the area as well as in two own shops/cafés in the city of Linz, where certified organic foods from allied manufacturers are offered, too. Resource protection and quality are put before availability; limited quantities should guarantee empty shelves at the end of the day, the few leftovers getting distributed to social markets.

4.3.1.3 Die Fairmittlerei

Type of company:	Association (e.V.)
Industry:	Social startup
Year of foundation:	2016
Employees:	Four board members, 12 volunteers
Mission:	Serve as hub for industry and NGO's to point out & utilize the potential of unused resources.
Business model:	Maximize material and energy efficiency, Repurpose for society/environment, (Inclusive value creation), Scale-up solutions (Crowdfunding)

"Die Fairmittlerei" – word play on "fair" and "vermitteln" (arrange, pass on) – is a Vienna-based non-profit organization founded in 2016. The idea of chairman Michael K. Reiter and his co-founders was to repurpose and redistribute unused goods (otherwise discarded along the production chain) and provide tangible assistance for the less fortunate and minimizing environmental pollution. Die Fairmittlerei connects for-profit manufacturing companies and local non-profit organizations, through the service of collecting, storing and redistributing product donations. Moreover, the volunteers engage in creating awareness in society for the potential of surplus resources and to put these products to good use; simultaneously providing large companies with an opportunity to prove corporate social responsibility in the real world. The members see themselves as nodes in a network, inspiring through interaction, co-creating value through shared passion and mobilizing and motivating – in the digital world or the analogue.

4.3.1.4 Blün

Type of company:	Limited liability company
Industry:	Agriculture
Year of foundation:	2016
Employees:	Four founders, one employee

| **Mission**: | Set an example for autonomous, future-proof farming with local & transparent processes. |
| **Business model:** | Closing resource loops – value from waste, Substitute with renewables and natural processes, Scale-up solutions (Crowdfunding) |

Vienna-based agriculture collective is working according to the principles of "local, transparent, eco-effective" since the formation in 2016. Co-founder Michael Berlin took over the family farm with a vision of autonomous agriculture, and has since pursued the idea to conjoin aquaculture and hydroponics with his business partners. Four farmers together operate Vienna's first aquaponics plant, with an annual production of 20 tons of fish (catfish) and 15 tons of vegetables (tomato, eggplant, pepper, cucumber). They commit to the Cradle-to-Cradle principle and are striving for constant improvement in all details of the concept. Processes take place in Vienna for Vienna; produce and artisanal products (e.g. ketchup, vegetable sauce, dog snacks made from fish skin) are distributed to restaurants, delivered via postal service or sold in the own farmers market among foods from fellow Viennese manufacturers. Blün also take on an educational task, offering guided tours around the production site to farmers, academic institutions or private individuals, proving their aim for transparency in practice.

4.4 Results – framework development

This framework for success factors seeks to "map the unmappable" – bridging individual qualities, ideology & cognitive aspects and applied innovation & business practice. Relevant aspects encompass (1) the individual level of sustainability startup founders/leading team members (including personal experience, ideology, character traits, leadership practice) as well as (2) the corporate level of sustainability startups (applied innovation practice in business modelling, design, communication and organizational culture). The identified non-quantifiable aspects can be categorized in three main dimensions of (1) Mindset, (2) Commitment and (3) Execution, leading further to a division in subcategories: Consciousness, Meaning, Proactive Attitude, Responsibility, Pioneering Role, Authenticity and Transparency. In the following, each factor is described and illustrated with examples and quotes from the interviews (see Figure 4.1).

4.4.1 Consciousness

Consciousness, as defined by the Merriam-Webster English dictionary, means (1) the quality or state of being aware especially of something within oneself, (2) the state or fact of being conscious of an external object, state or fact and (3) in the sense of "awareness", especially a concern for some social or political cause. Within the scope of this framework, this very definition is

Beyond the Business Model Canvas 63

integrated in the sustainability context and expanded in the following way. We describe Consciousness as an entrepreneur's awareness of their environment, surroundings and ecological, social, political or economic issues as well as of their own role, actions and reactions and their consequences in this environment. A dramatic personal experience of seeing petrol leakage burning convinced Michael Berlin (Blün) to pursue autonomy from fossil fuels, to leave the planet in a better state than it was.

The aspect of self-consciousness includes the ability, desire and active pursuit of reflecting on actions, especially in the sustainability context of entrepreneurial activity and corporate culture. The inherently democratic Fairmittlerei team discusses even the smallest decisions like printing a leaflet on recycled paper, weighing environmental and societal consequences while not disregarding the economic aspects.

Moreover, this point encompasses gratitude, not taking privilege for granted – like Stefan Faschinger's (Brotsüchtig) personal definition of success is the gratitude and reassurance he experiences when customers thank him for making good bread.

A positive, though essentially realistic and well-informed view on the present and outlook on the future is important, as well as a down-to-earth attitude towards business practice and different stakeholders, success and failure and not least to their own person and individual position. As failure is sometimes inevitable, one better comes prepared; Michaela Gahleitner and Klaus Buchroithner (Vresh) actively reinforce each other's optimistic and resilient attitude towards obstacles and difficulty and learning from temporary setbacks.

"When it comes to sustainability, of course, you also have to take long-term economic efficiency into account. Nobody wins when we play 'happy hippies' and sell potato bag attire – that's cool for exactly one month until we declare bankruptcy." (Klaus Buchroithner, Vresh)

"We have a vision, a utopia, we know that's the ideal, when financial resources are given... but we have to face reality and compromise sometimes. Many social entrepreneurs are publicly shamed because they do one small thing not perfectly right, that's terrible." (Sabine Brunnmair, Fairmittlerei)

(On failure) "I write it down. I keep it in my mind. And I don't do it again! You have to remember big crashes and learn from them." (Stefan Faschinger, Brotsüchtig)

"Big goals are nice, but when you split them up and achieve them step by step, you get the feeling that something is actually moving forward." (Michael Berlin, Blün)

4.4.2 *Meaning*

This category draws influence from psychology: the concept of Meaning coined by Austrian psychologist Viktor Frankl. He describes humans as being guided by conscience in their search for meaning; the desire to transcend

64 *Lisa Winkler*

human existence by a sense of higher meaning as the very essence of human existence itself (Frankl & Lorenz, 1979). In the business context of this framework, meaning is interpreted as an intrinsic motivation to give entrepreneurial activity a higher meaning. The respective business practice of the entrepreneur as an individual and the entire organization is designed for and influenced by the pursuit of aspirations linked to their personal idea of meaning in a sustainability context. This category also includes a shared vision and sense of meaning among the startup team members – a crucial factor for venture success, not only in sustainability startups (DeMol, 2019); placing a high value on vision, meaning and purpose; considering actions (of the company as an entity and of team members as individuals) meaningful and having a culture of respect towards different ways of thinking and working towards a common goal. Having a sense of meaning is of utmost importance for resilience in times of difficulty and provides an intrinsic motivation to pursue the business endeavour further.

"Sustainability for me is to actively initiate things… that make sense and have a meaning… in the long run… for humans and the environment." (Klaus Buchroithner, Vresh)

"When you unite various characters in a team, where everyone shares the same passion but brings in a different quality, that's something exciting, fruitful and motivating where one can learn a lot. And that from people you've known forever! They [my co-founders] teach me new things on a regular basis, that's beautiful." (Manfred Hlina, Fairmittlerei)

"I know that I will receive something in return somewhere, somehow. Monetary value is not always everything – and that, you don't learn in economics class or an entrepreneurship course. You have to be willing to give a little bit of your soul and put it into your work. And your soul is a part of what you make. Although it is demanding and sometimes exhausting." (Stefan Faschinger, Brotsüchtig)

"We started a vision process, vision 2040: Where do we want to be, where do we want to stand, when we pass on the farm to the next generation? What are the goals? We decided on pursuing independent, autonomous agriculture […] preferably in a circular system." (Michael Berlin, Blün)

4.4.3 *Proactive attitude*

The active pursuit of ideas that are considered meaningful by individuals is named Proactive Attitude. The term subsumes the desire to actively make a change in the world and to address contemporary issues at their very core, with the instrument of creating and modelling a business according to own visions, values and standards linked to sustainability. Thorough reflection and honest answers to the questions: "What can I do to make a change – and what is needed to do it the best possible way?" may lead the way to the creation of a successful business endeavour. Furthermore, it encompasses the approach of thorough research and development for products and processes, as well as a certain maker spirit and do-it-yourself-attitude of nascent entrepreneurs who are not afraid to get their own hands dirty and choose to actively work on their dream with any means necessary (self-evidently reasonable and justified according to personal sustainability ideology). The desire to inspire others to change their mindset and behaviour towards a more sustainable lifestyle is also a part of this category, and precedingly linked to point 4.5, taking on a Pioneering Role.

All of the entrepreneurs interviewed actively pursue a mission for sustainability, have overcome the obstacles of founding a new venture and surviving the first years in operation and are still undefeated in business, without taking their success for granted. Inspiring others to behaviour changes towards sustainability instead of pointing out negative aspects is inherent to all four companies, and the founders are willing to go the extra mile to do this well. Maker spirit and do-it-yourself attitude can be grasped at the store location of Vresh, where most of the furniture is made out of repurposed materials or purchased second hand and an additional location of Brotsüchtig is currently being planned by founder Stefan Faschinger himself, without previous architectural experience: "I am planning my bakery, I know what I will need because I am going to work in it. Not my architect."

"If you don't dare to try…"

"…you'll never know…"

"… and you won't learn." (Klaus Buchroithner & Michaela Gahleitner, Vresh)

"Sustainability is, in the bigger picture, to leave the world behind as good or even better as it has been given to us. And on a smaller scale, it's about the little things that can make a difference every day. Waste less, consume responsibly." (Manfred Hlina, Fairmittlerei)

"We wanted to have a positive effect on society when starting a business. It was not like 'let's make a bakery… okay, let's make it organic.' We wanted to create something sustainable… so what could we do? We, with our abilities, capabilities, knowledge and [immaterial] resources." (Stefan Faschinger, Brotsüchtig)

4.4.4 Responsibility

A sense and awareness of Responsibility for oneself and others is crucial for any entrepreneur – and in a sustainability context, the term puts them in charge in an even more wide-ranging way. This important factor includes (1) the entrepreneurs' individual physical and psychological health and well-being as base for any outwardly directed actions, (2) other people, on a small scale, such as private environment, employees and other corporate stakeholders, (3) the common good on a larger, societal and economic scale and (4) the environment as indispensable key stakeholder. This multifaceted responsibility is put into practice through collaborative and holistic approaches to conducting business and running an organization, and the commitment to a business endeavour that, by design, has an altruistic component and is neither just "for fun" or "for profit". This category also includes the differentiation from competitors being handled with respect and consciousness, as well as the openness for ways of cooperation (e.g. with competitors or fellow startup founders) that might not serve a company's pursuit of profit but a greater goal or common good. In the case of Blün's aquaponics facility, another responsibility is animal welfare; they sought advice from WWF (World Wide Fund for Nature) before starting to work with living fish. And flights are arguably not the most sustainable way of travelling; nonetheless Klaus Buchroithner (Vresh) sees them as a tool to maintain the valuable personal partnership with their manufacturers in Portugal.

"We are no samaritans, our aim is to make money – but there's more to our company than just myself saying 'I want to do this – or I don't.' Human beings and their jobs depend on it, we have a responsibility for them." (Klaus Buchroithner, Vresh)

"I know I will get from my supplier what I need, that's handshake quality, friendship, that's living together. Live and let live… and even more, because it's coexistence and not parallel existence. It's simply a bliss." (Stefan Faschinger, Brotsüchtig)

"I think that doing business is not about making gains to your personal advantage, it has to serve the common good, too." (Sabine Brunnmair, Fairmittlerei)

"The network of people is very important. If you're surrounded by good, honest people, you can be very successful. When everyone has similar ideas, ideals and interests, one can sleep more peacefully at night." (Michael Berlin, Blün)

4.4.5 Pioneering role

Sustainability innovation in a startup company is essentially taking a pioneering role in the respective sector, not only through new technology, but a holistic and profound take on innovation in business model setup, internal processes and organizational issues along the entire value chain from research & development, product and service design to marketing, distribution and corporate communication. In the companies investigated, innovation at business model level means combining more than one of the archetypes presented by Bocken et al. (2019). The founders discussed their own business models and considered other categories possible directions for future improvement. This passion for continuous improvement towards increased sustainability is facilitated by the agile nature of a startup; successful change and risk management requires to consider numerous aspects of economy, environment and society. A company's pioneering role includes their self-imposed educational task through informing, offering sustainable solutions and setting a positive example to lead others on a way to increased sustainability by attitude and behaviour change. Pioneering entrepreneurs need to be conscious

Beyond the Business Model Canvas 67

and accepting towards this added responsibility of being role models and live up to certain expectations – leading to aspect 4.6 Authenticity.

"We even wrote on the wall of our changing room: 'Buy less. Choose well. Make it last.' Yes, we are a retailer – still, this is important to us! We prefer you buy a single, high-quality item once in a while over you coming each month to buy a new shirt." (Michaela Gahleitner, Vresh)

"You can be someone who thinks ahead, a pioneer, and only if you live accordingly and set an example, people will start thinking, too." (Stefan Faschinger, Brotsüchtig)

"It's important for us not to say: "You, you, and you are bad," but to say: "Hey, look, that's how you could try doing it better!"" (Manfred Hlina, Fairmittlerei)

"We were able to build up everything according to our ideas without being stuck in old tracks that you'd have to painstakingly re-shape. And if you're a small business, you're more agile." (Michael Berlin, Blün)

4.4.6 *Authenticity*

"Authenticity" has deteriorated into an overused buzzword, but is nonetheless a crucial point for being successful. In the sustainability context, it can be described as the opposite of Greenwashing or superficial CSR (Corporate Social Responsibility) practices: Genuinely pursuing a course of business practice true to vision/mission, values, standards and meaning; respecting differences between humans as individuals, being fully aware of corporate responsibility towards all stakeholders and acting according to this very responsibility. The phrase "walk the talk" (acting according to what is preached) can be turned around – a successful sustainability startup "talks the walk": They do good, but not behind closed doors, as corporate communication is carefully designed and executed in a way that shows clearly and effectively the quality of the company's action, without appearing artificial or suspiciously overbold. For entrepreneurs, being authentic also means actively calling for feedback (e.g. from employees, customers, stakeholders) and working with the results towards creating real innovation; even if this means facing unpleasant reactions from stakeholders, it is fundamental to acknowledge criticism and consciously reflect on it in order to take action and strive for future improvement.

"There's very little that we don't actively communicate, because if there are things we don't like…" "…we don't do them!" (Michaela Gahleitner & Klaus Buchroithner, Vresh)

"The idea we had in our minds comes across without us having to bend in a different direction. That's true success to me, that is very cool." (Stefan Faschinger, Brotsüchtig)

"We're no activists, but we have a vision. We think it's great that something is done for the environment – and we offer an opportunity to take action!" (Sabine Brunnmair, Fairmittlerei)

68   *Lisa Winkler*

"We don't have seals of approval, we're not certified organic. We explain the reasons very clearly." (Michael Berlin, Blün)

4.4.7 *Transparency*

How transparency and trust oppose or relate to each other has been subject to discussions in the context of economy, society, globalization and digitalization. Here, we agree with the reflection given by Stefan Faschinger, cofounder of Brotsüchtig: "Trust has to grow and transparency can be given from one day to the next." It is indispensable for sustainable companies to be as transparent as possible in action and communication, making manufacturing processes and conditions visible to prove worthy of customers' trust, showing that values and promises are put into practice with honesty and authenticity. Seals of quality (e.g. for organic or fair trade products) can be useful in order to show upfront the standards that are met, yet sometimes entrepreneurs feel that requirements for certification do not match their efforts, and the plethora of existing labels confuse consumers. Therefore, choosing to communicate quality standards and corporate practices openly and truthfully "beyond the label" proved to be a definite success factor for sustainability startups. The term transparency also describes a respectful and open conduct towards all stakeholders, a company's willingness to open their doors, to proactively show their business practice, to meet and explain at eye-level and to share knowledge, competences or resources. The very term "transparency" was mentioned several times by each of the entrepreneurs, proving the significance of this value.

"We are doing our thing, and if someone doesn't take delight in that, that's their thing. We, Vresh, that's the two of us – so everything is very transparent by nature!" (Michaela Gahleitner, Vresh)

"[The suppliers], and also those who resell my products want to know things about me and my company: What we do, how we do it. So we just have to be transparent. And consistent. Steady. Of one piece." (Stefan Faschinger, Brotsüchtig)

"We've tried to act as professional as possible from the beginning. Also in our public image – to prove that we are not just an idea but a serious organization that donors and big corporations can identify with and would like to be associated with." (Manfred Hlina, Fairmittlerei)

"There's nothing we don't show. We can't afford to hide anything! And to alarming voices against factory farming, we simply respond: 'Come here. Take a look for yourself!'" (Michael Berlin, Blün)

Beyond the Business Model Canvas 69

	Factor	Comprised aspects	(1) Individual level (examples)	(2) Corporate level (examples)
(1) Mindset	Consciousness	Be aware of issues & surroundings and (re-)act accordingly, positive but realistic outlook on future, self-consciousness, down-to-earth, ability to reflect	Awareness of environment (ecological & business), thorough reflection on values and actions, motivation for sustainable action (threat or passion), use of language & terms during interview	Description of business idea, allocation of roles in company, "who works here & what are my tasks?", timing of foundation, clear vision/mission for business
	Meaning	Personal idea of meaning (linked to sustainability), consider actions meaningful, see a bigger picture, intrinsic motivation, vision, high value of meaning & purpose	Motivation & drivers, crucial points in life linked to business creation & practice, individual perception of vision & purpose, commitment, resilience	Vision/mission statement, shared values among team members, sense of "we/us", goals & success stories, handling setbacks & obstacles
(2) Commitment	Proactive attitude	Maker spirit, not afraid to get hands dirty, desire to actively make a change, inspire others to change mindset & behaviour, get to the roots of issues	research practice, opportunity recognition, "what can I do – how can I do it best, according to my skills and resources?", examples of do-it-yourself culture, business modelling practice	create & maintain a thriving business, research & development, method of financing (e.g. crowdfunding campaigns, recruiting investors), attitude towards obstacles & difficulties

(Continued)

70 *Lisa Winkler*

	Factor	*Comprised aspects*	*(1) Individual level (examples)*	*(2) Corporate level (examples)*
	Responsibility	Sense of responsibility for (1) self, (2) others, (3) common good, (4) environment, collaborative & holistic approaches, business practice neither only for fun nor for profit	"Who do I do it for?", personal well-being strategies, consideration of stakeholders and openness to cooperation, networking practice, perception of competition	Decision making processes, involvement of stakeholders in corporate processes (who, when, how), personal involvement of founders
Commitment/ Execution	Pioneering role	"vordenken", "vorzeigen", "vorleben" (setting example through informing, showing & living up to values), be in the vanguard in respective field, true innovation, accept being a role model, not necessarily swim with the tide	Individual background (e.g. by education, startup experience, industry skills, product knowledge), openness to innovation, change management practice, importance of educational task	Application & profundity of product & process innovation, corporate communication, agility in the face of change & obstacles, educational activity
(3) Execution	Authenticity	Walk the talk & talk the walk, genuineness, respect humans as individuals, pursue path according to values & vision, acknowledge feedback, no greenwashing/ cosmetic CSR,	Use of "we/ us" during interview, personal presence, media presence, behaviour during interview (dialogue or business presentation), profundity of personal reflection, use of humour	Management of public relations, sustainability practice when there is no audience, adjustment of business practice to vision/mission, organizational culture (e.g. rituals, habits, internal sustainable practices)

Factor	Comprised aspects	(1) Individual level (examples)	(2) Corporate level (examples)
Transparency	Truthfulness & honesty "beyond the label", respect shown towards all stakeholders, willingness to (1) show, (2) explain, (3) share; withstands close scrutiny as opposed to superficial greenwashing	Honest remarks & use of language and terms during interview, willingness to share detailed information going beyond interview questions,	Importance of certification & seals of quality, ways of tackling prejudice, sharing insights in development/ improvement, offer additional information (e.g. company visit)

4.5 Discussion

The factors of the framework build up on each other, are interconnected and partly overlap. For instance, the visionary aspect of (b) Meaning requires previous (a) Consciousness and reflection on personal ideologies and standards. The "vision" is closely linked to the entrepreneurs' definition of the term sustainability and also to whether they are motivated by threat (e.g. the problem of environmental destruction) or passion (e.g. the desire to bring people closer together) (Shepherd & Patzelt, 2018). The "mission" aspect of (b) Meaning connects to (c), Proactive Attitude, exemplified by asking: "What can I do to make a change, and how can I do it?" (d), Responsibility, in a sustainability context especially for the common good or environment, builds on this. Economic sustainability, i.e. being able to continue entrepreneurial activity, requires making profit within an inherently capitalist system. Balancing the three pillars of the triple bottom line, environment, society and economics (Elkington, 2013) can be challenging for entrepreneurs and requires a willingness to consider, reflect and actively make decisions that may turn out a compromise sometimes – an essential part of (a) Consciousness, linked to (c) Proactive Attitude. The case companies adhere to the definition of "economics" as essentially creating value for the common good (Felber, 2014) and not just for the sake of personal monetary gain. The desire to inspire others to change mindset and behaviour is part of an entrepreneur's (c) Proactive Attitude and, when it comes to communicating and acting upon this desire, (e) Pioneering Role – actively informing, providing solutions (i.e. products or services) and setting positive examples through sustainable behaviour, manifesting in a company's everyday actions and the entrepreneurs' demeanour. The latter is also part of (f) Authenticity, acting genuinely true

	factor	Comprised aspects	(1) Individual level (examples)	(2) Corporate level (examples)
(1) Mindset	Consciousness	Be aware of issues & surroundings and (re-)act accordingly, positive but realistic outlook on future, self-consciousness, down-to-earth, ability to reflect	Awareness of environment (ecological & business), thorough reflection on values and actions, motivation for sustainable action (threat or passion), use of language & terms during interview	Description of business idea, allocation of roles in company, „who works here & what are my tasks?", timing of foundation, clear vision/mission for business
	Meaning	Personal idea of meaning (linked to sustainability), consider actions meaningful, see a bigger picture, intrinsic motivation, vision, high value of meaning & purpose	Motivation & drivers, crucial points in life linked to business creation & practice, individual perception of vision & purpose, commitment, resilience	Vision/mission statement, shared values among team members, sense of „we / us", goals & success stories, handling setbacks & obstacles
(2) Commitment	Proactive Attitude	Maker spirit, not afraid to get hands dirty, desire to actively make a change, inspire others to change mindset & behavior, get to the roots of issues	research practice, opportunity recognition, „what can I do - how can I do it best, according to my skills and resources?", examples of do-it-yourself culture, business modelling practice	create & maintain a thriving business, research & development, method of financing (e.g. crowdfunding campaigns, recruiting investors), attitude towards obstacles & difficulties
	Responsibility	Sense of responsibility for (1) self, (2) others, (3) common good, (4) environment, collaborative & holistic approaches, business practice neither only for fun nor for profit	„Who do I do it for?", personal wellbeing strategies, consideration of stakeholders and openness to cooperation, networking practice, perception of competition	Decision making processes, involvement of stakeholders in corporate processes (who, when, how), personal involvement of founders
Commitment / Execution	Pioneering Role	„vordenken" - „vorzeigen" - „vorleben" (setting example through informing, showing & living up to values), be in the vanguard in respective field, true innovation, accept being a role model, not necessarily swim with the tide	Individual background (e.g. by education, startup experience, industry skills, product knowledge), openness to innovation, change management practice, importance of educational task	Application & profundity of product & process innovation, corporate communication, agility in the face of change & obstacles, educational activity
(3) Execution	Authenticity	Walk the talk & talk the walk, genuineness, respect humans as individuals, pursue path according to values & vision, acknowledge feedback, no greenwashing / cosmetic CSR,	Use of „we / us" during interview, personal presence, media presence, behavior during interview (dialogue or business presentation), profundity of personal reflection, use of humor	Management of public relations, sustainability practice when there is no audience, adjustment of business practice to vision/mission, organizational culture (e.g. rituals, habits, internal sustainable practices)
	Transparency	Truthfulness & honesty „beyond the label", respect shown towards all stakeholders, willingness to (1) show, (2) explain, (3) share; withstands close scrutiny as opposed to superficial greenwashing	Honest remarks & use of language and terms during interview, willingness to share detailed information going beyond interview questions	Importance of certification & seals of quality, ways of tackling prejudice, sharing insights in development / improvement, offer additional information (e.g. company visit)

Figure 4.1 Beyond the Business Model Canvas – proposed framework of soft success factors in sustainability startups (the author, 2019).

to visions and values, even when there is no audience. Being a pioneer for sustainability in the respective sector stands synonymous for sustainable innovation, the very core of this chapter's background. Innovative approaches in business model design and a company's offering require appropriate communication – turning the buzzphrase "walk the talk" (i.e. acting true to one's preaching and teaching) into "talk the walk." The good that is done has to be communicated properly, proactively and openly in order to lead a new venture to success, proving the importance of (f) Transparency to gain consumer trust. Holistic sustainability innovation stands clearly opposite to greenwashing practices in business or superficial CSR (Corporate Social Responsibility) measures. Certificates and seals of quality can help gain customers' approval, but for customers' empowerment to distinguish authentic sustainability practice from cosmetic measures, it is fundamental for small businesses and new ventures to show their company's practice, inviting to scrutinize that there is nothing to be hidden.

4.6 Conclusion

The term sustainability is used by politics, academia, media and in daily conversations, yet the word means "different things to different people" (White, 2013). Sustainable business modelling and innovation for sustainability have been subject to vast research in recent years and valuable analyses, tools and frameworks have been published to clarify what "sustainable" means in a business context and how it can be applied through systemic approaches (e.g. Triple Layer Business Model Canvas. Joyce & Paquin, 2016; Sustainable Business Model Archetypes. Bocken et al., 2019; Bocken et al., 2014; Value Mapping Tool. Bocken et al., 2013; or Ecologies of Business Models Experimentation Map. Bocken et al., 2019).

Scholars theorize SBMs in multiple directions, but the teaching practice in e.g. entrepreneurship courses is struggling to keep up with the state of the art in research. Additionally, those who have founded sustainable business endeavours might have never heard of the academic discourse and yet be running thriving companies, innovating towards true sustainability in entrepreneurship. In this chapter, we investigate success of sustainable businesses in a real-world context. Exploring an Austrian perspective on sustainable innovation in startup companies proved to be relevant, insofar as numerous new business endeavours in the country are setting sustainability as a standard and prerequisite for entrepreneurial action, going beyond it being but added value (De Chernatony et al., 2000) or superficial greenwashing.

New venture founding is encouraged by policy makers and the supportive offerings for nascent entrepreneurs have grown significantly in the past few years. Nonetheless, teaching and counselling practice focuses almost purely on the economic side of a business, making it even harder for founders with ambitions towards innovation for sustainability to bridge their vision or ideology and a viable, hands-on business application. This was mentioned with regret by startup founders during our field research; entrepreneurs with

74   *Lisa Winkler*

praiseworthy ideas for sustainability have fallen victim to new venture failure, others have given in and resorted to more conventional practice instead of pursuing holistic innovation for sustainability.

In our empirical research, we explore (1) aspects of business model and value creation process, (2) individual reason and vision, (3) corporate action and communication along the value chain and (4) resilience, failure experience and future optimism.

We work towards closing the gap between the individual level of vision and idea and the corporate level of applied innovative practice for sustainability, drawing influence from aspects of sustainability in economics, business modelling & innovation for sustainability and entrepreneurial cognition, contributing through empirical case study research in cooperation with four successful sustainability startups.

Profound insights were gathered with the process itself being a sensitive and intense task of reflection for everyone involved. Based on these findings, we propose a framework of "soft success factors," creating an outcome complementary to existing tools for sustainable business modelling that focus mainly on a company as an entity of (economic) value creation. We suggest a categorization of these factors in (1) Mindset, (2) Commitment and (3) Execution, subdivided into Consciousness, Meaning, Proactive Attitude, Responsibility, Pioneering Role, Authenticity and Transparency.

Existing research is extended on the following levels: (1) investigating and structuring "soft success factors," the non-quantifiable aspects of a business such as individual characteristics, entrepreneurial practice and organizational culture, (2) creating a framework of these factors as tool to enable startup entrepreneurs to systematically reflect on their sustainable business endeavour and (3) presenting future founders, teachers and counsellors in with aspects to take into consideration when starting a sustainability business.

4.6.1 *Limitations and suggestions for further research*

This chapter gives a truly Austrian perspective; all companies are founded and based in Austria, operating mainly on national level. The sustainability agenda is taken quite seriously by policy makers and economists, and the market for emerging businesses in this sector is relatively open. The public sustainability discourse is ongoing, allowing for high awareness and sensitivity, especially for environmental issues and the need to act on them. The framework should provide a more holistic and systematic understanding of applied sustainability innovation, not a complete list of factors for success or failure, but an overview of the human side of a business. The dimensions Mindset, Commitment, Execution, their subcategories and contents, we suggest, can be verified and expanded by further research; possibly including measurable features. Additionally, the suggested application of the framework as tool for education and future founders is hypothetical to this point, yet to be verified, evaluated and expanded through experimentation.

Beyond the Business Model Canvas 75

The case study methodology allows for in-depth insight in each company, but a generalizing model derived only from qualitative research might be incomplete. For the Business Opportunity aspect, we recommend taking a closer look on each company's own business model instead of only reflecting on the archetypes suggested by Bocken et al. (2019). Lastly, profound personal and emotional levels of reflection were reached during the interview process. Outcomes might therefore vary with each entrepreneur's willingness to enter a dialogue of reflection and show individual characteristics (as opposed to giving a presentation of the company), depending also on the person conducting the interview. Yet, as the sessions required a great deal of openness and trust, they showed to be fruitful and thought-provoking for both interviewer and interviewee.

Acknowledgements

The author would like to thank Michaela Gahleitner & Klaus Buchroithner (Vresh), Stefan Faschinger (Brotsüchtig), Manfred Hlina & Sabine Brunnmair (Die Fairmittlerei) and Michael Berlin (Blün) for providing valuable insight in their companies. Thank you for the time and transparency!

Thematic section two

The network perspective

5 Buyer–supplier collaboration for eco-innovations in a circular economy

A network theory approach

Maria A. Franco

5.1 Introduction

Eco-innovations are broadly understood as product, process, and organizational novelties that lead to a substantial reduction in environmental burdens, including environmental risk, pollution, and resource use (Horbach, Rammer, & Rennings, 2012; Kemp, 2010). Because innovation is a problem-solving task that requires firms to recombine existing knowledge into novel solutions, there is evidence that firms are increasingly relying on the competencies and resources of their supply network in order to innovate (Arlbjørn, de Haas, & Munksgaard, 2011; Lee & Kim, 2011; Narasimhan & Narayanan, 2013). Supply networks facilitate the development of eco-innovations because they serve as important conduits for knowledge access and act as catalysts for the development and dissemination of new ideas, applications, and supply chain practices (Bellamy, Ghosh, & Hora, 2014). An innovation-oriented supply network partnership is defined as a collaborative working relationship between partners in the supply network involved in the conception, testing, production, or marketing of a new product or technology (Anderson & Narus, 1990). A firm's supply network is made up of ties to its immediate suppliers, as well as to other suppliers who serve the requirements of the firm even when they do not interact directly with each other.

A network perspective on eco-innovations is needed because little is known about how the structural characteristics of a supply network influence the focal firm's eco-innovation performance. Also, even though the majority of existing research on supplier involvement in innovation remains linear and dyadic in focus (Kim, Choi, Yan, & Dooley, 2011), several supply chain researchers have emphasized the value of incorporating a supply network (SN) perspective when considering firms' innovation and performance implications (Arlbjørn & Paulraj, 2013; Autry & Griffis, 2008; van Bommel, 2011). Finally, very few publications have studied the role of eco-innovations in the transition to a CE (de Jesus, Antunes, Santos, & Mendonça, 2018; EIO, 2016) and almost none have highlighted the importance of buyer-supplier network collaboration in such a transition.

80   *Maria A. Franco*

This paper takes a network theory perspective to elucidate how supply networks support the development of eco-innovations for the advancement of the circular economy. Networks are of particular importance to the CE because of their capacity for increasing cooperation in research and development projects (R&D), sharing materials and by-products, and managing common utilities and infrastructures (de Jesus et al., 2018). If attention to innovation is key for the successful diffusion of CE principles across different levels (i.e., micro, meso, and macro), how can network theory shed light on how collaboration for innovation can be better secured in a supplier network? To answer this question, I posit the following research question: How can network theory help predict who will be more likely to eco-innovate in a buyer-supplier network? The remainder of this paper is structured as follows: Section 5.2 provides a literature review on eco-innovations and their connection to the circular economy, innovation in a supply network, and network theory. Section 5.3 introduces the theoretical propositions, while Section 5.4 presents the conclusions derived from this analysis. Finally, Section 5.5 discusses some of the limitations of this paper and proposes avenues for future work.

5.2 Literature review

5.2.1 Eco-innovations and the circular economy

The idea of developing innovations to solve environmental challenges and preserve the planet's natural resources has gained track among policy makers, academia, and businesses alike since the mid-1990s. Prominent labels used in the literature to denote concepts similar to eco-innovations include: sustainability-oriented innovations, green innovations, and environmental innovations. Although there is no agreement on weather all these definitions refer to the social, environmental, and economic aspects of innovations, most researchers use the terms "environmental," "green," and "eco" almost interchangeably to refer to innovations aimed at reducing the harm of the economic activities in the environment (Díaz-García, González-Moreno, & Sáez-Martínez, 2015).

In this paper, I use the definition proposed by de Jesus et al. (2018) and de Jesus and Mendonça (2018), who describe eco-innovations as any innovation that: (i) preserves resources, mitigates environmental degradation, and/or allows the recovery of value from substances already in use in the economy, (ii) results in new or improved goods and services, technological and non-technological processes, and organizational schemes, (iii) is incremental or radical, and (iv) involves an actor or a plurality of actors. This comprehensive definition fits the focus of this research because it does not only contemplate the development of eco-innovations for the reduction of negative environmental impacts (i.e., eco-efficiency), but also for the valuable recovery of goods already in the economy, thereby ensuring environmental sustainability (i.e., eco- effectiveness).

Eco-innovations have been identified as a core driver for change in the transition to a more sustainable society, and more importantly, as one of the key factors determining the possibility of businesses and countries of moving towards a CE (Potocnik, 2014; Smol, Kulczycka, & Avdiushchenko, 2017). The European Commission pointed out, for instance, that besides the establishment of enabling regulations and public and private investments, the CE requires the development of novel R&D-enabled solutions (European Commission, 2017). Table 5.1 shows how the CE can be viewed as a business policy that targets the redesign of entire value chains through pervasive product and technological innovations (Cainelli, D'Amato, & Mazzanti, 2017). At this point, it is important to note that most of the theoretical propositions presented in this paper will refer to eco-product innovations for the circular economy, and not to process, marketing, and organizational innovations (Boons, Montalvo, Quist, & Wagner, 2013; Carrillo-Hermosilla, Del Río, & Könnölä, 2010). Pujari (2006) defines eco-product innovations as new or significantly improved products and technologies (e.g., improvements in technical components, materials, and eco-technologies), whose environmental impact resides in their use and disposal stages, rather than in their production stage.

5.2.2 Supplier collaboration for innovation

In a world where eco-innovations are needed at every stage of the manufacturing value chain, I posit focal firms collaborate with partners within their supply network in order to bring novel products to the market (Arlbjørn & Paulraj, 2013; Hojnik & Ruzzier, 2016). Supplier involvement in innovation

Table 5.1 Types of innovation required across the circular value chain

Stages in the circular value chain	Type of innovation required
Design	– Basic materials and component parts to ensure product durability, quality, modularity, and recoverability – Innovative design protocols for disassembly, refurbishment, reuse, and recycling
Manufacturing and supply chain management	– Cleaner production technologies
Commercialization	– Business models and technologies to enable performance models such as leasing, sharing, or pay-per-use
Use and maintenance	– Business models and technologies to accurately manage product lifecycles
Take back, sorting, and reprocessing	– Business models and technologies for locating and exchanging waste, sorting, and recycling
Waste exchange (industrial symbiosis)	– Enabling technologies

82 *Maria A. Franco*

can be understood as "the resources suppliers provide, the tasks they carry out, and the responsibilities they assume regarding the development of a part, process, or service for the benefit of a buyer's current or future product development projects" (van Echtelt, Wynstra, van Weele, & Duysters, 2008). While connecting the concept of innovation to that of the supply networks, Narasimhan and Narayanan (2013) stated that "innovation is the process of making changes to products, processes, and services that result in value creation to the organization and its customers by leveraging knowledge efforts of the firm and that of its supply network partners."

Some of the reasons recorded in the literature for collaborating within the supply network include the achievement of market diversity, competitive pricing through efficiencies, flexibility, shorter product life cycles, and ultimately competitive advantage (Nyaga, Whipple, & Lynch, 2010; Soosay, Hyland, & Ferrer, 2008). Past research has also suggested customer firms can benefit from involving suppliers in NPD activities, rather than working independently, by enhancing product performance in terms of product innovativeness, development time, development cost, product quality, and time-to-market. Collaborating with suppliers can also help firms conserve resources, share risks, gain new competencies, and move faster into new markets because suppliers possess specialized product and process knowledge (Johnsen, 2009; Wagner, 2010). From the supplier's perspective, a buyer can bring value by performing direct and indirect functions, including the generation of profit and volume, the development of innovations, and the granting of market access (Walter, Ritter, & Gemünden, 2001).

Within the realm of the CE, some authors have already reported on the existence of buyer-supplier collaboration for innovation. Drabe and Herstatt (2016), for example, described how firms aspiring to get Cradle to Cradle (C2C) certified, "extensively exchanged knowledge with other companies in order to implement C2C standards" and that "the implementation of C2C guidelines spurred innovation among the companies involved." Similarly, Franco (2017) presented evidence of strong cooperation among the members of textile value chains for the development of circular products. In her study, buyer-supplier collaboration for the CE was pervasive among firms in the research sample and was observed in the form of: (i) modification or substitution of chemicals for C2C yarn and fabric manufacturing, (ii) co-development of innovative circular basic materials and component parts, and (iii) customization of existing basic materials for new textile applications.

5.2.3 From supply chains to supply networks

Because it is assumed that focal firms develop eco-innovations with the aid of their supply networks, the unit of analysis for this study is the larger network in which the focal firm is embedded, rather than the traditional dyadic buyer-supplier relationship so pervasive in the field of supply chain management (SCM). Some authors suggest linear buyer-seller relationships fail to capture the complexity needed to understand a firm's strategy, which depends on a larger supply network than the one the firm is embedded in (Choi & Kim, 2008).

To understand the change in focus from a single actor to a network view, one needs to understand the difference between all units of analysis in SCM. Hence, Cousins and Lamming (2008) note that the SCM literature has progressively developed in three stages: (i) dyadic linkages, (ii) a chain of suppliers, and (iii) the supply network. While the thread on dyadic relationships usually discusses issues of trust and cooperation between two firms (i.e., supplier and its customer), the supply chain thread goes no further than second-tier or immediate suppliers (Miemczyk, Johnsen, & Macquet, 2012). From the late 1980s onwards, researchers began to take a broader view of supply chains as networks concentrating not only on material and information flows, but also on collaborative learning and product development (Mills, Schmitz, & Frizelle, 2004). In supply networks, individual firms constitute nodes in the network (Choi, Dooley, & Rungtusanatham, 2001) and the scope of collaboration is not restricted to customers and their direct suppliers, but extends to suppliers who serve the requirements of a particular customer even when they do not interact directly with each other (i.e., third- or fourth-tier suppliers) (Saunders, 1997). In other words, a firm's SN "consists of ties to its immediate suppliers and customers, and ties between them and their immediate suppliers and customers, and so on" (Kim et al., 2011). The next section briefly describes what network theory is and why it was used to investigate eco-innovations between buyers and their suppliers (Figure 5.1).

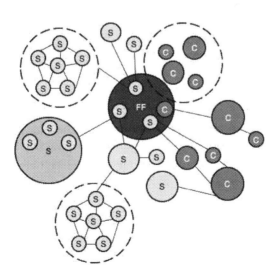

(S=supplier, FF=focal firm, C=customer)

Figure 5.1 The supply network from the perspective of the focal firm (Kemppainen & Vepsäläinen 2003).

84   *Maria A. Franco*

5.2.4 *Network theory*

Supply networks are characterized for being nonlinear, for showing complex multi-scale behavior, and for evolving and self-organizing through a complex interplay of its structure and function. The complex nature of supply networks provides the perfect foundation for elaborating theoretical propositions based on network theory. While a network is made up of actors or nodes connected by edges or ties (e.g., organizations, individuals), network analysis studies the patterns such ties form in a network. Network theory–related developments have been applied to various disciplines including sociology, epidemiology, management, and economics, in order to analyze topics ranging from friendship structure, to the spread of diseases, the diffusion of innovations, and the network effects on firm's performance.

Much of the theoretical wealth of network analysis resides in the study of the extent to which network structures and node positions have an effect on node and group outcomes (Borgatti & Halgin, 2011). Therefore, when using network theory in research, the hypotheses that are tested in empirical studies relate to features of the observed network to high-level outcomes such as organizational performance, and in this case, eco- innovative performance. As highlighted earlier, networks are of special importance for CE innovations because of their capacity for increasing cooperation in research and development projects (R&D), sharing materials and by-products, and managing common utilities and infrastructures (de Jesus et al., 2018).

5.3 Theoretical background and hypotheses development

Within the broader framework of innovation and sustainability, the following sections present a theoretical framework that integrates the literature on networks and eco-innovations for a CE.

5.3.1 *Power and innovation*

Power constitutes a central force in a network because it affects the control over resources and the tension between collaboration and competition (Zolkiewski, 2001). The dominant paradigm in SCM, and in this paper, is that power is a property of organizations as opposed to a property of individuals (Cox, 1999; Emerson, 1962; Wilkinson, 1996). As a basic working definition, I use Parson's definition of power, which states that "power is the capacity of actors to mobilize resources to achieve a certain goal" (Parsons, 1967). In this definition, resources are broadly defined as persons, assets, materials, or capital used to realize a certain goal, including human, mental, monetary, artefactual, and natural resources (Avelino & Rotmans, 2011). In relation to eco-innovations, power means that a firm, due to its position in a supply network, can exploit its influence on other actors to improve their sustainability performance, and more specifically their innovation performance (Meqdadi,

Johnsen, & Johnsen, 2017). For instance, in her study of textile value chains in Europe, Franco (2017) reports that the power balance between buyers and their suppliers greatly determined the willingness of either party to engage and invest in a joint eco-innovation effort for the CE.

Although previous literature has assumed that buyers have a dominant power over suppliers, who are susceptible to buyers' various demands (Yeniyurt, Henke, & Yalcinkaya, 2014), there is evidence that suppliers with special competencies could also occupy a powerful role within the supplier-buyer relationship because of the resources they possess. Key resources brought by a buyer in order to exert power over its supplier include its expenditure in terms of volume, regularity, and predictability, as well as its reputation in the marketplace. Similarly, key resources brought by a supplier in order to warrant influence over its buyer consist of its product/service offering and the organizational knowledge underpinning such offering (Cox, Sanderson, & Watson, 2001; Kähkönen & Lintukangas, 2010). Suppliers also bring value by creating awareness about solutions or directly satisfying customer needs (Johnsen, 2009). Depending on the relative power balance of the different network actors, scenarios displaying supplier dominance, buyer dominance, or power balance are possible. In all scenarios, the level of resource dependence of one actor over another determines the power of one of the parties. The powerful actor thus possesses resources that are relatively scarce, and highly desirable for the other party.

5.3.2 Traditional measures of power in networks

An actor's network role and network position are crucial when determining its power in a network (Kähkönen & Lintukangas, 2010). I operationalize an actor's network position by calculating its centrality score. Network centrality is a core concept in network research that characterizes a specific ego's power relative to other network alters (Kenis & Knoke, 2002). A high network centrality score allows an organization to get access to information faster and more effectively than nodes with low centrality. Centrality has not only been associated with concepts like power, but also with others such as popularity, social status, and prestige.

The three most prominent types of centrality metrics in the network literature are: (i) degree centrality, (ii) closeness centrality, and (iii) betweenness centrality (Everett & Borgatti, 1999). The first measure, degree centrality, computes how many connections one node has to other nodes. Actors with more ties may have multiple ways and more resources to reach their goals. This concept builds on the notion that the more links a node has, the more central the node is, and, as a result, the higher its score for degree centrality. Overall, the higher the degree centrality of a node, the more visible and powerful it is in the network (Marsden, 2002).

The second centrality concept is closeness centrality. This metric focuses on how short the distances between a node and the rest of the nodes in a

86 Maria A. Franco

network are. A node is central if it can quickly reach other nodes and that is why this measure includes direct ties. A node with high closeness centrality has more freedom from the influence of, and it is therefore more independent from and less reliant on, other nodes (Kim et al., 2011). Finally, betweenness centrality gives us an idea of how many shortest paths go through a certain node. That is, how many pairs of nodes would have to go through a node in order for them to reach one another in the minimum number of hops?

Brass and Burkhardt (1993) view the three measures of centrality as complementary since they all represent the two necessary conditions for power: "the potential for an individual to decrease dependence on others and to increase others' dependence on himself or herself." Therefore, in the absence of compelling theoretical arguments favoring one measure or the other, I posit all three centrality concepts influence the propensity of an actor to innovate in a network.

Proposition 1a: The propensity of a node to innovate with other network partners is directly correlated to its power, or centrality score, in a network.

5.3.3 Power in reference to others

The previous section used node-level network measures to assert that the actors bestowed with power are more likely to innovate and that, in general, the higher the degree centrality of an actor, the more powerful this actor is. This second part of the argument discriminates power from centrality by stating that the power of an actor cannot only reside on the number of nodes to which this actor is connected to, but also on the relative power of its neighbors. According to this argument, power is inversely correlated to the power of its neighbors, such that, for an equal number of ties, the actors linked to powerless others are powerful, and the actors tied to powerful others are powerless (Borgatti & Halgin, 2011; Bozzo & Franceschet, 2016).

For instance, in a dyadic relationship A–B, both parties are equally powerful. In a triad with nodes A–B–C, according to traditional measures of centrality, B is the most powerful node and A and C both depend on B. In a 4-node path A–B–C–D, actors B and C hold power, while A and D are dependent on either B or C. Finally, in a 5-node path A–B–C–D–E, the centrality measures discussed in the previous subsection would assert that C is the central or most powerful node. However, according to this second line or argumentation, B and D are the powerful ones because they are connected to the powerless (i.e., A and E). In sum, it can be argued that by being connected to a less powerful one, an actor becomes powerful because it controls the resources that create dependency on the other party.

Proposition 1b: The power of an actor is inversely correlated to the power of its neighbors, with the most powerful node being the most likely to eco-innovate.

5.3.4 Strong ties and incremental innovation

The previous propositions discussed how a firm's propensity to innovate with its buyer or supplier was contingent on the firm's power position in a network. The central premise of this section is that by relying on certain types of ties or inter-firm relationships, the focal firm can access strategic resources beyond its boundaries (Lewis, Brandon-Jones, Slack, & Howard, 2010). Because ties enable the acquisition and exchange of valuable knowledge and capabilities between buyers and suppliers in a network, they represent a fundamental driver for eco-innovations. Tie strength, therefore, stands as another important network feature worth being considered.

In particular, the existence of strong ties between a firm and its supply network has been found to be conducive to cooperative and innovative behavior between suppliers and buyers, as they facilitate knowledge and technology exchange during the product development process (Johnston, McCutcheon, Stuart, & Kerwood, 2004; Koufteros, Edwin Cheng, & Lai, 2007; Michelfelder & Kratzer, 2013). In relation to sustainability, strong ties between a buyer and its suppliers are needed to achieve environmental performance improvements and to foster knowledge exchange and innovation (Geffen & Rothenberg, 2000; van Bommel, 2011).

According to Granovetter (1973), the strength of a tie is a linear combination of: (i) the amount of time, (ii) the emotional intensity, (iii) the intimacy, and (iv) the reciprocal services experienced by the parties that make up the tie. Tie strength is thus characterized by strong interpersonal connections that are reflected in high levels of trust, cooperation, and a sense of mutual dependence among the parties in a relationship. Trust, in particular, has been a widely discussed concept in management studies and it reflects the buyer's or the supplier's belief in the other party's reliability and integrity. Besides uncovering the effect of power balance on the birth of eco-innovations, Franco (2017) also reported that collaboration for eco-innovation in a textile value chain depended on the level of trust between the engaged partners. Trust facilitated information exchanges and lowered the costs of engaging in arm's length contracts with suppliers. Several case-studies have also demonstrated that trust facilitated the implementation of sustainability practices across suppliers, including collaboration for innovation (Geffen & Rothenberg, 2000).

Although strong ties facilitate the recombination of knowledge for the development of eco- innovations, it is important to recognize the type of innovation we are referring to. Simard and West (2006) suggest that strong ties are characterized by redundant, homogeneous information, or in other words, by a situation in which the knowledge bases of the nodes in a network overlap. Information is redundant because nodes attached by strong ties tend to exhibit similar characteristics, such as comparable values, beliefs, or norms (a mechanism also known as "homophily"), this being the reason why the nodes got so closely connected in the first place. One could therefore assume that although strong ties lead to the formation of relational capital and, by extension, to the development of eco-innovations, these innovations are often incremental in nature (Roscoe, Cousins, & Lamming, 2016). In the context of the CE, this could mean that although network nodes connected through strong ties will tend to innovate, they will do so only incrementally. Marginal eco-improvements could include, for instance, alterations or modifications to existing materials and processes to fit the requirements of the CE.

Proposition 2: *A firm with strong ties to its buyer or supplier is more likely to develop incremental eco-innovations.*

5.3.5 Weak ties and radical innovation

The previous section argued that although strong ties facilitated the transfer of knowledge and, consequently, the development of innovations, actors embedded solely in strong-tie networks harmed their own performance, because of the self-inflicted bounded rationality of their group members. When a node's alters are strongly connected to each other, the information one alter possesses may also be possessed by other ego's alters, suggesting that a tie to both of them is redundant (Borgatti & Li, 2009), and that the innovations they develop are merely incremental in nature. In fact, the well-known notion of "overembeddedness" suggests that networks composed mostly of strong ties may threaten innovation, rather than enhance it (Uzzi, 1997).

The network literature suggests that in order for firms to enhance their opportunities for finding eco-innovations, not only do they need to maintain strong ties with strategic actors, but they must also create multiple weak ties with other actors in the network. Weak ties serve as bridges to different social circles and provide access to non-redundant, more novel information (Granovetter, 1973; Perry-Smith & Mannucci, 2017) (Figure 5.2).

When technological uncertainty is high and firms want to access the knowledge that their trusted, closest suppliers do not possess, firms must look for cooperation partners outside their traditional supply network. Here is where connections to weak ties can grant increased access to "outside perspectives" and novel knowledge (Burt, 1992, 2005). Because weak ties give

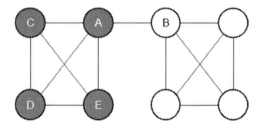

Figure 5.2 Representation of weak ties between nodes A and B.

firms access to non-redundant knowledge, it could be argued that they favor the development of radical innovations. Radical innovations introduce novel products to the marketplace and represent major departures from the current state of affairs in terms of product performance and technologies (Song & Di Benedetto, 2008). Radical eco-innovations for the circular economy are characterized by novel materials that allow not only the design of truly circular products, but also of novel technological solutions for circular manufacturing, commercialization, and post-processing.

Proposition 3: *Firms exhibiting multiple weak ties are more likely to develop radical eco- innovations than firms embedded in a strong-tied network.*

5.3.6 Innovation determined by spatial-linked collaboration

Industrial symbiosis (IS), one of the various concepts associated to the CE, has evolved from the study of industrial ecology and constitutes a prime element of the circular economy agenda because of its potential to turn one firm's waste into another firm's raw material (Ghisellini, Cialani, & Ulgiati, 2016; Lombardi & Laybourn, 2012). More specifically, IS refers to the physical exchange between two firms of materials, energy, water, and by-products, where the key is collaboration facilitated by geographic proximity (Chertow, 2000; Paquin & Howard-Grenville, 2012). Examples of IS include the use of non-toxic industrial waste to produce energy by incineration, or the use of excess heat and CO_2 from one firm to increase crop yields in a greenhouse.

Collaboration stands as one of the important concepts associated with industrial symbiosis. It refers to group efforts to achieve benefits beyond what the firm would normally aim to achieve in its self-interest, including network configurations for the development of eco-innovations (Zhu, Lowe, Wei, & Barnes, 2007). In other words, industrial symbiosis prompts firms to form networks for the development of eco-innovations that involve the identification of novel ways to source inputs and derive value from waste. As it is the case with typical eco-innovations, there is the perception that supplier-customer relationships in an IS context are somehow more intense than in traditional innovation scenarios, because IS partners must look for innovative resource exchanges that are beneficial for both of the parties involved.

Besides collaboration, the concept of exchanges (facilitated by geographical proximity) is also key in understanding industrial symbiosis relationships. Geographical proximity is defined as the spatial distance between actors, in absolute and relative meaning (Boschma, 2005). Geographical proximity has been regarded as a key factor in the functioning of the industrial ecosystem because of several reasons, namely: (i) the energy and transaction costs for closing resource loops are lower at a smaller spatial scale (Graedel, 1996) and (ii) the mental distance among collaborative parties is close in the face of geographical proximity. Extant literature suggests that because spatial proximity

90　*Maria A. Franco*

facilitates interaction by bringing people together, then knowledge exchange and innovation are more likely to take place. Conversely, when actors are spatially distant, knowledge exchange and transfer become more difficult (Boschma, 2005). Empirical studies seem to corroborate that firms located close to each other show a better innovative performance than firms located elsewhere (Audretsch & Feldman, 1996).

Spatial proximity is not only a requirement for partners in an industrial symbiosis arrangement, but also for other circular economy-related partnerships. For instance, firms in charge of sorting, dismantling, and reprocessing products might need to relocate to areas where they can be geographically close to product return flows. In sum, although we know that knowledge diffuses through social networks that are dispersed across the world, and not necessarily located within specific territorial boundaries or clusters, geographical agglomeration might be a requirement for the CE, especially for applications such as IS and reverse logistic networks.

Proposition 4: *Both in industrial symbiosis and in other related circular economy applications, firms located geographically close to each other will interact and eco-innovate more than firms that are located geographically distant from each other.*

5.4 Effect of buyer–supply network collaboration on innovation

It is a contention of this paper that certain properties of network nodes and ties facilitate the type of knowledge sharing that is conducive to eco-innovations. Hence, as supplier or buyer involvement in innovation increases, the eco-innovation performance of the focal firm increases accordingly (Yeniyurt et al., 2014). Although this paper is exclusively theoretical, extant literature provides numerous examples of how researchers have operationalized the dependent variable "eco-innovation."

Some of the most common approaches include evaluating: (i) the firm's R&D expenditures as a measure on innovation incentives or the start of innovation activities, and (ii) the firm's patenting activity as a measure of innovation intensity. Other authors like Wu, Wu, and Si (2016) have measured product innovation as the share of the new products a firm has launched over the total number of products it has sold. The percentage of new product sales is meant to indicate the realized commercial benefit of the firm's eco-innovation activities. Similarly, Wang and Hu (2017) assert there are other relative measures that could also reflect a firm' innovation performance. These measures include technological competitiveness, response to customer demand, number of new products or services, and the speed to market of new products. In a final representative example, Cheng, Yang, and Sheu (2014) used a 7-point Likert scale (1 = strongly disagree; 7 = strongly agree) to measure firm's degree of eco-product, eco-process, and eco-organizational innovative capacity in a Taiwanese context (Figure 5.3).

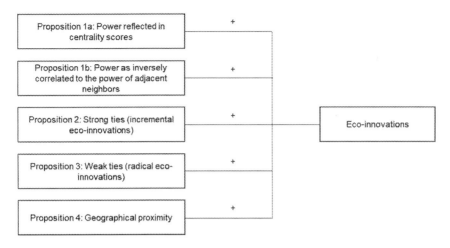

Figure 5.3 Conceptual model for studying eco-innovation outputs.

5.5 Conclusions

Eco-innovations encompass novel product or technological solutions aimed at reducing the environmental impact of industrial activity and allowing the value recovery of elements already in the economy. It has been a contention of this paper that for eco-innovations to materialize in a CE, collaboration with the focal firm's supply network is often key. To explain how supply network structure influences the development of eco-innovations, this paper proposes a conceptual framework backed up by four propositions.

First, I posit a network's most powerful firm, as reflected in is centrality scores and its relationship to power/powerless others, is more likely to eco-innovate. Power is contingent on the perception of actors and their position in the network and therefore, it conditions the behavior of buyers and suppliers to innovate (Cox et al., 2001). Propositions 1a and 1b indirectly highlight not only the fact that the most powerful node will be the most likely to start an eco-innovation project (most usually powerful suppliers, manufacturers, or retailers), but also the idea that "dominance or interdependency of organizations anywhere in the supply chain may influence individual buyer-seller relationships and can impact on their potential to manage a coherent chain" (Cox et al., 2001). Take, for instance, a power regime based on buyer dominance (e.g., A>B>C<D) where the end customer A apparently dominates the actions of all its suppliers upstream the supply chain. Although this is true for the relationship between A and B, and B and C, it does not hold true for the link between C and D. Here, C (the buyer) has a dependent relationship with D (the supplier) who has insufficient incentives to enter into a collaborative relationship with C. The supplier D has therefore all the leverage and incentives to manage the relationship with C according to its own interests.

Second, I have argued that trust developed from strong relational ties helps buyers and suppliers with information sharing and therefore with innovation. The stronger the ties between two or more parties, however, the more likely their social worlds and knowledge bases will overlap, and the more likely the innovations that result from their interaction will be incremental in nature. Third, partnering with nodes with whom the focal firm shares only weak ties is probably a better way to have access to unconventional and novel knowledge bases. Hence, it is hypothesized that building weak ties can lead to the development of radical eco-innovations. Innovative circular organizations will therefore exhibit a balance between dense and strong network relationships (for short-term modifications in the current range of products), as well as open and diverse circles where knowledge is novel and non-redundant (for the long-term development of radical eco- solutions).

Finally, I posit circular economy approaches such as industrial symbiosis and reverse logistics seem to thrive in network configurations where spatial proximity is present. Geography is thus an important factor in enabling circular firms to connect more easily. Theoretically, the propositions outlined in this paper contribute to the inter-organizational innovation literature by explaining how network features can impact the development of eco-innovations for the CE. Again, although a dyadic look at buyer-supplier relationships might reflect a landscape conducive to innovation, when studied through the perspective of networks, extended relationships may unveil faraway dependencies that could favor or hamper collaborative initiates either up or downstream the value chain. Managerially, this theory suggests that firms should consider a supplier's relationships with other organizations (i.e., its network) and not only its own resources and capabilities. For instance, firms should concentrate on building weak ties and therefore structural holes, as these relationships are more conducive to radical eco-innovations for the circular economy.

5.6 Limitations

One of the key limitations of this work is the lack of empirical validation of the theoretical propositions. Next steps, therefore, should include the application of social network analysis to operationalize and test the structural characteristics of nodes and ties in selected networks. Regression analysis, with the corresponding control variables, can then prove the relationship between the obtained network measures and firms' eco-innovation output. Finally, data collection to undertake such a study must be carefully planned, as it is a well-known fact that supply networks are inherently data intensive and that such data is often difficult to access (Waller & Fawcett, 2013).

6 Open innovation and sustainability

On potential roles of open innovation ecosystems for a sustainability transition

Dieudonnee Cobben, Dries Maes, and Nadine Roijakkers

6.1 The role of different ecosystems in sustainability transitions

This conceptual chapter explores the potential roles that different types of open innovation (OI) ecosystems (business, innovation, knowledge and entrepreneurial) could take up to enable sustainability transitions. Open innovation ecosystems involve complex, long-term networks that co-create and capture value collectively with direct and indirect partners (Leroi-Werelds, Pop, & Roijakkers, 2017). Ecosystem partners specialize and provide each other access to complementary assets to collaboratively develop innovative solutions (Gulati, Puranam, & Thusman, 2012). Although OI ecosystems are a fundamental part of open innovation processes, their socio-technical character represents an underexposed dimension in the ecosystem literature (e.g. Russel & Smorodinskaya, 2018). As a first step towards a larger framework of analysis, this chapter starts from a literature overview of current theoretical frameworks of ecosystems within transitions, and the chapter develops five propositions that explain relations between different ecosystem types and their potential contribution to sustainability transitions.

Open innovation ecosystems are increasingly forged around socio-technical challenges such as sustainability transitions (Dougherty & Dunne, 2011; Jarvi, Almpanopoulou, & Ritala, 2012). The advantages of OI ecosystems, such as increased innovative capacity, co-creation, co-specialization, and flexibility, could offer opportunities for the ecosystem to act as a niche to enable learning processes on multiple dimensions to establish new dominant designs and adjustments in the socio-technical regime (Geels & Schot, 2007; Walrave, Talmar, Podoynitsyna, Romme, & Verbong, 2018). Sustainability transitions can only take place when the dominant socio-economic regime is disrupted or changed. Open innovation ecosystems offer flexible, long-term multidisciplinary stakeholder networks that integrate knowledge exploration and exploitation to potentially contribute to these regime changes (Claudel, 2018; Walrave et al., 2018). Likewise, the long-term orientation of ecosystems and the related development of joint innovation strategies embedding sustainability targets by ecosystem partners are crucial elements in making

OI ecosystems powerful engines of sustainability transition trajectories. Sustainability transitions require path-breaking value propositions that can be challenging to implement as they conflict with elements of the dominant socio-technical regime (Geels, 2004; Geels & Schot, 2007). Organizations and policy makers have to be constantly working with ecosystem types to influence the likelihood to trigger sustainability transitions, at different levels. One framework that sheds light on different elements (e.g. regimes, landscape, niche) of sustainability transitions is the Multi-Level Perspective (MLP) (Geels, 2004; Geels & Schot, 2007). To realize a transition, a dominant social-economic system, also called regime, should be disrupted by niche-innovations. The regime is held in place by powerful incumbent actors that prefer to sustain existing development paths. New niche-innovations can challenge the regime or its specific elements. Replacing (parts of) the regime can be difficult, as niche-innovations have structural disadvantages in the selection environment. The only way for an innovation to grow into the existing socio-technical regime is to adapt or transform relevant societal sub-systems (Geels & Schot, 2007; Raven, 2007). Despite the potential of MLP to describe transitions, current research on MLP tends to take a technology focus, ignoring cultural and societal aspects that are important within sustainability transitions (Geels, 2005; Genus & Coles, 2008). Besides, transition literature has taken a linear rather than a systemic focus, ignoring the complexity of radical innovation adoption (Genus & Coles, 2008).

The step towards ecosystem analysis is not straightforward. The ecosystem concept is an umbrella term that includes a wide variety of ecosystem types that each have their unique characteristics and implications. Despite the increasing popularity of the OI ecosystem literature and the integration of other literature streams to explain their dynamics, the concept is still undertheorized (e.g. Jacobides, Cennamo, & Gawer, 2018). Research has not yet addressed the differences between ecosystem types with respect to their likelihood to contribute to sustainability transitions. First attempts have been done to integrate transition literature into OI ecosystem literature, but its application is still limited to radical and urban technology transitions led by corporates (e.g. Claudel, 2018; Walrave et al., 2018). As a result of the specific research environments that existing research offers, findings cannot be easily transferred to other open innovation contexts such as sustainability transitions. Transition literature scholars call for research on the interaction between niches and regimes in a network context to systematically understand transition development (Genus & Coles, 2008). Therefore scholars call for research on the intersection of different literature streams to enhance the understanding of the complexity of open innovation ecosystem literature in social value creation contexts such as sustainability transitions (e.g. Russel & Smorodinskaya, 2018).

The different ecosystem types have been inspired by different academic literature streams, such as natural ecosystem literature (e.g. Gunderson & Holling, 2001) and earlier network collaboration literature and exhibit

Open innovation and sustainability 95

therefore comparable structural features, such as strong interdependencies between partners, spatial co-location, and long-term commitment to the collaboration (Iansiti & Levien, 2004; Moore, 1993). These well-researched frameworks have been used to understand OI ecosystem's unique dynamics and characteristics (e.g. Spigel & Harrison, 2017; Walrave et al., 2018). Some scholars conclude that ecosystem types are complementary in explaining innovation processes (e.g. Claudel, 2018; Valkokari, 2015).

To understand the differences in potential influences that four ecosystem types could have on different elements of sustainability transitions, we explore how the ecosystem types influence the dynamics between niche-innovations and the dominant regime. These dynamics can influence the occurrence of sustainability transitions. As existing research has not been able yet to explain how ecosystem types could contribute to sustainability transitions, this conceptual research aims at contributing to a first understanding on the relationship between different ecosystem types and sustainability transitions. As such, well-researched literature frameworks will be reviewed to explore the potential roles that ecosystem types could play in transitions resulting in a number of propositions that could guide future (empirical) research. The chapter is structured as follows. First, the importance of sustainability transitions is discussed. Second, the different ecosystem types are elaborated upon recalling the earlier literature streams that they build upon. Third, the potential contribution of each ecosystem type for sustainability transitions is explained. Finally, five propositions are defined to guide future research, and boundary conditions for suitable research methodologies.

6.2 Sustainability transitions

Transition literature has been expanded in the last two decades, providing insights into different transition processes. Transitions involve *"outcomes of alignments between developments at multiple levels"* (p. 300), involving a change from one dominant system to another (Geels & Schot, 2007). Every transition includes a merger of social and technical elements to understand the complex system of interconnected levels of potential niche-innovations that have the potential to provoke the transformation of larger structures (Geels, 2004; Geels & Schot, 2007). Within the transition literature, several scholars have explicitly focused on transitions that require radical approaches and highly innovative abilities (Rauter, Perl-Vorbach, & Baumgartner, 2017; Wagner, 2009). Radical innovations often fail, as their value proposition conflicts with the dominant regime (Geels, 2004; Geels & Schot, 2007). The interdependence of the dynamics at different levels has been recognized in principle with research on technological evolution and industrial change, leading to an improved understanding and policies for *strategic niche management* (Kemp, Schot, & Hoogma, 1998), *transition management* (Rotmans, Kemp, & Asselt, 2001), or a *multi-level perspective* (MLP) (Geels, 2002).

The MLP framework offers a framework to conceptualize and explain socio-technical transitions. The regime (meso-level) is the dominant socio-technical system that specifies the economic and social character of a specific domain (Geels, 2004; Geels & Schot, 2007). The niche (micro-level) offers a protected space to nurture new (radical) niche-innovations. The exogenous landscape (macro-level) includes the broader, contextual societal developments (e.g. politics, economics, culture, etc.). Within the landscape, pressures can be developed that influence the dynamics between niches and the regime (Geels, 2004; Geels & Schot, 2007).The regime is often held in place, due to economies of scale and scope, by large and powerful incumbent actors that sustain certain development paths (Arthur, 1989; Geels, 2004). To maintain the regime, proven and existing innovations are preferred to keep the existing system in place (Adner & Snow, 2010). Interactions between and within different levels can modify or reproduce elements of the regime. Whether a regime is maintained or changed depends on the power relations between partners to influence rules and institutions (Geels, 2004). New niche-innovations can challenge the entire regime or specific elements. Replacing (parts of) the regime can be difficult, as niche-innovations have structural disadvantages in the selection environment. The only way for a niche-innovation to grow into the existing socio-technical regime is to adapt or transform relevant societal subsystems (Raven, 2007).

Alignment between niche-innovations, regimes and the exogenous landscape can result in a variety of transition pathways, depending on the timing and nature of interactions and on the interpretation and mobilization of actors. Four pathways are identified: (1) *technological substitution*, where interdependent niche-innovations disrupt the regime by landscape pressures, (2) *transformation*, where landscape pressures stimulate incremental innovations within the regime, (3) *reconfiguration*, where niche-innovations are implemented within regime, allowing future adjustments via landscape pressures, and (4) *de-alignment and re-alignment*, where landscape pressures are high, but niche-innovations are only able to co-create in a regime with other niche-innovations after a while. These transition pathways show that the dominant regime is often not entirely replaced by niche-innovations. Then, incumbent powerful actors (partly) influence the environment in which innovations develop and diffuse (Smink, Hekkert, & Negro, 2015). Despite having less ambitious environmental and social goals, incumbents have a more legitimate position in the market than niche-innovators (Hockerts & Wustenhagen, 2010). Incumbents can follow the niches, enter the niches, delay the transition or remain inert. In the latter, incumbents will not be able to sustain themselves in the long run (Mossel, Rijnsoever, & Hekkert, 2018). Transitions often include shifts between pathways that are influenced by landscape pressures, the role of incumbents, and the readiness of niche-innovations (Smink et al., 2015).

MLP integrates earlier conceptual frameworks such as strategic niche management (SNM) and transition management (TM). Strategic niche management (SNM) focuses on the management of experiments regarding technological innovations at the niche level. SNM is related to MLP, and focuses on the relation between the socio-technical regimes and the influence of niches on the regime (Kemp et al., 1998; Weber, Hoogma, Lane, & Schot, 1999). A niche offers a protected space for experimentation. Technologies and their contexts develop simultaneously, resulting in social and technical alignment within the niche. To understand the needs and required institutional changes, stakeholders co-create with customers to create an interactive learning environment. As a result, new technologies and social structures are developed. The experimental character of niches enables an ongoing search and learning environment (bottom-up) (Loorbach & Raak, 2006).

Transition management (TM) was developed around the same time as SNM and focuses on the change of regimes in social systems (Loorbach & Raak, 2006; Rotmans et al., 2000). TM provides a participatory framework to manage expectations within multi-stakeholder transition processes. Transitions are created by aligning strategic, tactical, and operational activities (Kemp, Loorbach, & Rotmans, 2007). A diverse set of partners, such as governments, companies, intermediary organizations, universities, and research organizations, interact at different levels to structure their shared problems with existing regimes and identify shared objectives and visions regarding future ones. Governmental organizations need to develop the required institutional environment for sustainable innovations (top-down). In addition, other actors collaborate in bottom-up initiatives to create inclusion, self-organization, and self-learning effects. In line with SNM, experiments regarding niche-innovations are important, to learn what a niche needs to grow into regime. After all, niche-innovations need safe and protected spaces. To summarize, TM focuses on transitions consisting of long-term, multiple domains, levels, and actors to develop the sustainable innovation that our society needs (Loorbach & Raak, 2006; Rotmans et al., 2001).

6.3 Ecosystem types and their characteristics

Different strands of ecosystem literature identify four types of ecosystems, centered respectively around the common creation of knowledge, innovation, businesses, and entrepreneurship. The four ecosystem types aim at shared value capture and creation between a group of actors, but each ecosystem type has unique implications regarding their geographical and temporal scope, partner types, knowledge flows, etc. As the ecosystem type literatures have been undertheorized, more well-researched frameworks, such as network collaboration literature, have been used to understand their unique dynamics and characteristics (Spigel & Harrison, 2017). Current network collaboration literature has not been able to explain the complexity of socio-technical transitions. Each literature can explain specific parts of the systemic changes that are required. Therefore a combination of literature streams is used to understand the dynamics and characteristics of OI ecosystems (Spigel & Harrison, 2017).

98   *Dieudonnee Cobben et al.*

6.3.1 Business ecosystem

The business ecosystem, initiated by Moore (1993), is defined as "*... loose networks ... affect, and are affected by, the creation and delivery of a company's own offerings.*" (Iansiti & Levien, 2004). Business ecosystems aim at building technological infrastructures, resulting in a technical/digital or local scale (Iansiti & Levien, 2004; Mäkinen & Dedehayir, 2013). The business ecosystem is the only ecosystem that specifically focuses on customer value creation, and does not take the customer for granted (Clarysse, Wright, Bruneel, & Mahajan, 2014; Valkokari, 2015). Business ecosystems serve different goals, such as building a strategy around a focal firm's value proposition or creating economies of scale (Clarysse et al., 2014). The leader is often a focal firm that aims at developing horizontal relations, expanding the ecosystem, developing an innovative community, setting directions, and providing key resources and infrastructures. The focal firm often has an important position in the network (Iansiti & Levien, 2004; Moore, 1996). Value is created by a variety of complementary, non-linear specialized individual skills and assets that provide directions within the continually changing environments (Clarysse et al., 2014; Valkokari, 2015). Value is captured by incubating and accelerating business activities. In terms of geographical scope, the system is a combination of global and local levels. Actors fulfill different roles within the ecosystem, such as keystone firm, niche player, dominator, or hub landlord. These roles can be supported by non-business actors such as governments and NGOs (Iansiti & Levien, 2004; Moore, 1993).

Business ecosystems are built around platforms providing complementary linkages between different stakeholders (Mäkinen, Kanniainen, & Peltola, 2014). Shared platforms for innovation are developed by the orchestrator of the business ecosystem, to develop a competitive advantage (Iansiti & Levien, 2004). Each platform will provide specific basic functionalities for the ecosystem (Tiwana, Konsynski, & Bush, 2010). As a result, the platform and business ecosystem both represent different organizational levels; the platform is the organization of things, whereas the ecosystem is the organization of related actors (Muegge, 2013). The organizational levels are interdependent and linked by institutional arrangements, governance, resource flows, etc. (Muegge, 2013). Platform literature has contributed to a better understanding of the value capture and creation mechanisms and the organizational structures of business ecosystems.

6.3.2 Innovation ecosystem

The innovation ecosystem, initiated by Adner (2006), is defined as "*...the collaborative arrangements through which firms combine their individual offerings into a coherent, customer-facing solution.*" (Adner, 2006, p. 2). The system focuses on the integration of exploration and exploitation (Valkokari, 2015).

Innovation ecosystems are applied to contexts such as knowledge hubs, crowdsourcing initiatives, and open source. The ecosystem is often led by a focal actor, such as a platform or firm, which starts the ecosystem to attract additional components that their innovation requires to work (Adner, 2006). The focal actor sets out the ecosystem strategy and governance model, often to control the technological architecture (Autio & Thomas, 2014). The extent to which an ecosystem is controllable, depends on the focal actor's ability to match their goals and the ecosystem goals, to design a clear structure, and the ability to influence and control. Each ecosystem has its own institutional climate that reduces the risks and stimulates trust-based relationships (Autio & Thomas, 2014). As a result, value is captured and created by actors within the system that combines their modular technologies into collective innovations. Each actor, both downstream and upstream, has its personal challenges that have to be resolved, to provide successful innovations (Adner & Kapoor, 2010). As a result of its modular focus, innovation ecosystems do not necessarily need a long-term focus as modular innovations mostly require adaptations to fit the technological structures (Autio & Thomas, 2014; Valkokari, 2015). Innovation ecosystems require close proximity in either geographical or cognitive sense. Stakeholders present in the network are NGOs, firms, intermediaries, funders, innovation brokers, governmental organizations, and other resource providers (Carayannis & Campbell, 2009).

The innovation ecosystem, seen as a specific subset of alliances, has a number of properties that distinguish them from alliances, such as their focus on long-term collaborative innovation and partner diversity (Adner, 2017; Gulati et al., 2012). The alliance literature has been extensively researched and provides interesting insights for the governance of collaborations. Within innovation ecosystem literature, the cluster is described as a type of innovation ecosystem that focuses on interactions with triple helix partners to continuously co-produce innovations. Clusters can evolve into innovation ecosystems, as soon as their focus shifts from short-term innovation to continuous innovations that require long-term complex collaborations (Porter & Ketels, 2009; Russel & Smorodinskaya, 2018). The cluster literature adds insights into geographically clustered multi-partner innovation processes. Last, innovation ecosystems are also linked to National Innovation Systems. NIS became difficult to maintain over time, as they could not handle increasing complexity of innovations, and were too much government-oriented for industry (too bureaucratic) (Russel & Smorodinskaya, 2018; Schot & Steinmueller, 2016). The innovation ecosystem offers solutions for these issues, by placing governments in a more passive role that aims at supporting rather than orchestrating collaborative innovation. Still, the NIS literature offers insights into the importance of governmental support to the innovation ecosystem literature (Russel & Smorodinskaya, 2018).

6.3.3 Knowledge ecosystem

The knowledge ecosystem, initiated by Van der Borgh, Cloodt, and Romme (2012), is defined as a "...heterogeneous set of knowledge-intensive companies and other participants that depend on each other for their effectiveness and efficiency, and as such need to be located in close proximity." (Van der Borgh et al., 2012, p. 151). The system aims at problem identification and search for knowledge exploration (Valkokari, 2015). This can involve long-term processes, requiring intensive partner commitment (Van der Borgh et al., 2012). Knowledge ecosystems offer ecosystem wide value sources, difficult to imitate value sources, and enhanced reputations (Van der Borgh et al., 2012). A university, public research organization, or external management team leads the ecosystem and provides the required social and economic environment and value sources (Clarysse et al., 2014). The knowledge ecosystem is the only ecosystem in which the leader is not directly competing with other ecosystem stakeholders. The ecosystem leader provides shared research facilities, convenient infrastructures, a meta-organization, and personalized services. The challenge for leaders is to find a balance between the member's own goals, and the ecosystem goals. Common and personal goals can be realized by business model innovation at the firm and ecosystem level to optimally capture and create value (Van der Borgh et al., 2012). Often, this ecosystem is applied to geographical or technological hotspots of co-located actors (Bathelt & Cohendet, 2014; Van der Borgh et al., 2012). Despite their local focus, knowledge ecosystems also need to integrate global resources as knowledge exploration sometimes needs to be complemented with knowledge that is not present within the local ecosystem (Van der Borgh et al., 2012).

The knowledge ecosystem literature is strongly related to the cluster literature. Cluster literature has provided insights into the mechanisms to benefit from a specific geographical location, such as providing supportive entrepreneurial environments for new ventures (Clarysse et al., 2014; Thomas & Autio, 2019). The main difference between both literature streams is the direction of collaboration; in cluster literature, collaboration is mostly vertically oriented, whereas in knowledge ecosystem literature collaboration can be both vertical and horizontal. Also the focus is slightly different as knowledge ecosystems focus mostly on knowledge exploration, whereas clusters aim at producing continuous innovations (Autio, Nambisan, Thomas, & Wright, 2018).

6.3.4 Entrepreneurial ecosystem

The entrepreneurial ecosystem, initiated by Isenberg (2011), is defined as "... entrepreneurs create new value, organized by a wide variety of governance modes, enabled and confined within a specific institutional context." (Stam, 2015, p. 1764). Entrepreneurial ecosystems aim at creating economic growth via entrepreneurship, often via one technology (Spigel,

2015). When growth is created, countries can flourish by job creation, and increased wealth, innovativeness, local entrepreneurship, etc. (Stam, 2015). The entrepreneurial ecosystem is used to explain how developing or emerging countries can or have grown into more wealthy economies, by stimulating entrepreneurship (e.g. Isenberg, 2011) or to explain the role of universities to create entrepreneurship within specific regions (e.g. Schaeffer & Matt, 2016). Governments, either local, regional, but often national, are responsible for creating the required institutional and economic climate for entrepreneurship (Isenberg, 2011). The government can support entrepreneurship by providing (in) direct support, organizing anchor events for network platforms, public policies, providing resources (e.g. financial), and stimulating stakeholders to overcome differences in objectives and expectations (Garud, Gehman, & Giulani, 2014; Stam, 2015). The entrepreneurial ecosystem is the only ecosystem type that has a government as leading actor. It can be difficult for governments to align the interest of all stakeholders. Especially entrepreneurs tend to search for legitimization before they consider to start with value creation processes (Kuratko, Fisher, Bloodgood, & Hornsby, 2017). Technology newness and legitimization influence the extent to which value can be created, and therefore governments have to provide the required institutional climate to provide required resources for radical innovations (Isenberg, 2011; Miller & Acs, 2017). Value is created and captured via collaboratively designing business environments for entrepreneurship. A variety of partners, such as firms, universities, NGOs, individuals, supporting organizations, and governmental organizations are part of the ecosystem. Each actor has an important role in supporting the government to develop the most optimal entrepreneurial climate and reduce possible barriers (Isenberg, 2011).

Entrepreneurial ecosystems are a specific cluster type, mainly as a result of their spatially confined character (Thomas & Autio, 2019). Entrepreneurial ecosystems are the only cluster type that focuses on shared business model innovation, rather than product or process innovation (Autio et al., 2018). The system also moves beyond a specific industry or technology-related knowledge base, towards shared business-process knowledge creation (Autio et al., 2018). Another difference is the nature of relationships; clusters tend to compete horizontally and connect vertically, whereas entrepreneurial ecosystems do it the other way around (Autio et al., 2018; Spigel & Harrison, 2017). The cluster literature provides insights into the importance of a shared focus and knowledge base between partners to make a collaboration successful. Entrepreneurial literature is related to the NIS literature. In both concepts, the role of the government is important for providing a required institutional climate for entrepreneurs. The governmental role within entrepreneurial ecosystems is a more passive compared to NIS, as entrepreneurial activities naturally co-locate resulting in a supporting instead of designing role of the government. As such, the NIS literature provides insights on the importance of governmental support.

6.4 Connecting different dimensions of ecosystems

Table 6.1 gives an overview of relations between network collaborations.

Each ecosystem type's objective contributes in its own way to the integrated value chain and interactive network to enable innovation processes (Xu, Wu, Minshall, & Zhou, 2018). Scholars have integrated separate ecosystem types into overarching frameworks to explain their complementary nature. Valkokari (2015) connects innovation, business, and knowledge ecosystems, and explains that the innovation ecosystem integrates the explorative character of knowledge ecosystems and the exploitative character of business ecosystems. Scholars such as Xu et al. (2018) agree that an innovation ecosystem is an integration of knowledge and business ecosystems, though their explanation is different. Valkokari (2015) describes ecosystems as complementary, whereas Xu et al. (2018) explain the relation between ecosystem types as several relating layers. Gomes, Salerno, Phaal, and Probert (2018) add that the business ecosystem is about value capture and integration, whereas the innovation ecosystem is about value co-creation and distributed challenges across partners. The combination of ecosystem types enables niche innovation to flourish and being exploited (Valkokari, 2015). Scholars have not explained the relation of entrepreneurial ecosystems and the other ecosystem types. This is probably the case as entrepreneurial ecosystems tend to have a national or regional scope, and therefore move beyond the geographical scope of other ecosystem types. Within entrepreneurial ecosystems, governments provide the required institutional environments for entrepreneurs to develop innovations (Clarysse et al., 2014). We assume that the entrepreneurial ecosystem provides the overall economic and institutional environments that the other three ecosystem types need to stimulate innovation processes.

Table 6.1 Relation between ecosystem types and network collaborations

Ecosystem type/network collaboration	Alliance	Cluster	NIS	Platform
Business	–	–	–	Value capture and creation, structure
Innovation	Collaborative governance	Multi-partner innovation	Governmental support	–
Entrepreneurial	–	Shared focus and knowledge base	Governmental support	–
Knowledge	–	Mechanisms for value creation and capture from geographical location.	–	–

6.5 Focus points for investigating combined roles of ecosystem types in a sustainability transition

Previously, unique characteristics of different ecosystem types have been explained. The ecosystem types stood in order of appearance in the literature. We now construct five propositions that show the potential roles that each ecosystem type could take to increase the likelihood of a sustainability transition. We move beyond the technological focus that transition literature tends to take, into the complexity of social and technical elements that are required for niche-innovations to grow into or change existing dominant regimes. Ecosystem literature has not yet addressed the differences between ecosystem types regarding their contribution to sustainability transitions. By combining both literature streams, we create an understanding of the complexity of niche-innovation within different ecosystem types to increase the likelihood of sustainability transitions.

Sustainability transitions require radical innovations that are able to disrupt the existing regime. To trigger sustainability transitions, experimentation with niche-innovation has to be stimulated. Experimentation involves both technical and social aspects (Geels, 2004; Geels & Schot, 2007). The technical experimentation of niche innovation requires the development of new technical knowledge, to understand how a specific technology works, and how it can be applied within certain contexts. Niche-innovations need a shared knowledge base, and geographical co-location to enable technical experimentation. The knowledge ecosystem aims at knowledge exploration and joint value networks (Bathelt & Cohendet, 2014). Despite their local focus, knowledge ecosystems also integrate global resources to complement local knowledge (Van der Borgh et al., 2012). Within sustainability transitions, the knowledge ecosystem can enhance the presence of a shared knowledge base and can work on enhanced learning processes. Therefore, we propose the following proposition:

> To the extent that knowledge ecosystems allow for a shared knowledge base, there is an increased speed and quantity of technical learning within niche experimentation.

Sustainability transitions move beyond the technical dimension, and need social experimentation. The contexts often develop in parallel with technological innovations. To understand the needs and the interactions with customers/users, organizations should co-create with customers. Customer value creation is more important than ever to increase the likelihood that users are willing to switch to new technologies (Geels, 2004; Geels & Schot, 2007; Valkokari, 2015). Business ecosystems offer the opportunity to understand how users would like to use technologies (Clarysse et al., 2014; Valkokari, 2015). Business ecosystems offer network effects; the more people use the ecosystem, the more attractive the sub-platforms become for potential ecosystem partners to develop additional components. Business ecosystems consist of interacting platforms, that provide specific sub-parts of the technological innovation (Mäkinen et al., 2014). The more consumers use a certain sub-part, the more stakeholders will join the ecosystem to provide additional technologies (Gawer & Cusumano, 2014). The business ecosystem offers a self-reinforcing effect. Therefore we propose the following:

> To the extent that business ecosystems allow for network externalities/ customer inclusion, there is an increased speed and quantity of social learning within niche experimentation.

Insights from social and technical experimentation need to be aligned and developed synchronously to create social and technical niche alignment. Within innovation ecosystems, a variety of stakeholders such as users and governments participate to enable co-learning between technology companies and other stakeholders. Co-learning offers insights into specific stakeholder needs and wishes for niche-innovations. The institutional context that is required for the niche-innovation can be developed, based on insights from co-learning. At the same time, technology companies combine their complementary technologies to build new technological innovations. Combining different modules is a learning process, as each company has challenges that need to be resolved before an innovation becomes successful (Adner & Kapoor, 2010). Innovation ecosystems offer room for continued experimentation by providing a system in which stakeholders can continue their understanding regarding societal and technical elements. The innovation ecosystem provides room for continued growth trajectories, by strengthening the competitive position of a niche-innovation and its potential to grow into a strong technology that can compete with existing regimes. We propose the following:

> To the extent that innovation ecosystems allow for a continued growth trajectory of experimentations, there is an increased speed and quantity of niches experiments developing into a regime.

Governments need to consider how to manage large-scale transitions, by developing pathways for niche-innovations to disrupt existing regimes. Diverse stakeholders have different objectives to collaborate and therefore sustainability is a social issue that needs clear guidance. In line with ecosystem literature, TM offers a multi-stakeholder approach for innovation trajectories. Governments need to consider strategic, tactical, and operational activities to stimulate transitions (Kemp et al., 2007; Rotmans et al., 2000). Strategic activities focus on the development of a clear, long-term vision that is directed at stimulating transitions at the landscape and system level. Tactical activities focus on the interaction between the landscape and the regime. Tactical activities are important to interpret the visions of the strategic activities on the regime. Tactical activities are used to understand the barriers that niche-innovations can encounter. Actors that could influence a transition are invited to implement the vision in their own business models. Operational activities involve experimentation and learning processes at the level of niche-innovations. As the vision and potential barriers are known, operational activities enable the filtering up and transformation of lower level structures into new or modified regimes (Kemp et al., 2007).

Entrepreneurial ecosystems offer the institutional climate that is required for change. National governments can provide the institutional frameworks that communicate a certain entrepreneurial vision. Instruments, such as subsidies, new laws and regulations, legitimization of certain technologies, etc. can be developed to put pressure on the landscape. As a result, niche-innovations can be nurtured and stimulated to influence the regime or the development direction of the dominant regime. Entrepreneurial ecosystems offer the governmental support that is required for niches to grow into new regimes or to modify them. They influence the exogenous context to put pressure on existing regimes. We propose the following proposition:

> To the extent that entrepreneurial ecosystems allow for entrepreneurial institutional climates, there is a higher frequency of new enterprises being created to compete with the regime.

Current incumbent actors (e.g. fossil fuel companies) prefer to keep the existing system in place. Therefore the dominant regime prefers incremental technologies on conventional technologies. Not all large incumbents react in a similar way when confronted with landscape pressures and niche developments. Some actors remain inert. Others engage with innovation actors with the intent to guide and delay radical transformations. Some incumbents engage in the transition by allowing an internal transformation. This way, some transitions may be enabled not only by growing niche developments, but also by transforming incumbent actors (Mossel et al., 2018; Smink et al., 2015). The interaction between a large incumbent actor and ecosystems is most outspoken within business ecosystems. Contrary to other ecosystem types, the business ecosystem is often centered around a focal private actor, being a large incumbent company. The business ecosystem can therefore play a crucial role in the internal transformation of the incumbent actor, triggering a gradual regime shift leading to a sector transition. This is not necessarily the case. The large incumbent focal actor may enter in the business ecosystem to "keep innovation on a leash" (Smink et al., 2015) or to develop new markets while keeping its traditional markets and regime activities intact. The difference between the two behaviors, between "stalling innovation speed" and "actively driving the innovation" in the business ecosystem, is determined by the type of activity that the incumbent is willing to engage in. An incumbent actor can participate in innovative business partnerships either to develop new peripheral markets and growing niches, or to transform its own core business. Only the last type of involvement of the incumbent actor

106   *Dieudonnee Cobben et al.*

indicates an alignment with the transition. As such the long-term strategy of focal actors within business ecosystems is highly indicative of the trajectory that is followed leading to sustainability transition. Therefore we propose the following:

> To the extent that focal actors in business ecosystems are engaging their core business in ecosystem activities, there is a faster occurrence of a regime shift leading to a sustainability transition.

It is important to understand the interaction between ecosystems in order to facilitate the transition towards more sustainable systems. Each ecosystem type contributes in its own unique way to specific elements of socio-technical transition processes. By combining different ecosystem types, niche-innovations can compete with existing regimes (MLS) and they will be more resilient against external shocks. Both technological and social experimentations are important to understand the specific requirements of new niche-innovations to grow into new dominant regimes or to modify them. Future research should focus on investigating the relationships between and the most optimal configuration of the different ecosystem types to understand how their synergy can contribute to sustainability transitions. In addition, particular (geographical or sectoral) contexts may reflect specific attributes for sustainability transitions. Therefore future research should focus on investigating the effectiveness of different ecosystem types in effectively contributing to sustainability transitions within different institutional contexts and industries.

6.6 Discussion

This chapter focuses on the relation between different OI ecosystems and their potential contribution to increase the likelihood of the occurrence of a sustainability transition. The ecosystem concept has yet to address how different ecosystem types can potentially support sustainability transitions. Transition literature on the other hand has not yet been able to explain the systemic nature of transitions. To understand the different roles that ecosystem types could take, the ecosystem, socio-technical transition, and network collaboration literatures have been reviewed to develop five propositions that explain how ecosystem types could increase the likelihood of the occurrence of a sustainability transitions.

Each ecosystem could potentially influence a specific element of the transition. The knowledge ecosystem offers the development of a shared knowledge base to enhance the required technological learning within niche experimentation. The business ecosystem focuses on the social learning required for niche experimentation, by co-construction with customers and users. The innovation ecosystem connects exploration and exploitation of knowledge and business ecosystems, and offers a continued growth trajectory

Open innovation and sustainability   107

for experimentation. To offer niche-innovations the protected space they need for the experimentations, the entrepreneurial ecosystem can create a stimulating entrepreneurial institutional climate. This climate can make the niche more attractive for enterprises, as it becomes easier for them to compete with the regime. In some cases, the incumbent firm(s) are responsible for the change of the dominant regime. Incumbents can take part in the transition, as they want to lower the potential dangers of the ongoing niche-innovations or to steer developments in their desired directions, or in some cases even lead their own transformation. Only in the last case, they are contributing to the sustainability transition by using their power and legitimacy to influence the future directions of the dominant regime. The five identified propositions could guide future research, to enhance our understanding of the potential influence that ecosystem types could have. Grasping the interactions of eco-system types can contribute to our understanding of how they can add to sustainability transitions.

The combination of ecosystem types can result in a local focus on nur-turing niches, with national support to provide room for growth and the stimulation of entrepreneurship. The differences in ecosystems' contributions to specific elements of sustainability transitions imply that firms and policy makers should combine ecosystem types to enable change. Policy makers and firms can create portfolios of different OI ecosystem types to enable social and technical niche experimentation. Each ecosystem type can contribute in its own, unique way to influence specific elements of the transition. When we understand the most optimal configuration of ecosystem types, policy makers and firms are better able to increase the likelihood of sustainable transitions. When each ecosystem has an optimal fit, sustainability transitions can be accelerated.

Acknowledgments

We are much indebted to the reviewers, in particular Dr. W. Ooms, for guidance and reflections on earlier versions of this text. This article reflects the position of the authors alone, and is not indicative of the position of the Flemish Government. All remaining errors are the sole responsibility of the authors.

7 Sustainable innovation

Drivers, barriers, and actors under an open innovation lens

Barbara Bigliardi, Serena Filippelli, and Francesco Galati

7.1 Introduction

Survival is the goal of any organization, but during recent decades, both academics and practitioners agreed in stating that simply bringing new products to the market is not sufficient to gain and maintain competitive advantages. In particular, the increasing rates of innovation, the complexity of global markets and the environmental problems companies are facing, are inducing firms to operate in a multi-stakeholder context (Holmes & Smart, 2009). Among all, sustainability, defined as business policies and practices that *"meet the needs of the present without compromising the ability of future generations to meet their own needs"* (World Commission on Environment and Development, 1987, p. 8), is receiving more and more attention. Indeed, environmental constraints may limit the growth of a company (De Medeiros, Ribeiro, & Cortimiglia, 2014). As a consequence, the concept of sustainable innovation (hereafter, SI) has emerged. SI was defined by Charter and Clark (2007) and Charter et al. (2017), as the

> process where sustainability considerations (environmental, social, and financial) are integrated into company systems from idea generation through to research and development (R&D) and commercialization. This applies to products, services and technologies, as well as to new business and organizational models.

Studies have shown that integrating customers, suppliers, and research institutions, among others, may enable companies to successfully develop SIs (Carrillo-Hermosilla, Del Rio, & Könnölä, 2010; De Medeiros et al., 2014). In particular, in the last two decades the way companies undertake SI has changed, and the use of external networks has greatly increased. Dealing with cooperation, the open innovation (OI) approach (Chesbrough, 2003, 2006) has been one of the topics most frequently discussed during recent years. It was first introduced by Chesbrough in 2003, meaning the *"paradigm that assumes that firms can and should use external ideas as well as internal ideas, and internal and external paths to markets, as the firms look to advance their technology"* (Chesbrough, 2003, p. 24).

110   *Barbara Bigliardi et al.*

Despite the recognized importance of both these concepts, and despite companies worldwide recognize the power of OI to fuel SI (Adamczyk, Bullinger, & Moeslein, 2011), practitioners and academicians yet question whether OI may contribute to SI (Mustaquim & Nyström, 2014). In particular, relatively little is known about OI in the context of SI, even if OI is recognized as increasingly relevant for SI (De Medeiros et al., 2014; Gabriele Arnold, 2011; Perl-Vorbach, Rauter, & Baumgartner, 2014). Specifically, open questions remain referring in particular to how sustainability can be fully integrated into an OI process (Hossain, 2015).

Based on these premises, this chapter attempts to remedy the situation by discussing the existing literature in the fields of SI and OI, with the twofold objective to (ii) show what has been done so far in this area, and (ii) identify the main drivers, barriers and actors involved in an SI process under an OI lens. Specifically, the present chapter highlights in which areas of SI can the concept of OI be applied, by addressing the following two questions:

1   Why companies adopt SI?
2   Which stakeholders should be involved in SI?

The chapter is structured as follows: Section 7.2 discusses the concepts of SI and OI; Section 7.3 explains the relationships existing between these concepts; and Section 7.4 discusses the main findings and draws relevant conclusions.

7.2 Sustainable innovation and open innovation: Definitions and peculiarities

7.2.1 Sustainable innovation

Innovation allows companies to reach a greater level of sustainability in their activities (Hansen & Grosse-Dunker, 2013; Hansen, Grosse-Dunker, & Reichwald, 2009). Innovations can take the form of traditional innovation, which is an innovation that contributes to an improvement in sustainability (such as process innovation), or a form which in and of itself generates greater sustainability (e.g., the introduction of a new product using different raw materials) (Steiner, 2008). Innovations that contribute to sustainability are referred to with the term SIs, or with synonymous such as eco-innovations, green innovations, sustainability-oriented innovations (Horbach, 2008; Rowley, 2017). The literature on SI discussed the following main issues: (i) definitions of SI, (ii) classification of SIs, (iii) drivers and barriers to SI, and (iv) actors involved in the development of SIs.

The terms sustainability and innovation are controversial concepts. Consequently, to date, no clear or general definition exists. Table 7.1 shows only some of the definitions proposed in the available literature. As appears evident from these definitions, SI concept entails economic, environmental, and social target dimensions along the innovation's lifecycle, from material flows to their ecological and social effects, as well as the whole value chain. The object of innovation may be a product, a process, a service, a technique, a business method, a methodological innovation as well as an organizational innovation. From the definitions reported in Table 7.1, also different SI orientations (specifically, four orientations) emerge. SI has always an environmental orientation, aiming to reduce negative environmental and/or social impacts, and not only to increase the economic success of the company. SI may also have a market orientation, aiming at the satisfaction of the customers' needs and their competitiveness in the market. Thus, the two-level classification of SI depicted in Table 7.2 may be provided, based on the type of SI and its orientation.

As for the type of SI, the definitions allowed to classify SI into three main types: (i) technological, (ii) organizational, and (iii) social. Technological SI refers to a company's implementation of a new product, process, and/or service, as well as to a modification of the existing products, processes, or services, that reduces the impact of firm's activities on the environment (Varadarajan, 2017). According to the classic taxonomy of innovation, technological SI may be divided into product SI and process SI. Product SI is the most investigated type of SI, defined as

> a firm's introduction of a new product or modification of an existing product whose environmental impact during the lifecycle of the product, spanning resource extraction, production, distribution, use, and post-use disposal, is significantly lower than existing products for which it is a substitute.
>
> "(Varadarajan, 2017, p. 17)

The same author further classified product SI into three sub-categories, namely: efficiency innovation, elimination innovation, and substitution innovation. Efficiency innovation refers, for example, to the reductions in the quantities of renewable and non-renewable resources used to develop the new product, or to a new product that incorporates in a single product different standalone products. Elimination innovation includes, for instance, the elimination of the need to use a complimentary product, or the incorporation of all product-related information in the product container thus eliminating additional packaging. Finally, substitution innovation refers to the change or substitution of non-biodegradable materials or non-renewable resources with biodegradable or renewable ones. Organizational SI includes the development or adoption of business methods, new or improved to the organization, or more in general to organization designs which results, throughout its life cycle, in a reduction of environmental risk, pollution and other negative impacts of resource use and which would lead a company to operate beyond the economic profit, creating social and environmental value (Buttol et al., 2012). Finally, social SI is described as new behaviors, new organization

112 *Barbara Bigliardi et al.*

models, and new ways of living, more sustainable than move toward more sustainable ways of living (Manzini, 2007).

As far as the orientation is concerned, from the company perspective, the environmental orientation of an SI is considered to be the most important (OECD, 2009) and also the most investigated (indeed, this orientation appears in all the definitions summarized in Table 7.1). According to the environmental orientation, the impact of SI refers to its effect on environmental conditions, either in terms of the product life cycle or some other relevant dimension (OECD, 2009). The marketing and social orientation have received almost the same attention in the literature (indeed, they appear in 14 and 15 definitions respectively). According to the marketing orientation, SI is seen as a means to successfully introduce an innovation in the market, and consequently, it is related to a company's marketing performance, measured in terms of market share, sales growth rate, customer satisfaction, customer

Table 7.1 Definitions of sustainable innovation

Definition	Reference
The process of developing new products, processes or services which provide customer and business value but significantly decrease environmental impact	Fussler and James (1996)
New products and processes that provide customer value, while using fewer resources and resulting in reduced environmental impacts	Johansson and Magnusson (1998)
All measures of relevant actors (firms, politicians, unions, associations, churches, private households) which develop new ideas, behaviour, products and processes, apply or introduce them and which contribute to a reduction of environmental burdens or to ecologically specified sustainability targets	Klemmer, Lehr, and Löbbe (1999) and Rennings (2000)
Innovation that serves to prevent or reduce anthropogenic burdens on the environment, clean up damage already caused or diagnose and monitor environmental problems	Markusson (2001)
Innovation which is able to attract green rents on the market	Andersen (2002)
New and modified processes, equipment, products, techniques and management systems that avoid or reduce harmful environmental impacts	Rennings and Zwick (2003)
The creation of new market space, products and services or processes driven by social, environmental or sustainability issues	Little (2005)
The creation of novel and competitively priced goods, processes, systems, services, and procedures designed to satisfy human needs and provide a better quality of life for all, with a life-cycle minimal use of natural resources (materials including energy, and surface area) per unit output, and a minimal release of toxic substances	Europa INNOVA (2006)
Any form of innovation aiming at significant and demonstrable progress towards the goal of sustainable development, through reducing impacts on the environment or achieving a more efficient and responsible use of natural resources, including energy	European Commission (2007)

Definition	Reference
A process where sustainability considerations (environmental, social, financial) are integrated into company systems from idea generation through to research and development (R&D) and commercialisation. This applies to products, services and technologies, as well as new business and organisation models	Charter and Clark (2007)
The production, assimilation or exploitation of a novelty in products, production processes, services or in management and business methods, which aims, throughout its life-cycle, to prevent or substantially reduce environmental risk, pollution, and other negative impacts of resource use (including energy)	European Commission (2008)
The production, assimilation or exploitation of a product, production process, service or management, or business method that is novel to the organisation (developing or adopting it) and which results, throughout its life cycle, in a reduction of environmental risk, pollution and other negative impacts of resources use (including energy use) compared to relevant alternatives	Kemp and Pearson (2008)
Whenever innovations contribute to sustainable development from an economic, ecological, and a social point of view	Steiner (2008)
Innovation that results in a reduction of environmental impact, whether such an effect is intended or not; its scope may go beyond the conventional organisational boundaries of the innovating organisation and involve broader social arrangements that trigger changes in existing socio-cultural norms and institutional structures	OECD (2009)
Innovations that consist of new or modified processes, practices, systems, and products which benefit the environment and so contribute to environmental sustainability	Oltra and Saint Jean (2009)
Innovation that improves environmental performance	Carrillo-Hermosilla et al. (2010) and Arnold and Hockerts (2011)
The production, assimilation or exploitation of a product, production process, service or management, or business method that is novel to the organization (developing or adopting it) and which results, throughout its life cycle, in a reduction of environmental risk, pollution and other negative impacts of resource use (including energy use) compared to relevant alternatives	Buttol et al. (2012)
Innovation that improves sustainability performance, where such performance includes ecological, economic, and social criteria	Boons, Montalvo, Quist, and Wagner (2013)
The commercial introduction of a new (or improved) product (service), product-service system, or pure service which – based on a traceable (qualitative or quantitative) comparative analysis – leads to environmental and/or social benefits over the prior version's physical life-cycle ("from cradle to grave")	Hansen and Grosse-Dunker (2013)

(Continued)

Definition	Reference
New products and processes that serve both an organization's self-interest, as well as social and environmental needs	Christensen, Raynor, and McDonald (2015)
Innovation that has to consider environmental and social issues as well as the needs of future generations	Ketata, Sofka, and Grimpe (2015)
Innovation towards more sustainable processes in which resource use and waste production remain within proper environmental limits	Kılkış (2016)
A mean through which organizations can actually foster sustainable development	Kennedy, Whiteman, and Van den Ende (2017)
Innovation which involves the precepts of the triple bottom line and requires: flexibility between ecological and economical concerns, a balance between economic and social factors, and tolerance between ecological and social issues	Pedro Filho, Lima, Neto, Muller, and Costa (2017)
Firm's implementation of a new product, process, or practice, or modification of an existing product, process, or practice that significantly reduces the impact of the firm's activities on the natural environment	Varadarajan (2017)
Innovations (new or improved processes, products, services, organizational and marketing methods) that significantly reduce negative or improve positive economic, environmental and/or social impacts	Xavier, Naveiro, Aoussat, and Reyes (2017)
Innovation that improves sustainability performance on the ecological, economic, and social domains	Reficco, Gutiérrez, Jaén, and Auletta (2018)
Innovations (new or improved processes, products, services, organizational and marketing methods) that significantly reduce negative or improve positive economic, environmental and/or social impacts	Aka (2019)

loyalty, and so on (Varadarajan, 2017). As far as social orientation is concerned, it deals with social value creation. It emphasizes the social impact of an SI. Social benefits include employment and access to products and services, earning money, providing solutions to problems of others (e.g., of societal groups lacking the resources or capabilities), or alleviating urgent social problems (Boons & Lüdeke-Freund, 2013). Finally, the financial dimension of SI is largely investigated, meaning the improvement of a company's financial performance (e.g., return on sales and return on investment) and economic impact, or the reduction of the negative one (Boons & Lüdeke-Freund, 2013).

Studies exist (e.g., Perl-Vorbach, Rauter, & Baumgartner, 2014) stressing that taking all dimensions of sustainability into account simultaneously would be the best option but is not an essential requirement. However, as

Table 7.2 The two-level taxonomy of sustainable innovation

	Type of SI			Orientation of SI			
Main references	Technological	Organizational	Social	Environmental	Marketing	Financial	Social
Fussler and James (1996)	X			X	X	X	
Johansonn and Magnusson (1998)	X			X	X	X	
Klemmer et al. (1999) and Rennings (2000)	X	X	X	X			
Markusson (2001)	X	X	X	X			
Andersen (2002)	X			X		X	
Rennings and Zwick (2003)	X	X		X			X
Little (2005)	X	X	X	X	X		X
Europa INNOVA (2006)	X	X	X	X	X		X
European Commission (2007)	X	X	X	X			X
Charter and Clark (2007)	X	X		X	X	X	X
European Commission (2008)	X	X		X	X	X	X
Kemp and Pearson (2008)	X	X		X			
Steiner (2008)	X	X	X	X	X	X	X
OECD (2009)	X	X	X	X	X	X	X
Oltra and Saint Jean (2009)	X	X		X			
Carrillo-Hermosilla et al. (2010) and Arnold and Hockerts (2011)	X	X	X	X			
Buttol et al. (2012)	X	X	X	X	X		
Boons et al. (2013)	X	X	X	X	X	X	X
Hansen and Grosse-Dunker (2013)	X	X		X			X
Christensen et al. (2015)	X			X		X	X
Ketata et al. (2015)	X	X	X	X	X		X
Kilkiş (2016)	X			X			
Kennedy et al. (2017)	X	X	X	X	X	X	X
Pedro Filho et al. (2017)	X	X	X	X	X		
Varadarajan (2017)	X	X		X		X	X
Xavier et al. (2017)	X	X		X	X	X	X
Reficco et al. (2018)	X	X	X	X		X	X
Aka (2019)	X	X	X	X	X	X	X

Perl-Vorbach et al. (2014) stress, *"we are aware that sustainability is a continually evolving concept, with no final or absolute boundaries"* (p. 5).

In addition to SI definitions and classifications, the extant literature also shows studies investigating the main drivers and motivation to adopt SI. The literature shows several studies reporting that the drivers of SI are interactive rather than mutually exclusive, and both internal and external (Porter & Kramer, 2006). Examples of internal drivers are compliance (and specifically the need to comply with regulatory and norms to maintain the license to operate) (Carroll & Shabana, 2010), opportunity and competitive advantage (Carroll & Shabana, 2010), voluntariness and top management commitment (del Brio, Fernández, Junquera, & Vázquez, 2001), and recruiting (indeed, many studies stressed that companies tend to develop SI to attract the attention of young and talented employees) (Bonini, Gorner, & Jones, 2010). Among external drivers, stakeholder pressure (that is the pressure generated by external stakeholders) (Paraschiv, Nemoianu, Langă, & Szabó, 2012) and other external pressure linked to the market in which a company operates and to the lack of available resources to generate a competitive advantage in the sustainability ambit (Paraschiv et al., 2012), can be cited. CSR initiatives can serve as both internal drivers (because they encourage employees to engage in sustainable business practices), and external drivers (because they raise competitive advantage and threats both within and across industries) (Ginsberg & Bloom, 2004; Porter & Kramer, 2006).

Besides, drivers of SI may be the same as traditional innovation. The traditional innovation literature, for example, mainly recognizes two drivers: technology push and market pull (Hamel & Prahalad, 1994). The driver of technology-oriented companies is to push the new technology to market and create a winning strategy, thus being the first to deploy that technology. Conversely, the main driver of market-orientated companies is to understand customer needs, and thus to develop innovative solutions by discovering hidden customer needs and new markets. In terms of SIs, technology is recognized as an important driver, allowing reducing the environmental impact of production processes, their energy consumption, or polluting emissions, but also producing more sustainable products by adopting organizational routines or specific knowledge developed within the company (e.g., Horbach, 2008). Technological advances, in particular, by developing efficient technologies to reduce resource depletion and pollution and new technologies raising rivalry and competition within and across industries, help companies in developing SI (e.g., Henderson, 2006). Similarly, a market pull SI innovation starts from the recognition of more or less explicit needs in the environment among customers or other traditional players in the market, thus leading a company to develop new solutions. Authors such as Ginsberg and Bloom (2004) or Goldstein (2000) emphasized the role of consumer demand in purchasing environmentally sound goods and services and leading changes in business practice. Nowadays, customers and consumers are more and more important to help companies developing their SIs because they are more and more concerned with the environmental and social sustainability of the products they buy (Kammerer, 2009).

Also, government intervention enforces compliance with regulations and provides incentives to improve environmental impact, thus acting as a driver to SI (Simpson, Taylor, & Barker, 2004). Dealing with SIs, other drivers have been highlighted in the literature, namely new meanings (Verganti, 2009), regulation (Rennings, 2000), and values (Walker, 2014). The former refers to the opportunity to propose and attach new meanings to products, with the final aim to address latent needs. Regulation drives companies to comply with existing regulations, change regulations, or anticipate future regulations (e.g., Khanna, Deltas, & Harrington, 2009). It opens up the numbers and types of stakeholders involved (Carroll & Buchholtz, 2014), from governmental bodies and local communities to demanding customers or suppliers, or NGOs and other non-governmental bodies. Finally, an additional driver for SI is also the conscience or values of the company (Walker, 2014).

Also, Varadarajan (2017) in his study proposed several drivers of SI. Building on institutional theory, he stressed that institutional pressures (coercive pressures, mimetic pressures, and normative pressures) may predispose firms towards an SI orientation. According to his research, also firm related factors (such as size, globalization, reputation, and slack) as well as industry-related factors (such as relative environmental impact of the industry, sustainability initiatives of firms in upstream supplier industries and downstream customer industries, and size of end-users' customer base) are drivers towards SI.

7.2.2 Open innovation

Since Chesbrough published his book on OI in 2003, there has been a proliferation of studies regarding this issue. For decades, companies have adopted a closed innovation model, but to survive in today's context, with increasing global competition and rising innovation costs, they need also external resources. In other words, companies have moved from the traditional (closed) model to a new (open) model of innovation, where the mindset can be reformulated as *"If we make the best use of both internal and external ideas, we will win"*. Paraphrasing Chesbrough (2003), OI is *"the use of purposive inflows and outflows of knowledge to accelerate internal innovation, and to expand the markets for external use of innovation, respectively"*. According to this paradigm, companies can and should use both external and internal ideas.

As stressed by Bigliardi and Galati (2018), a first stream of literature focuses on the actors of collaboration in an OI context. These may range from consumers and customers (Bigliardi & Galati, 2018; van de Vrande, De Jong, Vanhaverbeke, & De Rochemont, 2009), suppliers (Chesbrough & Prencipe, 2008), scientific partners such as universities and research organizations (Brunswicker & Vanhaverbeke, 2015), and also government (De Zubielqui, Jones, & Statsenko, 2016) and competitors (van Hemert, Nijkamp, & Masurel, 2013).

118 *Barbara Bigliardi et al.*

Another important stream of literature investigated the drivers that lead companies to adopt OI. The drivers can be mainly classified into two groups: entrepreneurial and financial reasons, and innovation reasons. Thus, the following factors are the most highlighted: revenues generation or costs reduction, operational flexibility increase, international growth (Spithoven, Vanhaverbeke, & Roijakkers, 2013), as well as the attainment to strong innovation performance, the successful development and commercialization of new products, acquisition of R&D services required in the innovation process, or the intention to serve customers effectively (Hossain, 2015). Several studies however exist (e.g., van de Vrande et al., 2009) stressing that the main reason to adopt an OI approach refers to collaborations: that is, to acquire missing knowledge and complementary resources and to enlarge their social networks. Finally, a recent and less explored reason is the development of SIs: Bocken, Farracho et al. (2014) claimed that SI is increasingly important, and hence they may adopt the OI paradigm to support such innovation.

As SI, OI also presents some barriers that have recently been classified by Bigliardi and Galati (2016) into four main types: knowledge, organizational, collaboration, and financial-strategic factors. The former ones refer to the loss of know-how, the risk of imitation by competitors, or the extent to which relevant knowledge is not available. Organizational barriers are related to a lack of the managerial skills required to establish an effective collaboration with external partners as well as to resistance to change. Collaboration barriers refer to the collaboration mechanisms behind OI, specifically to the loss of know-how, difficulties in finding the right partners, the risk of opportunistic behavior, and cultural differences with partners. Finally, the main and probably the most obvious barrier to OI is represented by economic and financial issues as well as by a lack of strategic vision.

7.3 Open sustainable innovation: Evidence from the literature

Based on the existing literature analyzed above, we can stress that the development of SI, as a consequence of its multidimensional complexities, requires a wide knowledge of environmental, marketing, financial, and social aspects that exceed the scope of one single organization. Indeed, to develop SIs, as well as to face their complexities and challenges, requires organizations to acquire new skills and knowledge and new competencies. These considerations suggest interaction with various stakeholders when carrying out innovation processes. Consequently, OI may help companies in enabling such stakeholder engagement and may be key to successfully develop and implement SIs (Van Kleef & Roome, 2007).

Open sustainable innovation (hereafter, OSI) is an outside-in process that can simply be defined as the use of OI in the development of any SI or, paraphrasing (Arcese, Flammini, Lucchetti, & Martucci, 2015), *"an approach by which open innovation practices merge with the sustainability concept"* (p. 8080).

While classical innovation and marketing processes are characterized by a uni-directional relationship, OI has reconceptualized these processes into a bi-directional relationship: indeed, according to an open approach to innovation, companies open up their boundaries and R&D departments, in particular, to allow insights to flow out, as well as to let new stimuli of information and knowledge flow in (Chesbrough, 2006). OSI generally integrates the interest groups into the innovation process; in other words, it aims to develop technological (i.e., products, processes or services), or organizational innovations, with the firm acting as the central actor, but with the integration of outside innovators into the inside innovation process (Hansen, Bullinger, & Reichwald, 2011). For the sake of clarity, OSI has not to be confused with traditional stakeholder integration. Indeed, while in the latter a continuous account of stakeholder needs and requirements concerning the overall company is taken, in OSI the focus is more on the entire innovation process (Achterkamp & Vos, 2006). Moreover, in an OSI approach, the collaboration with external actors and stakeholders happens systematically, and not occasionally.

Actors involved in the company's OSI system are different. Past research has classified actors of collaboration into two main groups: primary stakeholders and secondary stakeholders (Hall & Vredenburg, 2003). Examples of the former are customers/consumers and employees, while examples of the latter are NGOs/activists, communities, governments, that is stakeholders that are not directly involved in a market relationship with the innovating firm.

Among primary stakeholders, key actors for OSI are consumers and customers: the creation of OSI should come largely from the integration of their input and ideas into the process of innovation. Suppliers are also considered in the literature as key actors of collaboration because SI very often requires making changes in the raw materials or components and depends on the receipt of specific information from suppliers (De Marchi, 2012). This collaboration usually aims to both codevelop and verify their compliance, which makes the concept of OI a helpful instrument that can support this process. Among the secondary ones, firm-NGO collaborations represent informal collaborative arrangements between firms and NGOs concerning a broad range of environmental issues (Rivera-Santos & Rufin, 2010), and have the objectives of environmental and economic value creation (Waddock, 1988). Government (i.e., central and local governments, or government agencies) is considered another key actor with which companies can establish environmental collaborations, aimed at the definition of new environmental standards and new rules (Delmas & Terlaak, 2001).

Alternatively, scholars classified stakeholders as direct and indirect. According to Rowley (2017), direct stakeholders are *"actors related to an organization by direct exchange flows of resources"*, while indirect stakeholders are not related by such flows. Similarly, Freeman (2010a) described direct stakeholders as actors interacting directly with a system, and indirect stakeholders as actors affected by the use of the system. The involvement of customers or suppliers is an example of direct collaboration (Vachon & Klassen, 2008).

120   *Barbara Bigliardi et al.*

Among collaborations, the academic literature also lists inter-firm collaborations, which are collaborations between two or more firms (Dussauge, Garrette, & Mitchell, 2000). These collaborations may involve both companies upstream and downstream in the supply chain and also companies of the same supply chain stage (Seuring, 2004), or even with companies belonging to different supply chains (Heuer, 2011).

Finally, in the last decades, firms started collaborating with knowledge leaders (Siegel, Wessner, Binks, & Lockett, 2003), focusing on collaborative R&D, contract research, development and commercialization of technology through a firm owned partly by the academic inventor, and so on (Perkmann & Walsh, 2007). Even if only a few studies investigated collaborations between companies and universities and research institutions that are sources of environmental and technological expertise, such collaborations may play an important role when firms develop SI (Seuring, 2004).

Notwithstanding the benefits of collaborations for SI, OSI can also face relevant barriers (Boons & Berends, 2001). These barriers mainly refer to those related to OI (e.g., integration problems in general, the risk that actors do not share common perspectives and are unfamiliar with one another). Similarly, also the management of secondary stakeholders can be considered as a barrier. This complexity derives from the fact that secondary stakeholders may not be willing to engage or compromise, or because their positions are often difficult to identify beforehand (Hall & Vredenburg, 2005). All these barriers imply the need for and the importance of effective stakeholder management (Worley, Feyerherm, & Knudsen, 2010). Also, conflicts between new and existing way to operate and the consequent inertia to change and uncertainty about the "right" way to operate, can be cited (Chesbrough, 2010). Yoon, Shin, and Lee (2016) proposed the following difficulties that a company may face in a OSI context: the Not-Invented-Here (NIH) syndrome, the administrative burden for collaboration, additional time and cost for collaboration, lacking knowledge of administration and law, technological capabilities for collaboration, uncertainty about the capability and reliability of partners, conflicts with partners because of different operation policies and organizational cultures, communication difficulties because of geographical distance, different technological knowledge or a different language, conflict risks linked to IP for co-created innovation and different collaboration purposes.

7.4 Discussion of findings and implications for theory and practice

OI can be seen as a breakdown of values where knowledge is acquired through internal but also and in particular external partners (Chesbrough, 2006). Previous studies exist showing that SIs try to find benefits from such external knowledge sources (De Marchi, 2012). OI may also help companies focusing on environmental, marketing, social, and financial aspects of sustainability.

Sustainable innovation 121

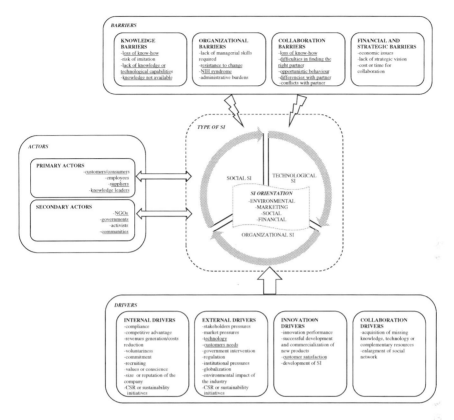

Figure 7.1 The OSI framework (author, 2020).

Figure 7.1 presents a model summarizing the main results of the chapter. It depicts the main issues investigated, and specifically the drivers and barriers that lead towards or hinder the adoption of OSI, and the main actors involved. The factors that emerged from both the SI and the OI literature are underlined.

Our analysis led to the identification of several challenges for the implementation of OI in developing SIs, while providing ideas for future research.

With a number of drivers (internal, external, innovation-related, or collaboration-related), companies are becoming more engaged in the development of SI. OI is recognized as an approach to helping companies in the process of SI development, to achieve environmental, economic, and social benefits. However, a number of barriers have been identified (knowledge, organizational, collaboration, and financial and strategic), representing significant challenges.

Finding the right partner is the most relevant challenges. In order to find the right partner, companies should rely more on professional actors such as innovation intermediaries, as the literature on matchmaking problems in networks suggests (e.g., Bigliardi & Galati, 2018). This has implications for academics, practitioners, and policymakers. As for the former, we suggest that future research could further explore the reasons why a company adopts OI or, conversely, chooses closed innovation when developing SIs. Managers could overcome this barrier using the expert advice of an innovation intermediary, or pursuing an adequate and transparent IPR strategy with partners aiming to avoid unclear or ambiguous situations that could compromise collaboration. Finally, policymakers could stimulate such collaborations through ad hoc financial incentives.

Thematic section three

The process perspective

8 The role of research centers in developing radical innovation for sustainability

Marianne Steinmo

8.1 Introduction

As the mitigation of environmental degradation gains prominence on the policy agenda, firms' innovation activities play a vital role in the transition to a more sustainable society (Cainelli, De Marchi, & Grandinetti, 2015). At the same time, firms must constantly create new products, services, and processes to acquire competitive advantage and survive in the long term (Kodama & Shibata, 2014). If firms are to contribute to sustainability, they need to improve their existing products and processes by making them more efficient (incremental innovation) (Schmidt & Calantone, 1998). However, radical innovation is the key to sustainability (Cainelli et al., 2015) and to firms' long-term competitive advantage (Kodama & Shibata, 2014) because this type of innovation involves the development of technologies that represent a fundamental change from firms' existing practices, knowledge, principles, and ideas (Dewar & Dutton, 1986).

Different types of innovation require various knowledge bases and types of expertise. Incremental innovation requires a deep and refined understanding of existing knowledge (Tsai, 2001), whereas radical innovation requires entirely new knowledge and skills that may introduce substantial changes to a firm's existing knowledge, capabilities, and routines (Benner & Tushman, 2002; Laursen & Salter, 2006). To access new knowledge, firms can engage in different types of innovation collaboration, defined as *"co-creation with (mainly) complementary partners through alliances, cooperation, and joint ventures during which give and take are crucial for success"* (Enkel, Gassmann, & Chesbrough, 2009, p. 313).

Although some firms succeed in capturing value from the strategies and capabilities associated with innovation collaboration, firms often fail to successfully implement innovation through collaboration (Knudsen & Mortensen, 2011; Laursen & Salter, 2006), and researchers have suggested that it is far from easy to identify and assimilate relevant external knowledge sources (Cohen & Levinthal, 1990). Moreover, firms find it difficult to implement comprehensive changes that will drive sustainability (Ionescu-Somers, 2012). Hence, more research is needed on the determinants of successful open innovation and on how firms can invest and build competencies and capabilities

126 *Marianne Steinmo*

that are focused on the exploration and exploitation of external knowledge (Lichtenthaler, 2009). This conceptual paper responds to these knowledge gaps by discussing the role of research centers for firms seeking to develop radical innovations focused on sustainability. Research centers are joint ventures among university, industry, and governmental funding organizations (Lind, Styhre, & Aaboen, 2013). They have become one of the predominant policy responses aimed at facilitating research solutions that require scientific and technical input from multiple disciplines and perspectives to address challenges that organizations are unwilling to address alone due to resource need and risk (Boardman, 2011). Research centers are therefore a unique setting in which firms might foster radical innovation for sustainability. Hence, this chapter addresses the following questions: (1) How can firms manage to develop radical innovation for sustainability? (2) What is the role of research centers in stimulating the development of radical innovation for sustainability?

To address these questions, this chapter first presents the literature on sustainable innovation, followed by a discussion of the role of incremental and radical innovation in sustainability. Then, the paper discusses the knowledge needed to develop different types of innovation (radical, in particular) and how firms can access that knowledge through different types of collaborations. The paper ends with a discussion of the role of the research center and how to enable firms to generate sustainable radical innovations in research centers. Radical innovation is the focus of this chapter, but discussions of incremental innovation are used for comparison.

8.2 Theoretical framework

8.2.1 Sustainability-oriented innovation

As environmental degradation demands increasing policy attention, firms' innovation activities play a vital role in the transition to a more sustainable society (Cainelli et al., 2015; Seebode, Jeanrenaud, & Bessant, 2012). Innovation (together with infrastructure) is strongly emphasized as one of the sustainable development goals adopted by the UN's General Assembly for the "2030 Development Agenda", in which 17 sustainability goals were announced as part of the vision for a sustainable future for humans and our shared planet (UN, 2015). Sustainability-oriented firms have shown that it is possible to be simultaneously socially responsible and profitable through sustainable innovation (Thu, Paillé, & Halilem, 2018).

Many studies still emphasize the intersection of the environmental and economic dimensions of the widely used "triple bottom line" framework (Rennings, 2000), often employing innovation in terms of "eco-innovation", "green" or "environmental" innovation (e.g. Horbach, Rammer, & Rennings, 2012; Schiederig, Tietze, & Herstatt, 2012). This chapter follows the definition of sustainability-oriented innovation provided by Arnold and Hockerts (2011), "*realized ideas that improve environmental and/or social performance compared with the current situation"* (p. 394), which implies products and processes that seek to improve environmental and/or social performance (Hansen & Grosse-Dunker, 2013). This term considers both the environmental and social dimensions of innovation and suggests that the performance improvement of both is necessary for the sustainable innovation performance of firms (Kennedy, Whiteman, & Van den Ende, 2017).

Sustainability-oriented innovation remains understudied (Hansen & Grosse-Dunker, 2013), and scholars often fail to differentiate between radical and incremental innovation (Dangelico, Pontrandolfo, & Pujari, 2013). Both types of innovation are important for sustainability and involve a continuum ranging from minor improvements of existing products and processes to a total change in their nature (Dodgson, Gann, & Salter, 2008). Hence, the role of different types of innovations for sustainability is discussed.

8.2.2 The role of incremental and radical innovation in sustainability

As shown in Table 8.1, incremental innovation involves cumulative improvements based on existing technological principles and continual changes in technologies and products (Schmidt & Calantone, 1998). Incremental innovation involves *"relatively minor changes in technology and provide relatively low incremental customer benefits per dollar"* (Chandy & Tellis, 1998, p. 476), and the knowledge and skills embodied in incremental innovation are mostly present within the firm (Robertson, Casali, & Jacobson, 2012). Firms benefit from incremental innovation because they produce more efficient products and processes that enhance and increase consumption experiences without disrupting customers' prior knowledge or requiring new learning (Menguc, Auh, & Yannopoulos, 2014).

Conversely, radical innovation involves the development of technologies that represent a fundamental change from firms' existing practices, knowledge, principles, and ideas (Dewar & Dutton, 1986). Ahuja and Morris Lampert (2001, p. 253) define radical innovation as *"those foundational inventions that serve as the basis for many subsequent technical developments"*, thereby defining radical innovation as a source for the subsequent development of incremental innovation (Schoenmakers & Duysters, 2010). Unlike incremental innovation, which mainly applies existing knowledge, radical innovation requires firms to come up with novel ideas that address customer problems through technologies that are distant from existing approaches (Zhou & Li, 2012). Well-known examples of radical innovation include the shift from pistol aircraft engines to turbojets and the change from steam to diesel electric locomotives (McDermott & O'Connor, 2002). Radical innovation is critical to long-term firm success and competitiveness because the potential rewards are much higher (McDermott & O'Connor, 2002). Furthermore, firms that create radical innovation are able to deliver breakthrough technologies that benefit customers and alter the ways new products and processes are experienced and used (Chandy & Tellis, 1998).

128 *Marianne Steinmo*

Table 8.1 Distinction between incremental and radical innovation

	Incremental innovation	Radical innovation
Definition	Cumulative improvements based on existing technological principles and continual changes in technologies and products (Schmidt & Calantone, 1998).	Development of technologies representing a fundamental change from firms' existing practices, knowledge, principles and ideas (Dewar & Dutton, 1986).
Knowledge and skills	Deep and refined understanding of existing knowledge (Tsai, 2001), mostly present within the firm (Robertson et al., 2012).	New and broad set of knowledge and skills that may introduce substantial changes in a firm's existing knowledge, capabilities and routines (Benner & Tushman, 2002; Laursen & Salter, 2006).
Risk	Less risky (Yamakawa, Yang, & Lin, 2011).	Highly risky (Yamakawa et al., 2011).
Time of diffusion	Short-term performance impact for firm (Yamakawa et al. 2011).	Long-term performance impact for firm (Yamakawa et al., 2011).
Type of collaboration	Deep collaboration with actors providing similar knowledge (Katila & Ahuja, 2002).	Collaborative breadth with a diverse set of resources providing new knowledge (King, Covin, & Hegarty, 2003).
Central collaborative partners	Suppliers (Sobrero & Roberts, 2002), customers (Von Hippel, 2007), and competitors (Gnyawali & Park, 2011).	Universities and public research organizations (Hall & Bagchi-Sen, 2007).
Potential for sustainability	Low potential for sustainability (Hellström, 2007) and failure to address the causes of unsustainable global problems (Whiteman, Walker, & Perego, 2013).	High potential for sustainability (Hellström, 2007).

Different levels of risks and diffusion time are associated with incremental and radical innovation. Because radical innovation requires new knowledge and represents a departure from existing practice, they tend to be more costly and associated with higher risks compared to incremental knowledge, which relies more on existing knowledge and existing markets (Germain, 1996; Yamakawa et al., 2011). Incremental innovation tends to take a shorter time to diffuse because it is more predictable, less risky, and more proximate to previous innovation compared to radical innovation, which takes more time to diffuse (Yamakawa et al., 2011).

In the context of sustainability, the changes that characterize incremental innovation mostly relate to add-on or end-of-pipe improvements to existing technologies and to reductions in resource inputs, materials, and waste, often referred to as "eco-efficiency" (Szekely & Strebel, 2013). Examples of incremental innovation for sustainability exist in a range of industries, such as building, manufacturing, electricity, and heat generation, and they are important for firms' competitiveness sustainability. However, while incremental innovation reduces waste and costs, they fail to address the causes of unsustainable global problems (Whiteman et al., 2013). Firms that only concern themselves with incremental innovation can suffer from a "carbon lock-in," where they repeatedly return to their fossil-fuel path dependency (Arthur, 1994; Unruh, 2000). This lock-in situation might lock out more radical innovation, which is essential for sustainability (Könnölä & Unruh, 2007) and for long-term firm success and competitiveness and has much higher potential rewards (McDermott & O'Connor, 2002).

Radical innovation for sustainability is key to achieving the UN goal of sustainability because such innovation often arises from changes in technological paradigms and is a driving force of technological, industrial, and societal change (Schoenmakers & Duysters, 2010). Hence, radical innovation for sustainability is needed to manage sustainability transitions, such as the shift from fossil fuels to solar energy (Fischer-Kowalski, 2011), the replacement of toxic substances, the creation of cradle-to-cradle loops, and the transformation of supply chains (Braungart, McDonough, & Bollinger, 2007; Young & Tilley, 2006). Because radical innovation is increasingly apparent in sustainability debates and is found to have higher potential for sustainability compared to incremental innovation (Hellström, 2007), this chapter further discusses the *knowledge* needed for radical innovation, which is recognized as one of the most important antecedents of innovation processes (Darroch & McNaughton, 2002).

8.2.3 Knowledge needed for the development of sustainability-oriented radical innovation

Although there are many arguments that innovation is necessary for a sustainable transition, it is less clear what skills, techniques, and approaches firms should use to develop radical sustainability-oriented changes (Seebode et al., 2012). The development of incremental innovation relies mainly on internal knowledge sharing, individually held know-how and the construction of deeper and more refined understandings of existing knowledge (Tsai, 2001) and is *"associated with recombination that consists of combining improved components that are already connected within a technological domain or from technologically proximate domains"* (Keijl, Gilsing, Knoben, & Duysters, 2016, p. 1026). In contrast, radical innovation requires an entirely new set of knowledge and skills that may introduce substantial changes in a firm's existing knowledge,

130 *Marianne Steinmo*

capabilities, and routines (Benner & Tushman, 2002; Laursen & Salter, 2006) (see Table 8.1). Firms' abilities to respond to market opportunities for radical innovation are enhanced by a broad knowledge base with varied accumulated observations and understandings of new information and knowledge (Chesbrough, Vanhaverbeke, & West, 2006). Diverse knowledge often stimulates various ideas that only touch the surface of emerging breakthroughs instead of digging down to their core, a situation that likely promotes incremental innovation (Laursen & Salter, 2006).

This chapter mainly explores radical innovation, which has strong potential to contribute to sustainability (Hellström, 2007). Therefore, the next issue to address is how firms can *obtain access* to a new set of broad and diverse knowledge bases and skill sets required for radical innovation for sustainability. Firms' access to the knowledge needed for radical innovation for sustainability relates to the UN's 17th sustainability goal, which indicates that collaboration plays an essential role in setting the world on a sustainable path (Schaltegger, Beckmann, & Hockerts, 2018; UN, 2015). Several sustainability researchers also consider the benefits of open innovation (Keskin, Diehl, & Molenaar, 2013) and collaboration (e.g. Lang et al., 2012; Wiek, Ness, Schweizer-Ries, Brand, & Farioli, 2012) to be critical to solving the complex challenges of sustainability.

8.2.4 The role of collaboration for radical innovation for sustainability

Considering the importance of going beyond the firm's organizational boundaries to gain access to the knowledge needed for innovation, collaboration with external actors is at the heart of the open innovation perspective (Chesbrough et al., 2006; Von Hippel, 2007). The idea that openness is beneficial for innovation is based on the premise that a single firm cannot innovate in isolation but must engage external actors (e.g., customers, suppliers, competitors, and R&D organizations) to obtain access to ideas and resources that enrich and expand its technological resource base (Dahlander & Gann, 2010). Scholars have identified collaboration as important to sustainable innovation because of its complexity and uncertainty (Adams, Jeanrenaud, Bessant, Denyer, & Overy, 2016; De Marchi, 2012) and have begun to consider the synergy between open innovation and sustainability (Slotegraaf, 2012).

Open innovation exists along a continuum that represents various levels of collaboration breadth and depth – in terms of knowledge and partnership – that might also influence the outcome of innovation (incremental vs. radical) (Kobarg, Stumpf-Wollersheim, & Welpe, 2019). Collaboration depth refers to the intensity and extent of the interaction between firms and their collaborative partners and determines opportunities for knowledge transfer and learning (Kobarg et al., 2019). Greater collaboration depth can facilitate trust between collaborative partners and ease both knowledge transfer and the acquisition of complex external knowledge (Lane, Koka, & Pathak, 2006).

The role of research centers   131

Incremental innovation is driven by improvements in existing knowledge, and the knowledge and skills embodied in these innovations are usually close to the firm's knowledge bases (Yamakawa et al., 2011). Therefore, repeated, deep collaboration can be used to develop incremental innovation because it gives firms access to familiar knowledge (Katila & Ahuja, 2002). Examples of collaborations where external partners possess similar knowledge include collaborations among suppliers, which often trigger improvements to existing products and processes (Sobrero & Roberts, 2002); collaborations with customers, who can be knowledge sources for new ideas about existing practices (Von Hippel, 2007); and collaborations with competitors, which give firms access to industry-specific knowledge (Gnyawali & Park, 2011).

Conversely, the breadth of collaboration for innovation can be defined as *"the number of external sources or search channels that firms rely upon in their innovative activities"*, and depth can be defined as *"the extent to which firms draw deeply from the different external sources"* (Laursen & Salter, 2006). Collaboration breadth can therefore be determined by the number and diversity of external partners, the variety of shared experiences (Kobarg et al., 2019), and the complexity of knowledge transactions (Sirmon, Hitt, Ireland, & Gilbert, 2011). Because radical innovation is primarily characterized by the newness of knowledge, is complex in nature and requires multiple connections to internal and external actors in the value chain (Dewar & Dutton, 1986), this type of innovation requires collaborative breadth (Kobarg et al., 2019). Moreover, greater collaborative breadth indicates diverse resources (King et al., 2003) that expand the resource base to share the risk associated with radical innovation (Green, Gavin, & Aiman-Smith, 1995).

Universities and R&D organizations are essential collaborative sources for firms seeking to develop radical innovation (Hall & Bagchi-Sen, 2007) because they provide firms with specialized and broad knowledge and give firms access to fundamental knowledge and the opportunity to conduct high-quality research (Laursen & Salter, 2006).

8.2.4.1 R&D collaboration for radical innovation for sustainability

Perkmann and Walsh (2009) identify four types of collaboration between firms and universities and R&D organizations (henceforth, R&D partners): knowledge generation, idea testing, technology development and problem solving. The goals of these collaborations can range from basic research projects steered by researchers to applied projects that solve firms' problems. These collaborations aim to develop new scientific and technical knowledge and involve different types of R&D partners (e.g., R&D organizations and universities) and firms of different sizes. The R&D partners are focused on the development of new knowledge, while firms explore and exploit the knowledge through innovative opportunities created through collaboration for economic benefits (McKelvey, Zaring, & Ljungberg, 2015). Research centers represent one essential type of collaboration between firms and R&D

132 Marianne Steinmo

partners that aims to cover the range of activities from knowledge generation to problem solving and thereby involves both firms' aim of developing innovation and R&D partners' aim of developing new knowledge. The next section discusses the role of research centers as instruments for radical innovation in sustainability.

8.2.4.2 The role of research centers for sustainable radical innovation

Research centers have become one of the predominant policy responses that facilitate research collaboration spanning the boundaries of government, R&D organizations, and industry. By joining firms with universities and R&D organizations, research centers aim to develop solutions that require scientific and technical input from multiple disciplines and perspectives to address challenges that organizations are unwilling to address alone due to resource requirements and risk (Boardman, 2011). A research center can be defined as a "joint venture between the university, industry and governmental funding organisations, identifying some domain of research where industry and academy can benefit from collaborating" (Lind et al., 2013, p. 910). Bringing together R&D partners and firms in research centers is an attempt to stimulate the production of academic research and radical innovation (Ponomariov & Boardman, 2010; Styhre & Lind, 2010) and to address social and economic problems (e.g., sustainability) that cannot easily be addressed by R&D actors, firms or the government (Stokols, Hall, Taylor, & Moser, 2008).

Research centers are a key solution to support sustainable development because they often focus on research and development that aims to be "transformative" and "paradigm-shifting"; their research is characterized as "bluesky" or as having a "high risk-high yield" (Boardman & Gray, 2010). With a broad and diverse set of collaborative partners, research centers provide firms with the specialized knowledge bases (Gulbrandsen, Thune, Borlaug, & Hanson, 2015) required for radical innovation (Kobarg et al., 2019). Moreover, R&D partners deliver scientific knowledge and highly skilled labor to the collaborative firms, which in turn provides R&D partners with funding, equipment and a range of research projects to pursue (Feller & Roessner, 1995). Research centers are also a valuable source of radical innovation collaboration due to their time horizon (usually five to eight years) (McKelvey, Alm, & Riccaboni, 2003), which supports the idea that radical innovation takes time to develop and that the partners (both R&D partners and firms) will most likely benefit from the results in the long run by identifying possible future economic applications of the innovations and deriving returns (O'Connor, Paulson, & DeMartino, 2008).

Research centers are university-based; they have clear, predefined tasks, obligations, and divisions of labor (Ménard, 2004) and represent higher structural levels of scientific and technical research compared to university-based research units in general, such as department laboratories (Friedman, 1982). Moreover, research centers can be relatively hierarchically structured. They may have a manager representing an R&D partner that establishes the overall goals, evaluates performance, and selects projects for the research activities within the centers, which are typically supported and controlled by an advisory board (Bozeman & Boardman, 2003).

In sum, research centers are a valuable source of radical innovation for sustainability. Their value stems from "structural reasons", such as their long-term orientation, focus on "blue-sky" innovation and access to a diverse and broad set of actors with the specialized knowledge bases required for radical innovation. Moreover, because firms find it difficult to implement a comprehensive change to drive sustainability (Ionescu-Somers, 2012) and to obtain support for long-term radical innovation that carries high risks (McDermott & O'Connor, 2002), research centers are a unique way for firms to share the risk with several actors and to obtain access to the resources needed to develop radical innovation.

8.2.5 Key enablers of firms seeking to develop radical sustainable innovation in research centers

Although research centers are a valuable tool for firms seeking support for radical innovation for sustainability, there are significant institutional and knowledge boundaries between firms and R&D partners that make such collaborations challenging (Galán-Muros & Plewa, 2016; Miller, McAdam, Moffett, Alexander, & Puthusserry, 2016; Steinmo, 2015). The next section discusses key enablers for firms to overcome potential challenges and thus manage long-term radical innovation development for sustainability in collaboration with R&D partners in research centers. Figure 8.1 illustrates the enablers of three central phases of a research center, (1) "steering enablers", (2) "knowledge transfer enablers", and (3) "forwarding enablers", which involve the establishment (before and when entering the collaboration), performance (during the collaboration) and end (last year(s) of collaboration) of research centers, respectively. It is worth noting that each of the discussed enablers is important throughout all the phases of a research center, but these enablers are of the utmost importance during the phase under which they are presented in the figure. Hence, in Figure 8.1, the most important enablers for each phase are marked in bold type.

8.2.5.1 Establishing phase – steering enablers

There are four aspects in particular that firms should consider when establishing a research center but that are also important in the performance phase: (1) coordination and internal firm management of involvement in the research center, (2) influencing research activities, (3) identifying crossover researchers, and (4) contractual provision. These enablers mostly pertain to important internal aspects of how the firm steers the research center at the very beginning to manage long-term radical innovation for sustainability.

134 *Marianne Steinmo*

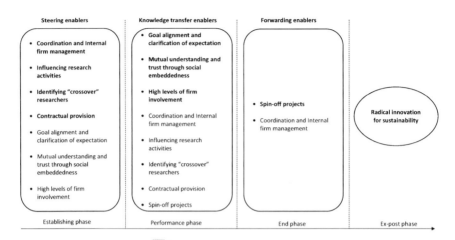

Figure 8.1 Firm enablers for managing radical innovation for sustainability in research centers (authors, 2020).

8.2.5.1.1 COORDINATION AND INTERNAL FIRM MANAGEMENT OF INVOLVEMENT

Schoenmakers and Duysters (2010) suggest the need for more coordination of internal firm management to acquire the knowledge necessary to develop radical innovation. This is an important requirement to consider when firms are invited by researchers to become partners in a research center. To this end, firms should ensure that the firm's strategy is in line with the firm's involvement in the research center and that the owners of the company have the patience to be involved in long-term radical innovation development. In this situation, an in-depth presentation of the aim and potential benefits of the research center to the firm's board of directors is essential. Such a presentation can ensure that board members dedicate the necessary resources to reap long-term benefits from the collaboration and that board members have the understanding and patience needed for radical innovation because a successful radical innovation will most likely benefit the firm in the long run. The board's resolution of the firm's involvement in the research center and its commitment to resource allocation will secure long-term involvement and prevent the firm from dropping out of the center prematurely.

Firms could also create a strategic plan for firm involvement and goals for their involvement in the research center. These plans and goals should articulate the firm's level of involvement as well as the personnel and resources required to achieve radical innovation development in the long run.

8.2.5.1.2 INFLUENCING RESEARCH ACTIVITIES

Because the research center's application often sets the agenda for the collaboration and acts as the foundation for continuing collaboration, firms should ensure that they obtain a complete overview of the thematic and working tasks of the research center, and they should influence and suggest user-oriented research activities that are in line with the interests of the firm. This influence on research activities is also important in the performance phase to increase the usefulness of the knowledge and research results developed. Therefore, firms should conduct thorough internal discussions to highlight themes relevant to the research center both in the application phase and during the collaboration to provide benefits to the firm.

However, because the outcome of radical innovation can rarely be anticipated and often requires a new set of knowledge and skills provided by universities and R&D organizations (Laursen & Salter, 2006), it is crucial that firms attend to their research partners' suggestions for long-term research activities to foster radical innovation and avoid excessive steering of the research activities, which may result in incremental innovation outcomes. Finding a balance between activities driven by researchers and by firms can be accomplished by including projects within the center with different time horizons (short and long term) and research orientations (basic and applied research). Some short-term applied research projects (one to two years) will likely contribute to more frequent research results for firms and greater motivation and patience to be involved in long-term research activities driven by researchers, thus preventing unsatisfied firms from dropping out of the center.

8.2.5.1.3 IDENTIFYING THE CROSSOVER RESEARCHERS

Because research centers often consist of a large range of diverse researchers (representing universities and R&D organizations), they usually include researchers with different academic orientations, such as those with an orientation toward a "fundamental understanding" or the "utility" of their research (Tijssen, 2018). Tijssen (2018) captures the use-inspired identity of researchers in three archetypes: (1) "science-oriented" researchers who perform scientific research with high levels of knowledge production, (2) "application-oriented" researchers who are highly concerned with technological development, and (3) "user-oriented" researchers who have high levels of interaction with users outside the research community who will use and/or benefit from the research results through commercialization and innovation. However, user-oriented researchers have been found to provide lower rates of academic output (Tijssen & Yegros, 2017). Tijssen and Yegros (2017) have identified a fourth type, "crossover" researchers, who tend to combine these three orientations. Crossover researchers often have prior employment experience in the business sector, are engaged with firms through joint research and commercialization activities, and show better research performance than their non-entrepreneurial peers (Abramo, D'Angelo, Ferretti, & Parmentola, 2012; Tijssen & Yegros, 2017). Several studies suggest that crossover researchers act as exchange agents between the worlds of science and the business sector (Mangematin, O'Reilly, & Cunningham, 2014).

136   *Marianne Steinmo*

Therefore, crossover researchers are of special importance for research centers that merge these two worlds to achieve long-term innovation goals by including numerous firm and R&D partners.

Arguably, firms involved in research centers should be attentive to the different research orientations of researchers to be more strategic about those with whom they establish research projects in the establishing phase (and in the performance phase) because researchers are likely to shape their research to achieve a particular outcome. Research projects shaped by application-oriented and user-oriented researchers will most likely yield development projects with incremental innovation outcomes because these types of researchers likely hold knowledge bases quite similar to those of firms. Hence, to promote long-term radical innovation performance as well as user-oriented research, firms mostly engage in projects with crossover researchers, which supports a threefold research orientation of scientific research, technological development and user orientation. Firms should therefore invest time in getting to know the researchers in the research center by asking questions about their research interests and orientations and their prior experience to identify and capitalize on relationships with crossover researchers.

8.2.5.1.4 CONTRACTUAL PROVISIONS

Academic research conducted in research centers has limitations regarding the disclosure and further development of research results, methods or materials (Lerner & Merges, 1998). Hence, the utilization of research results developed in a research center depends on contractual provisions – devised by the owners – that govern the access to and openness of the results and technologies. Because firms often strive to secure private financial results and universities and R&D organizations seek to commercialize research results, contractual agreements between the partners are important to control intellectual property (IP) (Czarnitzki, Grimpe, & Toole, 2014). A collaboration agreement that governs how the involved partners address research results and IP in a way that conforms to the regulations of the research center's funding is also important to build trust-based collaboration between firms and R&D organizations (Rappert, Webster, & Charles, 1999), which is a prerequisite of knowledge sharing (Steinmo & Rasmussen, 2016).

Hence, firms should consider and decide what research activities they can conduct in open innovation projects where the research results can be made publicly available for all partners as well as the activities and results that must be confidential and/or controlled through IP. Firms' ability to distinguish between knowledge and research results that should be open or secret requires internal discussion within the firms and thorough negotiations with the research partners early in the collaboration. These decisions should not be left to external actors (such as lawyers). Firms need control over specific research activities, and results can be achieved by negotiating contractual agreements that feature at least one research partner early in the collaboration that works with firm-specific research activities. These activities could also be addressed through parallel projects conducted outside the research center that translate the publicly available knowledge developed in the center to more specific and applied results that are useful for individual firms.

However, firms' demand for control is likely to hamper long-term radical innovation processes that require broad knowledge bases from different sources and openness from different firms during the knowledge-creation process. Firms should therefore be as open as possible in sharing the knowledge that contributes to a collective knowledge development process, which is required to achieve the goal of radical innovation for sustainability. This can be done by engaging in formal and informal meeting arenas in the research center where firm-specific knowledge and experience decided by the firm is shared. As such, the firm representatives who engage in the research center should be given a mandate from the firm to not only consider their operations and short-term benefits but also use their knowledge to identify and explore research possibilities with their partners, which is the likely starting point to develop radical innovation for sustainability. To secure an open knowledge-sharing process, contractual agreements that regulate access to and ownership of potential future innovation outcomes should be negotiated and established early in the collaboration to secure the firm's benefits of the knowledge it has contributed in the beginning of and during the innovation process. Such agreements will likely contribute to a more open knowledge-sharing process because the firms ensure long-term benefits of their contributions of "intellectual" assets. Such contractual agreements are typically negotiated at the end of R&D collaborations when solutions and research results are developed, but it is strongly recommended that they should be considered in the early phases of collaborations because it is easier to negotiate the IP of potential outcomes prior to its existence.

Because the knowledge and results developed in research centers cannot always be anticipated, continuous awareness of open vs. firm-specific knowledge and results is also important in the performance phase of a research center, when substantial research activities are established.

8.2.5.2 Performance phase – knowledge-transfer enablers

Firms should focus on three aspects during the performance phase of a research center: (1) goal alignment and clarification of expectations, (2) mutual understanding and trust through social embeddedness, and (3) high levels of firm involvement. These enablers mostly focus on how firms manage efficient knowledge transfer processes with R&D partners, which is a prerequisite for the enhancement of radical innovation for sustainability.

8.2.5.2.1 GOAL ALIGNMENT AND CLARIFICATION OF EXPECTATIONS

Differences in organizational structure, management, goals, and problem solving sometimes hinder collaborations between academic and commercial entities (Ambos, Mäkelä, Birkinshaw, & D'Este, 2008; Bjerregaard, 2010) and can lead to goal conflicts (Bozeman & Boardman, 2003). Whereas the aim of universities and R&D organizations is to educate and perform fundamental academic research, firms seek to develop commercially valuable products and services (Ambos et al., 2008). Furthermore, universities and R&D organizations often have a long-term orientation, whereas firms are more oriented toward short-term, applied research that can lead to solutions to current problems (Spithoven, Clarysse, & Knockaert, 2011). These differences might hamper the performance of radical innovation in research centers. Hence, to avoid goal conflicts, it is important that the partners conduct in-depth conversations to understand each other's interests and how they can contribute to radical innovation performance. These conversations can ease the process of formulating shared goals for the collaboration that are beneficial to both partners' involvement in radical innovation.

Because radical innovation requires time to develop, it is important to facilitate effective dialogue early in the collaboration process so that the partners can clarify their expectations, ask questions and develop an understanding of the different goals and requirements of their work in the research centers. Firms should also address unrealistic expectations and be patient because it takes time to manage a successful and vigorous collaboration with research partners to develop radical innovation.

8.2.5.2.2 MUTUAL UNDERSTANDING AND TRUST THROUGH SOCIAL EMBEDDEDNESS

As evidenced by the many unsuccessful attempts at knowledge transfer between firms and R&D organizations, it can be challenging to develop trust and establish a common understanding in communications and interactions between firms and academics (Santoro & Bierly, 2006; Steinmo & Rasmussen, 2016). Trust and common understanding are typically developed when firms are socially embedded (Boschma, 2005) in the research center and engaged with researchers in both formal (e.g., meetings and workshops) and informal arenas (ad hoc contact). Because similar partners are better able to transfer knowledge, social embeddedness is of the utmost importance to the development of a radical innovation that requires that *different* and often unknown partners collaborate. Hence, firms should understand how to manage and organize their social relationships with researchers and dedicate considerable time to engaging with unknown researchers when they begin collaborating and over time (Steinmo & Rasmussen, 2018).

8.2.5.2.3 HIGH LEVELS OF FIRM INVOLVEMENT

Firm involvement is an important premise for successful university-industry collaboration. Due to the challenge of collaborating with a diverse set of actors, as is required for radical innovation, high levels of interaction and firm involvement are needed in research centers (Gulbrandsen et al., 2015).

The role of research centers   139

When research centers are established and when firms have signed collaborative contracts and received grants from the support schemes, some firms might expect to have already achieved the "golden ticket" to innovation without making any appreciable contribution. Nevertheless, collaboration between firms and R&D organizations is a two-way engagement and requires contributions from both partners. When entering a research center, firms should therefore dedicate the resources needed to involve several employees (from the strategic to the more operative levels) to ensure successful collaboration with the research center. As such, firm leaders should explicitly focus on motivating and dedicating several employees to engage in frequent interaction with the research center. In particular, leaders should dedicate a boundary spanner who acts as the main firm representative in the research center. This person functions as the link between a unit and its environment and works in the interfaces with R&D partners, thus contributing to transferring new knowledge. The boundary spanner could be used to transfer the knowledge accessed in the research center to the firm level, which would likely strengthen firms' R&D robustness and reduce the potential vulnerability of relying solely on individuals who have acquired knowledge through the research center. The boundary spanner of the firm can discuss with firm employees the research results achieved by the research center and suggest research activities to the center based on the firm's needs. Moreover, firms should dedicate a boundary spanner with the skills to interact and create external relationships and with prior experience in collaborating with researchers, which has been shown to be an enabler of successful R&D collaboration (Steinmo & Rasmussen, 2016).

8.2.5.3 End phase – forwarding enablers

Because radical innovation for sustainability takes a long time to develop, firms should ensure that the knowledge and research results developed in the research center are developed further in new spin-off projects during the last year(s) of a research center's existence (ex-post phase).

8.2.5.3.1 SPIN-OFF PROJECTS

Because radical innovation for sustainability takes time to develop, the innovation processes that unfold in a research center most likely need to continue after the work of the research center ends if their full implementation potential is to be realized. Hence, in the last few year(s) of the research center's existence, firms should make sure that they continue the innovation processes by applying for subsequent projects that integrate the knowledge and learning derived from specific research center activities into new R&D funded projects. Previous research shows the value of prior contacts (Slavtchev, 2013) with common understanding (Steinmo & Rasmussen, 2016) for successful collaboration between firms and universities or R&D organizations.

140   *Marianne Steinmo*

Therefore, firms should capitalize on the relationships developed within the research center to kick-start new overlapping innovation projects for radical sustainable innovation.

8.3 Concluding remarks

To address the issues of how firms can develop radical innovation for sustainability and the role of research centers in that process, this conceptual chapter contributes by increasing our understanding of how radical innovation can be developed by accessing new knowledge from a diverse set of actors through collaboration with R&D partners in research centers. Furthermore, this chapter contributes to increased knowledge of how firm enablers can manage this process during the three phases of a research center.

First, in the establishing phase, firms should *coordinate a long-term radical innovation approach* to sustainability within the firm and *influence research activities* in line with the firm's needs while attending to R&D partners' thematic and long-term orientation. Finding this balance can be accomplished by including some short-term applied research activities based on the firm's needs and some long-term activities driven by researchers that support radical innovation performance. Some applied activities will likely produce more frequent research results for the firm and the motivation and patience to become involved in long-term research activities, which may prevent firms from dropping out from the center. Firms should also be strategic regarding the type of researcher with whom they establish research projects because researchers hold different research orientations that are likely to influence the research activities and potential results. As such, through close dialogue and interaction, firms should aim to identify and *establish research projects and activities together with "crossover" researchers* that support a threefold research orientation of scientific research, technological development and user orientation, which are all important to foster long-term radical innovation performance and provide firms with user-oriented research results. Finally, from the very beginning, firms should formulate contractual provisions of potential research results and innovation outcomes. As such, firms should consider what research activities they could conduct in open innovation projects where the research results could be made publicly available for all partners and the activities and results they need to keep secret and/or maintain control over through IP. However, to support long-term radical innovation processes, firms should be as open as possible in sharing the knowledge that contributes to the collective knowledge development process. This can be done by giving the firm representative a mandate from the firm to use his or her knowledge to identify and explore research possibilities with partners, which is likely to be the starting point to develop radical innovation for sustainability. To ensure an open knowledge-sharing process, contractual agreements that regulate access to and ownership of potential future innovation outcomes should be negotiated and established early in the collaboration.

In the performance phase, firms should be particularly attentive to knowledge-transfer enablers by *aligning goals and clarifying expectations* with R&D partners in a way that attends to both partners' interests. Firms should also accept R&D partners' long-term goals and orientations, which are essential for radical innovation. Moreover, *developing mutual understanding and trust through social embeddedness* and a high level of firm involvement are essential to managing knowledge transfer in the performance phase of a research center because radical innovation development requires collaboration with diverse partners who are often unknown. In the end phase, firms should ensure that they continue their innovation processes by *applying for subsequent projects* that integrate knowledge and learning from specific research activities from the center into additional R&D projects.

9 Making innovation sustainable

Lessons from an internal innovation idea challenge

Joon Mo Ahn and Jong Rak Kim

9.1 Introduction

Recent years have witnessed unprecedented quantum leap of technological development. Not only the advancement of each technology but also the rapid convergence of multiple technologies has destroyed the boundary of business domains (e.g., Uber moment[1]), which has made firms face fierce competition across industry sectors. Consequently, first movers as well as followers/imitators keep searching new ideas and are looking for more effective ways of innovation initiation and implementation. To cope with such tide, various strategies have been developed and suggested, and open innovation can be one of such strategic approaches, in that it helps firms to develop dynamic capability and establish sustainable innovation implementation.

Open innovation is innovating innovation (Chesbrough, 2003), so it breaks static equilibrium and brings in new changes. Open innovation pushes firms to deviate from their current routines and find better ways for doing innovation, which helps firms to find a new solution and enhance their dynamic capability (Ahn, 2020; Bogers, Chesbrough, & Strand, 2019). By its definition, open innovation stimulates firms to search and utilise new resources, and this increased openness can be an effective approach for the adaptation to the turbulent environment (Ahn, Mortara, & Minshall, 2018). As noted by Di Minin, Frattini, and Piccaluga (2010), open innovation adoption can transform a whole landscape of internal innovation in a firm, which increases the survival rate of the firm not only for the short term but also for the long term. Leveraging new resources would be clever improvising for a changing environment, and fundamental changes triggered by openness, such as business model restructuring and idea source diversification, can result in long term effective and sustainable changes for firms.

Further, open innovation can make innovation sustainable. As open innovation is a process of organisational routine change, it requires firms to track knowledge flow, establish an open innovation-friendly culture and make organisations flexible (Kim & Ahn, 2020). Firms establish knowledge management platforms to systematically screen and control knowledge, and active participation of internal members makes innovation implementation smooth, voluntary and sustainable. Open innovation expands the boundary of the innovation process from its R&D division to whole divisions in a firm, making innovation company-wide. This expansion enables firms to establish an internal system which is more structural and more sustainable than closed innovation.

Based upon this understanding, this chapter aims to explore how open innovation can be used for the establishment of sustainable innovation implementation. Innovation culture is not established by one-sided efforts, so bilateral efforts from both top management and employees are necessary. Using case study methodology, the current study illustrates the case firm's innovation journey. The case firm has attempted to change and cultivate a new innovative organisational culture by encouraging an internal idea competition platform, and this organisational experiment was led by stand-alone Change Agents in the firm. This chapter suggests practical implications by exploring what the firm has learned so far and what has to be amended in the future. The later part of this chapter is structured as follows. The next section explores the related literature to understand the theoretical background of the case firm's organisational experiment and the following section illustrates research methodology. The detailed case is explored in Section 9.4, and the chapter concludes with a discussion and implications.

9.2 Theoretical background

9.2.1 Sustainable innovation using open innovation

As the competition accelerates, the pressure for change is drastically increasing in firms. Open innovation is defined as 'a distributed innovation process based on purposively managed knowledge flows across organisational boundaries, using pecuniary and non-pecuniary mechanisms in line with the organisation's business model' (Chesbrough & Bogers, 2014, p. 17), and many firms have adopted open innovation to cope with such pressure for change. By its definition, open innovation attempts to leverage a variety of resources to drive innovation, which enables firms to continue to innovate in the long run (Ahn et al., 2018; Di Minin et al., 2010).

Open innovation was initially studied at the firm level as an alternative route for internal R&D, but its concept has evolved and its applications have disseminated to many different domains. Consequently, scholars have investigated open innovation from different perspectives, for example, its adoption in low as well as high technology industry and public as well as private organisations. This wide acceptance of open innovation was possible because open innovation can be easily integrated with other concepts. Open social innovation, which focuses on open innovation for public benefits (its adoption in public organisations), is such an example (Ahn, Roijakkers, Fini, & Mortara, 2019), and sustainable open innovation is another example. Sustainable open innovation is defined as 'a distributed innovation process which is based on purposively managed knowledge flows across organisational boundaries, using pecuniary and non-pecuniary mechanisms in line with the organisation's business

144 *Joon Mo Ahn and Jong Rak Kim*

model, thereby contributing to development that meets the needs of the present without compromising the ability of future generations to meet their own needs (Bogers, Chesbrough, Heaton, & Teece, 2019, p. 4). In their research, Bogers, Chesbrough, Heaton et al. (2019) investigated why Danish beer company Carlsberg opened their green fibre bottle technology to other firms and how such technology revealing established a sustainable innovation ecosystem for Carlsberg. Although Bogers, Chesbrough, Heaton et al. (2019) focused on environmental issues by investigating how the adoption of open innovation contributed to the use of less energy and eco-friendly material, this chapter focuses on another aspect of sustainability – 'able to continue innovation over a period of time in a stable way', and, for this, we explore the case of an innovation platform and the factors affecting the implementation of such platform.

By its definition, open innovation stresses knowledge flow across permeable boundary, so external knowledge has been relatively more emphasised. However, to exploit external knowledge, internal ability to learn – absorptive capacity – plays a vital role in successful knowledge acquisition (Spithoven, Clarysse, & Knockaert, 2011). It is also noteworthy that, even in the era of open innovation, internal employees are an essential source of innovation, and there are plenty of examples supporting this. For instance, *Google* has attempted to stimulate the creativity of employees by providing financial and non-financial incentives (Steiber & Alange, 2013). Therefore, for the successful and stable implementation of open innovation, encouraging individuals can be a good start to establishing an innovation friendly organisational culture, but not every such effort results in tangible success. Admittedly, many firms are not appropriately exploiting the immense potential of their employees, and this indicates that systematic knowledge management is necessary for them to harness employees' creativity.

Open innovation is innovating innovation (Chesbrough, 2003), so it not only uses a variety of knowledge resources but it also expands the boundary of innovation from internal R&D division to a whole company. This indicates that open innovation encourages the participation of all employees, which has the effect of spreading an innovation-friendly culture throughout organisations. Various factors can affect successful internal change for innovation. Full support from top management would be an important motivation, and systematic knowledge management is a vital medium for innovation (Ahn et al., 2016; Ahn, Minshall, & Mortara, 2017). Further, the role of internal facilitators, who are in charge of micro-tuning and encouraging participation is vital. In this respect, multiple elements, such as strong leadership, a systematic platform, and Change Agents, must be harmonised to accommodate a new organisational experiment and to make this new attempt sustainable.

9.2.2 Strong leadership for change

One of the important hurdles for organisational routine change is the ability of organisational members to embrace new changes, and this is promoted by

Making innovation sustainable 145

strong leadership (Ahn et al., 2017). The literature (e.g., Elenkov & Manev, 2016; Howell & Boies, 2004) emphasises the importance of leadership in change management, in that they can encourage their employees by providing necessary resources for voluntary engagement (Siebenhuner & Arnold, 2007). In many cases, employees do not resist the change itself but fight against uncertainty or a possible decrease of their pays, position and familiarity caused by a change (Jansen, 2002; Kitchell, 1997), and substantial prior research (e.g., Landau, 1999) has corroborated the fact that strong and enthusiastic leaders can lessen these concerns by offering empowerment or various incentives for changes (Ahn et al., 2017, Bogers, Foss, & Lyngsie, 2018). March and Shapira (1987) observed that Chief Executive Officers (CEOs) can trigger drastic strategic changes, and it was also found that entrepreneurial CEOs adopt innovative strategies boldly despite resistance and challenges (Howell & Higgins, 1990; Khandwalla, 1976/1977; Miller, 1983; Miller & Friesen, 1982). As noted by Di Minin et al. (2010), the high uncertainty of an open approach may demand that individuals would be more entrepreneurially oriented, and this entrepreneurial posture can significantly affect innovation method and tool selection at the firm (Cassia, Minola, & Paleari, 2011).

9.2.3 Systematic knowledge management: Idea Suggestion Platform

Open innovation is a new concept, but it is also rooted in classical innovation principles, such as idea generation and choice. Idea generation is an important means of competitive advantage (Gordon, Schoenbachler, Kaminski, & Brouchous, 1997), and one of the most effective sources of ideas is internal teams and employees. If strong support from top management is priming water for innovation initiation, systematic knowledge management, such as an idea competition platform, would be a vehicle for embracing the necessary innovation activities. This chapter pays attention to the Idea Suggestion Platform which not only generates creative and innovative ideas but also arouses the interests from participants (Ebner, Leimeister, & Krcmar, 2009). The first role of an Idea Suggestion Platform would be gathering new fresh ideas, but, in addition to this, idea platforms can play a vital role in spreading innovation within organisations. There may be various elements influencing idea platforms, but the following three factors are vital for a successful and sustainable idea platform. Firstly, an active and voluntary participation is important. Attracting as many participants as possible would be the key to success, and, according to Leimeister, Huber, Bretschneider, and Krcmar (2014), there is a core practice for this, such as an Information Technology (IT) based idea competition toolkit. Active user engagement can be encouraged by easy access to the Idea Suggestion Platform, and an IT suggestion box enables users to easily access without the time and location constraints while decreasing the cost for information management (Leimeister et al., 2014). Secondly, it is also important to stimulate the motivation of participants, and a suggestion platform can encourage both intrinsic and extrinsic motivations of participants.

Self-achievement in that 'my idea' is selected for implementation would be an intrinsic motivation, and recognition from colleagues or financial incentives can be an important extrinsic motivation (Leimeister et al., 2014). Lastly, reasonable and transparent evaluation of the suggested ideas is important (Ebner et al., 2009). The perception that a participant's idea is fairly assessed and reflected in the improvement process would be vital, in that this can be a positive signal that it is worth applying for idea suggestion. Considering these three aspects, many leading firms have used an IT-based idea competition toolkit to strategically manage bottom-up suggestions. For example, SAP introduced a multiple stage model. Ideas are generated and submitted in 'Pre-phase' and suggested ideas are further modified in 'Phase1'. In 'Phase 2', refined ideas are evaluated by the virtual community, and expert evaluations are conducted in 'Phase 3'. The ideas that survived in this evaluation process are finally selected in the last Phase (Ebner et al., 2009). As in the case of SAP, such efforts aim at attracting many participants and offering psychological incentives whilst eliminating challenges involved.

9.2.4 Change Agents as facilitators

Strong leadership can be a vital initiator of innovation, but it is not a necessary and sufficient condition of sustainable innovation. The bottom-up approach is a voluntary approach and may find a lower level of resistance, but it may not be sustainable in that a bottom-up approach is typically uncoordinated. Therefore, to disseminate full support from top management and encourage voluntary participation, a mediator role is necessary. If a leader is an initiator and an Idea Suggestion Platform is a vehicle for innovative change, a change agent would be a facilitator orchestrating the implementations. The role of a change agent lies in coaching and championing rather than in monitoring resistance against changes, so how much a firm is ready to change is highly related to the activities of Change Agents who significantly influence motivation, attitude and participation of target groups (Jansen, 2002). Organisational change is a dynamic and two layer process, in that unpredicted challenge and a mismatch between organisational and individual goals occurs. In this regard, swift response and continuous efforts are necessary to meet dynamic equilibrium, and a change agent will play an intermediary role in identifying and reporting necessary needs to top management while tuning unpredicted challenges. It is also important to synchronise organisational and individual goals, in that an individual's positive attitude towards the organisation can result in voluntary and sustainable innovation, which leads to resource allocation optimisation in organisations (Eby, Adams, Russell, & Gaby, 2000). Furthermore, a change agent plays a vital role in organisational learning. Even although they do not have an implementation function, they are still key players who encourage interactions between functional teams while leading organisational learning (Siebenhuner & Arnold, 2007).

9.3 Research method

This chapter attempts to explore sustainable innovation using an open innovation method, so, given the need for a holistic understanding of 'how firms can initiate and implement innovation in a sustainable way', an explorative inductive case study is adopted for analysis. The current chapter aims to add knowledge about factors affecting sustainable innovation, and the case study method, which is relevant to answering 'why' and/or 'how' research questions (Yin, 2009), would be an appropriate methodological choice for this work when considering the nature of our research question. We selected a large established ICT firm, as a single case, in the sense that it satisfies the three case choice criteria – critical, unusual, and longitudinal – suggested by Yin (2009). First, the case is unusual. The case firm used an IT platform as well as Change Agents, which is rare in practice. Second, the case is critical for this study, because this chapter investigates a firm that needs to cultivate a new innovative organisational culture to survive given rapid technological developments, such as Industry 4.0. The research question that we attempt to answer is what is the factor that allows employees to voluntarily participate in innovation by using strong leadership of top management and leading activities of Change Agents? Third, the case study enables us to observe how the case firm has developed its innovation strategy over time.

9.3.1 Data collection

Data were collected from three different data sources in order to increase construct validity. For data triangulation, semi-structured interviews, written documents and non-participant observations were adopted as multiple evidences. Ten semi-structured interviews that lasted one and a half hour and five workshops that lasted three hours on average were conducted (see Table 9.1). The interviews and conversations were carried out with top management, innovation program representatives, Change Agents, and innovation program participants. Notes were added to the interview transcript as soon as interviews

Table 9.1 Interview participants

Interviewee	Job title	Empirical data
Interviewee 1	Change agent 1	One interviews, two workshops
Interviewee 2	CHRO	Three interviews, two workshops
Interviewee 3	Innovation training participant 1	One interview, one workshop
Interviewee 4	Innovation training participant 2	One interview, one workshop
Interviewee 5	Innovation training participant 3	One interview
Interviewee 6	Innovation idea proposer	One interview
Interviewee 7	CEO	Two interviews

148 *Joon Mo Ahn and Jong Rak Kim*

were completed in order to reflect non-recordable aspects, such as subtle nuance and reactions. We also used written documents and non-participant observations as complementary data sources. Written documents, such as media releases, internal annual reports and external audit reports, were collected. Such written documents were very helpful for identifying the firm's strategic decision, catching up with innovation history and understanding the firm's technology and platform architecture. The collected data were analysed by integrating different data to reorganize the case story (Eisenhardt, 1989). First, we used written documents as a starting point for understanding the firm's situation. The interview guide was made based on the initial findings from written documents to draw further explanation. Also, non-participant observations were conducted between interview processes to complement the interview data, and additional written documents were analysed in parallel. All the data were decomposed and then restructured and combined to construct an overview of the findings and to understand the interactions between strong leadership, Change Agents and systematic platforms.

9.4 Case analysis

9.4.1 Research setting

9.4.1.1 Introduction of the case firm

The case firm is a large and leading IT (information technology) service firm in Korea, founded in 1987. The 6,500 employees work in consulting, system integration, IT outsourcing, and IT convergence in 12 countries around the world. The case firm has been pursuing various IT service projects in the field of e-government, transportation, and the manufacturing industry, including the projects for building the Korean e-Government system, LG Electronics smart factory, and the transportation card systems in Seoul, South Korea, Wellington, New Zealand, Bogota, Colombia, Athens, and Greece (see Table 9.2). It recorded sales of about 3.1 trillion KRW (approximately 2.3

Table 9.2 The case firm overview

Founded	January 1987
Number of employees	6,063 employees (as of 2018, including Korea & overseas)
Annual sales	3.1177 Trillion KRW
Business scope	Consulting, System Integration, Outsourcing, ERP/BI, IT Infra Solution, IT Convergence
Overseas Subsidiaries	China, Europe, Americas, India, Indonesia, Japan, Brazil, Colombia, Malaysia, Vietnam, Greece
Business references	Seoul Automatic Fare Collection System, the Seoul Transport Operation & Information Service, the Bus Management System project for Pasto in Colombia, Japanese Shinmine Solar Plant Project

billion EUR) in 2018. The former CEO set a challenging goal of achieving 10 trillion KRW in sales by 2020. For external growth, the case firm merged with an unmanned helicopter firm and started new businesses in the fields of electric vehicle battery charging and electric car-sharing service. However, new businesses, which the case firm entered without its own internal capability eventually became a deficit business. In 2015, a new CEO was appointed to clean up insolvent businesses and began to promote growth through sustainable innovation rather than external growth.

9.4.1.2 Reigniting innovation

Due to the waves of the Fourth Industrial Revolution (Industry 4.0), which began in 2016, many firms have been urged to adopt digital transformation. To support customer needs for digitalisation, firm A is developing new business solutions in Artificial Intelligence (AI), Big Data, Internet of Things (IoT), Cloud and so on, and promoting the skill transformation of the existing workforce so that its employees could use such new technologies to carry out projects for customers (see Figure 9.1). In order to survive in a rapidly changing market, the top management of the case firm set up innovation tasks, apart from the existing management tasks, and allocated them to each business division and department. However, its top executives have realised that a top-down approach to innovation alone is difficult to achieve. The reason was that the leaders of business field units, who had to lead such top-down innovation, were more concerned with the goals of achieving short-term management performance, which caused the majority of members to pay less attention to the sustainable innovation tasks.

Firm A's top management promoted the Idea Suggestion Program (ISP) to provide employees with opportunities to innovate voluntarily in the workplace so that they could reach consensus on such a sustainable innovation. The case firm started out with the ISP in the form of a pilot for about 1,300 people in 11 departments under a business division. The reasons why the ISP was conducted in the form of a pilot rather than the entire firm-wide innovation program was to ensure that the ISP worked well for the firm, and to expand the ISP to the whole firm in the future by supplementing them as they progress. Eleven departments involved in the pilot program consisted of five departments for business, three departments for technical implementation, and three departments for staff.

9.4.2 Strengthening sustainability through collective intelligence

9.4.2.1 What is the bottom-up innovation program?

The ISP is an idea proposal program that voluntarily proposes ideas that employees have found in their work enabling the firm to review and implement these ideas. Employees can suggest their ideas related to new business, technologies, and ways of working (work process and system) obtained from

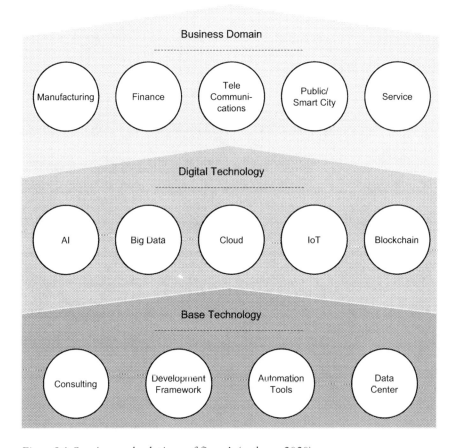

Figure 9.1 Services and solutions of firm A (authors, 2020).

business fields. The ISP is designed to reduce the employees' negative perception of innovation and encourages employees to propose lots of ideas so that they can participate positively in innovation. The case firm's innovation team expected that the consensus of innovation formed through the ISP would eventually have a positive effect on top-down innovation.

Firm A's innovation staff tried to convey the message to the employees that innovation is not a difficult thing, but a joyful and meaningful activity. The message of the ISP, 'my little idea can change the firm' was simple, but very powerful. One word for the slogan of the ISP, the 'little' gave the impression that even a small, simple idea can be an idea of innovation, which relieved employees of the burden of proposing innovative ideas. It gave employees a positive message that even small, trivial ideas offered by employees

Making innovation sustainable 151

could change their own and their colleagues' work and ultimately the firm. A change agent who participated in the innovation program said:

> We found that the innovation is not huge and difficult. We felt less burdensome by the slogan that the innovation starts with small ideas that change my business and workplace.
>
> (Change agent 1, 2019-04-19)

Chief Human Resources Officer (CHRO), the ISP's general director, commented:

> It is not innovations from grandiose slogans or innovations for solving main problems but small innovations, such as getting rid of a stone in front of us, can lead to practical activities for a big innovation because such small innovations gather and eventually form the big innovation. The problem is not that the mountain is high, but that there is a small stone in my shoes. When we get rid of a stone in our shoes we can climb the mountain.
>
> (CHRO, 2019-04-28)

9.4.2.2 Process of the Idea Suggestion Platform

Firm A's ISP consists of four steps. The outline of the process is shown in Figure 9.2.

Step 1 Build consensus for innovation

The first step in the ISP is to build a consensus with employees on the need for innovation and to train employees as to how to develop innovative ideas. The case firm produced a video clip on why the ISP is needed and all the employees were allowed to watch it. The seven-minute short video clip commended the sincere efforts of employees to sell their deficit business and

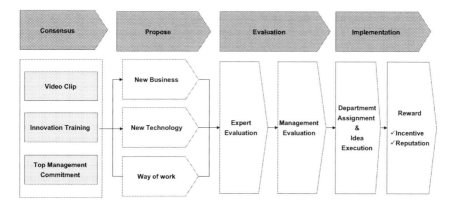

Figure 9.2 The four-step process of the ISP (authors, 2020).

rebuild the firm. Further, the video clip emphasised that innovation with employee engagement is necessary for growth through sustainable innovation. To prevent the spread of misunderstandings and negative perceptions about the ISP among employees, CHRO reviewed the storyline of the video clip. After watching the video clip, the employees of 11 departments participated in the offline innovation training program to learn how to develop innovative ideas. Firm A's top management gave a special lecture called 'Why Innovation Again?' to create consensus among employees about the necessity of bottom-up innovation. They frankly acknowledged the firm's difficult situation and the mistakes in decision-making by top management to employees who did not know the firm's difficult situation, and conveyed in a confident tone the need for innovation to make a new leap forward. This active participation of top management in the ISP has served as a starting point to make the employees, who have been negative about the innovation program, understand the need for innovation and transform into a positive mind set for innovation.

Step 2 Idea proposal

The second step of the ISP is the stage in which employees develop innovative ideas from their fields and suggest the ideas to the Innovative Ideas Proposal System – system is called 'I-TOGETHER' (i.e., online bulletin board for idea suggestion) – located in the enterprise portal. Program participants worked with colleagues to identify the current status and cause of problems in the field that needed improvement and to develop innovative ideas for solving the problem. Specifically, their ideas are divided into three categories and suggested by the employees to the I-TOGETHER. Each suggested idea includes the background of the idea proposal, solutions, the expected effects and difficulties and information from the department in charge. Every idea can be looked up by any employee. Employees can click the 'like' button (in the Facebook) on the ideas in I-TOGETHER and post their comments on them for feedback on the ideas. Idea proponents can supplement their ideas through peer feedback on their own ideas, and check the progress and adoption of ideas. Colleagues' behaviours of clicking the 'like' button and posting comments about the proposed ideas are meaningful as activities for indirect participation in the ISP with employees' interest.

Step 3 Evaluation of ideas

The third step of the ISP is the stage in which the proposed idea is evaluated by an evaluation committee. The evaluation committee includes a first-round professional review panel consisting of 56 experts and team leaders from each sector of the case firm and a second-round executives' review panel of 18 executives. The professional review panel is divided into a business division, a technology division, and a way of working division, and conducts the primary review of the proposed innovative idea with an average of three professional reviewers assigned to the review of one idea. The innovation manager assigns ideas to the first-round reviewer through the I-TOGETHER, and the reviewers evaluate them on a scale of 1 point (very bad) to 5 point (very good) and register their opinions. The first-round screening will be completed within one week after the idea proposal, and ideas with three or more points will pass the first screening and proceed to the second-round screening. In the second-round screening, 18 executives examine the ideas that passed the first-round screening. Ideas are assigned to two or three related department executives and are evaluated considering the effectiveness and feasibility of the idea. Ideas that have passed the second-round screening are subject to the final decision of the chief executive, according to the type of the adopted idea, and then transferred to a department to implement the idea.

Step 4 Implementation of ideas

The final step of the ISP is the stage in which the adopted idea is transferred to the department in charge of the execution of the idea at the firm. Firm A's innovation manager communicates with the team leader of the department in charge of the direction, planning and support for the idea adopted. In some cases, the implementation speed of an idea depends on the level of difficulty. It may take some time when the various departments have conflicting interests, technical difficulties or significant costs occur in implementing the idea. Because the executive of the department in charge already participates as the reviewer in the evaluation of the idea, the contents of the idea are understood by the head. Thus, the main focus of communication is on the priorities of the adopted idea in relation to the existing work being undertaken by the department. The case firm's innovation manager continues to monitor the implementation of the ideas transferred to the departments in charge and works together to resolve any problems in practice. The implementation of the idea is communicated to employees through the firm's electronic bulletin board (BBS).

9.4.3 Why is the ISP working well?

Firm A's innovation manager hoped that a culture of innovation would be settled down in the workplaces of employees for sustainable innovation, not one-off events. The manager found that it was important to build consensus on innovation among employees, to alleviate the input time and physical difficulties of employees in participating in the innovation program, and to communicate transparently about how the suggested idea was accepted by the firm. An employee who had attended the ISP said:

> Even if my idea is not adopted, it is important to share transparently the process by which the idea was evaluated. In previous innovation programs that we've experienced so far, frequently we could not get feedback properly and thus came to give up the proposal of innovative ideas.
>
> (Innovation training participant 1, 2019-04-29)

154 Joon Mo Ahn and Jong Rak Kim

Other participants who attended the innovation training program said:

> Because of the nature of IT projects, we have an excessive workload over a given amount of time. Thus, the reality is that we don't have the time and heart to suggest and implement such innovative ideas. I hesitate to suggest ideas because if I propose the idea, I have to do it so my workload would increase.
>
> (Innovation training participant 2, 2019-05-09)

The case firm's innovation manager set three ISP directions to increase the success rate of sustainable innovation. The first was to create many opportunities to communicate the need for innovation between top management and employees in order to create consensus because the formation of employee consensus is the first key to the success of innovation. The second was not to limit the scope of ideas to their work to reduce the burden of an idea proposal. Employees are free from the burden of implementing ideas when they propose a new business opportunity and technology ideas and solutions to work process problems they find during their work, because they are not their work. This is because the innovation program is likely to succeed when many ideas are proposed and the number of ideas surviving through the process of combination increases. Third, for sustainable innovation, Change Agents should voluntarily propagate and lead the culture of innovation at the sub-organisation level with confidence in the need for innovation. Sustainability of innovation ultimately depends on whether innovation can be reflected in the firm's business processes and organisational culture.

9.4.3.1 Forming a consensus of sustainable innovation

One of the important factors in the success of the case firm's sustainable innovation is the active participation and support of top management. Whereas chief executives of high-tech IT firms in the US, such as Google and Facebook, frequently communicate about the firm's management status and future directions in public places, chief executives of firms in Asia are not familiar with publicly communicating with employees. In particular, Korean CEOs generally deliver their messages via bulletin board systems (BBS) or e-mail rather than communicating with employees directly. Unlike the United States and Europe with active individualism, East Asian countries such as Korea, China, and Japan have a strong culture of family-ism, which is also reflected in the firm's organisational culture. In particular, because Korean firms have an organisational culture with a high hierarchy, CEOs are familiar with top-down communication rather than horizontal communication with employees. Top management's open communication with employees, other than a presence at formal events for business needs, rarely happens in Korean firms, compared to Western firms. Thus, millennial employees who do not hesitate to express their opinions on various issues of the firm need a system to communicate with the firm.

However, the case firm's top management was active in conveying the need for bottom-up innovation, unlike those of typical Korean firms. The workshops were held with executives from 11 departments, for which the ISP was implemented in the form of a pilot, to identify the progress of the ISP and encourage leaders to actively participate in it. Top management also attended the innovation training program and instructed employees to communicate their ideas about innovation directly. The active involvement and attention of top executives influenced employees to recognize the firm's commitment to innovation and needs for bottom-up innovation. The innovation training program attendant said:

> Previously the word innovation sounded very uncomfortable and negative. However, through the executive special lectures, we clearly understood why we need the bottom-up innovation. We've come to realize again that innovation is a matter of survival.
>
> (Innovation training participant 3, 2019-06-14)

The I-TOGETHER also serves as a channel through which employees communicate with the firm. Employees of the case firm did not have much opportunity to ask for improvements on their inconvenience in the business systems, work processes they found during their work. With the I-TOGETHER, however, they got a channel where they can suggest their ideas to the firm. In addition, peers' clicking 'like' and posting comments on the ideas they registered could convince employees that many people support their ideas. For example, employees are required to transform their main skills to those in new technologies such as Cloud, AI, and Big Data. In this situation, one employee proposed an idea of 'Cloud Playground' at which employees could practice various services offered by Amazon Web Service and Microsoft's Azure Cloud. The idea was supported and received encouragement by many employees, and is now adopted as an innovative idea. The employee proposing the "Cloud playground" said:

> I had a lot of pressure to do the project in a different cloud environment, unlike the previous project environment. The Cloud playground helps us to test the AI or other services that we need to perform on the project.
>
> (Innovation idea proposer 1, 2019-08-28)

The CEO of the firm A also showed interest in the idea and said:

> It is necessary for the firm to push employees to learn new skills, but the Cloud Playground is a very good attempt because it gives voluntary motivation to employees and provides them with a field to learn and practice new skills.
>
> (CEO, 2019-09-18)

156 Joon Mo Ahn and Jong Rak Kim

9.4.3.2 Beyond the scope of the idea proposal

Employees who have experienced various innovation programs in the past often have a negative perception of innovation (Chung, Choi, & Du, 2017). This is because in order to produce fruits of innovative activities, employees had to look for a task that will produce visible results in their own work, and had to make an extra effort to implement an idea for the task. To enhance the sustainability of innovation, the case firm's innovation team did not limit the scope of innovative ideas to the current work of each employee. They expanded the scope of the idea proposals from the idea of getting rid of the inconvenience in the daily task to the idea of changing the basis of a business, a technology or the way of working. Employees who felt a burden with respect to proposing new ideas were able to lower their mental burden up to proposing ideas to address the inconveniences they felt during their career, not improving their work. The types of ideas were divided into three categories: a new business, a new technology/knowledge assets, and the improvement of smart work (internal systems and processes related to work methods, and organisational culture) for the reviewing of ideas. By expanding the range of idea proposals in this way, the ISP naturally has the characteristic of separating the proponents and implementers of ideas. The ideas that passed the first-round and second-round screening are reported to the top management and transferred to the relevant departments through decision-making so that employees do not have to take responsibility for the implementation of the proposed ideas unless they come up with ideas related to their work.

9.4.3.3 Change Agent for ISP

Unlike top-down innovation, ISP is not compulsory and thus requires employees' voluntary involvement. The innovation team picked up 31 Change Agents recommended from 11 departments to lead the ISP in the department. And they trained the change agent as a trainer of the ISP. Change agents have been working part-time on leading changes, carrying out their existing tasks in parallel. At the beginning of the program, Change Agents had many complaints about being selected as change agent. They were involved in the program without hearing from the team leaders the background of their selection as change agent for ISP and their roles in ISP.

However, through the meeting with top management at a workshop for Change Agents, they recognized the firm's need for innovation and the importance of the change agent's role as a facilitator of field innovation. They served as instructors of the innovation training program, taught their colleagues how to develop innovative ideas and how to submit ideas through the I-TOGETHER. For lots of innovative ideas to come out, the Change Agents planned and promoted idea proposal events and provided an environment for employees to suggest ideas. Change Agents realized the importance of their role in ISP through positive responses from leaders and employees who attended ISP.

Making innovation sustainable 157

When I was designated as change agent, I had vagueness and fear about the role at first. It seemed like a role to give an additional burden on my busy colleagues. However, when I designed a meaningful and fun innovation program in which the members could participate casually the program drew a good response from the participants. In particular, I was encouraged by top management's statement that the adopted idea will be implemented by the corresponding department; the participants could propose much more ideas.

(Change Agent 2, 2019-08-28)

9.4.4 Current status of the Idea Suggestion Platform

9.4.4.1 Current status

The ISP that began with the innovation training program for 1,300 employees in 11 departments in April 2019 produced about 360 innovative ideas as of October 2019. Out of these, 155 ideas passed the first-round screening, 65 ideas are in the process of the second-round screening and 17 ideas passed the second-round screening. Eight ideas are being implemented by the department in charge. In the beginning, firm A planned to launch ISP for 11 departments in 2019 and to expand, by 2020, the program to about 5,000 employees in the rest of the firm after improving the complement found through the pilot program. The innovation manager of the case firm discovered some phenomena at about two thirds of the pilot program's process.

9.4.4.2 From the improvement of the inconvenience to the opportunity of the new business

The ISP of the case firm provides freedom to the range of idea suggestions so that they can propose content that is not relevant to their work, which has a positive effect on the various types of ideas being proposed. In addition to the idea of innovation in their work, employees are also proposing a variety of ideas to improve new business opportunities, skills, and the inconvenience of their working life. The area in which the most ideas have been proposed, accounting for about 70% of the proposed ideas, is the improvement of work processes. New ideas in the field of business or technology can be proposed by experienced employees in the area. However, suggestions for improvement in the way of working can be found in their own work or through conversation with colleagues. Moreover, innovative ideas on working methods have more viable characteristics than ideas in business and technology, and they have a strong impact on employees. One of the ideas for process improvement implemented is the idea of removing its X-ray security checkpoints to simplify the firm's procedures for entry and exit. Employees had to pass through a checkpoint with an X-ray scanner, installed to prevent unauthorized shipments of portable storage and others that were not reported to the firm on the security system. It was normal to stand in a long line at the gate when it was time for work. However, there were six employees who proposed the idea of improving access procedures, and the leader of the information security team who was reviewing the idea received reports of staff inconvenience and removed the X-ray checkpoints after reviewing whether there were any security issues. This saved the firm a million dollars a year in expenses, eliminating the employees' inconvenience of passing through X-ray security checkpoints that took long.

Another example of implementing a proposed idea is the application of a technology that can automatically register Customer Service Requests (CSRs) using Robotic Process Automation (RPA). At the case firm, many employees manage IT systems of their customers, and the number of times that customer service requests are processed forms the basis for billing customers. However, despite the CSR management system, there have been cases in which a customer sends service requests by messenger or by mail and a CSR registration is missing. To solve this phenomenon, an employee suggested an idea to automatically register the CSR management system by recognizing the texts related to the customer service requests from e-mails through RPA. The idea is in the process of pilot testing for actual application and will be spread to the firm's system management sites for its customers after verification. In addition, based on RPA technology, the case firm plans to develop a solution to automate the text-based works for customers.

I-TOGETHER plays a role as a pool of various innovative ideas for employees who need ideas to discover a new business opportunity and improve their work. Even when an idea was not selected as an excellent idea due to the low evaluation result at the time of screenings, it was discovered that the relevant departments were proceeding with the idea on their own after the related surroundings or situations changed.

9.4.4.3 Lessening the burden on innovators for sustainable innovation

When employees heard about the new innovation program their first reaction was that they had no time and heart to undertake innovation. This is because employees viewed ISP as similar to the previous innovation program in which they had to identify tasks to improve their areas of work and had to proceed with the idea to innovate the tasks on their own. However, ISP was totally different from such a concept. Employees only need to register their thoughts in the I-TOGETHER. Although the complexity of the idea may vary, employees could usually propose ideas by investing from three hours to a day. Firm A's innovation staffs tried to ease the burden of engaging in innovation training, discovering new ideas, identifying challenges in the work environment that requires innovation, practicing the process of finding solutions, and drafting innovative ideas proposals. Employees worked through the process of explaining their ideas to colleagues, listening to various feedback to see if their ideas worked well, and developing the proposed ideas by modifying them into viable ones. Of course, there have been cases where employees have developed ideas for needs to improve the process of their own work.

9.4.5 Challenges of the Idea Suggestion Platform

9.4.5.1 NIH syndrome in the execution of ideas

The ISP did not limit the scope of the idea proposals so that employees can participate in idea proposals easily and various innovative ideas come out. This resulted in the separation of proponents of the idea and executors. This separation helped to get many ideas, but it was found that there was an unexpected delay in implementing the ideas adopted by the department in charge. Even the best ideas adopted were mostly those in the state of a concept which omitted the detailed design needed to be implemented, and thus it was often necessary for the implementation department to develop the ideas further. Although implementing an idea for a business requires a close check of marketability, the feasibility of the technology, and the capacity of the firm, many of the proposed ideas were often suggested only with a certain potential. In some cases, before the proposal of the idea, the department in charge had already reviewed similar ideas and had determined that the idea is unviable. Another reason was that when additional tasks, not included in the task objectives of the department, were assigned to the department, the department in charge is often reluctant to accept transferred ideas. Because the department in charge already had a lot of priorities higher than the ideas transferred through the ISP, the execution was delayed. To address the delay in the implementation of the adopted ideas due to the Not-Invented-Here (NIH) syndrome (Katz & Allen, 1982), firm A's innovation team came to play more significant roles in the early stages of implementing the adopted ideas.

9.4.5.2 Different evaluation results among the idea reviewers

Another phenomenon is that there were differences in the screenings among the idea reviewers. Because technical experts from the field and team leaders from the department to implement the idea were assigned as the first-round reviewers, differences in the outcome of the screening were found between the two groups. After reviewing the results of the reviewers' evaluation, the technical experts often gave higher scores than the team leaders in the implementing departments. This is because the technical experts appreciated the various aspects of new technology usage, whereas the team leaders noticed the difficulties of technical implementation. In addition, as the names of the reviewers are disclosed in the I-TOGETHER, some reviewers wanted to avoid the burden of making negative decisions by making ambiguous assessments while they should clearly decide whether to adopt the idea considering feasibility and effectiveness. This phenomenon puts additional pressure on

160 *Joon Mo Ahn and Jong Rak Kim*

the innovation manager who needs to proceed with implementation through rapid decision-making with respect to adopting ideas.

9.4.5.3 Thinking about continuing ideas

Many ideas have been proposed since the opening of the I-TOGETHER, but over time the number of people accessing the system and the number of ideas proposed has been decreasing. While it may seem natural to see a decrease in the number of access moments and suggested ideas over time, constant control of the number and quality of the proposed ideas is required to establish an innovative culture in which employees propose ideas in their work and the firm executes them. To this end, the case firm's innovation team plans to provide quarterly incentives to the active innovators and best ideas to encourage employees to participate in ongoing idea-proposal activities. In addition, by announcing the implementation progress of the adopted ideas and best ideas through the firm's electronic bulletin board and digital signage installed in the firm, employees are encouraged to recognize the achievements of ISP activities and participate in activities for continuous idea proposals.

9.5 Conclusions

Innovation is an important source of organisational change, but it is not easy for a firm to sustain its change process. Open innovation not only enriches ideas but it also establishes and disseminates an innovation friendly culture, and, this chapter has explored how an open innovation mode, such as crowd souring, can be used to boost and support company-wide internal innovation. To be specific, this study has attempted to answer the question '*How can a firm make its innovation process sustainable by encouraging its employees' participation?*', and for this, the current chapter investigated the case firm's internal Idea Suggestion Platform and factors influencing its success and challenges. This program was adopted in order to nurture an innovation friendly firm culture by forming internal consensus for changes while minimizing the hurdles involved in the change process. Firms in East Asian countries typically have a very hierarchical culture, so they are accustomed to a top-down approach. To overcome this, the case firm has tried to encourage the motivation of employees in various ways. Unlike a general idea suggestion system, ISP separates suggestion and implementation to lessen the possible burden on a proposer of ideas. This encourages employees to voluntarily participate in the ISP without the burden of implementation, but at the same time it has resulted in an unexpected issue – NIH. NIH (Not-Invented-Here) syndrome refers to the psychological resistance against ideas from external organisations (Katz & Allen, 1982), and it is regarded as one of the critical challenges in the adoption of innovative ideas (Chesbrough, 2003). In our case, although ideas were generated inside an organisation, ideas from anonymous proposers are treated like external ideas. So, resistance from implementers was observed in the case.

This explorative case analysis provides rich implications. The case shows that (1) top managements' emphasis on innovation platforms and their commitment to create consensus inside a firm plays a vital role in making innovation sustainable, (2) IT based Idea Suggestion Platforms play an important role in gathering ideas and communicating with employees, and (3) separating the idea proponent and implementer alleviates the burden of participating in the innovation process and allows for a variety of ideas to be generated. The case firm's organisational experiment is a good example to be benchmarked by a firm which wants to make its innovation process more sustainable. However, as the analysis of the case firm shows, there are also challenges to be addressed, such as NIH and the constant motivation of employees through incentive system establishment.

Note

1 It is when the confluence of technology and social change upends an industry and creates massive dislocation in traditional business models (source: https://www.cumber.com/the-uber-moment-in-the-financial-advice-industry).

10 Shaping sustainable innovation based on cultural values

Jaap Boonstra and João Brillo

10.1 Introduction

Innovation has become essential for the future of organizations and is based on their capacity to share values within the organization that have high impact on business strategies, cultural change, and innovation. Cultural change and leadership for innovation are closely connected with value-based management, behavioral change and a vision of the future in which leaders walk the innovational path (Boonstra, 2013).

This chapter presents the case of the Global Alliance for Banking on Values (GABV, 2019a). The banking sector is one of the most internationalized services in the world, and there is a pressing social need to transform our financial institutions into more sustainable and value-driven businesses. The GABV is a network of leading bankers worldwide who are committed to advanced positive and innovative change in the banking sector (www.gabv. org). After exploring the relationships between sustainable innovation, organizational culture and leadership, a methodology for managing sustainable innovational values is introduced. This methodology can help organizations create values that support sustainable innovation. Sustainable innovation occurs best when members of the organization are passionate about their work because they share emotional as well as economic values, and when these values inform organization goals, mission, strategic objectives, processes, and initiatives, and when the values are embedded in the organizational culture (Brillo, Dolan, & Kawamura, 2014a).

The concepts of cultural change and leadership used in this chapter are based on multiple longitudinal case studies. Seventeen organizations who are successful in innovation have been studied over periods of five to ten years. The cases are based on factual and documentary studies and interviews with managers, employees, and customers (Boonstra, 2013). The in-depth case study of the GABV is based on five years of research collaboration between the members of the GABV and a research team from Esade Business School. Strategic developments and innovation initiatives are explored and studied using a research and feedback process in close collaboration between GABV members and the researchers. This method can be considered as action research in which researchers and participants explore new horizons and learn from each other. It is based on the assumption that actors in organizations have useful detailed practical knowledge and experience. Researchers, for their part, have experience in conducting research and theoretical knowledge about innovation and organizational change processes. Together, these two groups can examine the nature and causes of problems, make sense of research results, learn about the dynamics of organizational change and make decisions about interventions (Eden & Huxham, 1996). Action research can be used as a way to improve organizational change and to stimulate learning processes within and between organizations. Interactive feedback sessions on the results of the research offer people in organizations an opportunity to understand the reasons underlying failures and stimulate interaction as well as a joint search for alternative action (Argyris, Putnam, & McLain Smith, 1985). Making sense of the reasons underlying failure together can help people in organizations learn how to handle future change processes more effectively (Boonstra, 2004).

10.2 Organizational culture and business ideas for innovation

The competitive strength of businesses in the 21st century will depend mainly on using creativity to make innovations possible in collaboration with other businesses. Innovative enterprises are successful because they can create a balance between preserving their core values and stimulating renewal (Collins & Porras, 1996). There are two key elements to a vision: a clear identity and an image of the future. The identity is relatively stable, while the business strategy develops continuously subject to the changes in the demands of customers and the business environment. This value-driven perspective on a culture for innovation concerns the identity of an organization, its values and competencies, market position, customer value, and social meaning (van der Heijden, 2005). The business idea of an organization involves these four related points of view that together give shape to the creation of value for customers. Figure 10.1 presents a diagram of the business idea of an organization.

Working on the business idea centers on how organizations can retain their individual character, put their core values into action to realize renewal and make them stand out by creating value for their customers. The key question is how a business wants to position itself and distinguish itself by creating value for customers. Companies that are successful in strategic and organizational culture for innovation are clear about what they believe in and are aiming for. Not a crisis, but a clear business idea is at the root of a successful culture of innovation in organizations. It is therefore an essential condition of innovative culture in businesses. At least equally essential is a good definition of the customer and a clear picture of the customer value that the business wants to deliver (Boonstra, 2013).

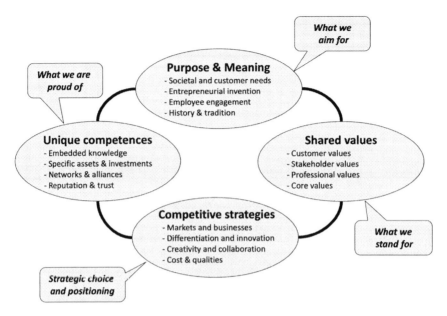

Figure 10.1 Business idea for innovation (Boonstra, 2019).

10.2.1 GABV: Business idea and guiding principles

Founded in 2009, the GABV is a growing network with commercial banks, banking cooperatives, credit unions, microfinance institutions, and community development banks from many parts of the world taking part. The collective goal of the alliance is to change the banking system so that it is more transparent, supports economic, social, and environmental sustainability and is composed of a diverse range of banking institutions serving the real economy. The Global Alliance consists of 43 financial institutions and seven strategic partners operating in countries across Asia, Africa, Australia, Latin America, North America, and Europe. Collectively the alliance serves more than 41 million customers, holds close to 127 billion USD of combined assets under management and is supported by more than 48,000 co-workers (GABV, 2019b).

The members of the GABV have one purpose in common: a shared mission to use finance to deliver sustainable economic, social, and environmental development, with a focus on helping individuals fulfill their potential and build stronger communities. The alliance is committed to financing change in communities. Below we explore the business idea as a core concept in greater depth paying special attention to cultural values and guiding principles (Figure 10.2).

10.2.1.1 Meaning

The members of the GABV are deeply involved with the people and the communities they serve and are accountable for the risks they both take and

Shaping sustainable innovation 165

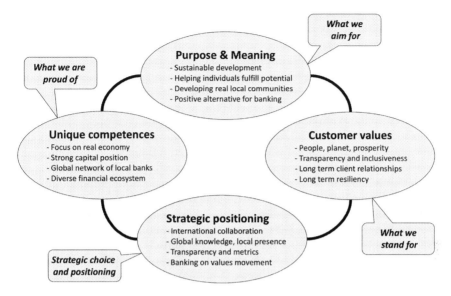

Figure 10.2 Business idea GABV (GABV, 2019c).

create for the people who use their products and services. This focus on inclusion puts basic banking products at the service of a greater number of people, rather than highly sophisticated products in the hands of a few. The members are very aware of the externalities produced by their banking activities through the projects and clients they finance. The GABV members want to ensure that banking is a healthy and productive system for society and develop a positive, viable alternative to the current banking system. The public is becoming increasingly aware of the interdependence of the real economy, social cohesion, and our natural ecosystem, something values-based bankers have long understood, and which lies at the heart of their business model. Knowing that people want to support positive change in society the GABV sees the opportunity to demonstrate a healthy transformation of the banking sector, a contribution to solving societal problems and a reference point for others along the way.

10.2.1.2 Uniqueness

GABV members have a strong belief in the values-based banking model and recent research backs this up, showing that lending to the real economy delivers better financial returns compared with the largest banks in the world (Khan, Serafeim, & Yoon, 2018). The GABV has achieved a strong capital position and steady financial returns through their focus on the real economy, with the values-based banking model providing a viable and much-needed alternative and adding strength to a diverse financial ecosystem. Another unique quality of the GABV is its strong global network of banks, rooted in local economies and drawing on the strength of collaborative experiences worldwide.

10.2.1.3 Values and guiding principles

The organizational glue of the GABV as an innovative alliance lies in their basic values and guiding principles such as transparency, long-term resilience, investment in the real economy and long-term client relationships. In the alliance, local banks are collaborating globally on the basis of shared principles and values. Corporate culture and management transparency are so important for the GABV that they have become core elements in the six principles they use to evaluate and promote values-based banking. Figure 10.3 provides a schematic presentation of the GABV's cultural values and principles (GABV, 2019c).

10.2.1.3.1 PRINCIPLE 1. TRIPLE-BOTTOM-LINE APPROACH.

Values-based banks integrate this approach by focusing simultaneously on people, planet, and prosperity. Products and services are designed and developed to meet the needs of people and safeguard the environment. Generating reasonable profit is recognized as an essential requirement of values-based banking but is not a stand-alone objective. Significantly, values-based banks embrace a proactive approach to triple-bottom-line business—they do not just avoid doing harm but actively use finance to do good.

10.2.1.3.2 PRINCIPLE 2. THE REAL ECONOMY

Values-based banks serve the communities in which they work, serve the real economy and enable new business models to meet the needs of both.

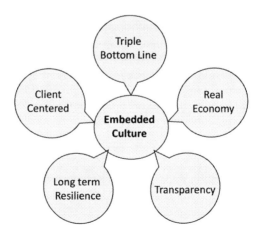

Figure 10.3 GABV cultural values and principles (GABV, 2019c).

They meet the financial needs of these geographic and sector-based communities by financing enterprises and individuals in productive and sustainable economies.

10.2.1.3.3 PRINCIPLE 3. TRANSPARENT AND INCLUSIVE GOVERNANCE

Values-based banks maintain a high degree of transparency and inclusiveness in governance and reporting. In this context, inclusiveness means an active relationship with a bank's extended stakeholder community and not only its shareholders or management.

10.2.1.3.4 PRINCIPLE 4. LONG-TERM, SELF-SUSTAINING, AND RESILIENT

Values-based banks adopt a long-term perspective to make sure they can maintain their operations and be resilient in the face of external disruptions. At the same time, they recognize that no bank, or its clients, is entirely immune to such disruptions.

10.2.1.3.5 PRINCIPLE 5. LONG-TERM RELATIONSHIPS WITH CLIENTS

Values-based banks establish strong relationships with their clients and are directly involved in understanding and analyzing their economic activities and assisting them in becoming more values-based themselves. Proper risk analysis is used in product development so that indirect risk management tools are neither adopted as a substitute for fundamental analysis nor traded for their own sake.

10.2.1.3.6 PRINCIPLE 6. PRINCIPLES EMBEDDED IN CULTURE

At the center of values are the cultural values because the other business values depend on the culture of the banking organization and the way of working on the daily financial services offered to customers. Values-based banks seek to embed these principles in the culture of their institutions so that they are routinely used in decision making at all levels.

10.2.1.4 Positioning

The GABV is a growing movement that influences the way people are doing business and earning a living. In Latin America GABV members are located in Bolivia, Ecuador, Peru, El Salvador, and Paraguay. The GABV is holding conversations with a couple of financial institutions in Brazil that may become members in the near future.

In our global world international collaboration in alliances is developing very fast. These alliances challenge existing business models through innovative power rooted in local knowledge and worldwide expertise. As a global

168 *Jaap Boonstra and João Brillo*

alliance, the GABV operates both within and outside the banking system. This inspires the GABV to consider all stakeholders as bankers, including their customers. Whether you are a values-based bank or banking cooperative, a banking professional or organization interested in creating more social, economic, and environmental impact, a policy maker or regulator interested in bringing progressive change to the sector or a member of the banking public, the GABV considers you as part of the growing global banking on values movement.

The member banks seek to embed the six principles in the culture of their institutions so that they are routinely used in decision making at all levels. Recognizing that the process of embedding these values requires deliberate effort, these banks develop human resources policies that reflect their values-based approach and develop stakeholder-oriented practices to encourage sustainable business models. These banks also have specific evaluation systems and reporting frameworks to demonstrate their financial and non-financial impact.

Based on this business idea the GABV can be seen as an innovative financial movement with a strong culture rooted in basic values and guiding principles.

10.3 Cultural change for sustainable innovation

Cultural change for innovation in organizations is not a goal in itself but is crucial for the strategy and future of the business. This means that there is a continual dialogue with all parties involved about achieving cultural change for innovation. The best way to achieve successful change is by giving meaning and value to the company, and what the company wants to signify for customers and for society. Successful leadership in organizational change for innovation is a function of people's conviction and vision of the future and not a formal position in the company: everyone can play a role in successful change. Innovation champions bring people together with an inspirational vision and move their organization forward to meet the future. Changes in organizations are most often approached as a planned or programmed effort but in the case of cultural change for innovation this planned approach is not fruitful. Innovation is like a journey through an unknown territory (Boonstra, 2019)

There is no single best way of changing organizations; it involves making conscious decisions each time about how to set up the concept of play by choosing and combining change strategies. Change starts with standing still. This not only means finding out the reason for the change but also thinking through a suitable change approach as to how to effect the desired transformations.

Theories about organizational change have described a number of strategies for change. In Figure 10.4 these theories are used to describe six approaches to strategic and cultural change in situations of uncertainty.

Power Strategy	Planned Strategy	Negotiating Strategy	Motivation Strategy	Learning Strategy	Interactive Strategy
Forcing	Pushing	Exchanging	Developing	Learning	Discovering
Steered from the top	Initiated at the top	Multiple actors	Transformative	Active & reflective	Interactive
Goal oriented	Solution oriented	Results oriented	Problem oriented	Transition oriented	Future oriented
Position power	Expert power	Position power	Seductive power	Informal power	Visioning power
Input controllers	Input consultants	Different coalitions	Employee input	Learner input	Collaboration
Linear process	Linear process	Iterative process	Iterative process	Circular process	Cyclical process
Pressure	Persuasion	Negotiation	Participation	Action learning	Mutual learning
Tell & Sell	Convincing	Compromising	Guiding	Coaching	Dialoguing

Figure 10.4 Approaches to cultural change in organizations (Boonstra, 2019).

In power strategies, top managers create urgency using threats from the business environment to galvanize people into action. The idea behind this is that people are cautious and only want to change under external pressure. With this approach conflicts and resistance to change are unavoidable and have to be overcome by force. Top managers determine goals and delegate implementation to middle managers. Controllers monitor whether goals are reached and top managers intervene if that is not the case. Desired behavior is rewarded and behavior that is not appropriate to the new values and standards is penalized.

In rational and planned strategies, the assumption is that people will always choose the most logical solution; the problem is to convince people what the best solution is. After the business environment has been analyzed, management develops a business strategy together with experts; they formulate objectives and implement changes. Experts and advisors have an important role in the problem analysis and formulation of the desired situation. In a planned approach, managers sometimes use large-scale cultural programs whose aim is to change the behavior of people in the organization.

Negotiating strategies are appropriate when parties with different interests and wishes need each other in order to realize their objectives. In this strategy people focus mainly on their own interests but take others into account if there is a need to collaborate. The idea is that personal interest may motivate people to change. This strategy aims at making force fields visible, articulating one's own advantage and trading interests to achieve a solution.

The idea behind motivating and development strategies is that people have the capacity to change as long as there is a good director who can get the best out of them. Creating a safe environment and offering clear structures reduces uncertainty and builds a foundation for change. The problem-solving capacities of the people involved are appealed to in the change process; the change is usually initiated and supported by top management. In this change strategy, people who are directly involved work together in the organization to realize the desired change.

The idea behind the learning strategy is that people act on the basis of assumptions, emotions, feelings, and almost unconscious patterns. Making

170 *Jaap Boonstra and João Brillo*

people aware of these assumptions and patterns and making it possible to discuss feelings creates space for learning processes in which people can change their behavior. The underlying idea is that learning is about overcoming limiting beliefs and the creation of new images of reality. Organizations that work successfully on strategic and cultural change almost always focus on opening up basic assumptions and patterns that may obstruct change for discussion.

In a dialogue strategy, people exchange perspectives on organizing, changing, and innovating; they experiment and initiate innovations that go beyond their own organization. The belief behind this strategy is that reality is not objective but anchored in people's hearts and minds. If this view of reality is linked with a future ideal, energy is created and people are motivated to act. This strategy involves multiple examination and interpretation of problems and stimulating interactions to produce various possible solutions. Meanings and basic assumptions are brought out into the open and alternative joint actions initiated which lead to the discovery of new futures and destinies.

One of the most complicated tasks for people who are engaged in organizational change is choosing and combining change strategies that enable sustainable innovation to take place. The first step in choosing and combining change strategies is to consider the dynamics of the business environment and define the business idea behind the change process. The second step is to consider the importance of the engagement of internal players: in crisis situations and under pressure from the transactional environment there is little room to maneuver. Time is limited and the compliance of employees is needed to make progress. In this situation a power and planned strategy might be suitable for stabilizing the situation and realizing changes that contribute to organizational survival. Where there is a need for quality improvement a rational and planned change strategy is useful for improving quality systems, while a motivation and development strategy is useful in getting people involved in the change process. A change approach based on motivation, learning, and development allows space for innovative experiments but needs time to share experiences and learn from them. Organizations that proactively want to be prepared for the future or focus on innovations take a long-term perspective and the engagement of internal players is usually easy. In this situation learning and dialogue strategies are a good combination. Figure 10.5 shows these views on choosing change strategies for innovation.

10.3.1 *GABV: innovation based on dialogue, learning, and development*

The change strategy of the GABV is very clear in the conscious choice of dialogue, learning, and development as an overarching combination of change strategies to make the global alliance grow and build a worldwide community that offers a positive alternative to current banking principles. A long-term perspective is dominant in the business concept and in the change process itself. The change is a step-by-step process based on small

Shaping sustainable innovation 171

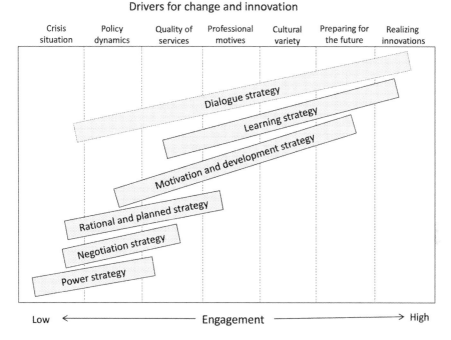

Figure 10.5 Choosing and combining change strategies (authors, 2020).

initiatives, experiments, reflection and learning; room to experiment is huge. The commitment of leaders and professionals is high because of the challenging business idea and their shared ambition to contribute to a better world.

Change in the GABV is a continuous process where bankers worldwide learn from each other's experiences and inspire each other. The change process is based on a challenging ambition to create a movement for values-based banking worldwide. Dialogue, learning, and development are the change strategies used to grow as a global movement. The banks in the alliance create impact by interaction with entrepreneurs, sustainable businesses, microfinance institutions, customers, and non-governmental organizations. Within the alliance, professionals share ideas using communities of practice, learning cycles, and regional chapters to share local experiments, development of new ideas and exchange of best practices.

At its heart, the GABV is a Chief Executive Officer network providing a unique space for collaboration for leaders who are committed to values-based banking. It also provides learning and development opportunities for senior executives, experts, and banking professionals at member banks through their communities of practice. The GABV takes a leading role in the debate about how to build a sustainable financial future by managing joint projects among members, experts, and partners to help deliver it and by advocating change.

172 *Jaap Boonstra and João Brillo*

The GABV supports banks in the alliance with respect to their local cultural embeddedness. The alliance initiated SFRE, a venture capital fund that offers venture capital for values-based banks globally. It invests in local experiments and developing new ideas and supports learning from useful experiences and best practices. The GABV has created communities of practice to develop knowledge and create mutual support. These communities of practice play an important role in the life and development of the GABV. They have opened the Alliance to member banks' subject matter experts and professionals, beyond CEO level.

GABV members meet annually in person to collaborate at regional levels. They reinforce relationships and advance shared agendas to support the growth of the GABV and values-based banking in their geographic areas. The GABV regional chapters act as round tables to provide knowledge and exchange perspectives on issues to the larger CEO group, programs, and communities of practice. Board members responsible for the region provide leadership of each chapter. These chapters are an additional infrastructure for dialogue, learning, and developing (Table 10.1).

The GABV uses impact stories to give meaning to their business idea and support the exchange of good practices. Exploring real-life examples of the communities, organizations, and initiatives have a positive impact on the life of people (GABV, 2019d). Behind every bank in the Alliance there are organizations, entrepreneurs, and investors using money to create positive economic, social, and environmental impact that affect the life of millions of people. These stories share a profoundly different perspective on how banking can and should work. This approach towards GABV storytelling was first launched at an exhibition during the 2013 GABV Annual Meeting in Berlin. The exhibition was accompanied by a book, *Change Makers – The Stories Behind the Values-based Banks Transforming the World*. During the Annual

Table 10.1 GABV communities of practice

Governing Board Forum to develop powerful insights into the unique approach to governance and leadership required to make values-based banks positive, proactive, and profitable agents of social, economic, and environmental change.

Human Development to connect HR experts from each bank, build foundational relationships, and facilitate in-depth sharing and open discussion about best practices in values-based banks.

Impact Metrics to play a key role in developing the GABV Scorecard, which has incredible value as a measuring and differentiating tool in assessing the qualitative and quantitative impact of values-based banking.

Marketing & Communications to collaborate on the worlds' first #Banking OnValues Day, an internationally coordinated initiative that is helping to build visibility and appetite for the values-based banking movement globally.

Risk & Control to work together and exchange knowledge to establish a common view on how to apply risk and control functions within a values-based banking environment by focusing on those characteristics that make this environment so special and closely connected to the six value principles.

Shaping sustainable innovation   173

Meeting 2017 in Kathmandu a deeper approach to storytelling was launched with the publication of the Stories of Systemic Change. The stories can be found at the GABV website.

The GABV is systemically analyzing data that compares the viability of values-based banking. In collaboration with independent financial institutions, comparisons are made between values-based banks and traditional banks and financial institutions. The data builds a business case that demonstrates that organizations can make good money by putting money to good uses (GABV, 2019e).

10.4 Leadership for sustainable innovation

Different leadership styles are distinguished in leadership theory (Yukl, 2009). These different styles are summarized in Figure 10.6 in relation to leaders in organizational culture for innovation. Successful organizational culture for innovation in existing companies mainly involves a combination of transformational and participative leadership; when starting their enterprises, the founders form the company culture. Entrepreneurs and innovation champions are usually charismatic with a high need for achievement that is associated with transactional leadership.

Transforming leadership—Transformational leaders have a deep understanding of the fundamental values of our society and of people's social and emotional needs; they are conscious of developments in the environment. Transformational leaders are curious, explorative, and have broad interests; they have a positive attitude to learning and know themselves and their strong and weak points. They are able to see connections between environmental developments, understand incidental disruption to a work system that can arise and the dynamics of fundamental change. They are aware of the values and standards of a social system and recognize when those rules have to be modified. They listen to others and have the ability to trust others and build trust. They are inspiring and they know how they solve conflicts and realize cultural changes (Kim & Mauborgne, 2005).

Participative leadership—Participative leaders know what is important, inside and outside the organization. They have social awareness and are

Autocratic leadership	Transactional leadership	Charismatic leadership	Participating leadership	Innovating leadership	Transforming leadership
Goal setting	Goal setting	Impressing	Guiding	Initiating	Sensing
Commanding	Informing	Speaking	Listening	Communicating	Sense-making
Intimidating	Managing	Building	Evaluating	Engaging	Vitalizing
Accounting	Performing	Achieving	Consulting	Appealing	Envisioning
Realizing	Stabilizing	Modeling	Delegating	Cultivating	Supporting
Punishing	Rewarding	Monitoring	Developing	Inspiring	Appreciating
Positioning	Controlling	Expecting	Encouraging	Learning	Empowering

Figure 10.6 Perspectives on leadership (Boonstra, 2013).

174 *Jaap Boonstra and João Brillo*

self-aware. Through sensitivity to what is happening in the environment, they see new possibilities. They know what is happening in the organization and what people allow themselves to be controlled by. This enables them to connect with the emotions and ambitions of others so they can direct people's energy in the organization to the future. They know who they are, and they know their own motives. They are approachable, ask others what they think, organize honest feedback and are not afraid to make emotions discussable. These leaders also know themselves and their strong and weak points and know when to consult others to correct their blind spots.

Innovative organizations invest in a leadership style that is based on transformational, charismatic, and participative leadership qualities. They guide young talents to become new leaders by leadership programs, encouragement of new initiatives, trust in delegation, teamwork, and collegial support.

Charismatic leadership—Meaningful leaders deliberately pay attention to specific cases and events; in crisis situations, they step forward to identify the situation and tackle it. They are explicit about what they believe is important, what they attach value to, and what they definitely do not want. They are initiators in cultural change and name events, share interpretations and invite others to share their vision. In this way they create space for dialogue and give it meaning. Through these interactions they form the culture of organizations together with others; they also tell inspiring stories.

Entrepreneurial leadership—Entrepreneurs want to start something new, something they believe in. They have huge drive, powerful motivation and a strong need for achievement. They ask others to share their dream and their vision of the future. These qualities make them charismatic. Entrepreneurs look for people who fit in with their dream and are willing to participate and support the initiative. They are founders of the business and create an organizational culture based on their values and drivers and they are usually inspiring and demanding. They are able to develop disruptive innovations that may threaten existing businesses.

10.4.1 GABV: leadership and innovation

Leadership in the GABV is charismatic, participative, and transformational. Building the alliance as a global movement requires an appealing future perspective. Charismatic leadership creates such a perspective, attracts new banks into the alliance and builds common ground to develop it. This future perspective creates new possibilities for collaborating with knowledge institutes and offers the alliance a visible position in international interest groups like the World Economic Forum. Participative leadership is needed to engage the local banks in the alliance and invite them to share experiences and develop new business concepts. The GABV has an executive director and a support staff that is mainly focused on building the alliance by inviting members to engage in innovative business concepts and communities of practice to share these concepts.

Shaping sustainable innovation 175

Being a manager or professional in a GABV bank is a somewhat difficult task since it is not concerned primarily with making money but about being reasonably profitable in a people-centered organization in which long-term orientation and respect are key values. This means that recruiting and promoting the right executives who combine experience and technical knowledge with the right values and change capabilities is one of the toughest challenges in the GABV network. The Communities of Practice and Chapters support leaders and professionals in exchanging ideas, learning from each other and taking a leading role in values-based banking.

The alliance offers a leadership academy and online courses for values-based banking. The GABV Leadership Academy is designed to help values-based bankers strengthen their leadership skills and capacity to help their respective banks address the challenges of our time. Over a period of eight months, participants in the Academy convene for three in-person modules and participate in coaching sessions and projects between the modules. The curriculum of the GABV Leadership Academy includes: Introduction to values-based banking, Purpose and mission of the GABV; Values-based Banking Models, Social Entrepreneurship, Client relationships in values-based banking, Digitalization, FinTech & values, The Role of Art for Social Change, The Role of Money in Society and Introduction to core concepts as well as tools on leadership.

From the subjects above and the learning design it can be seen that the learning process has several layers: developing and advancing one's own leadership capacity in the context of values-based banking, learning about and exploring a wide variety of values-based banking models, supporting financial and non-financial innovations, developing personal and cultural skills, practicing innovation techniques, initiating individual change projects, and exploring societal challenges and innovative solutions to address them.

10.5 Managing sustainable innovational values

The methodology of managing by sustainable innovational values (MSIV, Brillo, Dolan, & Kawamura, 2014b) is an extension and elaboration of both the Management by Values (Dolan, Garcia, & Richley, 2006) and the coaching by values concepts (Dolan, 2011). The MSIV model has been fundamental in addressing complexity within organizations in the 21st century and strengthening organizations' capabilities for developing a culture for innovation.

10.5.1 Managing cultural values and innovation

MSIV is a tri-intersectional model and asymmetrical cultural inquiry tool that may be used as the foundation for developing organizational culture (Brillo, Dolan, Kawamura, & Fernandez, 2015). MSIV suggests that a firm's central values, goals, and strategic objectives are circumscribed within the triangle that is formed by the following three complementary yet orthogonal axes: Economic-Pragmatic, Ethical-Social, and Emotional-Developmental. Economic-Pragmatic values are a set of values related to the criteria of competitiveness, discipline, economic growth, and efficiency, among others. These values guide the planning, quality assurance, and accounting activities in organizations; they are necessary for maintaining and unifying various organizational subsystems. Ethical-Social values represent the way people behave in groups guided by ethical values shared by members of that group. These values come from conventions or beliefs about how people should behave in public, at work, and in their relationships; they are associated with values such as commitment, awareness, generosity, and respect for people. These values are manifested in actions more than words. Emotional-Developmental values are essential for creating new opportunities for action. These values are related to intrinsic motivation which moves people to believe in a cause. Autonomy, creativity, enthusiasm, joy, passion, and playfulness are some examples of these values. Without them, people would be unable to make organizational commitments or be creative. Therefore, when designing an organizational culture for innovation, it is essential that people are able to do what they do differently and best in their jobs (Brillo et al., 2014a).

Figure 10.7 shows the MSIV model, extracting the values from the GABV's principles and describing an alignment of the three axes: economic-pragmatic values—competitiveness, economic growth, and economic success—,

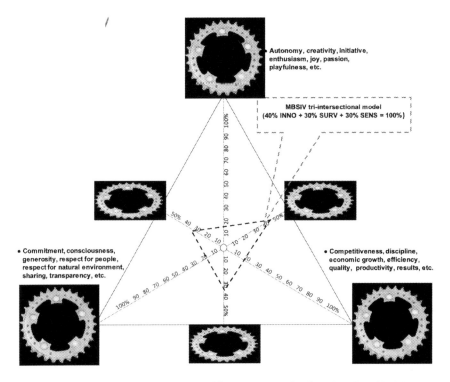

Figure 10.7 GABV's managing sustainable innovational values (GABV, 2019c).

Shaping sustainable innovation 177

ethical-social values—respect for people, respect for the environment—, emotional-developmental values—creative energy, enthusiasm, and passion— at their intersection points, which allows the GABV's leaders to focus on innovation linkage—intersection between the emotional-development axis and the economic-pragmatic axis—while keeping the sensitivity and survival linkages, increasing sensitivity, and making the organization socially and environmental responsible.

10.5.2 Values-based Strategy Map

The use of a strategy map, customized to an organization's particular strategy, describe how intangible assets drive performance enhancements to the organization's internal processes that have maximum leverage for delivering value to customers, shareholders, and communities. It provides a framework to illustrate how strategy links intangible assets to value-creating processes. The architecture of the cause and effect relationship linking the Financial Perspective—the outcomes of the strategy in traditional financial terms—, Customer Perspective—value proposition for the targeted customers, Internal Process Perspective—the small number of critical processes that are expected to have greatest impact on the strategy—, and the Learning and Growth Perspective—human, information, and organization capital required to support the value-creating internal processes—, define the chain of logic by which intangible assets will be transformed to tangible values, generating sustainable innovation (Brillo et al., 2014a).

The Values-based Strategy Map provides a visual representation of how companies' vision, mission, and values can be integrated. It is argued that sustainable innovation occurs best when organizational members share a high degree of Economic-Pragmatic/Emotional-Development/Ethical values and when these values are employed within the firm's strategic objectives, change initiatives and results and when these objectives, initiatives and results are effectively communicated and embedded within the organizational culture. The architectural relationships customized to an organization's particular strategy, linking the Values Perspective (the company's core economic, emotional, and social values), the Strategic Perspective (value proposition for the targeted vision and mission), Change Perspective (the critical processes that are expected to have greatest impact on the strategy), and Results (human, information and organizational capital required to support the value-creating processes). The Value-based Strategy Map generates better communication and an effective culture for innovation. The Values-Based Strategy Map in the GABV presented in Figure 10.8 shows an architecture of relationships linking strategic objectives, change process, and targets.

10.5.2.1 Strategic objective: Business development

Business development: To increase membership and membership categories, while remaining credible, diverse, and regionally representative. The GABV

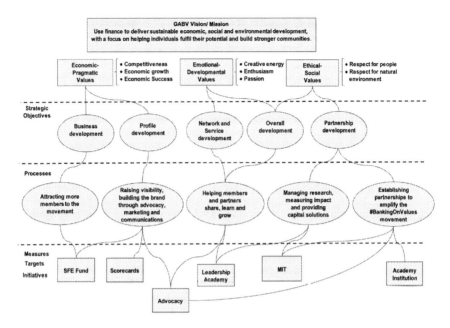

Figure 10.8 GABV's values-based Strategy Map (GABV, 2019c).

will also monitor and support members in expanding the quality and quantity of the economic, social, and environmental impact.

10.5.2.2 Change process and target: To attract more members to the movement

Full members: Expand to 60–75 members by 2020 with sufficient representation from different continents, serving 70–100 million customers and including mission-aligned banking-related holding companies (considered on a case-by-case basis).

Develop a new category for banks in transition to a values-based approach, based on compliance with the Principles of Sustainable Banking and Scorecard ratings.

10.5.2.3 Strategic objective: Profile development

Profile development: Establish the GABV as 'the' benchmark for values-based banking through a clearly defined position (based on content developed on the basis of the banking model of member banks and their impact); key relationships, strategic partnerships, and public profile opportunities.

10.5.2.4 Change process and target: To raise visibility through advocacy and communication

Advocacy: To provide an alternative point of view to the current banking system and its role in society; to advocate change in the banking system; to influence change in policy and regulation; to become a well-known, highly regarded and vibrant network of banks and influencing policymakers and regulators to develop a healthier banking system through trusted relationships with leading global actors e.g. World Bank and Asian Development Bank; to design Communities of Practice as key forums for sharing innovation and expertise within the Alliance to advance values-based banking.

Communication to develop a new category for banks in transition to a values-based approach, based on compliance with the principles of sustainable banking and scorecard ratings; to build the values-based banking movement, internally within the Alliance and its co-workers and externally with GABV partners and interested members of the public by a media strategy for web, social media, events, and publications; exchange their corporate identity and support co-branding with members and partners. Develop a media relations strategy and the next phase in the life of the GABV marketing and communications and the communities of practice.

10.5.2.5 Strategic objective: Partnership development

Partnership development: Help the GABV build relationships and collaboration with more external stakeholders in a more structured way. This in turn will build initiatives and innovations and amplify the #BankingOnValues movement and the global GABV brand. In 2016 a new category of membership was introduced to support this commitment formally.

10.5.2.6 Change processes and target: Partnerships and the #BankingOnValues movement

Support partners: Academic institutions or Independent research agencies who provide an alternative point of view to those of the current banking system; networks in different fields whose core values are similar to those of the GABV; development banks and other multilateral institutions; consulting organizations and private companies whose core values are similar to those of the Alliance; offer better help to banks transitioning to the values-based approach; amplify the experience and impact of GABV members through other networks and alliances, not necessarily exclusively in the banking field; identify and approach other values-based banks or transitioning banks in different parts of the world.

180 *Jaap Boonstra and João Brillo*

10.5.2.7 Strategic objective: Network and service development

Network and service development focuses on building the capacity of the GABV as a movement and as a network organization, positioning the Alliance to transition from start-up to growth phase, and readying the GABV for a renewed focus on member/business development

10.5.2.8 Change processes and targets: To help members and strengthen networking

Helping members: Help the Alliance improve the operational day-to-day management of activities through administrative, infrastructure, and process support; enhance the operational management of the Secretariat and Board of Directors; focus on process mapping and procedural improvements; implement an office management system, develop solutions, build processes, and implement improvements related to service providers, pipeline, and query management, team management, Executive Director support, financial management, and administration; implement IT and infrastructure solutions to ensure efficient and cost-effective operations; support the development of peer-to-peer exchange and use the forums to engage academic institutions for research purposes and in support of advocacy efforts; develop additional GABV Regional Chapters where local issues and positions can be addressed.

Networking: Provide support for GABV members to connect, collaborate, and create more impact; inspire GABV co-workers: remind them that they are part of something greater, something that can change the world, and how their passion and professionalism is fundamental; become better values-based bankers by networking, sharing, and learning from each other and reflecting on work in an international context; advance the field of values-based banking by educating GABV members about the movement, the innovations, and the potential; integrate performance plans for GABV co-workers involved in participating and supporting values-based banking activities; inter-member secondments and fellowships; GABV-member secondments; graduate classes of the GABV Leadership Academy; co-design the first open source online international training program and offer it every year as a Massive Open Online Course (MOOC).

10.5.2.9 Strategic objective: Overall development

Overall development: Focus on engagement through impact measurement and the development of a business case for values-based banking through research and proof points; the Scorecard; the creation of a knowledge-sharing platform to support Communities of Practices, hubs, and the growth of the values-based banking movement.

Shaping sustainable innovation 181

10.5.2.10 *Change processes and targets: Measuring impact and providing capital solutions*

Overall development: Conduct annual research updates including new members, issues and data; launch a reasonably independent Scorecard for assessing banks in terms of values-based banking and as a self-assessment tool for Executive Boards; publish annual results of Scorecards by all GABV members, SFRE Fund investees and other banks; periodically publish or cooperate in the publication of research papers or GABV position papers with a values-based focus; create a knowledge-sharing platform for GABV Member Banks, Partner Banks and Supporting Partners.

10.5.2.11 *Results*

Over the years the Alliance has evolved from an incubator of ideals, concepts, initiatives, connections and partnerships into a generator of sector and system positions, collaborations, operational alliances, and policy influencers. For example: the SFRE Fund, initiated by the GABV, is already a spin-off; advocacy is growing from a local and regional perspective to national and international action; the Scorecard has the potential to become an industry standard; the leadership academy has evolved from a values ambassador community of practice to an independent professionally accredited values-based banking leadership development program; the Massachusetts Institute of Technology massive open online courses, developed with input from the GABV, will change how banking professionals, policy makers, and the interested public view the potential for a different kind of banking system.

10.6 Conclusion

The example of the GABV shows that the alliance is at the forefront of a quiet revolution in banking based on an innovative business idea and innovative practices founded on a change strategy of engaging people, open dialogue, and a cycle of experimentation, reflecting, exchanging, and learning. Innovation based on sustainable values helps the GABV to develop as a movement dedicated to advanced positive change in the banking sector. Innovation and development are based on a challenging ambition to create a movement for values-based banking worldwide. The innovation activities used by the GABV are in accordance with the change strategy of dialogue, learning, and development. Every employee of the GABV and member banks is a member of the GABV community. They are invited to present new ideas and take initiatives for innovation as long as these are in accordance with the guiding principles. The example of the GABV may support other organizations in aligning sustainable innovation with cultural values, leadership practices, and change strategies.

Working on a clear business idea for sustainable innovation is concerned with how organizations can retain their individual character, put their core qualities into action to realize renewal or innovation, and differentiating themselves by creating value for their customers. The key question is how a business wants to position itself and distinguish itself by creating value for customers. The example of the GABV shows that cultural changes for innovation are not just a matter for top managers and directors; the initiative can be taken from any role and any position. Innovative leaders actively involve other members of the organization and external interested parties in the articulation of a meaningful, attractive, and feasible vision of the future.

The methodology of 'Managing by Sustainable Innovational Values' may support organizations in aligning sustainable innovation with cultural values and strategic initiatives through dialogue with internal and external stakeholders. It helped the GABV to align their strategic ambitions with change processes initiated by members within the alliance.

Thematic section four
The impact perspective

11 The role of sustainable innovation in building resilience

Matthew Kensen and Dan F. Orcherton

11.1 Sustainable innovation (SI) within the concept of climate change resilience

IPCC 5th Assessment Report on Urban areas highlights the fact that although much of the early innovation in ecosystem services and green infrastructure was to address water shortages or flooding, its importance for climate change adaptation is increasingly recognized (IPCC, 2014). Innovation within the context of climate change and resilience is easily understood, and those knowledge systems (respectful acquisition and transmission thereof), regarding climate change, can be divided into two main categories:

1 Knowledge and innovation for adapting existing and new infrastructure, and
2 traditional (or indigenous) climate knowledge (ICK) that develops from consistent innovation over time, based on ancestral teachings, ways of knowing of local climate systems

According to IPCC (2014), knowledge and innovation are required for adapting existing and new buildings or infrastructure. Affordable housing appropriate for health and citizen safety are built to climate-resilient standards and with the structural integrity to protect its occupants long-term against extreme weather (UNDRR, 2019). In addition, the implementation of social safety nets (SSN) is undertaken for the urban poor that get pushed to abject poverty where even basic lives and livelihoods are under threat. SSNs provide resilience of poor-quality housing, often at risk from extreme weather. SSNs can also be enhanced via structural retrofitting, interventions that reduce risks (for instance, expanding drainage capacity to limit or remove flood risks), and non-structural interventions (including insurance). Attention to all three is more urgent where housing quality is low, where settlements are on high-risk sites, and in cities where climate change impacts are greatest, enhancing the resilience of buildings that house low-income groups will usually be expensive and may face political challenges (Roaf, Crichton, & Nicol, 2009). The range of actors in the housing sector, the myriad connections to

11.2 Vulnerability

11.2.1 Vulnerability: A conceptual framework

The concept of vulnerability has been used widely in studies relating to both social and ecological systems. The concept of vulnerability was used mainly as a powerful analytical tool for describing the state of a system's susceptibility to harm, powerlessness, and marginality of both physical and social systems, and for guiding the normative analysis of actions so to enhance well-being through risk reduction (Adger, 2006). Vulnerability has no universally accepted definition (Downing & Patwardhan, 2004). The most often used and cited definition of vulnerability was the IPCC definition where it describes vulnerability as the degree to which a system is susceptible to and is unable to cope with the adverse effects of climate change (McCarthy, Canziani, Leary, Dokken, & White, 2001). Nunn and Mimura (1997) clearly exemplify the importance of vulnerability, stating that: Anxiety among Pacific peoples about the effects of future sea-level rise comes from their past experience and familiarity with the vulnerability of their island environments. This vulnerability includes physical (material) vulnerability, typified by the low islands of unconsolidated sand and gravel, which many atoll islanders inhabit, and socioeconomic vulnerability. Many Pacific island nations have fragile economies as most of their inhabitants grow their own food. In addition, undesired environmental changes are occurring increasingly in the name of development (p. 1). The concept of vulnerability can be understood from the viewpoint of the nomenclature of vulnerable situations as well as the classification scheme for vulnerability factor, for example, the external stressors that a system is exposed to from the internal factors that determine their impacts on that system (Füssel, 2007). A system experiences both external and internal stressors, which can determine the extent of its state of vulnerability. The terms 'external' and 'internal' are sometimes used to distinguish the 'external' structural economic or social factors such as that of the human ecology, political economy, and the entitlement theory from 'internal' agency-oriented factors as investigated in access-to-assets models, crisis and conflict theory, and action theory approaches (Bohle, 2001). As an isolated example from another region, in recent studies in Northern Canada, Petersen et al. (2014) highlighted the importance of vulnerability within a climate change concept, and the distinctions between climate exposure, sensitivity and Adaptive Capacity (Figure 11.1).

Climate *vulnerability* is the degree to which a system is susceptible to, or unable to cope with, adverse effects of climate change, including climate variability and extremes (Figure 11.1). Climate vulnerability depends on

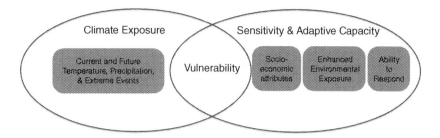

Figure 11.1 Climate *vulnerability* (IPCC, 2014).

exposure, sensitivity, and adaptive capacity. **Climate exposure** is the extent and magnitude of a climate and weather event. **Sensitivity** is the degree to which the area of concern is susceptible to a climate impact. **Adaptive capacity** it the ability of the area of concern to adjust or respond to the changing conditions.

In this study, Petersen et al. (2014) presented a framework for assessing the vulnerability of each key area of concern using the criteria of sensitivity and adaptive capacity (as defined above). The most vulnerable areas have the highest sensitivity and the lowest adaptive capacity. The least vulnerable areas have the lowest sensitivity and the highest adaptive capacity and McNamara and Buggy (2017), emphasized the emergence of community-based adaptation (CBA), driven by a number of factors: recognition of the human dimensions of changes; appreciation of the role of local knowledge for strengthening adaptive capacity; and a push to focus on the scale at which impacts are felt and link this action with pro-poor development outcomes (p. 1). Culturally and socioeconomically, the term "Innovation" in many parts of the Pacific Islands, therefore, denotes a blending of (locally focused) community-based or Regional levels of vulnerability and on-the-ground adaptation as focal points of community-based adaption (CBA). Community-based vulnerability and adaptation trials directly involving communities were tested in Fiji and surrounding Islands and atolls, as part of the work done by the Pacific Centre of Environment and Sustainable Development (PACE-SD) at The University of the South Pacific (Limalevu, 2012; McNamara, Hemstock, & Holland, 2012, 2015). The 'PACE-SD Methodology' as it was coined, relied on a comprehensive community-led participatory assessment that guided communities through a process in which to identify appropriate and sustainable activities to enhance their adaptive capacity to the impacts of climate change. Once a community has been identified to partake in climate change adaptation activities (based on the PACE-SD Rapid Assessment; (Limalevu, 2012), this V&A assessment was carried out. This implied that the project assessment team would have already visited the site during the process of site selection and would have some knowledge of the community and its vulnerability to the adverse impacts of climate change from the information gathered.

The V&A assessment usually takes between one to two days per community to complete, depending on weather conditions, and the availability of community members and leaders at the time of the visit.

The potential (for example) of vulnerability matrices or community-led participatory assessments, informs us of the complexities and possibilities that conceptually must be taken into consideration when researchers or authors 'describe' vulnerabilities specific to the Pacific Islands and the Caribbean, or other coastal regions with similar complexities as they relate to urban or rural populations or built environments. According to Allen (2014), in efforts to move forward with a local approach to addressing climate change under these circumstances, requires careful assessment of scientific data, conceptualization of meaningful impacts, and targeted prioritization and action (Allen, 2014).

11.2.1.1 Reducing vulnerability in urban centers and cities

Urban innovation is a key component of vulnerability as it relates to built environments. Lankao and Qin (2011) argue that just as the term 'vulnerability' is defined differently by different schools of vulnerability studies, current studies on urban vulnerability are based on different interpretations and paradigms which led on to the development of the three lineages of urban vulnerability study (Figure 11.1). The three lineages of urban vulnerability study assembled the urban vulnerability studies into three groups, namely, (1) urban vulnerability as impact, (2) inherent urban vulnerability and (3) urban resilience. It is thus important to understand the growth of urban vulnerability studies over the years and their categorization into the three lineages of urban vulnerability studies. The three lineages of urban vulnerability are discussed more in detail below:

11.2.2 Urban vulnerability as an impact

Urban vulnerability is perceived as an outcome in this lineage of urban vulnerability research. Studies within the natural hazards tradition conceive urban vulnerability to natural disasters as an outcome where the physical vulnerability of urban infrastructures, populations or activities are determined by their *sensitivity* to and their *exposure* to natural hazards resulting in the potential impacts (Blaikie, Cannon, Davis, & Wisner, 2014; Cutter, Boruff, & Shirley, 2003; Cutter & Finch, 2008; Godschalk, 2003; Pelling, 2003b; Romero-Lankao & Qin, 2011). These last authors pointed out the two types of research within this lineage, where the first explores how changes in parameters such as temperature and precipitation relates to impacts such as mortality and the second applies a scaled-down version of global change scenarios to urban centers to model how parameters such as temperature increases or sea-level rise will evolve in the future.

The first research type also explores how complex factors such as age, gender, and socioeconomic status affect the relationship between the hazard and the health impact (Bell et al., 2008; Grass & Cane, 2008; O'Neill, Zanobetti, & Schwartz, 2005). Other studies have also examined the geographical characteristics of urban settlements such as low elevation and proximity to coastal zones that makes city dwellers, especially the poor population to be vulnerable to the impacts of climatic and environmental changes (Bhattarai & Conway, 2010; CLACC, 2009; McGranahan, Balk, & Anderson, 2007; Prasad et al., 2009).

The second research type in this lineage on urban vulnerability uses climate change scenarios such as future climate hazards, for example, urban heat island effects, storm surges, and heat waves to estimate their impacts (Haines, Kovats, Campbell-Lendrum, & Corvalan, 2006; McCarthy et al., 2001; Romero-Lankao & Qin, 2011; Vörösmarty, 2000). In some cases, adaptation options were also explored under plausible socioeconomic scenarios to see how those impacts can be reduced (Kirshen et al., 2007; Knowlton et al., 2007; Nicholls et al., 2007; Rosenzweig et al., 2011; Sterr, 2008; Wilby, 2008). The *urban vulnerability as impact* lineage as discussed above addresses the issues of urban exposure and sensitivity to changes in hazards (Figure 11.2).

This figure depicts the evolution of research on urban vulnerability over time. The lighter-colored arrows represent narrower and more conventional studies, while the darker-colored arrows represent recent efforts within each lineage to converge with other traditions and develop a more integrated understanding of the different dimensions and determinants of urban vulnerability.

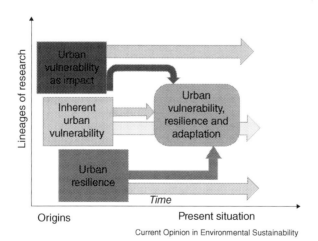

Figure 11.2 Lineages of urban innovation in vulnerability research.
Source: Adopted from Romero-Lankao and Qin (2011).

11.2.3 Inherent urban vulnerability

Inherent urban vulnerability lineage explores the questions as to how and why particular cities or populations are more vulnerable than others or more able to cope or adapt than others and by doing so they tend to differ in their scope of analysis and intervention (Romero-Lankao & Qin, 2011; Romero-Lankao, Qin, & Dickinson, 2012). Inherent or contextual vulnerability has evolved from livelihoods, political economy and later political ecology approaches (Adger, 2006; Eakin & Luers, 2006). For example, a livelihoods focus highlights the need to explore and reassert the building of assets at the individual, family and community level such as self-help housing and is seen as a fundamental mechanism to allow individuals and households to cope with the hazards they encounter (Moser & Satterthwaite, 2008; Pelling, 2003b; Wilbanks et al., 2007). It is yet problematic to up-scale these individual attempts to reduce vulnerability to the city level. This means that an individual attempt to reduce vulnerability does not in any way reduce the vulnerability of urban areas (Romero-Lankao & Qin, 2011). Recent research has focused on urban areas in the middle-income and low-income countries, which are thought to be affected more by the impacts of global climate and environmental change due to development and governance failures (Parnell, Simon, & Vogel, 2007; Wilbanks et al., 2007) (Figure 11.3).

Vulnerability is a function of (exposure × sensitivity) less the adaptive capacity of the community. As cities of high density get hit by natural disasters

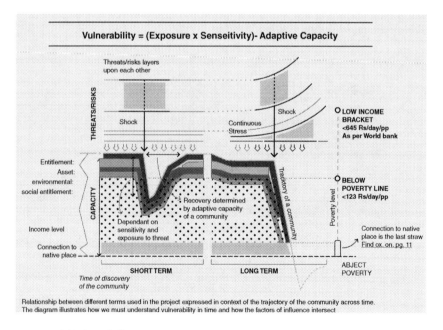

Figure 11.3 Vulnerability.
Source: Retrieved from Sensing Local-Urban Poverty (2007) https://www.sensinglocal.in/copy-of-urban-vulnerability.

or socioeconomic crises, it is urban poor that get pushed to abject poverty where even basic life and livelihood is under threat.

All these innovation studies seek to answer questions such as which urban areas are vulnerable, *who* within a city is vulnerable, and *how* and *why* particular urban populations are vulnerable. By doing so, this lineage of urban innovation in vulnerability helps to discover the common and diverse patterns including the processes in both direct and underlying socioeconomic and institutional determinants of urban vulnerability (Romero-Lankao & Qin, 2011). However, *urban inherent vulnerability* differs from the *urban vulnerability as an outcome* in several ways. Rather than viewing urban vulnerability as the end point of a linear process, the *urban inherent vulnerability* sees vulnerability as a dynamic process based on the decreasing ability of a city or its populations to cope with societal and environmental hazards and stresses. This decreasing ability is driven by the underlying socioeconomic and institutional factors such as the pathways of urban development and structural adjustment policies (Adger & Kelly, 1999; Romero-Lankao & Qin, 2011; Turner II et al., 2003). Research on the inherent urban vulnerability also has some limitations in its contributions to the understanding of the determinants of vulnerabilities across and within cities. One of the main shortfalls of this study is that in an attempt to illustrate the underlying socioeconomic and political dynamics that determines urban vulnerability, they also provide descriptions of inequities in resources distribution and access (Morello-Frosch, Jr, Porras, & Sadd, 2002; Sharkey, 2007) that lacks the provision of the whole sequence on how those changing inequities relate to differential impacts and susceptibility over time (Eakin & Luers, 2006) (Figure 11.4).

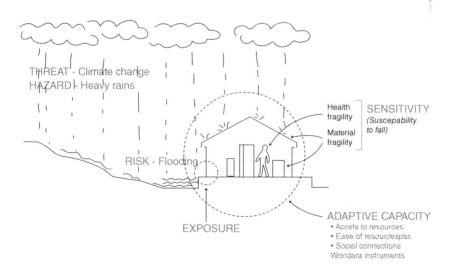

Figure 11.4 Social safety nets.
Source: Retrieved from Sensing Local-Urban Poverty (2007) https://www.sensinglocal.in/copy-of-urban-vulnerability.

Social safety nets in place by governments, however limited, are largely compensatory innovative instruments to help the affected, rather than protective instruments to safeguard the vulnerable from risks. They lack mechanisms to bridge the gap between critical points of weakness in vulnerable communities and help them become more resilient. 11.2.4 Innovative urban resilience in SIDS

Urban innovation in the face of climate change denotes building an *urban resilience* lineage. It has been documented that urban vulnerability studies move away from the traditional urban vulnerability to *a response capacity building* in an attempt to explore vulnerability and resilience as two overlapping inherent properties of urban areas which are people and places. It is the interaction of these properties with natural hazards and the coping and adaptation responses that can help reduce or enhance accumulative disaster impacts in urban areas. Different approaches to resilience such as the notion of tipping points have been used in recent studies to shed some light on the mechanisms that trigger short and long-term processes that shape the socio-economic and political threshold changes in urban areas (Resilience Alliance, 2016). In this lineage, disaster and resilience were observed to have a symbolic dimension where the urban actors' ability to recover and revive from natural disasters cannot be separated from their political history and cultural values and thus, resilience is always contested and conflict-ridden and is a function of power around which winners and losers emerge (Campanella, 2006; Romero-Lankao & Qin, 2011). This lineage has also contributed to the understanding of the human-environmental systems and how they allow or constrain their ability to cope with hazards and stresses. There are, however, some constraints in translating and contextualizing the concept of resilience to the analysis of urban vulnerability to climatic and environmental changes as reflected by some recent studies (Sherbinin, Schiller, & Pulsipher, 2007). Romero-Lankao and Qin (2011) stressed that the difficulties are often attributed to its (resilience's) socio-ecological systems version where resilience appears as a system's attribute of urban communities and regions and does not acknowledge the role of humans. This means that it does not see that rather than being passive receptors of stress, NGO's, organizations, households, and individuals are actively responding to and shaping the stresses and opportunities that are being presented to them by global climate and environmental change (Romero-Lankao & Qin, 2011).

11.3 Challenges involved in developing vulnerability indicators

Developing vulnerability indicators has proven to be a challenging practice. Defining *what* is to be indicated is one of the important phases in vulnerability indicator development. In the case of vulnerability to natural hazards, this would involve the vulnerability of an entity to natural hazards. There is a wide range of different and varying entities such as individuals,

The role of sustainable innovation   193

households, villages, communities, ecosystems, countries, regions and economic sectors are considered. In general, these entities can be conceptualized as socio-ecological systems (Gallopin, 1991) or they can be coupled as a human-environmental system (Turner II et al., 2003) as vulnerability is defined by the social or human and ecological or environmental sub-system interactions. The term 'system' is used by Hinkel (2008) as a synonym for an entity. Hence, defining an entity will subsequently involve defining a system's boundaries. Hinkel (2008) discusses two (2) unique challenges that correspond to the development of vulnerability indicators. The first was the difficulty that lies in defining exactly what the vulnerability entity is, particularly referring to the confusion that arises from the scale of the entity. Assessments have been made on systems with wider boundaries, for example, the vulnerability of a region or a country including their economic sectors and social groups to climate-related hazards and other hazards. On the contrary, local assessments that target individuals need to take account of the wide institutional, economic, political and social contexts that determines vulnerability, as expressed by the concept of "contextual vulnerability" (O'Brien, Eriksen, Nygaard, & Schjolden, 2007). The second challenge lies is in the forward-looking aspect of vulnerability when developing vulnerability indicators. Most indicators indicate a current state of vulnerability and not the potentiality of a future state (Birkmann, 2007; Eriksen & Kelly, 2007; Patt, Schröter, De La Vega-Leinert, & Klein, 2008) such as the HDI that was used to indicate the current state of development rather than the possibility of future development. Therefore, Hinkel (2011) proposed that developing vulnerability indicators must involve building a predictive model that will not only indicate the harm involved but also the vulnerability of a system to future harms in that it includes both the forward-looking aspect as well as the normative aspect of defining harm.

11.4 Conclusion

This exhaustive yet focused literature review, has attempted to review the concept of vulnerability, its assessments, analysis, and measurements together with vulnerability indicators as a way forward for measuring vulnerability to natural, technological and climatic hazards. The review also identifies the need to design and develop social vulnerability indicators that incorporate urban form categories for SIDS pertaining to natural disasters and climate change impacts on urban centers in SIDS. However, as highlighted in the literature review, one of the most obvious challenges in developing vulnerability indicators is its applicability, operability, and issues related to its downscaling to different scales of analysis to suit a specific study areas or specific social, cultural or institutional contexts. Previous studies that use case studies (Huang, Li, Bai, & Cui, 2012; Shah, Dulal, Johnson, & Baptiste, 2013) to develop vulnerability indicators fail to incorporate issues experienced in SIDS into the design and development of social vulnerability indicators to natural, technological, environmental and climate-related hazards. The dynamics within the social, economic, environmental, and political dimensions of SIDS are highly significant and needed to be explored and understood comprehensively as they have an impact on vulnerability indicators. Having an understanding of these dynamics can shed some light on how vulnerability indicators can be better designed, developed, and applied to suit certain geographical extents. A lack of integrating social and urban form issues faced in SIDS into formulating vulnerability indicators urges the need to have more clear and concise vulnerability indicators that can represent wholly the vulnerabilities experienced in urban centers in SIDS and thus the need for this research.

After exploring the use of green growth terminology as it relates to its widespread use in the Pacific, governments across the region have incorporated references to the green growth in National Development Plans and have advocated for improved environmental stewardship in international fora. International and regional nongovernmental organizations have increasingly deployed the term in their advocacy work. Green growth terminology now also informs the work of regional organizations, with a new regional agency having been established to promote the concept, and with the blue economy at the heart of the most recent key statement of regional identity (Dornan, Morgan, Cain, & Tarte, 2018).

12 Strategic or symbolic?

A descriptive analysis of the application of social impact measurement in Dutch charity organizations

Carly Relou and Frank Hubers

12.1 Introduction

Calls for professionalization and improved effectiveness of the charity sector have been raised more frequently in recent years. As a result, charity organizations are increasingly concerned with measuring and demonstrating their social impact (Ebrahim, 2019; Rogers & Weiss, 2007). This development means a shift away from focusing on output monitoring to improve efficiency, to outcome monitoring to improve effectiveness. Social Impact Management, which includes approaches such as Theories of Change, logic models and impact evaluations, is now widely advocated by philanthropic foundations and multilateral organizations. There is a strong belief that measuring impact enhances organizational learning, by providing information about which projects are successful and could be scaled up, and which ones are not and should be adjusted or discontinued. As information about social impact enables strategic decision making and organizational learning (Poister, Pitts, & Hamilton Edwards, 2010) it should guide charities to maximize their social impact (Coryn, Noakes, Westine, & Schröter, 2011).

However, institutional theory tells us that external pressure can force institutions to adopt policies that are not necessarily in their best strategic interests (DiMaggio & Powell, 1983). The wide adoption of impact measurement practices in the charity sector is thus by no means is an indicator of their strategic value. It could be a result of the charities' need to comply with increasing demands from donors and the public to demonstrate their impact. Implementing impact measurement is costly. Not only are there direct costs of performing impact management, but it also requires an organizational culture that stimulates learning and evidence-based decision making. Previous research demonstrates that external pressures on charity organizations can lead to a process of 'decoupling' in which the content of the social impact reports and the actual projects deviates significantly (Arvidson & Lyon, 2014). Moreover, there is some evidence that budget allocation for impact measurement is mostly driven by external pressures, whereas the actual use of impact measurement is driven by staff and board motivation (Barman & MacIndoe, 2012; MacIndoe & Barman, 2013).

196   *Carly Relou and Frank Hubers*

In this study, we propose a typology of practices of impact measurement, with the objective to differentiate between charities that merely use it symbolically and those that have actively adopted it to develop, adjust and refine a strategy to reach long-term objective. We base the typology on a wide range of literature on impact measurement and apply it to a sample of charity organizations. For this, we used survey data of over 450 registered Dutch charity organizations. This study provides insight into how charities use impact measurement practices. We find that only six out of ten of the charities that claim to measure their impact, can provide a coherent logic model, indicating their impact strategy. That implies that four out of ten charities were not able to logically connect their current activities to their long-term objectives. Only one out of ten organizations could be considered learning organizations: organizations that learn from or use evidence. Surprisingly, there is not much difference in the application of impact measurement practices among different non-profit sectors, although the size of the organizations matters: Larger organizations are more likely to adopt impact measurement for learning purposes.

This study is structured as follows. Section 12.2 provides an overview of the literature on impact measurement. Based on this review, we propose a typology that we describe at end of the section. In Section 12.3, we describe our data, survey process and sample. Section 12.4 shows the main results of this analysis. Section 12.5 concludes.

12.2 Measuring impact

12.2.1 Defining impact

Demonstrating the social impact of an organization is a challenge, not in the last place because of the increased pressures on charities to do so. Despite the increased popularity of social impact, there is still little consensus on the definition of the concept. The academic literature is dispersed, with different disciplines having different interpretations of the concept. There is limited empirical evidence to suggest that measuring impact will improve the allocation of charities' resources to more effective approaches. Clearly, the field of impact measurement is undertheorized (Ebrahim, 2009; Ebrahim & Rangan, 2014). Consequently, there are some very different perspectives on what impact measurement is and how charity organizations should use it.

There are many, often conflicting, definitions of impact measurement [see for example Maas and Liket (2011) for an overview]. One commonly applied definition comes from OECD/DAC, which describes impact as the "positive and negative, primary and secondary long-term effects produced by an [...] intervention, directly or indirectly, intended or unintended.[1]" Hulme (2000) defines impact as the "portion of the total outcome that happened as a result of the activity of an organization, above and beyond what would have happened anyway" which puts a stronger emphasis on causality than the definition of

OECD/DAC. Roche is more explicit about the type of change that should be achieved; he defines impact as "the lasting or significant changes in people's lives brought about by a particular intervention" (1999, p. 22). Despite the ambiguity of the concept, there are a few characteristics of social impact that appear in most definitions. First, social impact is the long-term result of an intervention. This long-term result has a certain value for society, although there are different perspectives on what constitutes as social value and who decides when it is significant. Another important characteristic is that impact is the causal effect of an intervention. We will discuss these characteristics and their influence on the debate on impact measurement below.

12.2.1.1 Long-term results and logic models

The idea of impact as a long-term result has its roots in programme planning and design. The appearance of the Logical Framework Approach (LFA) or Logframes in the development sector in 1969 by USAID meant the start of the wide usage of logic models in the development sector (Dale, 2003; Frumkin, 2010; Prinsen & Nijhof, 2015). The instrument that can be used for strategic planning and monitoring of development projects, divides the results of an intervention into short-, medium- and long-term results. This division is now commonly referred to as a logic model or results chain. Since the introduction of LFA in international aid, it has spread to other domains of the non-profit sector (Carman, 2009; Hall, 2014). LFA was soon adopted by multilateral donor organizations, and many funders still require a logic model in some form (Ringhofer & Kohlweg, 2019). As a result, logic models have become a central component impact measurement in charities.

Logframes were strongly criticized for their binary nature and lack of flexibility (Dale, 2003; Gasper, 2000; Prinsen & Nijhof, 2015). Because LFAs were mandatory in receiving funding from donor agencies, they were increasingly used for compliance rather than learning. This led to variety of other approaches that despite their greater flexibility, kept the idea of visualizing the (expected) results of an intervention in a logic model, containing short-, medium- and long-term objectives. Newer versions of the logic model visualize how interventions are expected to bring about long-term results through specifying inputs, activities, outputs, outcomes and the ensuing impact. The general assumption behind this is that a particular input (money, resources) will result (through activities) in a particular output, which will in turn lead to a particular outcome that then has a particular impact (Ebrahim, 2019; Hatton & Schroeder, 2007). As shown in Figure 12.1, impact is the effect expected to happen at the end of the impact chain. The further one goes

Figure 12.1 Steps in the logic model or results chain.

up in the chain however, the more the results are affected by external social, political and economic influences, and the greater the risk is that the intended results cannot be realized.

One of the most popular of these approaches is the Theory of Chance (ToC). As with the LFA, a ToC is a way to identify the causal link between the long-term objectives of and its (potential) projects, by identifying all intermediate steps. The LFA has a fixed number of steps, with each step accompanied by measurable indicators and a binary logic to achieve the next step. A ToC aims to identify every step or assumption that is required to get from the activities of the organization to achieve the desired impact. The ToC thus provides a theory with assumptions that can be verified and evaluated. Moreover, the process of designing a ToC could lead to new insight because of the identification of illogical and/or unproven assumptions (Prinsen & Nijhof, 2015). The assumptions in a ToC should also preferably be evidence-based (Brest, 2010; Weiss, 1995).

Most authors agree that an organization's intended impact should align with its social mission as the organization's mission statement reflects the ultimate social problem the organization intends to address (Ebrahim, 2019; Ebrahim & Rangan, 2014). A logic model specifies and visualizes how the activities are supposed to lead to the intended impact. A disadvantage of this focus on the organization's long-term objectives, is that it could overlook the perspective of the beneficiaries. Several authors claim that only the beneficiaries are able to determine whether the achieved impact is actually valuable (Chambers, 1994, 2009; Dart & Davies, 2003).

12.2.1.2 Evaluation

Whereas logic models are important in the design phase of an intervention, (ex-post) evaluations are important in the understanding of whether these results are realized. Evaluating the social impact of an intervention is methodologically challenging. Organizations only have limited control over realizing the social changes they aim to achieve due the influence of external factors (Ebrahim, 2019; Ebrahim & Rangan, 2014). This complicates determining a causal relation between activities—that what the organization is doing—and the resulting impact—the social change that the organization aims to achieve. In order to understand if and to what extent social impact is brought about by an organization's activities, it is necessary to know what would have happened if the intervention had not been implemented. This is considered as one of the core problems in impact evaluation and is often referred to as the counterfactual problem (Angrist & Pischke, 2008; Blundell & Costa Dias, 2000; Duflo & Kremer, 2005; Harrison & List, 2004).

The most common strategy to address the counterfactual problem is to form a control group of some kind: a group of individuals who in absence of the intervention would have had similar outcomes as the individuals that received the intervention, had they not received the intervention. However, simply comparing the group of participants with another group of individuals often leads to biased results, because of (self-) selection effects. The most valid approach to address this bias is via process of randomization in a randomized control trial (RCT) (Duflo & Kremer, 2005) or a field experiment (Harrison & List, 2004; List, 2007, 2011). In this approach, participants are randomly selected to participate in the intervention. Any changes in outcomes between these groups can then be confidently attributed to the programme (Angrist & Pischke, 2008). Randomized experiments have the highest validity and are therefore often referred to as 'The Golden Standard'. In practice, however, randomized field experiments are not always feasible, logistically complicated or too expensive. Alternative options are natural experiments, which exploit an exogenous shock: a third variable that it is correlated with the independent variable (whether or not the individual benefitted) but unrelated to any other endogenous characteristics of the individual[2] (Angrist & Pischke, 2008; Banerjee & Duflo, 2009; Newey & Powell, 2003). A more commonly applied method is the differences-in-differences (DD) approach, in which two groups of individuals are compared over time. The DD model assumes that the group of individuals that received the treatment would have followed a similar time trend as the control group. This is a strong assumption to make, for which the DD strategy is often criticized (Bertrand, Duflo, & Mullainathan, 2004).

An alternative approach to social impact assessment is using qualitative methods. Although these are popular among practitioners, they have a lower validity and are less reliable than the quantitative approaches mentioned above. Qualitative techniques find their origin in the humanities tradition. Their main features are an inductive approach, a focus on key informants, use of non-standardized interviews and storytelling, and a data analyst generally directly involved in data collection (Hulme, 2000). Although these techniques lack the rigour needed to make any valid statements about cause and effect, they are widely applied in impact assessments because of their relatively low costs and easy application. Moreover, storytelling is a popular strategy to visualize impact for fundraising and marketing purposes. There is substantial evidence that identifiable victims are often more appealing to the generable public than statistics (Karlan & Wood, 2017; Small, Loewenstein, & Slovic, 2007), making it more useful for marketing and fundraising purposes.

12.2.2 Learning and accountability

The question on how rigorous an impact evaluation should be and what approaches should be used is not merely a methodological one. The choice of method is largely determined by a certain the perspective on organizational learning and effectiveness, but it also is the result of institutional pressures forcing the organization to use a specific approach.

12.2.2.1 Organizational learning

The debate about the required rigor to evaluate interventions and learn about effectiveness, results in different beliefs and perspectives about how evaluations are best conducted and what type of knowledge can be generated from evaluation.

First, proponents of the *Effective giving* or *What Works Movement* argue that research validity can only be attained as long as rigorous scientific methods are used for impact evaluation (Hall, 2014). By establishing plausible causal links between activities and outcomes, organizations can learn about the effectiveness of interventions (White, 2019). The movement has resulted in several initiatives that aim to make evidence available to charities so it can be used in the planning phase of projects, for example to support the logic model. Since the early 2000s many impact evaluations have been carried out (many are done by affiliates of Abdul Latif Jameel Poverty Action Lab (J-PAL)). Duflo, Banerjee and Kremer, early advocates of this approach, won the Nobel Prize in Economic Sciences in 2019, underlining the influence of this movement. The evidence resulting from rigorous quantitative methods is gathered evidence in portals such as by International Initiative for Impact Evaluation (3ie) and the Campbell Collaboration to make them accessible. Other initiatives, such as Innovations for Poverty Action (IPA), wish to further connect as practitioners to existing evidence. These efforts are rooted in the idea that most interventions are not effective—rough estimates are at 80%—and that if existing evidence of effectiveness is used in planning the risk of spending money on interventions that do not deliver on outcomes is thwarted (White, 2019). When an intervention is promising but there is no evidence to support it, *Effective Giving* advocates would argue that the interventions should be tested and evaluated for it to estimate the impact.

Opposed to these rigorous methods is the view that outcomes emerge from a complex system of interactions, making causality intertwined and non-linear (Kurtz & Snowden, 2003). The approach is based on a view that contexts are diverse, interventions cannot be standardized or researched in isolation, causes of problems are multiple and control groups are rarely reliable, as there are many causal factors at play (Mayoux & Chambers, 2005). Therefore, causality between interventions and outcomes can never be established. Chambers argues that for this type of organization, learning requires an understanding of the experienced realities of beneficiaries' lives (2009, 2017). As these realities are more complex than can be expressed in measurable indicators, it is essential to capture stories of individuals who are targeted by an intervention (Chambers, 1994, 2009; Dart & Davies, 2003). The approach has fewer expectations of what results will be achieved than quantitative methods, allowing for more opportunity to detect unintended and unexpected effects (Chambers, 1994, 2009; Dart & Davies, 2003). According to this view, learning should emerge during implementation in each context (Chambers, 2017).

Taking the middle ground between these two views, is Ebrahim's classification of interventions based on two contingencies, causal uncertainty and charities' control over outcomes (2019, p. 35). He argues that the usefulness of a method (rigorous versus participatory) for the charity organization, depends on where the intervention of the charity organization is situated on these two contingencies. When the causal uncertainty is low, such as in basic health or sanitation services, organizations can learn from existing evidence about effectiveness, whereas in a high causal uncertainty environment, it is not possible to know which activities should be carried out to achieve results, for example in advocacy or human rights campaigns. Organizations that work in high causal uncertainty environments can at most expect to make claims about influence can be established (Ebrahim, 2019, p. 40). The control an organization has over outcomes depends on the complexity of interventions, such as the order in which they are implemented and their interaction, and on external factors, such as social or economic changes. In a high control environment, interventions are typically expected to result in linear change, so it is possible to measure outcomes. In environments where control over outcomes is low, for example because it aims at change at institutional or community level in which many forces and decision makers play a role, change will not occur linearly. For low control interventions, qualitative approaches and complex systems thinking as mentioned above are recommended (Ebrahim & Rangan, 2010).

12.2.2.2 Accountability

The primary reason that most non-profit organizations have increased their expenditure on impact measurement over the years is for accountability purposes (Ebrahim, 2003, 2005; MacIndoe & Barman, 2013). Accountability can be described as the means by which an organization reports to authorities and is held responsible for its actions (Edwards & Hulme, 1996). For charity organizations, with their high dependency on fundraising, multiple stakeholders and their moral obligation to "do good," accountability becomes a particularly difficult issue. Many authors have noticed that for non-profit organizations more accountability often leads to less organizational learning (Ebrahim, 2005). We will explore this apparent paradox in this section.

It was long assumed that more accountability is a good thing: The more transparent charities are about their spending, the more likely it is they invest wisely, and the more social impact is made. Many charities are accountable to numerous actors; each with its own accountability requirements (Lu Knutsen & Brower, 2010). Charities are dependent on fundraising, and their donors, whether they are small private donors or big multilateral organizations, want to know how their money is spent. As a result, the charity might be forced to report on their impact report via a Logframe for one funder, via a ToC to another, and will be required to evaluate one project with qualitative and another project with more rigorous approaches. These reporting requirements only describe upward accountability: the accountability towards the institutions on which the charities are financially dependent, like governments, private donors or multilateral organizations. Many argue that charities have a moral obligation to be downwardly accountable, or accountable towards their beneficiaries (Ebrahim, 2009). This is one of the motivations behind using participatory impact assessments, although it is often noted that the use these participatory methods alone is insufficient for ensuring downward accountability (Roche, 1999). Resource dependency theory predicts that, as a result of the power inequality between patrons and charities, charities will be more willing to invest upward than downward accountability.

The idea that accountability will lead to better performance and organizational learning has been brought into question by several scholars (Ebrahim, 2003, 2005; Roche, 1999) and the ideas of organizational learning and accountability are often put in juxtaposition. For example, Ebrahim (2005) argues that non-profit organizations could be hindered in achieving their long-term objectives by too much accountability. He claims that the accountability demands of different donors will lead to myopia, a preference on achieving short-term results over long-term goals and compliance to the requirements over organizational learning.

12.2.2.3 Institutional pressure

Institutional theory would predict that the accountability pressures on charities could eventually lead to a situation in which all charities would be demonstrating their impact without any organizational learning. In their famous contribution to institutional theory, DiMaggio and Powell (1983) argue that organizational practices are becoming more homogeneous through structuration of organizational fields and their striving for legitimacy, rather than competition and need for efficiency. This is particularly true for organizations with less measurable outcomes, like charities and other non-profit organizations. Coercive isomorphism, which is the result of institutional pressures on organizations to comply with certain societal expectations, may explain the adoption of social impact measurement practices. Coercive pressures include legislation and accountability expectations that organizations tend to conform in order to maintain or regain their legitimacy. This implies also that adopting the impact measurement practices is not necessarily beneficial to the organizations in the long run, but rather a strategy to safeguard their resources. Institutional theory could also explain why the choice of impact measurement tools also follows trends. For example, within a relatively short time period, Logframes fell out of favour with practitioners (Gasper, 2000) and were increasingly replaced by ToCs (Dale, 2003; Prinsen & Nijhof, 2015).

Besides compliance, there are other strategies that organizations might use to coop with these increasing accountability pressures. Meyer and Rowan (1977) describe a process of *organizational decoupling* as a coping mechanism to comply to an increasing number of rules that have no competitive advantage for the organization. They define decoupling as separating formal structure from practice. This implies that an organization can formally comply with requirements but follow different practices in reality. Arvidson and Lyon (2014) provide some evidence that this also applies for impact measurement in charity organizations. Using qualitative data, they find that decoupling is one of the strategies that charities use to cope with the increasing reporting pressures. They notice that not all charities simply accept or reject impact measurement requests from their funders, but that they choose a third option. These are the charities that are reluctant to comply to these requests, but fear damaging the relationship with the funder as well. This is symbolic compliance with minimal reporting. They might regard social impact measurement as an additional bureaucratic burden rather than a useful set of tools for organizational learning.

12.2.3 A typology on the application of social impact measurement

Our study aims to shed light on how charity organizations measure their impact and use the resulting data for learning and decision making. In this subsection we propose a typology for the use of impact measurement ranging from minimum reporting to having fully implemented impact measurement as a tool for organizational learning. Our typology distinguishes three types, with each type indicating a higher stage of development of impact measurement. This approach is inspired by Speckbacher, Bischof, and Pfeiffer (2003) who developed a typology for the use of the Balanced Scorecard (BSC), each type indicative of stages of development of the concept and implementation of the instrument. Whereas a typology for the use of BSC could be deduced by analyzing the work of its developers Kaplan and Norton, the impact literature is more ambiguous. Unlike BSC, there are no formal definitions or requirements of what good impact measurement practices are. Our proposed typology is based upon the wide range of impact literature:

12.2.3.1 Type 1: Symbolic logic model

This is the group that complies with the minimum requirements of having a logic model, but the logic model follows a faulty logic and/or is incoherent. Almost all literature agrees that impact measurement starts with some kind of logic model (Ebrahim, 2019; Gertler, Martinez, Premand, Rawlings, & Vermeersch, 2016; Ringhofer & Kohlweg, 2019; Stame, 2004; White, 2009), since it demonstrates that the organization has long-term objectives (impact-focused) and conducts activities that should lead to these objectives [at least in theory] (White, 2014). If the project does not logically contribute to the long-term goals or does not contribute to the mission, we consider it a Type 1 organization. In these cases, there is a logic model present, but the cause–effect relations are faulty. As Arvidson and Lyon (2014) demonstrate, the charity might have felt that the use of a logic model is forced upon them through accountability requirements or other institutional pressures. Instead of outright rejection of these requirements, they might go for the minimum reporting standard as a form of decoupling. A logic model will not guide decision making. Rather, we expect to see a project (that was already designed before the logic model was drawn up) that does not logically lead to the long-term goals.

12.2.3.2 Type 2: Coherent logic model

A logic model serves as the foundation for impact measurement within an organization. The coherent logic model indicates that the charity sets long-term objectives has a strategy to reach these. If the logic model is logically correct and clearly contributes to the mission, we consider the charity to be a Type 2 organization. The activities and projects of the charity logically lead to the outputs, outcomes and impact. The expected impact is aligned with the social mission of the organization.

12.2.3.3 Type 3: Learning organization

An organization that is serious about achieving its impact could be expected to evaluate their projects and be willing to adjust their projects when necessary. Evaluations should be used to test whether the activities indeed lead to the expected impact as described in the logic model (Weiss, 1995; White, 2009). Ideally, a logic model should be supported by evidence for the assumptions that are made and stakeholders, such as beneficiaries, should be invited to contribute to the validation of the logic model. An evaluation study should be conducted at the end of the project to determine whether the expected impact was realized. The organization learns from the conclusions of the evaluation and is willing to adjust its strategy accordingly (Chambers, 2009; Gertler et al., 2016; Stame, 2004; White, 2009).

In summary, an organization can progress from Type 2 to Type 3 if it has a system of learning and evaluation in place. Type 3 organizations use impact measurement practices voluntarily. Arvidson and Lyon (2014) show that even reluctant charities may eventually appreciate the value of impact measurement.

12.3 Data

This is an exploratory study, based on a survey data from a representative sample of Dutch charity organizations. Using the typology above, we explore how charities apply impact measurement within their organization.

12.3.1 Survey

The data were collected in collaboration with the Netherlands Fundraising Regulator (CBF).[3] CBF is an independent foundation that audits and certifies charity organizations on voluntary basis. In 2019, we collaborated with CBF which allowed us to add some additional questions to their yearly survey on social impact measurement.

The survey was sent out to all 547 charities that are certified by CBF. All respondents were asked to fill out an online survey. The majority of these questions were open-ended and could take some time to answer. We requested that the surveys were filled out by those in the organization most knowledgeable about impact measurement. Respondents were encouraged to base their answers on a best practice project or programme of their own choosing. The survey included both open and closed questions about impact measurement. The survey included four sections:

- Section I about the logic model, in which a basic template of a logic model was provided to be filled out by the respondents
- Section II about the use of evidence; sources of evidence and which part of the logic model is supported by evidence
- Section III about context: alternative solutions, awareness of other charities' approaches and the needs of the beneficiaries
- Section IV about evaluation and learning from evaluation

Open questions about the steps in the logic model were coded independently by two research assistants who were familiar with the concept of logic model. They received a training in coding steps in the logic model as logical or illogical based on research data from the previous year. As a part of the training they both coded 40 randomly selected charities. The codes they assigned were compared and discussed with one of the main researchers to ensure the coding criteria were clear to both. The open responses of the remaining charities were coded by one research assistant, each coding approximately half. As a final check of consistency in the coding, a z-test was used to compare the samples each of the research assistants coded. This revealed no significant differences between them.

12.3.2 Sample

The survey was sent out to 547 charities, to which 450 charities responded (a response rate of 82.3%). Our sample consists of a wide variety of charity organizations, working on a wide scale of social problems, and ranging from the very small to the very large. They have in common that they are fundraising charity organizations. Table 12.1 provides an overview of the sample of organizations in terms of size and sector. Although we do not have exact data about the size of each in organization in terms of annual budget, we know in which one of four categories of size each is. Category A contains the smallest charities: those with an annual budget of less than 100,000 euro. Category D contains the largest organizations: charities with an annual budget of more than 2 million euro. The frequency and proportion of each category are shown in Columns (1)–(4). Our sample has a good representation of each category, with only Category C (those with an annual budget between 500k and 2 million euro) a bit underrepresented.

206   *Carly Relou and Frank Hubers*

Table 12.1 also shows the six sectors the organizations are active in. The largest proportion of our sample is active in international aid. This sector includes poverty alleviation, international development and emergency aid. The sector 'Social' is the second largest group in the sample, and contains a wide variety of activities aimed at helping people, ranging from helping the poor, voluntary work for the elderly, etc. Both sectors generally seek to help the underprivileged, whereas the latter focusses merely on the Dutch society. Charities in the health sector are those that raise funds for research on diseases, whereas the sector 'Environment' contains all types of organizations that focus on animal welfare and/or the environment. The sector 'Religion' contains charities that have only religious or missionary objectives, such as spreading the religion. Organizations with religious roots that carry out charity work are not categorized as religious. Consequently, the sector 'Religion' is small compared to the others. The smallest category is the sector 'Culture', which contains charities devoted to the arts.

Figure 12.2 illustrates different types of organizations are represented in the sample. Out of the 451 organizations, 53 did not provide sufficient information about their logic model to be assessed (labelled: Type 0). Since we cannot determine whether they do no use a logic model or simply refused to collaborate, we will discard this group from the rest of our analysis, bringing the sample down to 398 (72.8%).

Table 12.1 Number of responding charities, categorized by industry and size

| Sector: | Size (annual budget): | | | | |
| | (1) | (2) | (3) | (4) | (5) |
	Cat A	Cat B	Cat C	Cat D	Total
International aid	52	42	16	51	161
	[32.3]	[26.1]	[9.9]	[31.7]	[35.7]
Social (national)	41	27	8	33	109
	[37.6]	[24.8]	[7.3]	[30.3]	[24.2]
Environment/animal welfare	9	10	19	33	71
	[12.7]	[14.1]	[26.8]	[46.5]	[15.7]
Health	20	18	11	18	67
	[29.9]	[26.9]	[16.4]	[26.9]	[14.9]
Religion	1	5	11	12	29
	[3.4]	[17.2]	[37.9]	[41.4]	[6.4]
Culture	1	1	2	10	14
	[7.1]	[7.1]	[14.3]	[71.4]	[3.1]
Total	124	103	67	157	451
	[27.5]	[22.8]	[14.9]	[34.8]	[100.0]

Notes: Size is based on the charity's annual budget in euros with Cat A: <100k; Cat B: between 100k and 500k; Cat C: between 500k and 2 million; and Cat D: > 2 million. Percentages in parentheses.

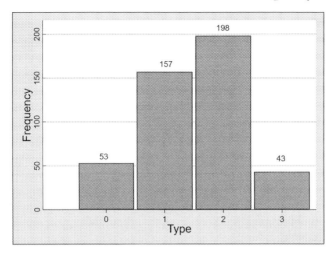

Figure 12.2 Number of charities per type.

12.4 Results

12.4.1 Main findings

Table 12.2 shows the indicators we used to categorize the impact practices into our typology, with Columns (1)–(3), showing the mean values per typology; Column (4) shows the total mean values. The differentiating indicator to be a Type 1 organization is to have a logic model. Organizations that failed to provide a logic model, were not included in this analysis. Each logic model was assessed and received a score between 0 and 4, based on the coherence and logic of the causal steps. An organization with a coherent logic model that is aligned with its social mission, is categorized as a Type 2 organization. Almost half of the organizations can be classified as such (49.7%). In order to be classified as Type 3 organization, the charity has to fulfil the same criteria as a Type 2 and answer positively to five questions that relate to learning and evaluation.

Based on the results, the three most distinguishing factors of a Type 3 organizations are its willingness to understand the needs of the target group, the consideration of alternative approaches in programme planning and its adjustments of programmes based on evaluation findings. Our results show that 60.6% of the organizations have a coherent logic model that, at least in theory, serves as a guide to achieve long-term objectives in line with their mission. However, still a significant proportion of organizations (39.4%) have logic model in place that is incoherent. Their logic model cannot be used be as a strategy to achieve long-term objectives, but rather seems to serve as a symbolic feature to comply with standard reporting requirements. What is also remarkable is that the proportion of organizations that could be regarded as learning organizations is small: Only 10.8% of all charities that claim to

208 *Carly Relou and Frank Hubers*

Table 12.2 Indicators used for typology

	Impact typology			
	(1)	(2)	(3)	(4)
	Type 1	Type 2	Type 3	Total
Logic model (1/0)	1	1	1	1
	(0)	(0)	(0)	(0)
Coherence of all steps in logic model	2.52	4	4	3.42
	(0.06)	(0)	(0)	(0.04)
Relation impact and social mission	0.85	1	1	0.94
	(0.03)	(0)	(0)	(0.01)
Evidence for assumptions	0.65	0.70	1	0.72
	(0.04)	(0.03)	(0)	(0.02)
Considered alternative approaches	0.50	0.49	1	0.55
	(0.04)	(0.04)	(0)	(0.03)
Needs assessment target group	0.46	0.29	1	0.43
	(0.04)	(0.03)	(0)	(0.02)
Impact evaluation	0.83	0.86	1	0.87
	(0.03)	(0.02)	(0)	(0.02)
Adjustments based on evaluation	0.54	0.63	1	0.64
	(0.04)	(0.03)	(0)	(0.02)
Observations	157	198	43	398

Notes: Standard errors in parentheses.

Table 12.3 Impact types per sector

	Impact typology		
	(1)	(2)	(3)
Sector:	Type 1	Type 2	Type 3
International aid	0.43★	0.48	0.10
	(0.04)	(0.04)	(0.02)
Social (national)	0.37	0.56	0.07
	(0.05)	(0.05)	(0.03)
Environment/animal welfare	0.29	0.63	0.08
	(0.06)	(0.06)	(0.04)
Health	0.38	0.45	0.17
	(0.06)	(0.06)	(0.05)
Religion	0.54★★	0.32	0.14
	(0.10)	(0.09)	(0.07)
Culture	0.39	0.39	0.23★
	(0.14)	(0.14)	(0.12)
Total	0.39	0.50	0.11
Observations	157	198	43

Notes: Standard errors in parentheses. Significance is level determined using multinomial logit with lvl2 and sector Environment/Animal Welfare as base outcomes: ★★ $p<0.05$; ★$p<0.10$.

measure impact have a system for evaluation and learning in place. This is an estimation. The real number might be even lower, since the indicators we use to identify Type 3 organizations are all self-reported.

12.4.2 Typology per size and sector

Our sample contains a wide variety of organizations. As a result, we might expect that many of the differences between the level of impact and learning are caused by these differences. It might be unfair to expect a small organization with merely volunteers to have a similar evaluation and learning system in place as a large international organization like Oxfam or Red Cross. Tables 12.3 and 12.4 explore the differences in typology between sector and size, respectively. Table 12.3 shows the typology for each sector, with Columns (1)–(3) showing the proportion (or mean values) of each sector in Types 1–3, respectively. We estimate whether differences are significant using a multinomial logit with the impact typology as dependent variable. Table 12.4 has a similar structure but shows the typology per size.

Table 12.3 illustrates that there are only a few significant differences in impact measurement practices between the sectors. One would expect that organizations working in the international aid or health sector would be more advanced in using impact measurement, given their history in evaluation. On the contrary, international aid organizations are more likely to be in the Type 1 category than those active in other sectors. We observe small significant differences for the religious and cultural sectors too. However, since the samples of religious and cultural organizations are relatively small, this might slightly distort the apparent diversity in impact measurement.

Size appears to be a determinant factor in impact practices. Table 12.4 shows that organizations in the larger categories are also more likely to be Type 3 organizations. Column (3) shows a clear increasing trend in proportion, when organization increase in size. Column (1) appears to show the opposite effect, whereas the proportion of Type 2 organization remains rather stable irrespective of the size.

12.4.3 Evaluation and impact practices

In this last section, we like to explore the common practices in impact measurement. Table 12.5 shows the different methodologies and evaluations are used. Columns (1)–(3) show the mean values of Types 1–3, respectively. Column (4) shows the overall score. Column (4) shows that the vast majority of the charity organizations that classify as Types 1–3, do some kind of process or outcome evaluation: 95% conducts process evaluations, and 93% also evaluates what outcomes are achieved. Only half (51%) of the organization measures and compares the impact of their interventions.

It appears that the more an organization is committed to impact measurement, the more different approaches it applies. Moving up from Type 2 to

210   *Carly Relou and Frank Hubers*

Type 3 all mean values increase—instead of an increase in the value of one particular method versus another. This is interesting because it is often assumed that organizations substitute one approach for another.

Table 12.4 Impact type per size (budget per year)

	Impact typology		
	(1)	*(2)*	*(3)*
Size	*Type 1*	*Type 2*	*Type 3*
Category A: <100k	0.44	0.52	0.04
	(0.05)	(0.05)	(0.02)
Category B: between 100k and 500k	0.51	0.44	0.05
	(0.05)	(0.05)	(0.02)
Category C: between 500k and 2 million	0.31	0.52	0.17★★
	(0.06)	(0.07)	(0.05)
Category D: >2 million	0.31	0.51	0.18★★
	(0.04)	(0.04)	(0.03)
Total	0.39	0.50	0.11
Observations (N)	157	198	43

Notes: Standard errors in parentheses. Significance is level determined using a multinomial logit regression with type2 and category A as base outcomes: ★★★ p<0.01; ★★p<0.05

Table 12.5 Evaluation practices per typology

	Impact typology			
	(1)	*(2)*	*(3)*	*(4)*
	Type 1	*Type 2*	*Type 3*	*Total*
Evaluates implementation of project (process evaluation)	0.94	0.95	1	0.95
	(0.02)	(0.02)	(0)	(0.01)
Evaluates whether project has the expected outcomes	0.92	0.92	1	0.93
	(0.03)	(0.02)	(0)	(0.01)
Evaluates impact compared to alternative projects	0.55	0.34	1	0.51
	(0.05)	(0.04)	(0)	(0.03)
Uses quantitative indicators	0.63	0.62	0.85	0.66
	(0.04)	(0.04)	(0.06)	(0.03)
Uses systematic qualitative review	0.27	0.28	0.40	0.29
	(0.04)	(0.04)	(0.08)	(0.03)
Conducts interviews	0.48	0.47	0.63	0.49
	(0.05)	(0.04)	(0.06)	(0.03)
Illustrative stories	0.34	0.30	0.45	0.34
	(0.04)	(0.04)	(0.08)	(0.02)
Observations	157	198	43	398

Notes: Standard errors in parentheses.

12.5 Conclusion

The use of social impact measurement practices is spreading throughout the charity sector. The popularization of the practices can be the result of several factors. One of them could be that charities truly find social impact measurement valuable as a method to aid organizational learning. On the other hand, as many charities face pressure from donors to demonstrate their effectiveness for accountability-related expectations, they might adopt social impact measurement practices symbolically. Institutional theory posits that external pressures may force organizations to adopt practices to signal legitimacy instead of out of their value for the organization (DiMaggio & Powell, 1983). Strategic decoupling could occur in these situations, when organizations formally engage in impact measurement while not doing it in practice.

In this study, we explored how charities adopt and apply practices of social impact measurement—analyzing a dataset of over 450 Dutch charity organizations. For this purpose, we developed a typology. Although the concept of social impact is ambiguous and the field undertheorized, there are universally recognized factors that are regarded as vital for the strategic use of impact measurement. We identify three types: Type 1 organizations are characterized by an incoherent logic model, indicating a more symbolic use of impact measurement. Type 2 organizations are characterized by the adoption of a coherent logic model, but a lack of organizational learning. This indicates that the organization has a strategy in place to reach long-term objectives, but this strategy might not be supported by evidence. Type 3 organizations are those with proper logic model and a system for evaluation and learning. In our sample, this group is by far the smallest: only 10.8% of the organizations fall into this type. Almost half of the charity organizations are Type 2 organisations. They have a strategy to achieve long-term objectives with logical chain of expected events between their activities and the intended impact, but they do not test their assumptions, measure their impact and/or adjust their projects according to the conclusions of the evaluation. The size of the Type 1 category charities is remarkable: four out of ten charities that claim to measure their impact do not have a coherent logic model. In other words, their projects do no logically align with their intended long-term objectives.

Our conclusion is that a large proportion of charities are using impact measurement symbolically rather than strategically. Type 1 organizations have an illogical logic model, suggesting the model is not used in practice to guide decision making. This indicates that a process of decoupling is occurring in some charity organizations. Type 2 charities, with a coherent logic model in place, are engaged in strategic impact planning, but do not evaluate or look for evidence to support their assumptions. Apparently, these organizations do not see the added value of becoming a learning organization or they are still developing into learning organizations. Type 3 organizations have adopted a comprehensive evaluation and learning system, suggesting they experience benefits of engaging in social impact measurement. Our data suggests that larger organizations are more likely to be a Type 3 organization.

Acknowledgements

We thank Fenna ten Haaf and Robert Praas for their dedication, support and critical attitude in the data analysis. Also, we would like to thank *Centraal Bureau Fondsenwerving* (CBF) for the collaboration and support.

Notes

1 OECD/DAC guidelines at https://www.oecd.org/dac/evaluation/49756382. pdf, (visited on 1 February 2020).
2 One popular adaptation is the regression discontinuity (RD) design, which can be applied when the organization implements certain rules about participation in the programme or has a waiting list (Imbens & Lemieux, 2008; Thistlethwaite & Campbell, 1960).
3 In Dutch: Centraal Bureau Fondsenwerving (CBF).

13 Impact of sustainable innovation on organizational performance

Egbert Dommerholt, Mariusz Soltanifar, and John Bessant

13.1 Introduction

Sustainable development, and along with it, corporate sustainability, corporate social performance, creating shared value and similar concepts accentuating the business–society relationship, ranks high on societal and corporate agendas nowadays. Numerous sustainability-related concepts have been used interchangeably and morphed over the years to describe organizations' efforts to make their operations sustainable. Some scholars believe that the sustainable development discussion commenced in the mid-1950s, whereas others claim the emergence of this concept goes back to the 19th century. According to Aguirre (2002), the sustainable development concept has a more recent date and gained momentum in the mid-1980s through the publication of the United Nations' World Commission on Environment and Development's publication *Our Common Future* (World Commission on Environment and Development [WCED], 1987). While others believe that sustainable development as a concept dates back to the 19th century (Sociaal Economische Raad, 2001), at that time such a term was not present in the literature or business practice.

To adhere to the concept of sustainable development, firms are increasingly expected to develop innovations that reconcile economic, environmental, and social goals (i.e., sustainable innovations) (e.g., Silvestre & Țîrcă, 2019). Therefore, the understanding and application of sustainable development is important because sustainable development aims to meet the needs of the present without compromising the ability of future generations to meet their own needs (WCED, 1987). For instance, we cannot continue using resources at current levels as this will not leave enough for future generations. For that, stabilizing and reducing carbon emissions is key to living within environmental limits in a world exposed more and more often to natural disasters. Interestingly, the line between sustainability and sustainable innovation is quite blurry. What some refer to as sustainability, or corporate social responsibility, is referred to by others as sustainable innovation (Inigo, 2019; Ratten, Pasillas, & Lundberg, 2019). As Business Insider (2019) reported recently, 'being socially and environmentally responsible' jumped from sixth to third place in terms of priorities for companies surveyed in Europe and North America. Moreover, the companies that are already thinking about their energy responsibility are expected to prosper the most and forecast to increase their revenue by more than 20% over the next five years. These findings indicate the additional importance placed on the issue of sustainability nowadays.

But what causes companies and other organizations to pay attention to sustainability-related issues in the first place? There are a number of answers to this question, such as reduced company costs, recruiting and retaining eco-conscious employees, taking advantage of tax incentives, image and reputation building, access to grants and loans, consumers recognizing green companies, stimulating innovation by going green, helping the environment, building brands, positioning themselves as a thought leader, providing a healthier work environment, and contributing to the sustainability of the planet (e.g., Kerényi & McIntosh, 2020). Basically, we can distinguish three broad categories of reasons why companies and organizations pay crucial attention to sustainability-related issues, which encompass all the above-mentioned arguments. Organizations go sustainable mainly for the three following reasons: profitability, environmental policy and stakeholder pressure (Naidoo & Gasparatos, 2018).

Entities that invest in technology and integrate sustainable energy into their core company values can expect improved brand reputation (Business Insider, 2019). The main motivator for companies to seek a green or sustainable orientation seems to be gaining a competitive advantage and boosting profitability (Papadas, Avlonitis, Carrigan, & Piha, 2019). This may cause people to think that corporate sustainability, and along with it, sustainable innovation, is primarily about serving organizations' self-interest (e.g. Karnani, 2011), or to put it provocatively, that contributing to society is a mere by-product of enhancing financial performance, which is basically grounded in the neoclassical economic view voiced by Milton Friedman in the 1970s. In this traditional or conventional economic view, innovations, be they sustainable or otherwise, will be effectuated only if they contribute to creating shareholder value, irrespective of the societal value that is being, or might be, created. This means that, from a neoclassical perspective, creating societal value is a random and hence unpredictable process. But is that really the case in practice?

In this chapter we seek to answer this question using the sustainability performance construct developed by Dommerholt (2019), which we elaborate in detail in Section 13.2. In contrast to other constructs accentuating the business–society relationship, the sustainable performance construct specifically takes regime–transition orientation and single–multiple creation as the starting point. Existing concepts are not sufficiently adequate to bring about the required social and economic system transformation (e.g., Loorbach & Wijsman, 2013). Although for this chapter we review relevant literature on corporate sustainable innovation as opposed to collecting primary data, we are confident that this chapter provides insights for further research and managerial practice. For practitioners, this framework can be perceived as a useful explanatory lens for coping with practical sustainability-related issues. However, the sustainability performance construct is still very much in its infancy and needs further testing and populating.

13.2 Defining sustainable innovation

> Sustainability is a major and growing driver of business change. Its implications for innovation are clear – living and working in a world of up to 9 billion people with rising expectations; providing energy, food and resource security; dealing with climate change, ecosystem degradation, a widening economic divide and a host of other interdependent issues that all require a massive change in products, services, processes, marketing approaches and the underlying business models which frame them.
>
> (Seebode, Jeanrenaud, & Bessant, 2012, p. 1)

The works of Seebode et al. (2012) provide a broader understanding of the new approaches to innovation management. Drawing on case studies of a variety of organizations the authors indicate practical actions that might be taken to respond to the growing pressures and emerging opportunities in the 'sustainability' agenda.

There are numerous approaches to sustainable innovation. A recent study by Cillo, Petruzzelli, Ardito, and Del Giudice (2019) aimed at organizing previous research regarding sustainable innovation. The 69 papers used for the literature review were organized according to three key perspectives: *internal managerial, external relational,* and *performance evaluation.* The findings have demonstrated that the first perspective, incorporating diverse internal managerial aspects, is the most frequently considered in research on sustainable innovation, whereas the second and third perspectives remain underdeveloped. This additionally strengthens the reasoning behind our chapter as next we highlight the innovation compass and discuss different innovation spaces. While engaging in this discussion and analysing the differences between incremental and radical innovation, we propose our own definition of sustainable innovation.

13.2.1 Innovation compass and innovation spaces

The research on innovation continues to expand. As such, the innovation compass has become a popular self-audit tool that guides companies in identifying unforeseen problems and designing a plan to improve their new product development (NPD) process (Bessant, 2019; Radnor & Noke, 2002). *The 4Ps innovation compass* developed by Bessant (2018) provides an overview of key themes, tools, and activities to help explore further. Each innovation takes place along a spectrum of novelty (including product, process, paradigm or position of such innovation). At one end, we have incremental innovation,

216 *Egbert Dommerholt et al.*

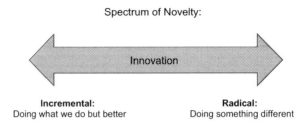

Figure 13.1 Incremental versus radical innovation (Bessant, 2018).

essentially doing what we do, but better. At the other end of the spectrum, we have radical innovation, which is doing something completely different. We can innovate anywhere along that spectrum (Bessant, 2018).

The main criterion for distinguishing between the types of innovation is the spectrum of novelty (Bessant, 2018). Regardless of whether the innovation is incremental or radical in nature, both types of innovation are adopted in the firm's pursuit of competitive advantage (Soltanifar, 2016).

Furthermore, the innovation compass assesses the firm's capacity to implement the strategies and how efficiently they can be adapted, corresponding to the NPD process, resource commitment, internal/external communication, and leadership (Radnor & Noke, 2002). Radnor and Noke (2002) propose a framework for developing the innovation compass. The framework consists of inner and outer circles. The inner circle of the compass envisions the company's structure, teams, output and leadership. The inner circle gives the company an opportunity to benchmark itself on a quantitative basis against competitors. In the outer circle of the compass, the 'social, economic, political, and competitive environment in which the company operates' are envisioned (Radnor & Noke, 2002).

13.2.2 Incremental and radical innovation

Innovation literature is very broad and results in many definitions and types of innovation. For the purpose of this chapter, we focus on describing the two most common types of innovation by the degree of novelty and their magnitude, such as incremental and radical innovation, which can be seen as representing opposite ends of a novelty spectrum (Nakao & de Andrade Guerra, 2019). By *magnitude*, we refer to the degree of novelty that the innovation brings. In general, incremental innovation represents a small change to existing routines and practices (Jia, 2020), whereas radical innovation introduces fundamental changes and departs from the existing practices of the organization (Domínguez-Escrig, Mallén-Broch, Lapiedra-Alcamí, & Chiva-Gómez, 2018).

Incremental innovation has been defined in many ways. One of the definitions of incremental technology innovation refers to 'a quality of newness that is less drastic and represents the cumulative improvement of existing knowledge, capabilities, or technologies' (Chan & Parhankangas, 2017, p. 6). As such, incremental innovation could also be seen as a competitive advantage in firms by 'allowing partners to understand more easily the underlying mechanisms and enabling better separation of tasks, reducing the risk of knowledge leakage and opportunistic behaviour' (Bouncken, Fredrich, Ritala, & Kraus, 2018, p. 392). Incremental innovation, representing the other end of the novelty spectrum, is characterized as a change that implies small adaptations to the status quo (Cammarano, Michelino, & Caputo, 2019), and it is often described as a step-by-step process. In this chapter we refer to *incremental innovation* as a minor change in the technology or design of products or services that offer improved efficiency, competitive advantage and productivity.

Similarly, over the years, *radical innovation*, also interchangeably called discontinuous or breakthrough innovation (Crossan & Apaydin, 2010), has been defined in many ways. Nagy, Schuessler, and Dubinsky (2016) define radical innovations as 'innovations with new functionality or with new materials or production processes [that] dramatically alter or disrupt existing organizational structure, strategy, context, and use' (p. 121). Radical innovations are different from what is typically seen in the (product) market or in a completely new product category (Chan & Parhankangas, 2017). Although there are other definitions of the concept, the common feature is the effect of the change on the resources or technology of an organization. As such, a new product, service, process or strategy when introduced to a market makes a significant impact by completely replacing existing technologies and methods. In this chapter, we refer to *radical innovation* as products or services with breakthrough functions that offer a new perspective on how we view and use the changed products and services.

To conclude, form and magnitude of innovation are closely related to the spectrum of novelty: incremental innovation is often associated with product or process innovation, while radical innovation is more often associated with business model innovation, in line with the innovation compass workbook developed by Bessant (2018).

13.2.3 Proposed definition of sustainable innovation

In order to formulate our own definition of sustainable innovation, we build upon earlier works on sustainable innovation that embody the means through which organizations nurture sustainable development (Kumar et al., 2017). We take into consideration previous studies on the triple bottom line approach, which includes economic growth (Lucía et al., 2019), social inclusion (e.g., Chaouachi et al., 2016), and environmental protection (e.g., Kiefer, Carrillo-Hermosilla, Del Río, & Callealta Barroso, 2017). As a result, we base our definition on the converged approach to sustainable innovation which refers to improving sustainability performance and includes

218 *Egbert Dommerholt et al.*

ecological, economic, and social criteria. Subsequently, we offer the following definition of sustainable innovation:

> *Sustainable innovation* is a process where sustainability, ecological, economic, and social considerations are integrated into company systems from idea generation to research and development to commercialization, resulting in societally desirable outcomes that enhance economic growth.

Indeed, the ecological, economic, and social developments that lie at the heart of sustainable innovation lead to advances in research and practices relating to the interconnected nature of firms' innovation undercurrents and sustainability. As such, finding out how organizations can strategically and efficiently accommodate sustainability and innovation, improving our understanding of the role of innovation in public sector organizations, focusing on the environmental pillar of the triple bottom line in private firms and linking these three areas with the role of the individual entrepreneur in bringing about sustainable innovation, are the four major reasons for sustainable innovation to become a truly mainstream practice in business.

13.3 Sustainability performance construct

If we aim to evaluate whether sustainable innovations contribute to societal good, we need to take refuge in constructs that are transition – and hence innovation – prone. However, none of the business–society construct to date is aimed at, nor adequately epitomizes, a social, environmental and economic system transformation or paradigm shift (Loorbach & Wijsman, 2013). A system transformation or transition is a prerequisite because of pressing issues, such as resource depletion, climate change, and social inequality that we are facing as a global community. To evaluate sustainable innovation we use the sustainability performance construct developed by Dommerholt (2019) because this construct takes the transition and value dimensions into account, both of which are of eminent importance when it comes to innovations and innovation decisions (Breuer & Lüdeke-Freund, 2017).

In general, sustainability performance conveys the relationship between businesses or other organizations on the one hand and society on the other. In this sense, the construct fits in quite nicely with existing constructs. However, it differs from these in terms of contextuality because it adds a regime and transition orientation perspective and stratification, indicating that it is a 'layered' construct. The concept itself is graphically represented in Figure 13.1 and will now be explained. The sustainability performance concept is the primary consideration for the rest of the chapter and forms the basis of the sustainable innovation analysis framework (see Figure 13.2). This framework should first and foremost be perceived as a useful explanatory lens

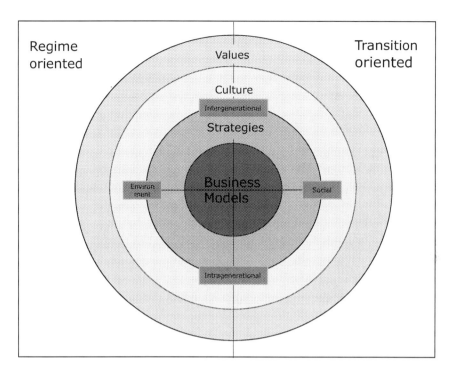

Figure 13.2 Sustainability performance construct (Dommerholt, 2019).

that still needs further testing and populating. It is not so much our intention to add to a new construct to the wealth of constructs already available.

Before pursuing sustainable development, many companies are convinced that the more environmentally friendly they are, the higher their costs will be, which will ultimately lower their financial benefits. However, according to the research of Nidumolu, Prahalad, and Rangaswami (2009), companies that are environmentally friendly lower their input usage and thus reduce costs.

13.3.1 Context

From a transition theory perspective, businesses are either regime oriented or transition oriented (Geels, 2002). A *regime orientation* means that organizations are focused on the existing regime, where a regime reflects the existing situation consisting of rules, skills and institutions, as well as the way societies function and how people view and deal with problems and the subsequent solutions that are being proposed to solve them, etc. The linear economy is such an existing regime. Within it, innovation is primarily focused on using resources more efficiently and on doing things better, implying that innovation is mainly of an incremental nature. A *transition orientation* means that

220　*Egbert Dommerholt et al.*

organizations are moving away from the current regime towards a circular sustainable economy, implying that innovation is about doing things differently. This is because the transition is, to a large extent, shaped by so-called niches. Niches can best be seen as fertile ground for new ideas and radical innovations. Experimenting and pioneering are important aspects of this and take place in both physical and virtual spaces.

13.3.2 Values

The Cambridge English Dictionary generically defines the word 'value' as 'the importance or worth of something to someone' (Cambridge English Dictionary, n.d.). Within the context of this chapter, values will be defined as 'notions of the desirable' or 'desirable goals that motivate action' (Breuer & Lüdeke-Freund, 217, p. 16), meaning that values represent what is worthwhile, or what is considered desirable. Values, in particular shared values, are crucial for an organization because of their directive, integrative and generative function (Breuer & Lüdeke-Freund, 2017). This implies that adopting values that relate to sustainable development can give rise and direction to completely new frameworks and solutions. Values are therefore crucial when it comes to finding answers to contemporary social, ecological and societal issues. In other words, values are critical when it comes to innovation.

However, we should bear in mind that societal values are by no means carved in stone and may prove to be quite flexible over time. If values evolve, companies and other organizations need to respond to these changing values to warrant their legitimacy, and along with it, their license to operate. Shifting values have an impact on how society perceives innovation and how this can trigger a search for radical innovation and a shift to better-perceived products and services (Ringberg, Reihlen, & Rydén, 2019). Society's perception of innovation is concerned with social mobilization and impact, where the values are shifting towards sustainability (Petteri & Kaisa, 2019). This defines *social innovation*.

13.3.3 Organizational culture

Generally speaking, we can say that organizational culture is the taken-for-granted behaviours and assumptions that make sense of people's organisational context and therefore contributes to how people or groups of people respond and behave in relation to issues they face (Johnson, Whittington, & Scholes, 2017). Organizational culture is first of all driven by the values an organization adheres to, and which permeate the organization, pervading all parts, units, policies, procedures, programmes, strategies and business models. Thus, values are inextricably connected to organizational culture.

13.3.4 Strategies

The sustainable development concept is believed to comprise three principles: social, ecological, and economic. The *social* principle is based on the notion that everyone, regardless of their heritage or talents, should be treated fairly and honestly, whereas the *ecological* principle highlights the vulnerability and protection of natural resources, ecosystems and biodiversity. The *economic* principle refers to the universal right of access to at least the basic necessities of life (e.g., access to education and healthcare) as well as the right to be treated respectfully.

Additionally, the sustainable development concept has an inter- and intragenerational perspective. The intergenerational perspective is mainly about the gap between current and future generations ('now and in the future'), while the intergenerational perspective is about the gap within generations ('there and here') (Dommerholt, 2019). Based on the generational perspective and the social, environmental, and economic dimensions of sustainable development, four types of strategy can be distinguished (where we combine social and economic dimensions): first, *intragenerational social strategies* that contribute to the social dimension of sustainable development; second, *intragenerational environmental strategies* that aim at narrowing the current accessibility gap of, for example, resources, energy, and water between 'here and there'; third, *intergenerational environmental strategies* that focus on closing intergenerational environment-related gaps; and lastly, *intergenerational social strategies* that aim at ensuring that both current and future generations can continue to meet their needs, indicating that we must be careful with the resources and energy reserves that are still available.

13.3.5 Business models

Despite the fact that all organizations have a business model, there is still no universally accepted definition of what that entails (Zott, Amit, & Massa, 2011). So far, many attempts have been made to come to a general definition. The following definition is one such attempt: a business model is 'the blueprint of a firm's business logic' (Lüdeke-Freund, 2009). In other words, a business model describes the logic or the reason(s) behind why and how organizations create value.

Business models are closely connected to business strategy, but do not coincide with it (DaSilva & Trkman, 2014). Furthermore, a business model is an organization's centrepiece because it defines its value proposition and how value is being created and captured. *Value creation and delivery* is at the very core of every business model (Bocken, Short et al., 2014). It includes all activities, partners, (distribution) channels, technologies, etc. that are needed to create value. The *value proposition* indicates which quantitative (e.g., price, speed of delivery) or qualitative (e.g., design, experience) value is created for which market segment (Vorbach, Müller, & Poandl, 2019). A business model also comprises the *value capture* element. This element describes how income is generated and what the associated cost structure looks like (Bocken et al., 2014).

Furthermore, having a clear business model is particularly beneficial for new businesses as it allows them to communicate a holistic and clear perspective of their organisational structure, value proposition, goals, and

222 *Egbert Dommerholt et al.*

future plans. Lastly, in recent years, another definition that has gained popularity is the sustainable business model. The core ingredients for sustainable innovation business models are integration and reconfiguration within the corporate culture, company capabilities, stakeholder relationship management, knowledge, and leadership (Adams, Jeanrenaud, Bessant, Overy, & Denyer, 2012).

13.4 Sustainable innovation analysis framework

In the previous section the sustainable innovation concept was explained. However, this concept is highly context prone. Figure 13.3 highlights the sustainable innovation analysis framework (SIAF) that will be used as a tool to gain a better and more comprehensive insight into the sustainable innovation concept. The SIAF has been derived from the sustainability performance construct discussed earlier, which will now be explained. Strategies are embedded in organizational cultures, which, in turn, are shaped and supported by the values an organization adheres to and that guide organizational behaviour. Furthermore, the context (transition oriented vs. regime oriented) in which an organization operates also plays an important role, since values, strategies and business models are directly connected to the business context.

Dommerholt (2019) and Geels (2002) conceptualize sustainability performance as regime oriented and transition oriented. Regime-oriented businesses are focused on the existing rules, skills, institutions and situations. These businesses focus on innovation at an incremental level and resources are used efficiently. Transition-oriented businesses are making a shift from regime oriented to be sustainable economic and environmentally friendly enterprises. Moreover, transition-oriented businesses can be defined as favourable financial entities that deliver social needs and beneficial environmental impact.

In the sustainability performance construct, values guide organizational behaviour. These values can be viewed as endogenous or as input variables because of their directive, integrative, and generative functions. On the other hand, organizations also create values that are the outcome of a process and can for that matter be perceived as exogenous or output variables. Of course, these value types are related because the values an organization will deliver in the end are closely connected to the values the organization adheres to. In Figure 13.3, 'values' should be interpreted as endogenous variables. Also, as societal norms and values evolve, organizational values have to evolve along with them to warrant legitimacy (Dowling & Pfeffer, 1975), and if organizational values evolve, so will the values that are being created. If the institutional pressure on organizations to embark on the transition towards a circular economy is mounting, these organizations had better conform to these pressures to avoid their license to operate being withdrawn and losing their societal acceptance, which is likely to have dire consequences for profitability rates.

Value creation comes in two extremes: single and multiple value creation. Single value creation is about putting financial value creation at the core,

Impact of sustainable innovation 223

or in neoclassical terms, maximizing financial value. In this case, social and ecological value creation is merely a by-product of financial value creation. On the other hand, multiple value creation is about simultaneously creating social, ecological and economic value, whereby financial value creation can be regarded as the by-product of social and ecological value creation. Ultimately, the choice between financial or multiple value creation is a fairly fundamental one, as an organization cannot simultaneously serve two masters: it cannot view shareholders, society and its stakeholders as equally important. This means that an organization cannot focus on maximizing financial and societal value at the same time (Tapaninaho & Kujala, 2019). The reason is that the intentions and consequently the internal value systems between the two differ completely.

If we take value creation as a starting point and link this to the context in which sustainable action takes place, Figure 13.3 emerges. The figure consists of two axes, on the basis of which four different sustainability strategies can be identified. The first is the regime orientation vs. transition orientation axis, while the second is the single value creation (=financial value creation) and multiple value creation axis.

Based on Figure 13.3, sustainability performance can be expected to take place within four mutually fairly exclusive ideal typical perspectives or strategies. These strategies are of an ideal typical nature, meaning that they accentuate an array of key characteristics and elements but may not fully comply with reality. We elaborate on each strategy and give examples below.

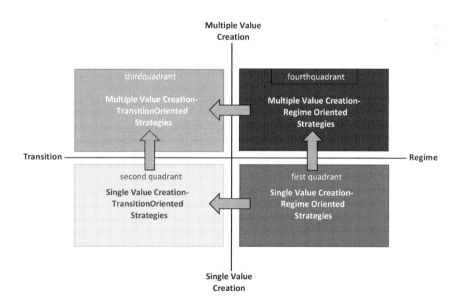

Figure 13.3 The sustainable innovation analysis framework (SIAF) (Dommerholt, 2019).

224 *Egbert Dommerholt et al.*

Each quadrant can be seen as a static or steady state. As discussed by Dosi (1982), a technological paradigm can be seen as a 'model' and a 'pattern' of a solution to selected (technological) problems, based on selected principles and materials technologies, bearing similarities to what Geels (2002) refers to as a regime. Solutions to sustainability-related challenges take place within the confines or boundaries of that particular paradigm or regime. These are what Dosi (1982) refers to as trajectories. These trajectories are very powerful in the sense that it is quite difficult to switch from one trajectory to another because of path dependency issues.

The green arrows in Figure 13.3 represent transition directions. Starting with the first quadrant, representing a conventional strategy, which is compliant with neoclassical economic thinking, the first most obvious choice for an organization is a transition towards a circular or sustainable economy (quadrant two) because the focus on single value creation remains intact. The second most obvious choice is a transition towards multiple value creation (quadrant three) because organizations are still very much regime oriented. The most complicated and impactful choice is for a simultaneous transition towards a circular or sustainable economy and multiple value creation.

The choice to move between quadrants may be voluntary if a shift in value creation activities is driven by intrinsic motives. Organizations may, at some point, because of ethical reasons, decide to contribute to the betterment of society. The shift may also be the result of coercive forces pressuring them to move in another direction. If these pressures are exerted by salient stakeholders, organizations most likely have no other option but to conform to these pressures.

The SIAF also bears some resemblance to the final model of sustainability-oriented innovation by Adams, Jeanrenaud, Bessant, Denyer, and Overy (2016). This model has three sustainability levels or stages. The first or 'operational optimization' level refers to 'doing things the same, but better', with a focus on compliance and efficiency and incremental improvements to business as usual, and gears very much towards commercial value creation. In Figure 13.3, this level very much resembles the first quadrant. The focus of the second level is on 'doing good by doing new things', which requires a fundamental shift in the firm's values, resulting in novel products, services, and business models. This is by and large what happens in quadrants two and four in Figure 13.3. Level three represents the highest sustainability level and is about 'doing good by doing things with others', which focuses on creating positive net societal value and extends beyond the norm to drive institutional change. In Figure 13.3, the highest sustainability level is represented by the third quadrant.

13.4.1 Single value creation–regime-oriented strategies

The single value creation–regime-oriented strategies quadrant represents conventional business strategies, which are rooted in neoclassical economics.

The focus is on serving shareholders and profit is the value to be maximized. Furthermore, the linear economy leads, which limits the scope for innovation. Single value creation is paramount, meaning that only sustainable innovations that contribute to profit maximization are considered. Because of the regime orientation, sustainable innovations are predominantly aimed at making things better (incremental innovation). This is not to say that radical innovations (doing things differently) do not occur, but the focus is on incremental innovation.

13.4.2 Single value creation–transition-oriented strategies

Single value creation–transition-oriented strategies are of a circular nature, since these contribute to an economic paradigm shift towards a circular economy. This transition causes great challenges for companies and other organizations because they have to level all kinds of barriers such as consumer awareness and organizational culture (Kirchherr, Piscicelli, Bour, Kostense-Smit, & Muller, 2018). On their way to the circular economy they also have to tackle all kinds of technological challenges. By consequence, organizations will have to move away from doing things better to doing things differently. However, since the focus is still on profit maximization, only those innovations that contribute to this focus will be taken into consideration.

13.4.3 Multiple value creation–transition-oriented strategies

Multiple value creation–transition-oriented strategies accentuate the twin transition that is moving away from a regime orientation towards a circular or sustainable economy, while simultaneously heading for multiple value creation instead of merely concentrating on financial value creation. This also means that things have to be done differently from both an economic and a value creation perspective, which obviously also has consequences for the kind of sustainable innovation.

13.4.4 Multiple value creation–regime-oriented strategies

Multiple value creation–regime-oriented strategies particularly concentrate on creating multiple values; that is, serving their stakeholders (including the natural environment) and society within a mainly linear economic setting. Taking the first quadrant as the starting point, this means that organizations need to modify the values they adhere to, which is easier said than done because it requires moving away from the still widely endorsed put-the-shareholders-first adage to putting society first. This paradigm shift requires that organizations start concentrating on doing things differently (radical innovation) instead of merely making some minor adjustments to the current system (incremental innovation).

226 *Egbert Dommerholt et al.*

13.4.5 Business model innovation

Taking Figure 13.3 as a starting point, we can identify four ideal typical business models that match with each of the four identified ideal typical strategies discussed above.

The first quadrant captures regime-oriented–single value creation strategies. A reference business model that fits this quadrant is that of Osterwalder and Pigneur (2010), because this model is rooted in conventional economic thinking. This model is based on the balanced scorecard approach by Kaplan and Norton (Osterwalder, 2004), implying that it is driven by financial performance.

Following the green arrows in Figure 13.3 requires novel individual and organizational mindsets, and hence different sets of values that the organization adheres to. It is about doing things (completely) differently and can hence be qualified as a radical innovation. So, organizations embarking on a paradigm shift from financial value creation to multiple value creation, as well as the shift from a regime orientation to a transition orientation, will have to radically innovate their business models. In contrast, optimizing business models within each of the four quadrants can be classified as incremental innovation.

However, mainly due to the fact that business model innovation is an emergent phenomenon (Hossain, 2017), the term 'business model innovation' has not yet been clearly defined. Many descriptions are rather fuzzy and imprecise, articulating terms like 'reconfiguration of activities', 'what value a firm is providing to its customers', 'adding new activities', 'novel opportunities portfolios', and 'new ways to create and capture value for its stakeholders' (Hossain, 2017).

Moving away from a conventional to a circular business strategy includes a novel value proposition because in a circular economy, products and services have to become circular. To add to the circular economy, products need to be circular and are increasingly offered as a service, and new revenue models emerge, such as pay per service, pay per use, and performance-based contracting (Lewandowski, 2016). To make a circular business model work, take-back systems and channels need to be developed, different types of networks and partnerships need to be explored, the production process needs to be reviewed, product redesign becomes more important, etc. Shifting from a conventional business strategy to a multiple value creation strategy also requires business model innovation of a radical sort. A reference model related to such a multiple value creation strategy is the triple layered business model (TLBM) developed by Joyce and Paquin (2016). Key to this business model is that it explicitly includes social, environmental, and economic dimensions, which are highly intertwined; activities in the social component also impact the economic and/or environmental components of the model. The same goes, *mutatis mutandis*, for the environmental and economic components. This implies that an offering in the TLBM also has an economic, environmental, and social dimension. The products and services that create value for a specific customer segments are clarified (value proposition), as well as the total amount of a physical product delivered (functional value), and the value that an organization creates for its stakeholders and society at large (social value). The same applies to the value creation and delivery component of the TLBM. Furthermore, the value capture component of the business model not only takes the financial costs and benefits into account, but also the environmental and social costs and benefits.

13.5 Conclusion

From a traditional or conventional economic perspective, sustainable innovations will be effectuated only if they contribute to creating shareholder value, irrespective of the societal value that is being, or might be, created. This means that, from a neoclassical perspective, creating societal value is a random and therefore unpredictable process. But is that really the case in practice? Much depends on the values an organization adheres to because these also determine the type of value that will ultimately be created. These values are either focused on serving the organization (and its shareholders) or serving society (and its stakeholders). This is a matter of 'either/or': an organization cannot simultaneously serve two masters. This implies that innovations aimed at serving society are obviously likely to have a greater positive impact on society than innovations aimed at pleasing shareholders. The former contributes to a paradigm shift towards multiple value creation. But it also matters if innovations are regime or transition oriented. In the case of transition orientation, the innovation contributes to a paradigm shift towards the circular or sustainable economy. In this case, an organization cannot serve two masters because it either stays within the current regime or contributes to bringing a circular or sustainable economy to life. Organizations may contribute to either paradigm shift voluntarily or because of coercive forces exerted upon them by their stakeholders.

Making a paradigm shift happen requires significant changes that vary depending on the spectrum of novelty, as measured by the innovation compass: as a part of incremental innovation, deploying a variety of sensors to measure temperature, water, airflow, and gas to make sure there are no inefficient parts of a company's operations, or movement detectors in office spaces that make it possible to program lights and heating systems so they are only used when someone is in the room; from major business model innovation adaptations for a circular economy to moving away from a conventional business model because it requires that things are being done 'differently', instead of simply being done 'better', as a part of radical innovation. Other innovation types may very well have a positive societal impact, but our impression is that business model innovation belonging to the radical innovation category contributes the most. In a regime setting, sustainable innovations are, to a large extent, aimed at optimizing economic processes within a linear economic setting. Furthermore, we also posit that whatever type of value creation an organization is opting for (single vs. multiple value creation), and whatever the context of an organization (regime vs. transition orientation), radical innovation seems to have a much higher societal impact than incremental innovation.

Acknowledgements

We acknowledge, with much appreciation, the many constructive contributions to this chapter from Yoanna Petkova, International Business School of the Hanze University of Applied Sciences, Groningen, the Netherlands. Thank you for your great input, commitment, and passion that together have increased the quality of this work. We wish you all the best in your future and we are looking forward to seeing your sustainable innovation-related activities in action. You definitely are a great asset to any potential employer.

14 Sustainable innovation and intellectual property rights

Friends, foes or perfect strangers?

Carolina Castaldi

14.1 Introduction

Incentives for firms to engage in sustainable innovation are becoming stronger, both as internal drivers and as external pressures (Berrone, Fosfuri, Gelabert, & Gomez-Mejia, 2013). While for some firms sustainable innovation might come as an offset of organizational changes, mostly prompted by external pressures (Porter & Van der Linde, 1995), increasingly companies innovate sustainably as a strategy on which to build their competitive advantage. If this is the case, appropriability questions should become strategic for companies, both the large incumbents shifting to more sustainable directions and the new entrants pioneering sustainable alternatives. These questions are about how to appropriate the returns from sustainable innovation and develop a viable business model to convince market investors. Innovation is about generating new ideas that are partly non-rival and non-excludable, implying that the innovator bears the costs of generating those new ideas, but might not collect the full returns if the ideas (partly) spill over to other economic actors. The appropriability question is a longstanding one within innovation management (see the seminal framework by Teece, 1986). Quite surprisingly, there is little research on how this question applies to the case of sustainable innovation and the little research is highly fragmented.

The profiting from technological innovation (PFI) framework of Teece has highlighted how companies can use a whole range of tools, both formal and informal, to capture the economic returns of their innovation efforts (Teece, 1986). Intellectual property rights (IPR) fall under the formal weapons available to innovators, with different degrees and objects of protection (Hall, Helmers, Rogers, & Sena, 2014; Seip, Castaldi, Flikkema, & de Man, 2019). Yet, the PFI framework appears only partially applicable to companies engaged with sustainable innovation. Two specific issues might make the relation between sustainable innovation and IPRs more complex than for other types of innovation.

First, the very use of IPRs might clash with the core values considered legitimate in relation with sustainability. The profit logic behind appropriation strategies can create tensions with the moral/societal value logic that is expected to come with embracing sustainability. Sustainable innovators might resort to alternative solutions that hardly rely on IPRs, for instance by leverage open innovation solutions (Ahn, Roijakkers, Fini, & Mortara, 2019). Alternatively, sustainable innovators might turn to IPRs with very specific motives. For instance, they might care about claiming ownership with the idea of facilitating access through licensing or with the intent to control the responsible use of their innovation (Eppinger et al., 2019).

Second, sustainable innovation typically entails commitment to sustainability in the entire value chain (Jolink & Niesten, 2015). Such commitment will prompt sustainable innovators to interact intensively with partners of all kinds, in particular suppliers and also distributors, to align the sustainability promise along the value chain. Few leaders might even opt for keeping the whole value chain in-house to claim total control (see the case of Tesla), but for most firms the dependence upon other organizations will be a defining element of their sustainable business models. IPRs as ownership rights can act as coordination mechanisms, but they will need to be in line with other more informal and trust-based governance mechanisms.

These two specific issues put together might prompt rather original solutions to be observed for companies involved with sustainable innovation and rather unique sets of motives to rely or not on IPRs. For instance, a number of sustainable technological fields has witnessed the phenomenon of 'patent commons', collections of free to use patents shared by large players in the fields. Building legitimacy for new technologies and achieving momentum by facilitating timely use might be more relevant for sustainable innovation than fencing ideas with property rights. Yet, these initiatives have not been entirely successful in promoting knowledge diffusion, suggesting that motives of individual companies and their strategies need to be better understood (Contreras, Hall, & Helmers, 2018).

This chapter aims at discussing the relation between sustainable innovation and IPRs starting from the motives that sustainable innovators might have either to leverage or not to leverage IPRs in their strategies. This discussion is highly relevant in light of the current academic and policy debates on the societal effects of IPR systems. Critical observers have voiced serious concerns on whether IPRs are really serving societies in facilitating innovation (Heller, 2010). There is mounting evidence of strategic practices of IPR filing whereby large corporations erect barriers to entry for newcomers and block sustainable progress in many ways (Bessen, Bessen, & Meurer, 2008; Shiva, 2001). At the same time, IPR offices worldwide also try to link their work to the Sustainable Development Goals (see for instance https://www.wipo.int/sdgs/en/story.html). It remains unclear what (legal or strategic) space sustainable innovators have to engage with IPR in their own specific ways, for instance by filing IPRs but then sharing them or making them available in their own ways.

The chapter is organized as follows. The next session will briefly sketch three types of sustainable innovations (product, process and service) and link them to the applicability of three key IPRs (patents, trademarks and design rights). Section 14.3 will discuss motives of sustainable innovators to use or not to use each IPR, while Section 14.4 will conclude by linking the understanding of motives to current debates on the role of IPRs for sustainability transitions and sketch a research agenda.

14.2 Sustainable innovation and IPRs: What are the options?

14.2.1 Archetypes of sustainable innovation

'Sustainable innovation' is a very broad term that has been linked to many different definitions. The sustainability element of the label typically refers to the three dimensions of environmental, social and economic sustainability, with most of the focus in the literature going to the first one, but increasingly also on the second one (Calabrese, Castaldi, Forte, & Levialdi, 2018). For the purpose of identifying the 'innovation' element of the definition, I will consider three broad categories of sustainable innovation: product, process and service innovation.

Sustainable product innovation takes the form of tangible products that can be adopted by consumers to move to sustainable consumption or by firms to implement sustainable production. Examples include LED lights and solar panels on the environmental and economic dimension, but also products like the Dutch Fair Phone aiming to contribute to both the environmental and social dimension of sustainability (https://www.fairphone.com/en/story/).

Sustainable process innovation concerns changes to production and organizational processes in the direction of making those processes more sustainable. Examples include not only changes towards increased energy-efficiency but also rethinking of value chains like in circular economy initiatives including recycling and upcycling. Process innovations are typically developed and applied within the same organization, but sustainable process innovation refers more often to systems and multiple organizations connected within value chains.

Finally, sustainable service innovation tends to have a more intangible nature as it is about novel solutions provided to meet specific needs of users. Often these service innovations are part of novel business models that challenge the existing way for firms to fulfill specific functions, so-called sustainable business models (Bocken, Short et al., 2014). Clear examples are mobility services and the shift towards sharing models instead of ownership models. Other examples from retail are novel solutions for more sustainable logistics. In the Netherlands the Bewust Bezorgd (loosely translated as 'responsibly delivered') initiative couples online purchase systems of large e-retailers to a menu where buyers can consider different options for delivery after being informed about their respective environmental impact (https://bewustbezorgd.thuiswinkel.org/).

232   *Carolina Castaldi*

14.2.2 IPRs applicable to sustainable innovation

I focus here on the three most used formal IPRs: patents, trademarks and design rights.[1]

A patent "describes an invention and creates a legal situation in which the patented invention can normally only be exploited (manufactured, used, sold, imported) with the authorization of the owner of the patent" (WIPO, 2004, p. 17). Inventions are defined to be solutions to specific technological problems. Patent registration comes after complying with strict and often complex-to-prove conditions: the invention must refer to patentable subject matter, it has to be industrially applicable, it must be novel and non-obvious, and the information needed to realize the invention must be disclosed in the patent description. It should be possible to build and apply the patented invention by someone skilled in the art, which means that publication of a patent releases knowledge that can in principle be put to use. Of course, actual use is controlled by the patenting company, but the inventor can decide to license out the technology for use by others, for several reasons. This is not to say that all patents are actually used, as in fact a large portion of patents remains unexploited, which is a much debated issue in the societal discussion around patent systems (Jaffe & Lerner, 2011).

A trademark is "any sign that individualizes the goods of a given enterprise and distinguishes them from the goods of its competitors." (WIPO, 2004, p. 54). The main rationale behind trademark systems is to facilitate the functioning of markets and avoid market failures derived from information asymmetries between buyers and sellers. As such, trademarks function as information signals that are supposed to reduce the transaction costs in markets. On the sellers' side, trademarks are used to indicate the source of products and services and thereby allow differentiation strategies. They are a way for firms to signal the quality of their offerings; hence they are also key to build reputational assets. Firms have strong incentives to maintain the informational value of their trademarks; hence, they will engage in activities to strengthen the signal (through complementary advertisement and marketing investment) and protect it from dilution (through product recall campaigns in case of negative publicity but also legal trademark enforcement against improper use of trademarks or court cases against competing trademarks). On the buyers' side, trademarks are expected to reduce search costs by allowing to discriminate better among competing offerings in the marketplace. They also offer a retaliation weapon against sellers in case of lower quality. Trademarks are used across all sectors of the economy since they can be used in all markets, from products to services. They will be part of the market strategies of innovative companies.

Design rights "protect the original ornamental and non-functional features of an industrial article or product that result from design activity" (WIPO, 2004). In the United States design rights are protected through the patent system via so-called design patents, different from utility patents, while in Europe design rights are administered by the same office that handles trademark registrations, the EUIPO. The registration of design rights requires proving novelty in the sense of originality.

Given the specific properties of the three IPRs discussed here, one can link each IPR to specific types of sustainable innovation (see Table 14.1).

Patents will be relevant for both sustainable product and process innovation, as long as the innovation has a clear technological dimension. Instead, patents will be less relevant for new services and business models, with the notable exception of countries where business methods and software can be patented. This is the case in the United States, but other countries have instead been reluctant to extend the applicability of patents to these domains since it remains unclear whether this extension of patentable subject matters really delivers societal benefits (Hall, 2003).

Trademarks are mostly relevant for sustainable product and service innovation, less so for process innovation given that the focus of process innovation is not on commercialization but use in production. Trademarks are used to flag the value proposition of the innovation at market introduction, using words and slogans or even figurative and design elements (shape, colors).

Design rights apply to sustainable product innovation whenever the sustainability dimension is about the actual physical properties of the product, think of packaging. For product innovation, sustainability can come together with innovative packaging which reduces transportation costs or uses more sustainable materials. Design can also have a less functional role, if it is about communicating or aligning with the value propositions in the shapes and colors chosen for the product. For service innovation, design is a key component since many new services rethink the interfaces of service provision, often exploiting digital platforms (Calabrese et al., 2018). Design thinking helps here to translate the user perspectives and practices in the architecture of the solution and hence relates to the social component of sustainable innovation.

Of course, that an IPR can be filed does not mean that it will be. In order to better understand the conditions under which sustainable innovation might be protected with any of these three IPRs, the next section will dig into the specific motives underlying IPR strategies of sustainable innovators.

Table 14.1 Archetypes of sustainable innovation and applicable IPRs

	Sustainable product innovation	*Sustainable process innovation*	*Sustainable service/ business model innovation*
Examples	*LED light bulb*	*Eco-design*	*Bike-sharing*
	Organic food	*Recycling*	*Pay-per-light*
	FairPhone	*Energy-saving*	*'Bewust Bezorgd'*
Dimensions and relevant IPRs			
Technology	Patents	Patents	
Market	Trademarks		Trademarks
Design	Design rights	Design rights	Design rights

14.3 Motives (not) to file IPRs for sustainable innovation

14.3.1 Patents

Motives to patent innovation are several and range from straightforward appropriation motives related to controlling use of the patented invention either through own use or use by others upon payment of licensing fees, to motives related to building assets that innovators can use in bargaining for access to other technologies (Blind, Edler, Frietsch, & Schmoch, 2006; Cohen, Nelson, & Walsh, 2000).

Out-licensing might be a valid strategy for companies to benefit from their sustainable technologies, especially when they do not have the scale or resources to translate the technologies into actual products and services (Lane, 2011). In turn, in-licensing of other companies' sustainable technologies can provide opportunities for new ventures with the right business model to use those technologies in the markets. All in all, licensing is a major component of the open innovation model, where given companies patent and own technologies but share access to those patents through licensing agreements (Alexy, Criscuolo, & Salter, 2009). In such a setting, patent rights can work as efficient allocation mechanisms.

Surprisingly, companies might also give away patents for free through donations to public entities like universities or through participation to patent commons (Ziegler, Gassmann, & Friesike, 2004). These initiatives are relevant for sustainable innovation, as there have been a few important cases related to patents of green technologies. The carmaker Tesla made the headlines when announcing that it would open up its patent portfolios to boost technological advances in battery technology. A larger initiative has been one of green patent commons (Contreras et al., 2018)

In some cases innovators might delay patenting to delay knowledge disclosure and hence competition (Desyllas & Sako, 2013). This buys innovators time to experiment further. Some innovators may not patent at all even if they could. This could be a strategic move, whenever innovators prefer secrecy for instance to build a first-mover advantage (Arundel, 2001). It might also be wise for small and/or young firms that lack the resources to enforce patents anyway (Leiponen & Byma, 2009).

14.3.2 Trademarks

Companies embracing sustainable innovation clearly choose for a differentiation strategy. They choose not to compete on prices and costs, but rather to develop a value proposition that can justify a premium pricing (Delmas & Colgan, 2018). Higher prices are also consistent with the idea of a fair retribution of all parties involved in the supply chain. If this is the case, then a strategy of brand investment appears the most sensible option. Moreover, sustainable products and service are typically 'credence goods', where reputation matters significantly for consumers to establish quality.

The sustainability of products is typically not a property that consumers can assess themselves. Instead, markets for sustainable products are characterized by strong information asymmetries given that suppliers hold the full information on the whole production chain behind a product while consumers cannot even fully experience the sustainability of products after purchase. There are different ways in which companies can deliver a trustworthy claim that consumers can rely upon.

Companies can design their own sustainable brands or private labels and protect them with trademarks or rely on labels developed by third-party organizations. These labels can for instance be issued by a coalition of multiple commercial parties or by independent organizations (e.g. Marine Stewardship Council) that monitor whether companies comply with certification schemes. Within these practices one also finds so-called greenwashing practices, of different nature, but involving different degrees of misalignment between claims and actual behavior. Delmas and Colgan (2018) suggest that purposefully misleading claims are only a minority of greenwashing cases. In fact when a greenwashing company associates a trademark to its practice, this gives a weapon of retaliation to (non-greenwashing) competitors and activist organizations that represent civil society. Lane (2011) documents several court cases where trademark claims around sustainability have been challenged in court. Moreover, non-profit organizations increasingly use name-shaming and brand-shaming as strategy to expose misconduct (see for a recent report Greenpeace, 2019).

There are also reasons why companies choose not to trademark. Lack of knowledge and resources is a straightforward argument that applies to small and/or young firms (Block, Fisch, Hahn, & Sandner, 2015). But other reasons might also play a role. Athreye and Fassio (2019) find that the more collaborative the nature of the innovation the less likely innovators are to trademark. The reason is that a trademark comes with commercial appropriation and such a strategy can clash with collaborative nature of the collaboration. In the case of sustainable innovation an additional motive might be that moral, sustainability-driven, drivers of innovation do not appear compatible values with commercial appropriation. Social entrepreneurs struggle with combining a business attitude with their drive for a societal contribution. They can either disregard or even be completely uninformed about IPRs or about trademarks specifically. In the context of the creative sectors, where actors also struggle with competing logistics (in that case artistic vs commercial) Castaldi (2018) found that trademarks might be disregarded specifically or just broadly as all other IPRs.

14.3.3 Design rights

Design rights protect the visual appearance of artifacts, either physical or digital. Ghisetti and Montresor (2019) find that firms investing in design tend to produce more eco-innovation. The whole idea of 'eco-design'

236 *Carolina Castaldi*

Table 14.2 Motives for (sustainable) innovators to apply or not to apply for the patents, trademarks, and design rights

	Motives to	Motives NOT to
Patent	• Appropriate rents from technology from own use • To license-out inventions • Owning to share, for ex. Through participation in patent commons • Delay competition and have time to experiment	• Lack of expertise/ knowledge • No technological invention • Secrecy is chosen, to have first-mover advantage or for lack of resources
Trademark	• Flagging market introduction • Legitimizing identity • Establishing market position and allow differentiation strategy • Attracting external funding • Complementing patents or substituting them	• Lack of expertise/ knowledge • Collaborative nature of the project • Clash of commercial vs sustainability value/ logics
Design rights	• Protection of design from imitation • Control design-mediated communication to users • Complementing other IPRs	• Lack of expertise/ knowledge • Design not recognized as strategic function

revolves around the transformational role that design can play in rethinking the processes and practices behind products and services. That said, one thing is taking a design perspective and another thing is wanting to make it proprietary through design rights. Seip et al. (2019) find that design rights are used in very specific sectors and by specific firms. Sectors include contexts where the design function is considered highly strategic and is internalized within organizations rather than outsourced to external contractors. In terms of firms, one finds that large IPR-active firms will tend to leverage all possible IPR types and hence will also appear as intensive users of design rights. These are large firms that can rely on expertise to draft IPR applications and financial resources to monitor and enforce rights as well. Instead, most designers and other creative entrepreneurs will neither have the knowledge nor the resources to embrace the opportunities from IPRs (Castaldi, 2018; Vankan, Frenken, & Castaldi, 2014) (Table 14.2).

14.4 Conclusions: Towards a research agenda on IPRs for sustainable innovation

There seem to be enough reasons to believe that IPRs can ideally support sustainable innovation by providing rights that empower innovators towards different ends. Profit making is one end but social impact can in principle also be aligned to a well-crafted IPR strategy, for instance through selective licensing. Yet, we see many instances when IPRs appear to be acting as impediments rather than incentives.

While the literature seems to focus either on the positive or negative effects, little attention has been given to the consideration that most firms engaged with sustainable innovation will neglect IPRs and may be perfectly fine doing so unless they become embroiled in legal cases they did not foresee. In fact, we lack systematic evidence on the actual practices of IPR use by sustainable innovators and their desirability from a societal point of view. Further conceptual and empirical research could focus upon four promising research avenues.

A *first* open question relates to the ongoing debate on reforming IPR systems to fix emerging distortions (Dosi, Marengo, & Pasquali, 2006; Henry & Stiglitz, 2010). The current trend for almost all IPR laws has been one of extending the applicability of rights towards new domains with the natural implication that IPR filings have been increasing exponentially. At the same time the reviewing process and the monitoring have not been tightened, resulting in lower quality of the granted rights, for instance, too incremental patents, only filed for strategic purposes. Increasingly, IPR systems appear to be serving the predatory strategies of a few (large) companies which have the resources to hire expansive lawyers, win court cases and leverage all legal opportunities by stacking different IPRs as well. If this is the case, then a pressing question is whether smaller and less experienced firms still have proper access to IPR systems: are sustainable innovators able to leverage the opportunities of IPR systems?

A *second* research trajectory could focus on specific sustainable innovation cases, to collect best practices and common bottlenecks in leveraging IPRs. A very interesting context is one of circular economy initiatives, which often involve sharing of materials and components across different organizations and places, with complex questions of ownership. In fact, several studies by now have shown how IPRs often act as impediments, for instance because of exclusive contracts forced by original equipment manufacturers that frustrate attempts a refurbishing and extending product life-cycles. Yet, the Right to Repair initiative is gaining momentum both in Europe and in the United States. Trademark or patent-protected spare parts could still thrive next to unprotected ones in a situation where consumers would be empowered to choose their preferred option. Research should look into cases of specific industries and investigate actual and possible governance solutions.

A *third*, and related, research domain concerns how IPRs can facilitate the mainstreaming of sustainable innovation by diffusing knowledge and showcasing practices. On the one hand, the poor performance of patent commons sheds major doubts on the effectiveness of patent systems to spur knowledge diffusion; on the other hand, there might be ways to align private and public incentives better, through institutional changes at the levels of norms and/or legislations. There is a much broader range of ways of leveraging IPRs than the most common practices biased towards 'closed models' (Vimalnath, Tietze, Eppinger, & Sternkopf, 2019).

A *fourth* research opportunity could be to broaden the geographical reach of current studies. More inclusive studies capturing the experience of the Global south, not only as victims or laggards, but as providing frugal solutions tweaked in environments where actors cannot rely on strong IPRs. The current norms around IPR systems stem from the choices of a few developed economies, most significantly the United States (Henry & Stiglitz, 2010). A genuine debate on the efficiency of strong IPR systems should take seriously the practices emerging in weak IPR contexts.

A *fifth* and last research agenda item concerns conceptual work. Can we elaborate a responsible IPR framework that can guide not only firms but also IPR institutional actors into more sustainable practices? It appears that current institutions offer enough regulatory space for economic actors to engage with IPRs according to very different norms: some actors can use this space to devise strategic practices, others will use it to put forward inclusive and sustainable practices of IPR use. Several factors might play a role in facilitating the second choice, for instance the type of pressures from customers, suppliers or investors. A conceptual framework on responsible IPR could build upon firm-level theories such as resource-dependence (Pfeffer & Salancik, 2003) or institutional economics (Scott, 2013) to understand motivations and processes. Such a conceptual framework could then be translated into an organizational tools for companies that want to make responsible IPR practices an integrated element of their sustainability goals.

Note

1 There are other, more specialized, IPRs that also matter for sustainability. The protection of plant varieties is a particularly debated topic.

15 Challenges in measuring sustainable innovations performance

Perspectives from the agriculture plantations industry

AD Nuwan Gunarathne and Mahendra Peiris

15.1 Introduction

The achievement of sustainable development goals (SDGs) by 2030 requires urgent action on many fronts, including the promotion of innovations that address not only economic development but also social equity and environmental conservation. Innovations oriented towards sustainability referred to as sustainable innovations hereafter, are considered vital in the transition towards more sustainable economies and societies while mitigating the "the traditional dichotomy between competitiveness and sustainability" (Kiefer, Carrillo-Hermosilla, Del Río, & Callealta Barroso, 2017, p. 1494).

Policymakers and decision-makers in organizations need a systematic process for evaluating sustainable innovation performance in order to justify the investments, to assess their efficiency and to reward those involved in the process (Gunarathne, 2019). Despite considerable efforts made towards developing measures to evaluate sustainable innovations at national and firm levels, there seems to be little consensus on what should be measured and how they could be measured (Birchall, Chanaron, Tovstiga, & Hillenbrand, 2011; Gunarathne, 2019). As many scholars have pointed out, "you cannot manage what you do not measure." There should be sound theoretical and methodological approaches, which are also practical for measuring, analysing, evaluating, and communicating sustainable innovation performance for achieving corporate and sustainability goals. Measurement of sustainable innovation performance is a complex and challenging process given the multitudinous impacts the innovations can have on the economic, social, and environmental dimensions (Bocken, Short et al., 2014; Gunarathne, 2019). The approaches and frameworks for measuring sustainable innovation performance globally remain at a rudimentary and fragmented level (Birchall et al., 2011; Bocken, Short et al., 2014; Gunarathne, 2019; Rauter, Globocnik, Perl-Vorbach, & Baumgartner, 2019).

This chapter aims to explore the challenges in sustainable innovation performance measurement at the firm level by focusing on the plantation agriculture industry. Although this research is not very common in sustainable innovation literature, it is of considerable relevance to sustainable innovation performance measurement. The plantation agriculture industry is a form of commercial agriculture found in tropical countries, in which specialized perennial crops[1] (e.g., bananas, coffee, tea, rubber, and cacao) are grown primarily for export (Park & Allay, 2014). Currently, large extents of land are used for plantation agriculture in developing countries such as Latin America, Asia, and Africa, where there is a tropical climate. In many countries, the area under plantation crops has expanded rapidly in the last few decades, resulting in a massive loss of native forest cover (Hartemink, 2005).

Despite its close connectivity with the environment and communities, the plantation agriculture industry has not witnessed many innovations that address the industry's economic, environmental, or social problems (Gunarathne & Peiris, 2017; Joseph, 2014; Oxford Business Group, 2016). This is an anomaly as sustainable innovation is said to be strongly associated with the sector in which a given firm operates, with firms from more environmental and social impact sectors characterized by a higher number of sustainable innovations adoption (Przychodzen & Przychodzen, 2018).

In addition to the economic, environmental, and social significance of this industry in developing countries in the tropics, plantation agriculture is different from other sectors such as manufacturing or services for several reasons. These distinctive features of the industry offer many challenges in measuring sustainable innovation performance.

- First, plantation agriculture is typically large-scale and export-oriented and a primary foreign exchange earner in the developing countries which are engaged in it. However, for the plantation companies, it poses additional uncertainty as their output is subject to world market agricultural commodity price variations and forex fluctuations (Hartemink, 2005). Therefore, there is a challenge in measuring the economic gains of sustainable innovations that aim to increase the crop yield consistently.
- Second, due to the labour-intensive nature of the industry (Gunarathne, 2020; Joseph, 2014), to be successful, any sustainable innovations should receive the support of its field-level employees who are often not well educated and are resistant to change. The performance of sustainable innovation at the field level can significantly vary with the level of support of the employees.
- Third, in many countries, plantation agriculture is highly dependent on weather conditions. Extreme dry or wet seasons, sweeping changes in climate, and other natural disasters significantly affect crop yield. Hence, there is a high level of uncertainty about the outcomes of sustainable innovations at the field level.
- Fourth, the plantations industry is typified by the possession of a considerable number of biological assets, which are defined as living animals (such as pigs, poultry, cattle) or plants (annual and perennial crops). Since biological assets are living or have an active component that is difficult to

Challenges in measuring sustainable innovation 241

maintain, they are subject to a natural transformation process of growth, degeneration, production, and procreation that causes qualitative or quantitative changes in a biological asset. These assets create significant variability in the performance of sustainable innovations.

Due to these reasons, the plantation agriculture industry offers a useful context to explore the challenges in measuring sustainable innovation performance.

The rest of the chapter is organized as follows: the section titled "Sustainable innovations" provides an overview of sustainable innovations by focusing on different definitions and classification methods. "Sustainable innovation performance and measurement" presents what constitutes sustainable innovation performance, measurement aspects, and challenges. The next section, "Sustainable innovations in the plantation agriculture sector," covers two areas: the tea industry and the sustainable innovations applied in the industry. "Challenges in the measurement of sustainable innovation performance" provides a detailed analysis of the sustainable innovation performance challenges from the plantation agriculture industry, followed by a discussion of the solutions in the "Possible solutions" section. The last section states the conclusions.

15.2 Sustainable innovations

Understanding what constitutes sustainable innovation is essential as the nature and type of innovation can significantly influence its performance measurement and related challenges.

The notion of sustainable innovation is not a stable, monolithic concept but interpreted flexibly and subject to multiple, often contested, framings, and definitions (Colombo, Pansera, & Owen, 2019). There is limited conceptualization of sustainable innovation due to its multifaceted character and diversity (Kiefer et al., 2017; Silvestre & Țîrcă, 2019). Various institutions and scholars have provided different definitions and explanations on sustainable innovations, mostly in parallel with eco-innovations (Adams, Jeanrenaud, Bessant, Denyer, & Overy, 2016; Przychodzen & Przychodzen, 2018). In this respect, eco-innovations are defined as "new or modified processes, technologies and products, which are eco-friendlier and enable the company to avoid or mitigate environmental damage" (Przychodzen & Przychodzen, 2018, p. 3558). Since the focus of eco-innovations is on the environmental dimension only, sustainable innovations should, therefore, encompass social and economic dimensions on equal terms alongside environmental aspects (Adams et al., 2016; Calik & Bardudeen, 2016; Gunarathne, 2019). Przychodzen and Przychodzen (2018) define sustainable innovations as "an introduction of a new or modified solution (either product/service or process), which creates both environmental and social value–added parallel to increased economic profit for the initiating company" (p. 3558). In another definition that is closely in line with the notion of sustainable development, Rauter et al.

(2019) emphasize that sustainable innovations should result in less negative environmental and/or increased social impacts from a full life-cycle perspective and consider the needs of future generations.

Along with an improved understanding of what sustainable innovations entail, scholars have provided different classifications of sustainable innovations. They can be categorized by the size (e.g., small and large innovations), novelty (e.g., new and old innovations or new-to-the firm or new-to-the-market innovations), magnitude of change (e.g., radical or incremental innovations), or nature/object (process, product, organizational and marketing innovations) (Kiefer, Carrillo-Hermosilla, & Del Río, 2019; OECD, 2009; Rennings, Ziegler, Ankele, & Hoffmann, 2006). Among these different types of sustainable innovation classifications, one that merits extra attention in performance measurement is the innovation types by nature/object. Both product innovations, which encompass improvements of goods or services or new product development, and process innovations that enable the production of a given output with fewer inputs are technical. However, organizational innovations (e.g., new forms of management systems such as total quality management) and marketing innovations are non-technical (OECD, 2009; Rennings et al., 2006).

15.3 Sustainable innovation performance and measurement

Sustainable innovation performance is the extent to which the innovation output/results have improved the firm's sustainability success (Calik & Bardudeen, 2016; Rauter et al., 2019). Sustainable innovation performance is the output/results of sustainable innovations reflecting the degree of success of the innovation in achieving the expected economic, social, and economic output/outcomes (García-Granero, Piedra-Muñoz, & Galdeano-Gómez, 2018; Gunarathne, 2019). Since sustainable innovations improve sustainability performance along economic, environmental, and social dimensions, their performance measurement has to capture these dimensions of innovative outcomes (Carrillo-Hermosilla, Del Río, & Könnölä, 2010; Rauter et al., 2019). According to Birchall et al. (2011), there is a 'measurement crisis' of innovation performance as there are so many different models attempting to quantify too many things, some of which are not even important. They suggest that the critical challenge is to ensure that the measurement of innovations leads to improved decision making.

Although equal emphasis should be placed on the measurement of the three dimensions of sustainability performance, a strong focus has been placed traditionally on the economic performance dimension (Rauter et al., 2019). This view has been widely criticized in the traditional performance measurement literature, notably by Kaplan and Norton (1996), who suggested broadening the measurement dimensions to provide a balanced view of performance.

To address the multi-dimensionality of sustainable innovation performance, Rauter et al. (2019) have developed a new scale by defining five dimensions to consider in innovation performance measurement. These dimensions include sustainable product design, resource/process efficiency, environmental pollution, social responsibility and economic perspective.

Along with these normative discussions of the measurement approaches and scales, some authors have documented the measurement challenges as well. These sustainable performance measurement challenges are the identification of sustainable innovation performance indicators in the economic, environmental, and social spheres; quantification of sustainable innovation performance indicators; problems associated with the determination of system boundary measurements; determination of the suitable period for measurement and benchmarking of sustainable innovation performance (Birchall et al., 2011; Cillo, Petruzzelli, Ardito, & Del Giudice, 2019; Gunarathne, 2019). Having analysed the literature on sustainable innovations, Cillo et al. (2019) identify four main research gaps in measuring sustainable innovation performance (see Table 15.1). These issues are rooted in the sustainable innovation performance measurement challenges, which have been highlighted by Gunarathne (2019).

The lack of standard measurement frameworks and approaches can lead to a poor interpretation of the performance of sustainable innovations. This can inevitably lead to flawed decision making at firm and national policy levels (Birchall et al., 2011). Failure to measure performance accurately can result in uncertainty regarding sustainable innovations in many ways. It can cause uncertainty over its *commercial viability* (i.e., uncertainty associated with the possibility of creating a market for an innovation), *organizational appropriability* (i.e., uncertainty associated with the potential to reap the benefits of the innovation and how easily it could be imitated) and *societal acceptability* (i.e., uncertainty associated with the potentially detrimental societal side effects) (Dyck & Silvestre, 2019).

Table 15.1 Challenges in measuring sustainable innovation performance (Gunarathne, 2019)

Main research gaps	Challenge
Lack of fundamental evidence about cause-and-effect relationships between the various measures	Identification issue
To account for differences in innovation performance between organizations with diverse sustainability goals	Benchmarking issue
To distinguish between innovating firm, stakeholder, and society when assessing the impacts of sustainable innovations	Scope issue
To distinguish between short-and long-term performance evaluation measures	Time issue

15.4 Sustainable innovations in the plantation agriculture sector

This chapter uses two sustainable innovations [i.e., *"strip-spreading of tea bushes"* (SSTB) and *"herbicide-free integrated weed management"* (HFIWM)] that have been applied in the tea plantation industry in Sri Lanka in discussing the challenges of measuring innovation performance.

15.4.1 Tea industry in Sri Lanka

Tea is an important form of plantation agriculture practised in Sri Lanka. Tea was first introduced by the British in the mid-19th century on a commercial scale by clearing montane forests in the Central Highlands[2] of the country (Wickramagamage, 2017). Like in many other developing countries where tea is produced, the tea industry forms an important economic sector in Sri Lanka that provides a valuable source of employment and foreign exchange earnings (Gunarathne & Peiris, 2017). For instance, the tea industry contributes to over 65% of the country's agricultural revenue and 13.5% of the export revenue and accounts for about 2% of GDP while offering over 1 million direct jobs and 2.5 million indirect jobs (Bloomfield, 2020). Over an extended period, Ceylon tea (tea produced in Sri Lanka) has earned a reputation for its high quality and demanded premium prices (Sri Lanka Tea Board – SLTB, 2018). As most of the tea plantations are located mainly in the Central Highlands of the country, which are home to an extraordinary range of flora and fauna, including several endangered species, tea is also crucial from an environmental perspective (Peiris & Gunarathne, 2020).

The tea industry in Sri Lanka has recently faced many challenges owing to declining productivity, increasing costs of production, labour shortages, fluctuations in world tea market prices, adverse weather conditions and climate change (Gunarathne & Peiris, 2017; Munasinghe, Deraniyagala, Dassanayake, & Karunarathna, 2017). As Munasinghe et al. (2017) point out, increased cost of production of tea together with declining international prices have led to severe economic, social, and environmental repercussions such as lower profit margins for producers and tea suppliers, stagnation or cuts in payments to employees, inadequate investments in efficient technologies and soil quality management. Not only do these affect the quality of the tea in the long run but they also adversely affect a range of actors in the supply chain and the economic activities reliant on the tea industry. Due to the widespread allegation that glyphosate was causing kidney disease[3] in some parts of the country, the government imposed a ban on the chemical (Jayawardana, 2018), leaving the tea industry with limited options to control weeds in their tea estates. Moreover, the health concerns developed at the consumer end due to the presence of permitted maximum residue levels (MRLs) of agro-chemicals in the tea they drink has also created tremendous

Challenges in measuring sustainable innovation 245

pressure on the industry. The future of the commercial tea industry has become uncertain and volatile with calls for innovations in productivity improvements, environmental conservation and social development (Oxford Business Group, 2016).

The prevailing situation in the Sri Lankan tea industry has led to some field-level innovations that address economic, environmental, and social challenges. This section next presents two important sustainable innovations, which were the brainchild of one of the authors of this chapter.

15.4.2 Strip-spreading of tea bushes (SSTB)

Periodic pruning to rejuvenate tea bushes to maintain the quality of the tea yield and worker productivity is a compulsory agricultural operation in the commercial tea industry. Usually, pruned tea bushes are ready for the first harvest in 90 days after pruning if the growing conditions are favourable. Conventionally, the tea bushes are grown to a level parallel to the ground at the first harvest itself forming a plucking table. SSTB is a method that promotes a quick re-establishment of a bush canopy of tea bushes after periodic pruning by the radial spread of growing shoots using parallel strips arranged along the rows of tea bushes. Here, the branches are temporarily held by tight parallel strips that allow them to shoot up more. Therefore, this process allows the tea bushes to grow larger than under conventional tipping. This simple technique exposes a tea bush to more sunlight enabling it to grow larger and wider and forming a thicker and broader canopy over the ground.

Note: In the SSTB method, there is a developed canopy closing the ground. However, in the traditional method, there is only partially developed bush canopy exposing the ground which leads to wastage of natural and synthetic resources.

15.4.3 Herbicide-free integrated weed management (HFIWM)

HFIWM is a scientifically developed method that selectively controls troublesome weeds in the tea land while promoting the growth of harmless weeds without chemical weed control. This method is specially designed to control the appearance of herbicide-tolerant weed species and other troublesome weeds in commercial tea fields by establishing a cover of harmless and beneficial weeds on the ground. Typically, healthy ecosystems permit robust self-resistance mechanisms against new arrivals of plant species into a system. This usually happens through competition for sunlight, space, moisture, nutrients, and also with the production and secretion of growth-suppressive chemicals on neighbouring plants by the established plants. This phenomenon is termed "*ecosystem immunity.*" The HFIWM process promotes identification and periodic selective removal of troublesome weeds by hand pulling.

Once the troublesome weed species are removed, the rest of the friendly weeds remaining in the soil gradually spread and cover the ground, thus establishing a beneficial weed cover over time. The friendly weeds occupy the area initially occupied by the troublesome weeds while minimizing their recurrence. The green matter produced by the friendly weed cover is slashed down periodically, thus enriching the soil carbon stock, nutrient status and soil biological activity.

Table 15.2 provides an overview of these two sustainable innovations.

These two innovations exhibit a greater potential to contribute to many of the SDGs (see Table 15.3).

Table 15.2 An overview of the two sustainable innovations in the tea industry

	Sustainable innovation	
	SSTB	*HFIWM*
Principal drivers of the innovation	• Quick re-establishment of tea canopy after pruning, improved resource utilization and boosting the yield	• Debilitation of tea bushes
Underlying reasons	• Variations in health and size of the tea bush canopy	• Increased use of herbicides • Ground exposure to natural forces such as air, wind, and sunlight • Improper use of agro-chemicals
Expected outcomes	• Increase in crop yield • Increased income for plantation workers • Suppressed weed growth	• Non-use of weedicides • Healthy and toxic free environment and clean drinking water for workers • Cost savings • Reduced soil erosion • Productive use of agro-chemical inputs
Application	• Applied in the tea industry since 2015 • Over 100 smallholder farmers and several large plantation companies follow this method	• Used in the tea industry since 2012 • More than 100,000 farmers have been educated through Rainforest Alliance farmer training programs, and nearly 50% of them practice this method
Recognition	• Winner of the best national level Blue Economy Eco-Innovation Concept Award in 2016	• Nominated for Global Tea Sustainability Award in 2015 • Rainforest Alliance has incorporated this method in its farmer training programs.

Source: Adopted from Gunarathne (2020).

Challenges in measuring sustainable innovation 247

Table 15.3 Contribution of the sustainable innovations to SDGs

Strip-spreading of tea bushes (SSTB)

SDG	Description
Foster industrial innovation	This is an innovative technology developed to solve many burning issues faced by the present Ceylon tea industry.
Promote decent work and economic growth	Increased tea yield leads to an increase in the income to the plantation workforce while contributing to economic growth and foreign exchange earnings.
Ensure availability of clean water	Increased ground cover by enlarged tea bush canopies minimizes soil erosion through interception, enhances soil water retention, reduces flash flood damage, and improves drinking water quality for the communities.
Ensure responsible consumption & production	Improved resource use efficiency minimizes pollution and wastage of agricultural inputs while reducing the resource demand. It further increases both product quality and profitability of the business.

Herbicide-free integrated weed management (HFIWM)

Foster industrial innovation	This is a process innovation applied in the tea industry and it has the potential to apply in many other perennial agricultural systems.
Protect and restore life on land	In situ generation of green matter upgrades the degraded soils by substantial volumes. It further enhances and protects above- and below-ground biological activity.
Combat climate change	Increased green matter generation leads to a higher level of carbon fixing in the tea fields.
Conserve life below water	Herbicide-free conditions contribute to improved drinking water quality and aquatic life locally, nationally, and globally.
Ensure responsible consumption & production	HFIWM is a breakthrough invention that reduces the use of chemicals and other synthetic agricultural inputs leading to higher resource use efficiency and greater product quality.

15.5 Challenges in the measurement of sustainable innovations

The success or failure of any innovation mainly depends on its ability to win the support of stakeholders, especially of decision-makers and policymakers who have the power to decide on investing or subsidizing investments (Birchall et al., 2011). Thus, the performance measurement of sustainable innovations should depend on the information needs of users. Understanding the requirements of information users is one of the primary challenges in sustainable innovation performance measurement.

Keeping information users in mind, this section discusses the specific challenges in measuring sustainable innovation performance by drawing examples from the perspective of a firm in the plantation agriculture industry (the

248   *AD Nuwan Gunarathne and Mahendra Peiris*

tea industry in Sri Lanka) regarding SSTB and HFIWM methods. These challenges are discussed below:

15.5.1 Determination of the dimension of sustainability performance to be measured

When attempting to measure sustainable innovation performance, a fundamental yet essential issue that arises is the difficulty in determining the dimensions to be measured (Gunarathne, 2019). There are two interconnected issues here.

First, due to the interconnected nature of the sustainability performance, there is a difficulty in deciding the economic, environmental, or social dimension under which the sustainability performance should be assessed. Silvestre and Țîrcă (2019) consider this as a "complexity," which is one of the fundamental characteristics of sustainable innovation. The complexity of sustainable innovation is caused by a large number of interconnected factors that impact, or are impacted by, the other factors (Bocken, Short et al., 2014; Silvestre & Țîrcă, 2019). For instance, when a sustainable innovation leads to an increase in the level of production or worker efficiency given that the employees' remuneration is correlated to production, a fundamental question that arises is under which dimension, i.e., economic or social, should this increase in employee earnings be accounted for. More specifically, in the context of the tea industry, the SSTB method increases the tea crop. Since the greater part of the earnings of the estate workers depends on the quantity of the plucked tea, an increase in tea yield also leads to a rise in the earnings of the estate workers. Should this be assessed under the economic or social dimension? If the performance of sustainable innovation is assessed in totality, variations in the dimension under which the benefits are accrued do not matter. However, for someone interested in the performance of a particular dimension, this can pose a challenge.

Second, even if the first issue is to overcome or to agree upon, there is another challenge to determine the sub-dimensions under which sustainability performance is assessed. For instance, increased coverage of the tea bush canopy under the SSTB method results in larger bush frames with additional wood biomass with fixed carbon. Due to the quick re-establishment of the tea canopy, there are many other environmental benefits such as retention of groundwater storage, increase in soil moisture supply for tea crop, enhancement of the water supply in the downstream catchment areas for other agricultural crop production during dry periods, minimization of soil erosion, and control of the incidence of floods at lower elevations. From a social perspective, it improves the quality of drinking water and lengthens the duration and quantity of drinking water availability. Hence, due to the availability of multitudinous aspects to consider, the determination of the dimensions under which the sustainability performance is accrued is one of the fundamental challenges in the measurement of sustainable innovation performance.

15.5.2 Measurement of the sustainability performance under different dimensions

Even after deciding on the sub-dimensions for measurement of the sustainable innovation performance, the real challenge is confronted in the ensuing stage. For instance, under both SSTB and HFIWM methods, there is a difficulty in measuring the environmental impacts such as the root growth of tea bushes, nutrient use efficiency, improvements in soil conditions, the extent of carbon fixing in the tea bushes, other resource use efficiency such as sunlight and water and actual biomass production.

15.5.3 Establishment of accurate measurement methods which are easy to communicate

Due to the variety of benefits and sub-dimensions to consider, it will be necessary to find new measurement approaches and tools to assess the performance of sustainable innovations. However, this can easily be subject to criticism and scepticism. Since it is the innovation performance that determines the viability and acceptance of sustainable innovation, there is a challenge to win legitimacy and approval from stakeholders who are concerned about a sustainable innovation. As most of the sustainable innovations disrupt the status quo of any industry, there are always actors who resist the acceptance of sustainable innovations. Vague or novel measurement approaches that are not yet widely accepted and fine-tuned can easily be targeted by these actors who oppose the innovations. This is particularly so in industries such as plantation agriculture where there is nexus between stakeholders with varying interests (Gunarathne, 2020). Hence, there is a challenge to find measurement and evaluation tools and approaches of high precision and wide acceptance.

15.5.4 Determination of the system boundary for the measurement of sustainability performance

Another critical challenge that arises in the measurement of sustainable innovation is related to the decision on the system boundary for the measurement. For instance, the reduced input use and minimization of input wastage of synthetic agro-chemicals (fertilizer and herbicides) lead to many benefits that can be recognized at different levels. As a direct consequence, less use of agro-chemicals reduces the cost of production and enables a company to earn premium prices while strengthening the market image of its tea. Since this is a direct economic benefit, the evaluation of the performance of sustainable innovation does not offer a problem (Rauter et al., 2019). Many other benefits are enjoyed at different levels of society. Lower use of agro-chemicals reduces the exposure of estate workers to their harmful impacts. Besides, the minimal escape of these inputs into the environment improves the water quality of the people who are dependent on the water sources originating from the Central Highlands of Sri Lanka. Minimization of agro-chemicals also brings down agro-chemicals residue levels of a product, in this case, the "*made tea*" benefiting the end consumers who are mostly in different countries.

Hence, it will be necessary to have a clear idea of the assessment of sustainable innovation performance such as the company level, estate worker level, regional level, national level, or international level. As Kiefer et al. (2019) highlight, sustainable innovations produce results at macro, meso and micro levels. In assessing sustainable innovation performance, the determination of the boundary for the measurement of sustainable innovation will be a critical challenge.

15.5.5 Determination of the time horizon for the measurement of sustainability performance

Particularly in the plantation agriculture industry in which the perennial crops are grown, it takes a considerable amount of time to witness the full effects of the impact of sustainable innovations (Gunarathne & Peiris, 2017). As Berrone and Gomez-Mejia (2009) note, since the link between environmental (or sustainable) actions and financial performance is not straightforward, it takes time for the sustainable performance to come to fruition. For instance, the extension of the canopy of tea bushes under the SSTB method gives an increased yield over many years. Similarly, the improvements in the soil conditions and the health of the tea bush due to the absence of herbicides in the HFIWM method can give benefits to a plantation company over a considerable period, sometimes over the full life cycle of a tea bush.

If a short period is considered for the assessment of the performance of sustainable innovations, some of the benefits will be underestimated, and hence, the innovation may be underrated. However, a more extended period may not be feasible due to changing climatic conditions, fluctuations in the market conditions, and other factors that are unpredictable and uncontrollable. This challenge is rooted in the "dynamism" of sustainable innovations in which interconnected factors of change and evolve over time, leading to varying results (Silvestre & Țîrcă, 2019). Therefore, there is a challenge in selecting the most suitable period for the assessment of sustainable innovations.

15.5.6 Variability in the sustainability performance on the nature of the biological assets

As already mentioned, the plantation agriculture, pulp and paper, forestry, and farming industries are characterized by the possession of biological assets that are subject to a natural and mostly uncontrollable transformation process. This unique feature of the industry can lead to complications in the measurement of sustainable innovation performance. For instance, the health and vigour of a tea bush can have a significant impact on the recovery of tea bushes after pruning. It leads to a varying number of shoots that arise from a pruned tea bush and the subsequent yield. Hence, this variability of sustainable innovation performance due to the nature of the biological asset poses another major challenge in determining the level of innovation performance. This challenge can again be traced to the character of "dynamism" in sustainable innovations (Silvestre & Țîrcă, 2019).

15.5.7 Variability of the sustainability performance on the innovation process

The two innovations described in the chapter can be identified as process innovations that involve a series of inter-related steps that should be performed with caution. Accordingly, in the SSTB method, factors such as the pruning height from the ground level and the size and spread of branch frame left after pruning can affect the number of branches, their length, and the time taken to grow and attain the required maturity. The post-pruning activities such as proper and timely mossing and ferning, weed management methods, appropriate nutrient management, and maintenance of healthy soil conditions too impact on the post-pruning recovery of tea bushes and the yield. The process involved in sustainable innovation (e.g., pruning and post-pruning activities) will inevitably determine the extent of the sustainable innovation performance and hence leading to changing performance outcomes.

15.5.8 Variability of the sustainability performance on uncontrollable factors

In addition to some of the factors described above, a host of socio-cultural, economic, environmental and technological factors can significantly decide the sustainability performance of the innovations. For instance, in the tea industry, weather and soil conditions, the presence of pests and diseases, and time of the year during which pruning is undertaken, too, are a few other factors that decide the post-pruning behaviour of tea bushes and the subsequent crop yield. While these uncontrollable factors result in a wide variability of sustainable innovation performance, the simultaneous presence of many factors also poses a challenge in isolating the impacts separately.

15.6 Possible solutions

While most of the possible solutions that aim to overcome the sustainable innovation measurement challenges are interconnected, this section provides them with each challenge.

15.6.1 Determination of the dimension of sustainability performance to be measured and measurement of the sustainability performance under different dimensions

As explained in the previous section, due to the multidimensional nature of sustainable innovations, there are many dimensions to consider under measurement (Adams et al., 2016; Gunarathne, 2019; Rauter et al., 2019). The consideration of too many dimensions can result in too much data (Birchall et al., 2011). This drowning in data can, therefore, lead to a 'measurement crisis' where the information users such as decision-makers and policymakers can often be confused (Birchall et al., 2011). As the importance of sustainable performance information mostly depends on the users of such information, it is necessary to decide which dimensions are essential for measurement. For instance, in implementing the SSTB method, top management will be interested in the financial returns for the company. In contrast, policymakers will be keen to know the impact on the broad environment (e.g., beneficial effects on flood control in the downstream areas) or society (e.g., the social benefits of reduced flood risk).

The solution would be to decide on the 'material' aspects (or dimensions) for measurement, depending on the users of sustainable innovation performance information. Even if these material dimensions are determined, the next challenge is connected with measurement. In areas where monetary valuations are difficult to make, economic valuation methods[4] should be used, such as the "market-price method" or "cost-based method" (Hoevenagel, 1994). For instance, the beneficial impact of SSTB on flood control could be measured as saving of the cost of flooding.

15.6.2 Establishment of accurate measurement methods which are easy to communicate

In determining the tools for measuring performance, it is essential to understand and anticipate the demands of the users of sustainable innovation performance. As 'use acceptance' is critical in sustainable innovations (Carrillo-Hermosilla et al., 2010), it is necessary to find the 'right' measurement tool depending on the user group. For instance, in communicating the performance of sustainable innovations to the top management of a company, it is essential to highlight the financial returns to the firm over a long period. However, when promoting a sustainable innovation to policymakers, it is crucial to highlight the monetized societal benefits. Hence, the promoters of sustainable innovation should use reliable and acceptable tools and techniques that are capable of measuring the economic, environmental, and social benefits in monetary terms.

15.6.3 Determination of the system boundary for the measurement of sustainability performance

As explained earlier, the selection of the boundary depends on the requirements of the targeted stakeholder group or information users. A broad scope

Challenges in measuring sustainable innovation 253

or narrow scope could be selected. There will be many different aspects to cover if a broad scope is selected, and the evaluation process can be too complicated. On the other hand, working on a narrow scope boundary could hide much valuable information needed to convince the stakeholders. This could underrate the value of sustainable innovations. Due to the "double externality" problem, where sustainable innovations produce positive externalities for a company during the innovation phase and for society during the diffusion stage, the private returns for a firm can be less than the social gains of an innovation (Rennings, 2000). This calls for policy-level interventions such as "regulatory-push" effects to incentivize the investments at the firm level.

15.6.4 Determination of the time horizon for the measurement of sustainability performance

Since sustainable innovations have long-term implications, it will be necessary to set apart an adequate period for measuring innovation performance. Consideration of a very long period can also distort the measurement process as there can be many variables that can affect innovation performance in the long run. A possible solution would be to conduct several parallel trials simultaneously under different conditions representing a wide range of (environmental) conditions. Following an approach of that kind to measure sustainability performance along the appropriate dimensions will facilitate the propagators of sustainable innovations to reach more practical and applicable solutions within the shortest possible time while gaining social acceptance.

15.6.5 Variability in the sustainability performance based on the nature of the biological assets

A solution to this challenge would be to use an average value that broadly represents the nature of the biological assets (see Table 15.4 for more details).

15.6.6 Variability of the sustainability performance on the innovation process

This challenge could be overcome through the standardization of the process (see Table 15.4 for more details).

15.6.7 Variability of the sustainability performance on the uncontrollable factors

A possible solution would be to develop a range of region-specific innovations with customized steps and remedial actions (see Table 15.4 for more details). The implementers of innovation can then select the most relevant innovation solution to suit their conditions. This approach would level the degree of performance to a great extent while facilitating the performance measurement process and subsequent data analysis.

254 *AD Nuwan Gunarathne and Mahendra Peiris*

Table 15.4 Sustainable innovation performance measurement challenges and possible solutions

Measurement challenge	Sources of the challenge in the tea industry	Possible general solution/s
Determination of the dimension of sustainability performance to be measured *E.g., Groundwater storage and water quality has many sub-dimensions*	• Increase in groundwater storage affects many sub-dimensions such as water availability, water quality, and prevention of soil erosion	• Identification of the material sub-dimensions depending on the interests of the information users
Measurement of the sustainability performance under different dimensions *E.g., Measurement of extended water availability, improvement in water quality, and prevention of soil erosion*	• Measurement of extended water availability during water stress periods for crop production	• Use of innovative and logical measurement approaches consistently *E.g., Extended water availability can be measured as the cost of irrigation during water stress periods*
Variability of the sustainability performance on the nature of the biological assets *E.g., Different properties of the tea crop species can affect the crop quality and quantity*	• Different cultivars of crop with a variety of growth habits and other characteristics such as pest and disease resistance	• Evaluation of the innovative application under different performance categories determined by the nature of the assets
Variability of the sustainability performance based on the environmental factors *E.g., Variations of the bush coverage and crop*	• Variation of performance level due to climatic conditions and soil conditions	• Assessment of response to the innovative application by different conditions.
Variability of the sustainability performance based on the innovation process *E.g., Pruning and post-pruning practices can affect the crop yield*	• Different pruning heights adapted and post-pruning practices can affect the subsequent crop yield	• Standardization of the innovation process

Table 15.4 provides a summary of the possible solutions in addressing several critical sustainable performance measurement challenges.

15.7 Conclusions

Despite the importance of sustainable innovation for the achievement of SDGs, the measurement of innovation outcomes is still at a rudimentary level. Without developed tools and approaches for innovation performance

Challenges in measuring sustainable innovation 255

measurement, the justification of the investments in and promotion of sustainable innovation becomes challenging as decision-makers and policymakers do not have reliable information about the outcome of the innovations. However, the measurement of sustainable innovation performance is inherently problematic.

Drawing applied sustainable innovation examples from the agriculture plantation industry; this chapter provides a comprehensive discussion of these challenges at the firm level. While most of the challenges are common to any sector (identification of the measurement dimension, system boundary, time period, measurement methods and tools and innovation process adopted), some of the challenges (the variability of performance due to the nature of assets and uncontrollable factors) can be industry-specific. The chapter stresses the need to consider the requirements of the sustainable innovation performance information users in seeking possible solutions to address the measurement challenges. It offers some possible generalized solutions for overcoming the measurement challenges.

The discussion made in this chapter opens several avenues for a future research agenda to include sustainable innovation performance measurement. First, there should be further research covering different industries to identify the unique industry-specific challenges in the measurement of sustainable innovation. Second, general or industry-specific research is needed for the development of measurement approaches to assess the various sub-dimensions of sustainable innovation performance. While offering different options for the assessment of multiple sub-dimensions, these studies can finally lead to a general acceptance of the measurement approaches. Third, as highlighted in the study, it will be useful to explore how user expectations affect the measurement of sustainable innovations. This will enable researchers (and innovation propagators) to identify the different levels at which sustainable innovation performance should be measured (e.g., firm, region, national or community), and the suitable measurement approaches. Fourth, there should be future research to identify the innovation performance measurement challenges in assessing the other types of innovation, as suggested by Rennings et al. (2006) and OECD (2009), such as product and service, organizational, and marketing innovations. Finally, researchers should identify and explore various alternatives to account for the variability of sustainable innovation performance due to uncontrollable factors. This is another important factor to consider as the measurement of sustainable innovation performance involves forecasting future benefits and costs. These benefits and costs can be dependent on many uncertainties, such as consumer demand, technological advances, climatic conditions, and socio-economic factors that are beyond the control of innovators. Such variations in the measurement approaches inevitably poses challenges in comparing different alternative innovations. It will, thus, be equally important for future researchers to come up with possible benchmarking mechanisms when innovation performance follows different paths.

Notes

1 Compared to "annual crops", which are cultivated (or sown/planted) at high densities and the economic benefits are obtained within a short period of time, "perennial crops" takes several years to mature and give the intended economic returns. Perennial crops are usually cultivated at relatively low densities and are considered as long-term investments (Hartemink, 2005).

2 The Central Highlands is the mountainous centre of Sri Lanka of which the elevation ranges from 300 to 2500 m (Peiris & Gunarathne, 2020). This region has been recognized as a "super-biodiversity hot spot" in the planet by the International Union for Conservation of Nature (IUCN) due to its significance of the natural ecosystems (ICUN, 2017).

3 This serious health problem called "chronic kidney disease of unknown aetiology (CKDu)" in rural areas of Sri Lanka has shown some association with the farming communities (Rajapakse, Shivanthan, & Selvarajah, 2016). This disease has taken the lives of nearly 20,000 people and sickened up to 400,000 people over the few years. However, due to the complaints made by the tea industry that their plantations becoming plagued by weeds, and resulting in a drastic drop in production, the government of Sri Lanka lifted the ban on glyphosate only for tea industry in July 2018.

4 These economic valuation methods include revealed preference methods (e.g. market value, cost and Hedonic pricing methods) and stated preference methods (e.g. contingent valuation or choice experiment method) for the valuation of ecosystem goods and service [see Hoevenagel (1994) for more details].

References

Abramo, G., D'Angelo, C. A., Ferretti, M., & Parmentola, A. (2012). An individual-level assessment of the relationship between spin-off activities and research performance in universities. *R&D Management, 42*(3), 225–242.

Achterkamp, M. C., & Vos, J. F. (2006). A framework for making sense of sustainable innovation through stakeholder involvement. *International Journal of Environmental Technology and Management, 6*(6), 525–538.

Adamczyk, S., Bullinger, A. C., & Moeslein, K. M. (2011). Commenting for new ideas: Insights from an open innovation platform. *International Journal of Technology Intelligence and Planning, 7*(3), 232–249.

Adams, R., Jeanrenaud, S., Bessant, J., Denyer, D., & Overy, P. (2016). Sustainability-oriented innovation: A systematic review. *International Journal of Management Reviews, 18*(2), 180–205. doi:10.1111/ijmr.12068

Adams, R., Jeanrenaud, S., Bessant, J., Overy, P., & Denyer, D. (2012). *Innovating for sustainability. A systematic review of the body of knowledge.* Ontario: Network for Business Sustainability.

Adger, W. N. (2006). Vulnerability. *Global Environmental Change, 16*(3), 268–281.

Adger, W. N., & Kelly, P. M. (1999). Social vulnerability to climate change and the architecture of entitlements. *Mitigation and Adaptation Strategies for Global Change, 4*, 253–266.

Adner, R. (2006). Match your innovation strategy to your innovation ecosystem. *Harvard Business Review, 84*(4), 98–107.

Adner, R. (2017). Ecosystem as structure: An actionable construct for strategy. *Journal of Management, 43*(1), 39–58.

Adner, R., & Kapoor, R. (2010). Value creation in innovation ecosystems: How the structure of technological interdependence affects firm performance in new technology generations. *Strategic Management Journal, 31*, 306–333.

Adner, R., & Snow, D. (2010). Old technology responses to new technology threats: Demand heterogeneity and technology retreats. *Industrial and Corporate Change, 19*(5), 1655–1675.

Aguirre, B. E. (2002). Sustainable development as collective surge. *Social Science Quarterly, 81*(1), 101–118.

Ahn, J. M. (2020). The hierarchical relationships between CEO characteristics, innovation strategy and firm performance in open innovation. *International Journal of Entrepreneurship and Innovation Management, 24*, 31–50.

258 References

Ahn, J. M., Ju, Y., Moon, T. H., Minshall, T., Probert, D., Sohn, S. Y. & Mortara, L. (2016). Beyond absorptive capacity in open innovation process: The relationships between openness, capacities and firm performance. *Technology Analysis & Strategic Management, 28,* 1009–1028.

Ahn, J. M., Minshall, T., & Mortara, L. (2017). Understanding the human side of openness: The fit between open innovation modes and CEO characteristics. *R&D Management, 47,* 727–740.

Ahn, J. M., Mortara, L., & Minshall, T. (2018). Dynamic capabilities and economic crises: Has openness enhanced a firm's performance in an economic downturn? *Industrial and Corporate Change, 27,* 49–63.

Ahn, J. M., Roijakkers, N., Fini, R., & Mortara, L. (2019). Leveraging open innovation to improve society: Past achievements and future trajectories. *R&D Management, 49,* 267–278.

Ahuja, G., & Morris Lampert, C. (2001). Entrepreneurship in the large corporation: A longitudinal study of how established firms create breakthrough inventions. *Strategic Management Journal, 22*(6–7), 521–543.

Aka, K. G. (2019). Actor-network theory to understand, track and succeed in a sustainable innovation development process. *Journal of Cleaner Production, 225,* 524–540.

Alexy, O., Criscuolo, P., & Salter, A. (2009). Does IP strategy have to cripple open innovation? *MIT Sloan Management Review, 51*(1), 71.

Allen, R. (2014). It's time: Address climate change. *Peninsula Daily News.*

Ambos, T. C., Mäkelä, K., Birkinshaw, J., & D'Este, P. (2008). When does university research get commercialized? Creating ambidexterity in research institutions. *Journal of Management Studies, 45*(8), 1424–1447.

Andersen, M. M. (2002). Organising interfirm learning – As the market begins to turn Green. In T. J. N. M. de Bruijn & A. Tukker (Eds.), *Partnership and leadership – Building alliances for a sustainable future* (pp. 103–119). Dordrecht: Springer.

Anderson, J. C., & Narus, J. A. (1990). A model of distributor firm and manufacturer firm working partnerships. *Journal of Marketing, 54*(1), 42–58. doi:10.2307/1252172

Angrist, J. D., & Pischke, J.-S. (2008). *Mostly harmless econometrics: An empiricist's companion.* Princeton, NJ: Princeton University Press.

Arcese, G., Flammini, S., Lucchetti, M. C., & Martucci, O. (2015). Evidence and experience of open sustainability innovation practices in the food sector. *Sustainability, 7*(7), 8067–8090.

Ardichvili, A., Cardozo, R., & Ray, S. (2003). A theory of entrepreneurial opportunity identification and development. *Journal of Business Venturing, 18*(1), 105–123.

Argyris, C., Putnam, R., & McLain Smith, D. (1985*). Action science.* San Francisco, CA: Jossey Bass.

Aristoteles. (1880). *Politik.* Übersetzt von J. H. v. Kirchmann. (Philosophische Bibliothek Band 7). Leipzig: Verlag der Dürr'schen Buchhandlung.

Arlbjørn, J. S., de Haas, H., & Munksgaard, K. B. (2011). Exploring supply chain innovation. *Logistics Research, 3*(1), 3–18. doi:10.1007/s12159-010-0044-3

Arlbjørn, J. S., & Paulraj, A. (2013). Special topic forum on innovation in business networks from a supply chain perspective: Current status and opportunities for future research. *Journal Supply Chain Management, 49,* 3–11. doi:10.1111/jscm.12034

Arnold, M. G., & Hockerts, K. (2011). The greening dutchman: Philips' process of green flagging to drive sustainable innovations. *Business Strategy and the Environment, 20*(6), 394–407.

References 259

Arthur, B. W. (1989). Competing technologies, increasing returns, and lock-in by historical events. *The Economic Journal, 99*(394), 116–131.

Arthur, W. B. (1994). *Increasing returns and path dependence in the economy*. Ann Arbor: University of Michigan Press.

Arundel, A. (2001). The relative effectiveness of patents and secrecy for appropriation. *Research Policy, 30*(4), 611–624.

Arvidson, M., & Lyon, F. (2014). Social impact measurement and non-profit organisations: Compliance, resistance, and promotion. *VOLUNTAS: International Journal of Voluntary and Nonprofit Organizations, 25*(4), 869–886. doi:10.1007/s11266-013-9373-6

Aspara, J., Lamberg, J. A., Laukia, A., & Tikkanen, H. (2011). Strategic management of business model transformation: Lessons from Nokia. *Management Decision, 49*(4), 622–647.

Athreye, S., & Fassio, C. (2019). Why do innovators not apply for trademarks? The role of information asymmetries and collaborative innovation. *Industry and Innovation, 27*(1–2), 1–21.

Audretsch, D. B., & Feldman, M. P. (1996). R&D spillovers and the geography of innovation and production. *The American Economic Review, 86*(3), 630–640.

Autio, E., Nambisan, S., Thomas, L. D. W., & Wright, M. (2018). Digital affordances, spatial affordances, and the genesis of entrepreneurial ecosystems. *Strategic Entrepreneurship Journal, 12*, 72–95.

Autio, E., & Thomas, E. D. W. (2014). Innovation ecosystems: Implications for innovation management? In M. Dodgson, D. M. Gann, & N. Philips (Eds.), *The Oxford handbook of innovation management* (pp. 204–228). Oxford: Oxford University Press.

Autry, C. W., & Griffis, S. E. (2008). Supply chain capital: The impact of structural and relational linkages on firm execution and innovation. *Journal of Business Logistics, 29*(1), 157–173. doi:10.1002/j.2158-1592.2008.tb00073

Avelino, F., & Rotmans, J. (2011). A dynamic conceptualization of power for sustainability research. *Journal of Cleaner Production, 19*(8), 796–804. doi:10.1016/j.jclepro.2010.11.012

Azzone, G., Brophy, M., Noci, G., Welford, R., & Young, W. (1997). A stakeholders' view of environmental reporting. *Long Range Planning, 30*(5), 699–709.

Baden-Fuller, C., & Mangematin, V. (2013). Business models: A challenging agenda. *Strategic Organization, 11*(4), 418–427.

Banerjee, A. V., & Duflo, E. (2009). The experimental approach to development economics. *Annual Review of Economics, 1*(1), 151–178.

Barman, E., & MacIndoe, H. (2012). *Institutional pressures and organizational capacity: The case of outcome measurement 1*. Paper presented at the Sociological Forum.

Barr, P. S., Stimpert, J. L., & Huff, A. S. (1992). Cognitive change, strategic action, and organizational renewal. *Strategic Management Journal, 13*(S1), 15–36.

Bathelt, H., & Cohendet, P. (2014). The creation of knowledge: Local building, global accessing and economic development – Toward an agenda. *Journal of Economic Geography, 14*(5), 869–882.

Baxter, P., & Jack, S. (2008). Qualitative case study methodology: Study design and implementation for novice researchers. *The Qualitative Report, 13*(4), 544–559. Retrieved from https://nsuworks.nova.edu/tqr/vol13/iss4/2

Brehmer, M., Podoynitsyna, K., & Langerak, F. (2018). Sustainable business models as boundary-spanning systems of value transfers. *Journal of Cleaner Production, 172*, 4514–4531.

260 *References*

Bell, M. L., O'Neill, M. S., Ranjit, N., Borja-Aburto, V. H., Cifuentes, L. A., & Gouveia, N. C. (2008). Vulnerability to heat-related mortality in Latin America: A case-crossover study in Sao Paulo, Brazil, Santiago, Chile and Mexico City, Mexico. *International Journal of Epidemiology, 37*(4), 796–804.

Bellamy, M. A., Ghosh, S., & Hora, M. (2014). The influence of supply network structure on firm innovation. *Journal of Operations Management, 32*(6), 357–373. doi:10.1016/j.jom.2014.06.004

Benner, M. J., & Tushman, M. (2002). Process management and technological innovation: A longitudinal study of the photography and paint industries. *Administrative Science Quarterly, 47*(4), 676–707.

Berrone, P., Fosfuri, A., Gelabert, L., & Gomez-Mejia, L. R. (2013). Necessity as the mother of 'green' inventions: Institutional pressures and environmental innovations. *Strategic Management Journal, 34*(8), 891–909.

Berrone, P., & Gomez-Mejia, L. R. (2009). Environmental performance and executive compensation: An integrated agency-institutional perspective. *Academy of Management Journal, 52*(1), 103–126.

Bertrand, M., Duflo, E., & Mullainathan, S. (2004). How much should we trust differences-in-differences estimates? *The Quarterly Journal of Economics, 119*(1), 249–275.

Bessant, J. (2018). *Exploring innovation space.* Retrieved from https://johnbessant.org/wp-content/uploads/2020/01/Workbook-2-The-4Ps-innovation-compass.pdf

Bessant, J. (2019). *Creating innovation spaces.* Retrieved from http://johnbessant.org/2019/06/29/creating-innovation-spaces/

Bessen, J. E., Bessen, J., & Meurer, M. J. (2008). *Patent failure: How judges, bureaucrats, and lawyers put innovators at risk.* Princeton, NJ: Princeton University Press.

Bhattarai, K., & Conway, D. (2010). Urban vulnerabilities in the Kathmandu Valley, Nepal: Visualizations of human/hazard interactions. *Journal of Geographic Information System, 2*(2), 63–84.

Bigliardi, B., & Galati, F. (2016). Open innovation and incorporation between academia and food industry. In C. Galanakis (Ed.), *Innovation strategies in the food industry* (pp. 19–39). Amsterdam: Elsevier-Academic Press.

Bigliardi, B., & Galati, F. (2018). An open innovation model for SMEs. In F. Frattini, M. Usman, N. Roijakkers, & W. Vanhaverbeke (Eds.,) *Researching open innovation in SMEs* (pp. 71–113). Singapore: World Scientific Publishing.

Birchall, D., Chanaron, J. J., Tovstiga, G. & Hillenbrand, C. (2011). Innovation performance measurement: Current practices, issues and management challenges. *International Journal of Technology Management, 56*(1), 1–20.

Birkmann, J. (2007). Risk and vulnerability indicators at different scales: Applicability, usefulness and policy implications. *Environmental Hazards, 7*(1), 20–31.

Bjerregaard, T. (2010). Industry and academia in convergence: Micro-institutional dimensions of R&D collaboration. *Technovation, 30*(2), 100–108.

Blaikie, P., Cannon, T., Davis, I., & Wisner, B. (2014). *At risk: Natural hazards, people's vulnerability, and disasters.* London: Routledge, Taylor & Francis Group.

Blind, K., Edler, J., Frietsch, R., & Schmoch, U. (2006). Motives to patent: Empirical evidence from Germany. *Research Policy, 35*(5), 655–672.

Block, J. H., Fisch, C. O., Hahn, A., & Sandner, P. G. (2015). Why do SMEs file trademarks? Insights from firms in innovative industries. *Research Policy, 44*(10), 1915–1930.

Bloomfield, M. J. (2020). South-South trade and sustainable development: The case of Ceylon tea. *Ecological Economics, 167*, 106393.

References 261

Blundell, R., & Costa Dias, M. (2000). Evaluation methods for non-experimental data. *Fiscal Studies, 21*(4), 427–468.

Boardman, C. (2011). Organizational capital in boundary-spanning collaborations: Internal and external approaches to organizational structure and personnel authority. *Journal of Public Administration Research and Theory, 22*(3), 497–526.

Boardman, C., & Gray, D. (2010). The new science and engineering management: Cooperative research centers as government policies, industry strategies, and organizations. *Journal of Technology Transfer, 35*(5), 445–459.

Bocken, N., Boons, F., & Baldassarre, B. (2019). Sustainable business model experimentation by understanding ecologies of business models. *Journal of Cleaner Production, 208*, 1498–1512.

Bocken, N., Lenssen, G., Painter, M., Ionescu-Somers, A., Pickard, S., Short, S., . . . Evans, S. (2013). A value mapping tool for sustainable business modelling. *Corporate Governance, 13*(5), 482–497.

Bocken, N., Short, S., Rana, P., & Evans, S. (2013). A value mapping tool for sustainable business modelling. *Corporate Governance, 13*(5), 482–497.

Bocken, N. M., Short, S. W., Rana, P., & Evans, S. (2014). A literature and practice review to develop sustainable business model archetypes. *Journal of Cleaner Production, 65*, 42–56.

Bocken, N. M. P., Farracho, M., Bosworth, R., & Kemp, R. (2014). The front-end of eco-innovation for eco-innovative small and medium sized companies. *Journal of Engineering and Technology Management, 31*, 43–57.

Bogers, M., Chesbrough, H., Heaton, S. & Teece, D. J. (2019). Strategic management of open innovation: A dynamic capabilities perspective. *California Management Review, 62*, 77–94.

Bogers, M., Chesbrough, H., & Strand, R. (2019). Sustainable open innovation to address a grand challenge: Lessons from Carlsberg and the Green Fiber Bottle. *British Food Journal, 122*, 1505–1517.

Bogers, M., Foss, N. J. & Lyngsie, J. (2018). The "human side" of open innovation: The role of employee diversity in firm-level openness. *Research Policy, 47*, 218–231.

Bohle, H.-G. (2001). Vulnerability and criticality. *International Dimensions Programme on Global Environmental Change*. Retrieved from https://www.researchgate.net/profile/Hans_Georg_Bohle/publication/305477730_Bohle_2001_Vulnerability_and_Criticality_Perspectives_from_Social_Geography/links/5790b23508ae108aa04016d1/Bohle-2001-Vulnerability-and-Criticality-Perspectives-from-Social-Geography.pdf?origin=publication_list

Bond. (2016). 50 Innovative business models. Retrieved from https://www.bond.org.uk/sites/default/files/resource-documents/50_innovative_business_models_2.pdf

Bonini, S., Gorner, S., & Jones, A. (2010). How companies manage sustainability: McKinsey Global Survey results. *McKinsey Quarterly (March)*.

Boons, F., & Berends, M. (2001). Stretching the boundary: The possibilities of flexibility as an organizational capability in industrial ecology. *Business Strategy and the Environment, 10*(2), 115–124.

Boons, F., & Lüdeke-Freund, F. (2013). Business models for sustainable innovation: State-of-the-art and steps towards a research agenda. *Journal of Cleaner Production, 45*, 9–19.

Boons, F., Montalvo, C., Quist, J., & Wagner, M. (2013). Sustainable innovation, business models and economic performance: An overview. *Journal of Cleaner Production, 45*, 1–8. doi:10.1016/j.jclepro.2012.08.013

262   *References*

Boonstra, J. J. (2004). *Dynamics of organizational change and learning*. Chichester: Wiley.

Boonstra, J. J. (2013). *Cultural change and leadership in organizations. A practical guide to successful organizational change*. Chichester: John Wiley & Sons.

Boonstra, J. J. (2019*). Organizational change as collaborative play*. Deventer: Management Impact.

Borgatti, S. P., & Halgin, D. S. (2011). On network theory. *Organization Science, 22*(5), 1168–1181. doi:10.1287/orsc.1100.0641

Borgatti, S. P., & Li, X. U. N. (2009). On social network analysis in a supply chain context. *Journal of Supply Chain Management, 45*(2), 5–22. doi:10.1111/j.1745-493X.2009.03166

Boschma, R. (2005). Proximity and innovation: A critical assessment. *Regional Studies, 39*(1), 61–74. doi:10.1080/0034340052000320887

Bouncken, R. B., Fredrich, V., Ritala, P., & Kraus, S. (2018). Coopetition in new product development alliances: Advantages and tensions for incremental and radical innovation. *British Journal of Management, 29*(3), 391–410.

Bozeman, B., & Boardman, P. C. (2003). *Managing the new multipurpose, multidiscipline university research*. Washington, DC: IBM Center for the Business of Government.

Bozzo, E., & Franceschet, M. (2016). A theory on power in networks. *Communications of the ACM, 59*(11), 75–83. doi:10.1145/2934665

Brass, D. J., & Burkhardt, M. E. (1993). Potential power and power use: An investigation of structure and behavior. *The Academy of Management Journal, 36*(3), 441–470. doi:10.2307/256588

Braungart, M., McDonough, W., & Bollinger, A. (2007). Cradle-to-cradle design: Creating healthy emissions–A strategy for eco-effective product and system design. *Journal of Cleaner Production, 15*(13–14), 1337–1348.

Brest, P. (2010). The power of theories of change. *Stanford Social Innovation Review, 8*(2), 47–51.

Breuer, H., & Lüdeke-Freund, L. (2017). *Values-based innovation management*. London: Palgrave.

Brillo, J., Dolan, S., & Kawamura, K. (2014). Coaching by sustainable innovational values: The 40-30-30 tri-intersectional model. *Effective Executive*, IUP Publication.

Brillo, J., Dolan, S., & Kawamura, K. (2014). Coaching by sustainable innovational values: The case of the 40-30-30 tri-intersectional model. *Esade Working Paper*. Barcelona: Esade.

Brillo, J., Dolan, S., Kawamura, K., & Fernandez, X., (2015). Managing by sustainable innovational values. *Journal of Management and Sustainability, 5*(3), 61–82.

Brundtland, G. (ed.) (1987). *Our common future*. WECD (World Commission on Environment and Development). Oxford: Oxford University Press, ISBN 019282080X.

Brunswicker, S., & Vanhaverbeke, W. (2015). Open innovation in small and medium-sized enterprises (SMEs): External knowledge sourcing strategies and internal organizational facilitators. *Journal of Small Business Management, 53*(4), 1241–1263.

Business Insider. (2019). *How businesses can be responsible with energy in today's demanding world*. Retrieved from https://www.businessinsider.com/sc/how-businesses-can-be-more-sustainable-2019-9?international=true&r=US&IR=T

Bussy, G., & Tims, M. (1980). *Pioneers for peace: Women's International League for Peace and Freedom 1915–1965*. London: WILPF British section.

Buttol, P., Buonamici, R., Naldesi, L., Rinaldi, C., Zamagni, A., & Masoni, P. (2012). Integrating services and tools in an ICT platform to support eco-innovation in SMEs. *Clean Technologies and Environmental Policy, 14*(2), 211–221.

References 263

Buysse, K., & Verbeke, A. (2003). Proactive environmental strategies: A stakeholder management perspective. *Strategic Management Journal, 24*(5), 453–470.

Buzzfeed. (2019). *WWF funds guards who have tortured and killed people.* Retrieved from https://www.buzzfeednews.com/article/tomwarren/wwf-world-wide-fund-nature-parks-torture-death

Cainelli, G., D'Amato, A., & Mazzanti, M. (2017). Resource efficiency, environmental policy and eco-innovations for a circular economy: Evidence from EU firms. *SWPS 2017–24.* doi:10.2139/ssrn.3070397

Cainelli, G., De Marchi, V., & Grandinetti, R. (2015). Does the development of environmental innovation require different resources? Evidence from Spanish manufacturing firms. *Journal of Cleaner Production, 94*, 211–220.

Calabrese, A., Castaldi, C., Forte, G., & Levialdi, N. G. (2018). Sustainability-oriented service innovation: An emerging research field. *Journal of Cleaner Production, 193*, 533–548.

Calik, E., & Bardudeen, F., (2016). A measurement scale to evaluate sustainable innovation performance in manufacturing organizations. *Procedia CIRP, 40*, 449–54.

Cambridge English Dictionary. (n.d.). *Value.* Retrieved at 25 March 2020, from https://dictionary.cambridge.org/dictionary/english/value

Cammarano, A., Michelino, F., & Caputo, M. (2019). Open innovation practices for knowledge acquisition and their effects on innovation output. *Technology Analysis & Strategic Management, 31*(11), 1297–1313. doi:10.1080/09537325.2019.1606420

Campanella, T. J. (2006). Urban resilience and the recovery of New Orleans. *Journal of the American Planning Association, 72*(2), 141–146.

Carayannis, E. G., & Campbell, D. F. J. (2009). 'Mode 3' and 'Quadruple Helix': Toward a 21st century fractal innovation ecosystem. *International Journal of Technology Management, 46*(3/4), 201–234.

Carman, J. G. (2009). Nonprofits, funders, and evaluation: Accountability in action. *The American Review of Public Administration, 39*(4), 374–390.

Carrillo-Hermosilla, J., Del Río, P., & Könnölä, T. (2010). Diversity of eco-innovations: Reflections from selected case studies. *Journal of Cleaner Production, 18*(10–11), 1073–1083.

Carroll, A. B., & Buchholtz, A. K. (2014). *Business and society: Ethics, sustainability, and stakeholder management.* Toronto: Nelson Education.

Carroll, A. B., & Shabana, K. M. (2010). The business case for corporate social responsibility: A review of concepts, research and practice. *International Journal of Management Reviews, 12*(1), 85–105.

Casadesus-Masanell, R., & Zhu, F. (2013). Business model innovation and competitive imitation: The case of sponsor-based business models. *Strategic Management Journal, 34*(4), 464–482.

Cassia, L., Minola, T., & Paleari, S. (2011). Entrepreneurship, technology and change: A review and proposal for an interpretative framework. In L. Cassia, T. Minola, & S. Paleari (Eds.), *Entrepreneurship and technological change* (pp. 1–16). Cheltenham: Edward Elgar Publishing Limited.

Castaldi, C. (2018). To trademark or not to trademark: The case of the creative and cultural industries. *Research Policy, 47*(3), 606–616.

Cavalcante, S., Kesting, P., & Ulhøi, J. (2011). Business model dynamics and innovation: (Re) establishing the missing linkages. *Management Decision, 49*(8), 1327–1342.

Ceptureanu, S. I., Ceptureanu, E. G., Orzan, M. C., & Marin, I. (2017). Toward a Romanian NPOs sustainability model: Determinants of sustainability. *Sustainability, 9*(6), 1–26.

264   *References*

Chambers, R. (1994). The origins and practice of participatory rural appraisal. *World Development, 22*(7), 953–969.

Chambers, R. (2009). So that the poor count more: Using participatory methods for impact evaluation. *Journal of Development Effectiveness, 1*(3), 243–246.

Chambers, R. (2017). *Can we know better? Reflections for development.* Warckwickshire: Practical Action Publishing.

Chan, C. S., & Parhankangas, A. (2017). Crowdfunding innovative ideas: How incremental and radical innovativeness influence funding outcomes. *Entrepreneurship Theory and Practice, 41*(2), 237–263. doi:10.1111/etap.12268

Chandy, R. K., & Tellis, G. J. (1998). Organizing for radical product innovation: The overlooked role of willingness to cannibalize. *Journal of Marketing Research, 35*(4), 474–487.

Chaouachi, A., Bompard, E., Fulli, G., Masera, M., De Gennaro, M., & Paffumi, E. (2016). Assessment framework for EV and PV synergies in emerging distribution systems. *Renewable and Sustainable Energy Reviews, 55*(3), 719–728. doi:10.1016/j.rser.2015.09.093

Charter, M., & Clark, T. (2007). *Sustainable innovation.* Farnham: The Centre for Sustainable Design.

Charter, M., Gray, C., Clark, T., & Woolman, T. (2017). The role of business in realising sustainable consumption and production. In *System Innovation for Sustainability 1* (pp. 56–79). Milton Park, Abingdon: Routledge-Taylor & Francis group.

Cheng, C. C. J., Yang, C.-l., & Sheu, C. (2014). The link between eco-innovation and business performance: A Taiwanese industry context. *Journal of Cleaner Production, 64*, 81–90. doi:10.1016/j.jclepro.2013.09.050

Chertow, M. R. (2000). Industrial symbiosis: Literature and taxonomy. *Annual Review of Energy and the Environment, 25*(1), 313–337. doi:10.1146/annurev.energy.25.1.313

Chesbrough, H. (2003). *Open innovation: The new imperative for creating and profiting from technology.* Boston, MA: Harvard Business Press.

Chesbrough, H. (2006). *Open business models: How to thrive in the new innovation landscape.* Boston, MA: Harvard Business Press.

Chesbrough, H. (2010). Business model innovation: Opportunities and barriers. *Long Range Planning, 43*(2), 354–363.

Chesbrough, H., & Bogers, M. (2014). Explicating open innovation: Clarifying an emerging paradigm for understanding innovation. In H. Chesbrough, W. Vanhaverbeke, & J. West (Eds.). *New Frontiers in Open Innovation* (pp. 3–28). Oxford: Oxford University Press.

Chesbrough, H., & Prencipe, A. (2008). Networks of innovation and modularity: A dynamic perspective. *International Journal of Technology Management, 42*(4), 414–425.

Chesbrough, H., Vanhaverbeke, W., & West, J. (2006). Open innovation: A new paradigm for understanding industrial innovation. In In H. Chesbrough, W. Vanhaverbeke, & J. West (Eds.) *Open innovation: Researching a new paradigm* (pp. 1–12). Oxford: Oxford University Press.

Choi, T. Y., Dooley, K. J., & Rungtusanatham, M. (2001). Supply networks and complex adaptive systems: Control versus emergence. *Journal of Operations Management, 19*(3), 351–366. doi:10.1016/S0272-6963(00)00068-1

Choi, T. Y., & Kim, Y. (2008). Structural embeddedness and supplier management: A network perspective. *Journal of Supply Chain Management, 44*(4), 5–13. doi:10.1111/j.1745-493X.2008.00069

Christensen, C. M., Raynor, M. E., & McDonald, R. (2015). What is disruptive innovation. *Harvard Business Review, 93*(12), 44–53.

Chung, G. H., Choi, J. N., & Du, J. (2017). Tired of innovations? Learned helplessness and fatigue in the context of continuous streams of innovation implementation. *Journal of Organizational Behavior, 38*, 1130–1148.

Cillo, V., Petruzzelli, A. M., Ardito, L., & Del Giudice, M. (2019). Understanding sustainable innovation: A systematic literature review. *Corporate Social Responsibility & Environmental Management, 26*(5), 1012–1025. doi:10.1002/csr.1783

CLACC. (2009). *Climate change and the urban poor: Risk and resilience in 15 of the world's most vulnerable cities. Capacity strengthening in the least developed countries for adaptation to climate change (CLACC) Programme.* London: IIED.

Clarkson, M. E. (1995). A stakeholder framework for analyzing and evaluating corporate social performance. *Academy of Management Review, 20*(1), 92–117.

Clarysse, B., Wright, M., Bruneel, J., & Mahajan, A. (2014). Creating value in ecosystems: Crossing the chasm between knowledge and business ecosystems. *Research Policy, 43*, 1164–1176.

Claudel, M. (2018). From organizations to organizational fields: The evolution of civic innovation ecosystems. *Technology Innovation Management Review, 8*(6), 34–47.

Cohen, W. M., & Levinthal, D. A. (1990). Absorptive capacity: A new perspective on learning and innovation. *Administrative Science Quarterly, 35*(1), 128–152.

Cohen, W. M., Nelson, R. R., & Walsh, J. P. (2000). Protecting their intellectual assets: Appropriability conditions and why US manufacturing firms patent (or not) (No. w7552). National Bureau of Economic Research. Retrieved from https://www.nber.org/papers/w7552.pdf

Collins, J., & Porras, J. (1996, September–October). Building your company's vision. *Harvard Business Review.*

Colombo, L. A., Pansera, M., & Owen, R. (2019). The discourse of eco-innovation in the European Union: An analysis of the Eco-Innovation Action Plan and Horizon 2020. *Journal of Cleaner Production, 214*, 653–665.

Contreras, J. L., Hall, B. H. & Helmers, C. (2018), *Green technology diffusion: A post-mortem analysis of the eco-patent commons.* NBER working paper.

Coryn, C. L., Noakes, L. A., Westine, C. D., & Schröter, D. C. (2011). A systematic review of theory-driven evaluation practice from 1990 to 2009. *American Journal of Evaluation, 32*(2), 199–226.

Cousins, P., & Lamming, R. (2008). *Strategic supply management: Principles, theories and practice.* Essex: Pearson Education.

Cox, A. (1999). Power, value and supply chain management. *Supply Chain Management: An International Journal, 4*(4), 167–175. doi:10.1108/13598549910284480

Cox, A., Sanderson, J., & Watson, G. (2001). *Power regimes: A new perspective on managing in supply chains and networks.* Paper presented at the 10th International Annual IPSERA Conference Jönköping, Sweden.

Crossan, M. M., & Apaydin, M. (2010). A multi-dimensional framework of organizational innovation: A systematic review of the literature. *Journal of Management Studies, 47*(6), 1154–1191. doi:10.1111/j.1467-6486.2009.00880.x

Cutter, S. L., Boruff, B. J., & Shirley, W. L. (2003). Social vulnerability to environmental hazards. *Social Science Quarterly, 84*(2), 242–261.

Cutter, S. L., & Finch, C. (2008). Temporal and spatial changes in social vulnerability to natural hazards. *Proceedings of the National Academy of Sciences of the United States of America, 105*(7), 2301–2306.

266   *References*

Czarnitzki, D., Grimpe, C., & Toole, A. A. (2014). Delay and secrecy: Does industry sponsorship jeopardize disclosure of academic research? *Industrial and Corporate Change, 24*(1), 251–279.

Dahlander, L., & Gann, D. M. (2010). How open is innovation? *Research Policy, 39*(6), 699–709.

Dale, R. (2003). The logical framework: An easy escape, a straitjacket, or a useful planning tool? *Development in Practice, 13*(1), 57–70.

Daly, H. E., & Daly, H. E. (Eds.). (1973). *Toward a steady-state economy (Vol. 2).* San Francisco, CA: WH Freeman.

Dangelico, R. M., Pontrandolfo, P., & Pujari, D. (2013). Developing sustainable new products in the textile and upholstered furniture industries: Role of external integrative capabilities. *Journal of Product Innovation Management, 30*(4), 642–658.

Darroch, J., & McNaughton, R. (2002). Examining the link between knowledge management practices and types of innovation. *Journal of Intellectual Capital, 3*(3), 210–222.

Dart, J., & Davies, R. (2003). A dialogical, story-based evaluation tool: The most significant change technique. *American Journal of Evaluation, 24*(2), 137–155.

DaSilva, C., & Trkman, P. (2014). Business models: What it is and what it is not. *Long Range Planning, 47*(6), 379–389. doi:10.1016/j.lrp.2013.08.004

Daub, C. H., Scherrer, Y. M., & Verkuil, A. H. (2014). Exploring reasons for the resistance to sustainable management within non-profit organizations. *Sustainability, 6*, 3252–3270.

De Chernatony, L., Harris, F., & Dall'Olmo Riley, F. (2000). Added value: Its nature, roles and sustainability. *European Journal of Marketing, 34*(1/2), 39–56.

de Jesus, A., Antunes, P., Santos, R., & Mendonça, S. (2018). Eco-innovation in the transition to a circular economy: An analytical literature review. *Journal of Cleaner Production, 172*, 2999–3018.

de Jesus, A., & Mendonça, S. (2018). Lost in transition? Drivers and barriers in the eco-innovation road to the circular economy. *Ecological Economics, 145*, 75–89.

De Marchi, V. (2012). Environmental innovation and R&D cooperation: Empirical evidence from Spanish manufacturing firms. *Research Policy, 41*(3), 614–623.

De Medeiros, J. F., Ribeiro, J. L. D., & Cortimiglia, M. N. (2014). Success factors for environmentally sustainable product innovation: A systematic literature review. *Journal of Cleaner Production, 65*, 76–86.

De Zubielqui, G. C., Jones, J., & Statsenko, L. (2016). Managing innovation networks for knowledge mobility and appropriability: A complexity perspective. *Entrepreneurship Research Journal, 6*(1), 75–109.

Del Brío, J. Á., Fernández, E., Junquera, B., & Vázquez, C. J. (2001). Environmental managers and departments as driving forces of TQEM in Spanish industrial companies. *International Journal of Quality & Reliability Management, 18*(5), 495–511.

Della Corte, V., & Del Gaudio, G. (2014). A literature review on value creation and value capturing in strategic management studies. *Corporate Ownership & Control, 11*(2), 328–346.

Delmas, M. A., & Colgan, D. (2018). *The green bundle: Pairing the market with the planet.* Stanford, CA: Stanford University Press.

Delmas, M. A., & Terlaak, A. K. (2001). A framework for analyzing environmental voluntary agreements. *California Management Review, 43*(3), 44–63.

References 267

DeMol, E. (2019, March 21). What makes a successful startup team? *Harvard Business Review*. Retrieved from http://hbr.org/2019/03/what-makes-a-successful-startup-team#

Dentchev, N. A., & Heene, A. (2004). Toward stakeholder responsibility and stakeholder motivation: Systemic and holistic perspectives on corporate sustainability. In S. Sharma & M. Starik (Eds.) *Stakeholders, the environment and society: New perspectives in research on corporate sustainability*. Cheltenham, UK: Edward Elgar Publishing. (pp. 117–139).

Dentchev, N., Rauter, R., Jóhannsdóttir, L., Snihur, L., Rosano, M., Baumgartner, R., . . . Jonker, J. (2018). Embracing the variety of sustainable business models: A prolific field of research and a future research agenda. *Journal of Cleaner Production, 194*, 695–703.

Desyllas, P., & Sako, M. (2013). Profiting from business model innovation: Evidence from Pay-As-You-Drive auto insurance. *Research Policy, 42*(1), 101–116.

Dewar, R. D., & Dutton, J. E. (1986). The adoption of radical and incremental innovations: An empirical analysis. *Management Science, 32*(11), 1422–1433.

Di Minin, A., Frattini, F., & Piccaluga, A. (2010). Fiat: Open innovation in a downturn (1993–2003). *California Management Review, 52*, 132–159.

Díaz-García, C., González-Moreno, Á., & Sáez-Martínez, F. J. (2015). Eco-innovation: Insights from a literature review. *Innovation, 17*(1), 6–23.

DiMaggio, P. J., & Powell, W. W. (1983). The iron cage revisited: Institutional isomorphism and collective rationality in organizational fields. *American Sociological Review, 48*(2), 147–160.

Dmitriev, V., Simmons, G., Truong, Y., Palmer, M., & Schneckenberg, D. (2014). An exploration of business model development in the commercialization of technology innovations. *R&D Management, 44*, 306–321.

Dodgson, M., Gann, D. M., & Salter, A. (2008). *The management of technological innovation: Strategy and practice*. New York: Oxford University Press on Demand.

Doganova, L., & Eyquem-Renault, M. (2009). What do business models do?: Innovation devices in technology entrepreneurship. *Research Policy, 38*(10), 1559–1570.

Dolan, S. L. (2011). *Coaching by values. A guide to success in the life of business and the business of life*. Bloomington, MN: IUniverse Inc.

Dolan, S., Garcia, S., & Richley, B. (2006). *Managing by values: A corporate guide to living, being alive, and making a living in the 21t Century*. Hampshire: Palgrave Macmillan.

Domínguez-Escrig, E., Mallén-Broch, F., Lapiedra-Alcamí, R., & Chiva-Gómez, R. (2019). The influence of leaders' stewardship behavior on innovation success: The mediating effect of radical innovation. *Journal of Business Ethics, 159*(3), 849–862. doi:10.1007/s10551-018-3833-2

Dommerholt, E. (2019). *Prutsenderwijs duurzaam presteren; Over het wat, waarom en hoe van duurzame ontwikkeling en de circulaire economie*, 1st ed. Soest: Boekscout.

Donghyun, K., & Lim, U. (2016). Urban resilience in climate change adaptation: A conceptual framework. *Sustainability, 8*, 405.

Dornan, M., Morgan, W., Cain, T. N., & Tarte, S. (2018). What's in a term? "Green growth" and the "blue-green economy" in the Pacific islands. Retrieved from doi:10.1002/app5.258

Dosi, G. (1982). Technological paradigms and technological trajectories. *Research Policy, 11*(3), 147–162.

268   *References*

Dosi, G., Marengo, L., & Pasquali, C. (2006). How much should society fuel the greed of innovators?: On the relations between appropriability, opportunities and rates of innovation. *Research Policy, 35*(8), 1110–1121.

Dougherty, D., & Dunne, D. D. (2011). Organizing ecologies of complex innovation. *Organization Science, 22*(5), 1214–1223.

Dowling, J., & Pfeffer, J. (1975). Organizational legitimacy: Social values and organizational behavior. *Pacific Sociological Review, 18*(1), 122–136.

Downing, T. E., & Patwardhan, A. (Eds.). (2004). *Adaptation policy frameworks for climate change: Developing strategies, policies and measures.* Cambridge: Cambridge University Press.

Doz, Y. L., & Kosonen, M. (2010). Embedding strategic agility: A leadership agenda for accelerating business model renewal. *Long Range Planning, 43*(2), 370–382.

Drabe, V., & Herstatt, C. (2016). *Why and how companies implement circular economy concepts – The case of cradle to cradle innovations.* Paper presented at the R&D Management Conference "From Science to Society: Innovation and Value Creation", Cambridge, UK.

Duflo, E., & Kremer, M. (2005). Use of randomization in the evaluation of development effectiveness. *Evaluating Development Effectiveness, 7*, 205–231.

Dussauge, P., Garrette, B., & Mitchell, W. (2000). Learning from competing partners: Outcomes and durations of scale and link alliances in Europe, North America and Asia. *Strategic Management Journal, 21*(2), 99–126.

Dyck, B., & Silvestre, B. S. (2019). A novel NGO approach to facilitate the adoption of sustainable innovations in low-income countries: Lessons from small-scale farms in Nicaragua. *Organization Studies, 40*(3), 443–461.

Dziallas, M., & Blind, K. (2019). Innovation indicators throughout the innovation process: An extensive literature analysis. *Technovation, 80*, 3–29.

Eakin, H., & Luers, A. L. (2006). Assessing the vulnerability of social-environmental systems. *Annual Review of Environment and Resources, 31*(1), 365–394.

Ebner, W., Leimeister, J. M, & Krcmar, H. (2009). Community engineering for innovations: The ideas competition as a method to nurture a virtual community for innovations. *R&D Management, 39*, 342–356.

Ebrahim, A. (2003). Accountability in practice: Mechanisms for NGOs. *World Development, 31*(5), 813–829.

Ebrahim, A. (2005). Accountability myopia: Losing sight of organizational learning. *Nonprofit and Voluntary Sector Quarterly, 34*(1), 56–87.

Ebrahim, A. (2009). Placing the normative logics of accountability in "thick" perspective. *American Behavioral Scientist, 52*(6), 885–904.

Ebrahim, A. (2019). *Measuring social change: Performance and accountability in a complex world.* Stanford, CA: Stanford University Press.

Ebrahim, A., & Rangan, V. K. (2010). *The limits of nonprofit impact: A contingency framework for measuring social performance* (No. 10-099). Harvard Business School.

Ebrahim, A., & Rangan, V. K. (2014). What impact? A framework for measuring the scale and scope of social performance. *California Management Review, 56*(3), 118–141.

Eby, L. T., Adams, D. M., Russell, J. E., & Gaby, S. H. (2000). Perceptions of organizational readiness for change: Factors related to employees' reactions to the implementation of teambased selling. *Human Relations, 53*(3), 419–442.

Eden, C., & Huxham, C. (1996). Action research and the study of organizations. In S. R. Clegg, C. Hardy, & W. R. Nords (Eds.), *Handbook of organization studies* (pp. 526–542). London: Sage.

References 269

Edwards, M., & Hulme, D. (1996). Beyond the magic bullet: NGO performance and accountability in the post-cold war world, 377–439.

EIO. (2016). *Policies and practices for eco-innovation uptake and circular economy transition. Eco-innovation observatory.* Brussels: European Commission & Eco-Innovation Observatory (EC&EIO).

Eisenhardt, K. M. (1989). Building theories from case study research. *Academy of Management Review, 14*(4), 532–550.

Eisenhardt, K. M., & Graebner, M. E. (2007). Theory building from cases: Opportunities and challenges. *Academy of Management Journal, 50*(1), 25–32.

Elenkov, D. S. & Manev, I. M. (2016). Top management leadership and influence on innovation: The role of sociocultural context. *Journal of Management, 31*, 381–402.

Elkington, J. (1994). Towards the sustainable corporation: Win-win-win business strategies for sustainable development. *California Management Review, 36*(2), 90–100.

Elkington, J. (2013). Enter the triple bottom line. In A. Henriques & J. Richardson (Eds.) *The triple bottom line* (pp. 23–38). New York: Routledge.

Emerson, R. M. (1962). Power-dependence relations. *American Sociological Review, 27*(1), 31–41. doi:10.2307/2089716

Enkel, E., Gassmann, O., & Chesbrough, H. (2009). Open R&D and open innovation: Exploring the phenomenon. *R&D Management, 39*(4), 311–316.

Eppinger, E., Bocken, N., Dreher, C., Gurtoo, A., Chea, R. H., Karpakal, S., . . . Vimalnath, P. (2019). *The role of intellectual property rights in sustainable business models: Mapping IP strategies in circular economy business models.* Presented at the 4th International Conference on New Business Models, Berlin on 1–3 July 2019.

Eriksen, S. H., & Kelly, P. M. (2007). Developing credible vulnerability indicators for climate adaptation policy assessment. *Mitigation and Adaptation Strategies for Global Change, 12*(4), 495–524.

European Commission. (2017). *Circular economy research and innovation: Connecting economic and environmental gains.* Retrieved from Brussels, Belgium https://ec.europa.eu/programmes/horizon2020/sites/horizon2020/files/ce_booklet.pdf

European Commission. Directorate-General for Economic. (2008). *EMU@ 10: Successes and challenges after 10 years of Economic and Monetary Union* (No. 2). Brussels: European Communities.

Evans, S., Vladimirova, D., Holgado, M., Van Fossen, K., Yang, M., Silva, E. A., & Barlow, C. Y. (2017). Business model innovation for sustainability: Towards a unified perspective for creation of sustainable business models. *Business Strategy and the Environment, 26*(5), 597–608.

Everett, M. G., & Borgatti, S. P. (1999). The centrality of groups and classes. *The Journal of Mathematical Sociology, 23*(3), 181–201. doi:10.1080/0022250X.1999.9990219

Felber, C. (2014). *Die Gemeinwohl-Ökonomie: Erweiterte Neuausgabe.* Vienna: Paul Zsolnay Verlag.

Felber, C. (2016). *Die Gemeinwohl-Ökonomie: Ein Wirtschaftsmodell mit Zukunft.* Begegnung und Gespräch, 175, 1/2016. Retrieved from http://christian-felber.at/artikel/pdf/BuG_175_1-2016.pdf

Feller, I., & Roessner, D. (1995). What does industry expect from university partnerships? *Issues in Science and Technology, 12*(1), 80–84.

Fischer-Kowalski, M. (2011). Analyzing sustainability transitions as a shift between socio-metabolic regimes. *Environmental Innovation and Societal Transitions, 1*(1), 152–159.

270   *References*

Foss, N. J., & Saebi, T. (2017). Fifteen years of research on business model innovation: How far have we come, and where should we go? *Journal of Management, 43*(1), 200–227.

Franco, M. A. (2017). Circular economy at the micro level: A dynamic view of incumbents' struggles and challenges in the textile industry. *Journal of Cleaner Production, 168*, 833–845. doi:10.1016/j.jclepro.2017.09.056

Frankl, V. E., & Lorenz, K. (1979). *Der Mensch vor der Frage nach dem Sinn: eine Auswahl aus dem Gesamtwerk.* München: Piper.

Freeman, R. E. (1984). *Strategic management: A stakeholder approach.* Boston, MA: Pitman.

Freeman, R. E. (2010a). Managing for stakeholders: Trade-offs or value creation. *Journal of Business Ethics, 96*(1), 7–9.

Freeman, R. E. (2010b). *Strategic management: A stakeholder approach.* Cambridge: Cambridge University Press.

Friedman, R. S. (1982). The role of university organized research units in academic science. Springfield, VA: National Technical Information Service [NTIS].

Frumkin, P. (2010). *The essence of strategic giving: A practical guide for donors and fundraisers.* Chicago, IL: University of Chicago Press.

Füssel, H. -M. (2007). Vulnerability: A generally applicable conceptual framework for climate change research. *Global Environmental Change, 17*(2), 155–167.

Fussler, C., & James, P. (1996). *Eco-innovation: A breakthrough discipline for innovation and sustainability.* London: Pitman.

Gabriele Arnold, M. (2011). The role of open innovation in strengthening corporate responsibility. *International Journal of Sustainable Economy, 3*(3), 361–379.

GABV. (2019a). [Corporate website: Homepage] Retrieved from www.gabv.org

GABV. (2019b). [Corporate website: About us page] Retrieved from http://www.gabv.org/about-us

GABV. (2019c). [Corporate website: Our principles page] Retrieved from http://www.gabv.org/about-us/our-principles

GABV. (2019d). [Corporate website: Our bank stories page] Retrieved from http://www.gabv.org/the-impact/our-bank-stories

GABV. (2019e). *Real economy – Real returns. The business case for values-based banking.* Zeist: GABV.

Galán-Muros, V., & Plewa, C. (2016). What drives and inhibits university-business cooperation in Europe? A comprehensive assessment. *R&D Management, 46*(2), 369–382.

Gallopin, G. C. (1991). Human dimensions of global change: Linking the global and the local processes. *International Social Science Journal, 43*(4), 707–718.

García-Granero, E. M., Piedra-Muñoz, L., & Galdeano-Gómez, E. (2018). Eco-innovation measurement: A review of firm performance indicators. *Journal of Cleaner Production, 191*, 304–317.

Gartner, W. B. (1988). "Who is an entrepreneur?" is the wrong question. *American Journal of Small Business, 12*(4), 11–32.

Garud, R., Gehman, J., & Giulani, A. P. (2014). Conceptualizing entrepreneurial innovation: A narrative perspective. *Research Policy, 43*(7), 1177–1188.

Gasper, D. (2000). Evaluating the 'logical framework approach' towards learning-oriented development evaluation. *Public Administration and Development, 20*(1), 17–28.

Gatto, M. (1995). Letter to the editor. *Ecological Applications, 5*(4), 1181–1183.

Gawer, A., & Cusumano, M. A. (2014). Industry platforms and ecosystem innovation. *Journal of Product Innovation Management, 31*(3), 417–433.

Geels, F. W. (2002). Technological transitions as evolutionary reconfiguration processes: A multi-level perspective and a case-study. *Research Policy, 31*(8), 1257–1274.

Geels, F. W. (2004). From sectoral systems of innovation to socio-technical systems. Insights about dynamics and change from sociology and institutional theory. *Research Policy, 33*, 897–920.

Geels, F. W. (2005). Co-evolution of technology and society: The transition in water supply and personal hygiene in the Netherlands (1815–1930) – A case study in multi-level perspective. *Technology in Society, 27*, 363–397.

Geels, F. W., & Schot, J. (2007). Typology of sociotechnical transition pathways. *Research Policy, 26*, 399–417.

Geffen, C. A., & Rothenberg, S. (2000). Suppliers and environmental innovation: The automotive paint process. *International Journal of Operations & Production Management, 20*(2), 166–186. doi:10.1108/01443570010304242

Geissdoerfer, M., Savaget, P., & Evans, S. (2017). The Cambridge business model innovation process. *Procedia Manufacturing, 8*, 262–269.

Geissdoerfer, M., Vladimirova, D., & Evans, S. (2018). Sustainable business model innovation: A review. *Journal of Cleaner Production, 198*, 401–416.

Genus, A., & Coles, A. (2008). Rethinking the multi-level perspective of technological transitions. *Research Policy, 37*, 1436–1445.

Germain, R. (1996). The role of context and structure in radical and incremental logistics innovation adoption. *Journal of Business Research, 35*(2), 117–127.

Gertler, P. J., Martinez, S., Premand, P., Rawlings, L. B., & Vermeersch, C. M. (2016). Impact evaluation in practice. The World Bank.

Ghisellini, P., Cialani, C., & Ulgiati, S. (2016). A review on circular economy: The expected transition to a balanced interplay of environmental and economic systems. *Journal of Cleaner Production, 114*, 11–32.

Ghisetti, C., & Montresor, S. (2019). Design and eco-innovation: Micro-evidence from the Eurobarometer survey. *Industry and Innovation, 26*(10), 1208–1241.

Ginsberg, J. M., & Bloom, P. N. (2004). Choosing the right green marketing strategy. *MIT Sloan Management Review, 46*(1), 79–84.

Gnyawali, D. R., & Park, B.-J. (2011). Co-opetition between giants: Collaboration with competitors for technological innovation. *Research Policy, 40*(5), 650–663.

Godschalk, D. R. (2003). Urban hazard mitigation: Creating resilient cities. *Natural Hazards Review, 4*(3), 136–143.

Goldstein, D. B. (2000). 'Green' and 'Growth' are not mutually exclusive. *Business Week*.

Gomes, L. A. d. V., Salerno, M. S., Phaal, R., & Probert, D. R. (2018). How entrepreneurs manage collective uncertainties in innovation ecosystems. *Technological Forecasting & Social Change, 128*, 164–185.

Gordon, G. L., Schoenbachler, D. D., Kaminski, P. F. & Brouchous, K. A. (1997). New product development: Using the salesforce to identify opportunities. *Journal of Business & Industrial Marketing, 12*, 33–50.

Graedel, T. E. (1996). On the concept of industrial ecology. *Annual Review of Energy and the Environment, 21*(1), 69–98. doi:10.1146/annurev.energy.21.1.69

Granovetter, M. S. (1973). The strength of weak ties. *American Journal of Sociology, 78*(6), 1360–1380. doi:10.1086/225469

272   *References*

Grass, D., & Cane, M. (2008). The effects of weather and air pollution on cardiovascular and respiratory mortality in Santiago, Chile, during the winters of 1988–1996. *International Journal of Climatology, 28*(8), 1113–1126.

Green, S. G., Gavin, M. B., & Aiman-Smith, L. (1995). Assessing a multidimensional measure of radical technological innovation. *IEEE Transactions on Engineering Management, 42*(3), 203–214.

Greenpeace. (2019), Throwing away the future: How companies still have it wrong on plastic pollution "solutions". Retrieved from https://storage.googleapis.com/planet4-international-stateless/2019/09/8a1d1791-falsesolutions2019.pdf

Gulati, R., Puranam, P., & Thusman, M. L. (2012). Meta-organization design: Rethinking in interorganizational and community contexts. *Strategic Management Journal, 33*(6), 571–586.

Gulbrandsen, M., Thune, T., Borlaug, S. B., & Hanson, J. (2015). Emerging hybrid practices in public-private research centres. *Public Administration, 93*(2), 363–379.

Gunarathne, A. D. N., & Peiris, H. M. P. (2017). Assessing the impact of eco-innovations through sustainability indicators: The case of the commercial tea plantation industry in Sri Lanka. *Asian Journal of Sustainability and Social Responsibility, 2*(1), 41–58.

Gunarathne, A. D. N. (2020). Making sustainability work in plantation agriculture: The story of a sustainability champion in the tea industry in Sri Lanka. In P. Flynn, M. Gudić, & T. Tan (Eds.), *Global champions of sustainable development* (pp. 49–63). London: Routledge.

Gunarathne, N. (2019). Sustainable innovation measurement: Approaches and challenges. In N. Bocken, P. Ritala, L. Albareda, & R. Verburg (Eds.), *Innovation for sustainability* (pp. 233–251). Cham: Palgrave Macmillan.

Gunderson, L. H., & Holling, C. S. (2001). *Panarchy: Understanding transformations in human and natural systems.* New York: Island Press.

Hadida, A. L., & Paris, T. (2014). Managerial cognition and the value chain in the digital music industry. *Technological Forecasting & Social Change, 83*, 84–97.

Hailey, J. (2014). *Models of INGO sustainability: Balancing restricted and unrestricted funding.* Retrieved from https://www.intrac.org/resources/briefing-paper-41-models-ingo-sustainability-balancing-restricted-unrestricted-funding/

Haines, A., Kovats, S. R., Campbell-Lendrum, D., & Corvalan, C. (2006). Climate change and human health: Impacts, vulnerability and public health. *Public Health, 120*(7), 585–596.

Hall, B., Helmers, C., Rogers, M., & Sena, V. (2014). The choice between formal and informal intellectual property: A review. *Journal of Economic Literature, 52*(2), 375–423.

Hall, B. H. (2003). Business method patents, innovation, and policy (No. w9717). National Bureau of Economic Research.

Hall, J., & Vredenburg, H. (2003). The challenge of innovating for sustainable development. *MIT Sloan Management Review, 45*(1), 61.

Hall, L. A., & Bagchi-Sen, S. (2007). An analysis of firm-level innovation strategies in the US biotechnology industry. *Technovation, 27*(1–2), 4–14.

Hall, M. (2014). Evaluation logics in the third sector. *VOLUNTAS: International Journal of Voluntary and Nonprofit Organizations, 25*(2), 307–336.

Hamel, G., & Prahalad, C. K. (1994). Competing for the future. *Harvard Business Review, 72*(4), 122–128.

References   273

Hansen, E. G., Bullinger, A. C., & Reichwald, R. (2011). Sustainability innovation contests: Evaluating contributions with an eco impact-innovativeness typology. *International Journal of Innovation and Sustainable Development, 5*(2/3), 221–245.

Hansen, E. G., & Grosse-Dunker, F. (2013). Sustainability-oriented innovation. In: S. O. Idowu, N. Capaldi, L. Zu, & A. Das Gupta (Eds.), *Encyclopedia of corporate social responsibility* (pp. 2407–2417). New York: Springer.

Hansen, E. G., Grosse-Dunker, F., & Reichwald, R. (2009). Sustainability innovation cube – A framework to evaluate sustainability-oriented innovations. *International Journal of Innovation Management, 13*(04), 683–713.

Harrison, G. W., & List, J. A. (2004). Field experiments. *Journal of Economic Literature, 42*(4), 1009–1055.

Hartemink, A. E. (2005). *Plantation agriculture*. Wallingford: CABI Publishing.

Hatton, M. J., & Schroeder, K. (2007). Results-based management: Friend or foe? *Development in Practice, 17*(3), 426–432.

Heller, M. (2010). *The gridlock economy: How too much ownership wrecks markets stops innovation, and costs lives*. New York: BasicBooks.

Hellström, T. (2007). Dimensions of environmentally sustainable innovation: The structure of eco-innovation concepts. *Sustainable Development, 15*(3), 148–159.

Henderson, H. (2006). Twenty-first century strategies for sustainability. *Foresight, 8*(1), 21–38.

Henry, C., & Stiglitz, J. E. (2010). Intellectual property, dissemination of innovation and sustainable development. *Global Policy, 1*(3), 237–251.

Heuer, M. (2011). Ecosystem cross-sector collaboration: Conceptualizing an adaptive approach to sustainability governance. *Business Strategy and the Environment, 20*(4), 211–221.

Hinkel, J. (2011). Indicators of vulnerability and adaptive capacity: Towards a clarification of the science-policy interface. *Global Environmental Change, 21*, 198–208.

Hinkel, J. (2008). *Transdisciplinary knowledge integration. Cases from integrated assessment and vulnerability assessment* (Ph.D thesis), Wageningen University, Netherlands.

Hockerts, K., & Wustenhagen, R. (2010). Greening Goliaths versus emerging Davids – Theorizing about the role of incumbents and new entrants in sustainable entrepreneurship. *Journal of Business Venturing, 25*, 481–492.

Hoevenagel, R. (1994). A comparison of economic valuation methods. In R. Pethig (Ed.), *Valuing the environment: Methodological and measurement issues* (pp. 251–270). Dordrecht: Springer.

Hojnik, J., & Ruzzier, M. (2016). What drives eco-innovation? A review of an emerging literature. *Environmental Innovation and Societal Transitions, 19*, 31–41. doi:10.1016/j.eist.2015.09.006

Holmes, S., & Smart, P. (2009). Exploring open innovation practice in firm-nonprofit engagements: A corporate social responsibility perspective. *R&D Management, 39*(4), 394–409.

Horbach, J. (2008). Determinants of environmental innovation—New evidence from German panel data sources. *Research Policy, 37*(1), 163–173.

Horbach, J., Rammer, C., & Rennings, K. (2012). Determinants of eco-innovations by type of environmental impact – The role of regulatory push/pull, technology push and market pull. *Ecological Economics, 78*, 112–122.

Hossain, M. (2015). A review of literature on open innovation in small and medium-sized enterprises. *Journal of Global Entrepreneurship Research, 5*(1), 6.

274   *References*

Hossain, M. (2017). Business model innovation: Past research, current debates, and future directions. *Journal of Strategy and Management, 10*(3), 1–19.

Howell, J. M. & Boies, K. (2004). Champions of technological innovation: The influence of contextual knowledge, role orientation, idea generation, and idea promotion on champion emergence. *The Leadership Quarterly, 15*, 123–143.

Howell, J. M. & Higgins, C. A. (1990). Champions of technological innovation. *Administrative Science Quarterly, 35*, 317–341.

Huang, Y., Li, F., Bai, X., Cui, S. (2012). Comparing vulnerability of coastal communities to land use change: Analytical framework and a case study in China. *Environmental Science & Policy, 23*, 133–143.

Hulme, D. (2000). Impact assessment methodologies for microfinance: Theory, experience and better practice. *World Development, 28*(1), 79–98.

Iansiti, M., & Levien, R. (2004). Strategy as ecology. *Harvard Business Review, 82*(3), 68–78.

Imbens, G. W., & Lemieux, T. (2008). Regression discontinuity designs: A guide to practice. *Journal of Econometrics, 142*(2), 615–635.

Inigo, E. A. (2019). Sustainable innovation: Creating solutions for sustainable development. In W. Leal Filho, A. Azul, L. Brandli, P. Özuyar, & T. Wall (Eds.), *Decent work and economic growth. Encyclopedia of the UN sustainable development goals.* doi:10.1007/978-3-319-71058-7_51-1

INNOVA, E. (2006). Thematic workshop: Lead markets and innovation. *Munich, June,* 29–30.

International Union for Conservation of Nature. (ICUN). (2017). *Central highlands of Sri Lanka 2017 conservation outlook assessment.* Gland: ICUN.

Ionescu-Somers, A. (2012). Going, going…”: The long term sustainability impacts of short term focus. *European Business Review.* Retrieved from https://www.europeanbusinessreview.com/going-going-the-long-term-sustainability-impacts-of-short-term-focus/.

IPCC. (2014). Urban areas in climate change 2014: Impacts, adaptation, and vulnerability. Part A: Global and sectoral aspects. Contribution of working group II to the fifth assessment report. Retrieved from https://www.ipcc.ch/report/ar5/wg2/

Isenberg, D. (2011). The entrepreneurship ecosystem as a new paradigm for economic policy: Principles of cultivating entrepreneurship. *Babson Entrepreneurship Ecosystem Project,* 1–13. Retrieved from https://www.innovationamerica.us%2Fimages%2Fstories%2F2011%2FThe-entrepreneurship-ecosystem-strategy-for-economic-growth-policy-20110620183915.pdf

IUCN. (2019). Human-elephant conflict mitigation around the refugee camp of Cox's Bazar (Phase 2: 2019). Retrieved from https://www.iucn.org/asia/countries/bangladesh/human-elephant-conflict-mitigation-around-refugee-camp-coxs-bazar-phase-2-2019

Jackson, T. (2009). *Prosperity without growth: Economics for a finite planet.* London: Routledge.

Jacobides, M. G., Cennamo, C., & Gawer, A. (2018). Towards a theory of ecosystems. *Strategic Management Journal, 39*(8), 2255–2276.

Jaffe, A., & Lerner, J. (2011). *Innovation and its discontents: How our broken patent system is endangering innovation and progress, and what to do about it.* Princeton, NJ: Princeton University Press.

Jamieson, D. (1998). Sustainability and beyond. *Ecological Economics, 24*(2–3), 183–192.

References 275

Jansen, K. J. (2000). The emerging dynamics of change: Resistance, readiness, and momentum. *People and Strategy, 23*(2), 53.

Jarvi, K., Almpanopoulou, A., & Ritala, P. (2018). Organization of knowledge ecosystems: Prefigurative and partial forms. *Research Policy, 47*, 1523–1527.

Jaskyte, K. (2004). Transformation leadership, organizational culture, and innovativeness in nonprofit organizations. *Nonprofit Management and Leadership, 15*(2), 153–168.

Jayawardana, S. (2018). Glyphosate ban lifted. Retrieved from http://www.sundaytimes.lk/180715/news/glyphosate-ban-lifted-302600.html, accessed 24 November 2019

Jia, J. Y. (2020). Micro-innovations: Incremental process improvements. In *The corporate energy strategist's handbook*. Cham: Palgrave Macmillan. doi:10.1007/978-3-030-36838-8_18

Johansson, G., & Magnusson, T. (1998). Eco-innovations-a novel phenomenon? *Journal of Sustainable Product Design, 7*, 7–18.

Johnsen, T. (2009). Supplier involvement in new product development and innovation: Taking stock and looking to the future. *Journal of Purchasing and Supply Management, 15*(3), 187–197. doi:10.1016/j.pursup.2009.03.008

Johnson, G., Whittington, R., & Scholes, K. (2017). *Exploring strategies; texts and cases.* Essex: Pearson Education.

Johnston, D. A., McCutcheon, D. M., Stuart, F. I., & Kerwood, H. (2004). Effects of supplier trust on performance of cooperative supplier relationships. *Journal of Operations Management, 22*(1), 23–38. doi:10.1016/j.jom.2003.12.001

Jolink, A., & Niesten, E. (2015). Sustainable development and business models of entrepreneurs in the organic food industry. *Business Strategy and the Environment, 24*(6), 386–401.

Joseph, K. J. (2014). Exploring exclusion in innovation systems: Case of plantation agriculture in India. *Innovation and Development, 4*(1), 73–90.

Joyce, A., & Paquin, R. L. (2016). The triple layered business model canvas: A tool to design more sustainable business models. *Journal of Cleaner Production, 135*, 1474–1486.

Kähkönen, A.-K., & Lintukangas, K. (2010). Dyadic relationships and power within a supply network context. *Operations and Supply Chain Management, 3*(2), 59–69.

Kammerer, D. (2009). The effects of customer benefit and regulation on environmental product innovation: Empirical evidence from appliance manufacturers in Germany. *Ecological Economics, 68*(8–9), 2285–2295.

Kaplan, R. S., & Norton, D. P. (1996). Linking the balanced scorecard to strategy. *California Management Review, 39*(1), 53–79.

Karlan, D., & Wood, D. H. (2017). The effect of effectiveness: Donor response to aid effectiveness in a direct mail fundraising experiment. *Journal of Behavioral and Experimental Economics, 66*, 1–8.

Karnani, A. (2011). Doing well by doing good: The grand illusion. *California Management Review, 53*(2), 69–86.

Katila, R., & Ahuja, G. (2002). Something old, something new: A longitudinal study of search behavior and new product introduction. *Academy of Management Journal, 45*(6), 1183–1194.

Katz, R. & Allen, T. J. (1982). Investigating the Not Invented Here (Nih) syndrome – A look at the performance, tenure, and communication patterns of 50 R-and-D project groups. *R&D Management, 12*, 7–19.

276 References

Keijl, S., Gilsing, V., Knoben, J., & Duysters, G. (2016). The two faces of inventions: The relationship between recombination and impact in pharmaceutical biotechnology. *Research Policy, 45*(5), 1061–1074.

Kemp, R. (2010). Eco-innovation: Definition, measurement and open research issues. *Economia Politica, 27*(3), 397–420. doi:10.1428/33131

Kemp, R., Loorbach, D., & Rotmans, J. (2007). Transition management as a model for managing processes of co-evolution towards sustainable development. *International Journal of Sustainable Development & World Ecology, 14*, 1–15.

Kemp, R., & Pearson, P. (2008). Measuring eco-innovation, final report of MEI project for DG Research of the European Commission. *Pobrane z.* Retrieved from https://search.oecd.org/env/consumption-innovation/43960830.pdf, accessed 28 October 2019

Kemp, R., Schot, J., & Hoogma, R. (1998). Regime shifts to sustainability through processes of niche formation: The approach of strategic niche management. *Technology Analysis & Strategic Management, 10*(2), 175–198.

Kemppainen, K., & Vepsäläinen, A. P. J. (2003). Trends in industrial supply chains and networks. *International Journal of Physical Distribution & Logistics Management, 33*(8), 701–719. doi:10.1108/09600030310502885

Kenis, P., & Knoke, D. (2002). How organizational field networks shape interorganizational tie-formation rates. *The Academy of Management Review, 27*(2), 275–293. doi:10.2307/4134355

Kennedy, S., Whiteman, G., & Van den Ende, J. (2017). Radical innovation for sustainability: The power of strategy and open innovation. *Long Range Planning, 50*(6), 712–725.

Kerényi, A., & McIntosh, R. (2020). *Sustainable development in changing complex earth systems.* Cham: Springer.

Keskin, D., Diehl, J. C., & Molenaar, N. (2013). Innovation process of new ventures driven by sustainability. *Journal of Cleaner Production, 45*, 50–60.

Ketata, I., Sofka, W., & Grimpe, C. (2015). The role of internal capabilities and firms' environment for sustainable innovation: Evidence for Germany. *R&D Management, 45*(1), 60–75.

Khan, M., Serafeim, G., & Yoon, A. (2018). Corporate sustainability: First evidence on materiality. *The Accounting Review, 91*(6), 1697–1724.

Khandwalla, P. N. (1976/1977). Some top management styles, their context and performance. *Organization and Administrative Science, 7*, 21–51.

Khanna, M., Deltas, G., & Harrington, D. R. (2009). Adoption of pollution prevention techniques: The role of management systems and regulatory pressures. *Environmental and Resource Economics, 44*(1), 85–106.

Kiefer, C., Carrillo-Hermosilla, J., Del Río, P., & Callealta Barroso, F. (2017). Diversity of eco-innovations: A quantitative approach. *Journal of Cleaner Production, 166*, 1494–1506. doi:10.1016/j.jclepro.2017.07.241

Kiefer, C. P., Carrillo-Hermosilla, J., & Del Río, P. (2019). Building a taxonomy of eco-innovation types in firms. A quantitative perspective. *Resources, Conservation and Recycling, 145*, 339–348.

Kılkış, Ş. (2016). Sustainable development of energy, water and environment systems index for Southeast European cities. *Journal of Cleaner Production, 130*, 222–234.

Kim, N. K., & Ahn, J. M. (2020). What facilitates external knowledge utilisation in SMEs? – An optimal configuration between openness intensity and organisational moderators. *Industry and Innovation, 27*, 210–234.

References 277

Kim, Y., Choi, T. Y., Yan, T., & Dooley, K. (2011). Structural investigation of supply networks: A social network analysis approach. *Journal of Operations Management, 29*(3), 194–211. doi:10.1016/j.jom.2010.11.001

Kim, W., & Mauborgne, R. (2005). *Blue ocean strategy. How to create uncontested market space and make competition irrelevant.* Boston, MA: Harvard Business Review Press.

King, D. R., Covin, J. G., & Hegarty, W. H. (2003). Complementary resources and the exploitation of technological innovations. *Journal of Management, 29*(4), 589–606.

Kirchherr, J., Piscicelli, L., Bour, R., Kostense-Smit, E., & Muller, J. (2018). Barriers to the Circular economy: Evidence from the European Union (EU). *Ecological Economics, 150*, 264–272.

Kirshen, P., Watson, C., Douglas, E., Gontz, A., Lee, J., & Tian, Y. (2007). Coastal flooding in the Northeastern United States due to climate change. *Mitigation and Adaptation Strategies for Global Change, 13*(5–6), 437–451.

Kitchell, S. (1997). CEO characteristics and technological innovativeness: A Canadian perspective. *Canadian Journal of Administrative Sciences-Revue Canadienne Des Sciences De L Administration, 14*, 111–125.

Klemmer, P., Lehr, U., & Löbbe, K. (1999). *Environmental innovation: Incentives and barriers.* Berlin: Analytica.

Klotz, A. C., Hmieleski, K. M., Bradley, B. H., & Busenitz, L. W. (2014). New venture teams: A review of the literature and roadmap for future research. *Journal of Management, 40*(1), 226–255.

Knowlton, K., Lynn, B., Goldberg, R. A., Rosenzweig, C., Hogrefe, C., Rosenthal, J. K., & Kinney, P. L. (2007). Projecting heat-related mortality impacts under a changing climate in the New York City region. *American Journal of Public Health, 97*(11), 2028–2034.

Knudsen, M. P., & Mortensen, T. B. (2011). Some immediate – But negative – Effects of openness on product development performance. *Technovation, 31*(1), 54–64.

Kobarg, S., Stumpf-Wollersheim, J., & Welpe, I. M. (2019). More is not always better: Effects of collaboration breadth and depth on radical and incremental innovation performance at the project level. *Research Policy, 48*(1), 1–10.

Kodama, M., & Shibata, T. (2014). Strategy transformation through strategic innovation capability – A case study of Fanuc. *R&D Management, 44*(1), 75–103.

Könnölä, T., & Unruh, G. C. (2007). Really changing the course: The limitations of environmental management systems for innovation. *Business Strategy and the Environment, 16*(8), 525–537.

Koufteros, X. A., Edwin Cheng, T. C., & Lai, K.-H. (2007). "Black-box" and "gray-box" supplier integration in product development: Antecedents, consequences and the moderating role of firm size. *Journal of Operations Management, 25*(4), 847–870. doi:10.1016/j.jom.2006.10.009

Kumar, A., Sah, B., Singh, A., Deng, Y., He, X., Kumar, P., & Bansal, R. (2017). A review of multi criteria decision making (MCDM) towards sustainable renewable energy development. *Renewable and Sustainable Energy Reviews, 69*, 596–609.

Kuratko, D. F., Fisher, G., Bloodgood, J. M., & Hornsby, J. S. (2017). The paradox of new venture legitimation within an entrepreneurial ecosystem. *Small Business Economics, 49*, 119–140.

Kurtz, C. F., & Snowden, D. J. (2003). The new dynamics of strategy: Sense-making in a complex and complicated world. *IBM Systems Journal, 42*(3), 462–483.

278   *References*

Landau, J. (1999). Champions of change: How CEO's and their companies are mastering the skills of radical change. *International Journal of Selection and Assessment, 7,* 52–53.

Lane, E. L. (2011), *Clean tech intellectual property: Eco-marks, green patents and green innovation.* Oxford: Oxford University Press.

Lane, P. J., Koka, B. R., & Pathak, S. (2006). The reification of absorptive capacity: A critical review and rejuvenation of the construct. *Academy of Management Review, 31*(4), 833–863.

Lang, D. J., Wiek, A., Bergmann, M., Stauffacher, M., Martens, P., Moll, P., . . . Thomas, C. J. (2012). Transdisciplinary research in sustainability science: Practice, principles, and challenges. *Sustainability Science, 7*(1), 25–43.

Lankao, P., & Qin, H. (2011). Conceptualizing urban vulnerability to global climate and environmental change. *Current Opinion in Environmental Sustainability, 3*(3):142–149. doi:10.1016/j.cosust.2010.12.016

Laursen, K., & Salter, A. (2006). Open for innovation: The role of openness in explaining innovation performance among UK manufacturing firms. *Strategic Management Journal, 27*(2), 131–150.

Lee, K.-H., & Kim, J.-W. (2011). Integrating suppliers into green product innovation development: An empirical case study in the semiconductor industry. *Business Strategy and the Environment, 20*(8), 527–538. doi:10.1002/bse.714

Leimeister, J. M., Huber, M., Bretschneider, U., & Krcmar, H. (2014). Leveraging crowdsourcing: Activation-supporting components for IT-based ideas competition. *Journal of Management Information Systems, 26,* 197–224.

Leiponen, A., & Byma, J. (2009). If you cannot block, you better run: Small firms, cooperative innovation, and appropriation strategies. *Research Policy, 38*(9), 1478–1488.

Lerner, J., & Merges, R. P. (1998). The control of technology alliances: An empirical analysis of the biotechnology industry. *The Journal of Industrial Economics, 46*(2), 125–156.

Leroi-Werelds, S., Pop, O-M., & Roijakkers, N. (2017). Value creation in alliance ecosystems: Insights from marketing. In T. K. Das (Ed.), *Managing alliance portfolios and networks* (pp. 1–31). Charlotte, NC: Information Age Publishing.

Lewandowski, M. (2016). Designing the business models for circular economy – Towards the conceptual framework. *Sustainability, 8*(1). Retrieved from https://www.mdpi.com/2071-1050/8/1/43/htm

Lewis, M., Brandon-Jones, A., Slack, N., & Howard, M. (2010). Competing through operations and supply: The role of classic and extended resource-based advantage. *International Journal of Operations & Production Management, 30*(10), 1032–1058. doi:10.1108/01443571011082517

Lichtenthaler, U. (2009). Absorptive capacity, environmental turbulence, and the complementarity of organizational learning processes. *Academy of Management Journal, 52*(4), 822–846.

Limalevu, L. (2012). Rapid assessment: Site selection process and criteria. Pacific Centre for Environment and Sustainable Development: The University of the South Pacific, Suva, Fiji.

Lind, F., Styhre, A., & Aaboen, L. (2013). Exploring university-industry collaboration in research centres. *European Journal of Innovation Management, 16*(1), 70–91.

Lindgardt, Z., & Shaffer, B. (2012). Business model innovation in social-sector organizations: Meeting the need. Retrieved from https://www.bcg.com/publications/2012/innovation-business-unit-strategy-business-model-innovation-social-sector-organizations.aspx

References   279

List, J. A. (2007). Field experiments: A bridge between lab and naturally occurring data. *The BE Journal of Economic Analysis & Policy, 5*(2).

List, J. A. (2011). The market for charitable giving. *Journal of Economic Perspectives, 25*(2), 157–180.

Little, A. D. (2005). How leading companies are using sustainability-driven innovation to win tomorrow's customers. *Innovation High Ground Report.* Retrieved from https:// www.adlittle.com%2Fsites%2Fdefault%2Ffiles%2Fviewpoints%2FADL_Innovation_High_Ground_report_03.pdf

Lombardi, D. R., & Laybourn, P. (2012). Redefining industrial symbiosis. *Journal of Industrial Ecology, 16*(1), 28–37. doi:10.1111/j.1530–9290.2011.00444.x

Longoni, A., & Cagliano, R. (2018). Sustainable innovativeness and the triple bottom line: The role of organizational time perspective. *Journal of Business Ethics, 151*(4), 1097–1120.

Loorbach, D., & Wijsman, K. (2013). Business transition management: Exploring a new role for business in sustainability transitions. *Journal of Cleaner Production, 45,* 20–28.

Loorbach, D. A., & Raak, R. v. (2006). Strategic niche management and transition management: Different but complementary approaches. Retrieved October 30, 2019 from Erasmus http://hdl.handle.net/1765/37247

Lu Knutsen, W., & Brower, R. S. (2010). Managing expressive and instrumental accountabilities in nonprofit and voluntary organizations: A qualitative investigation. *Nonprofit and Voluntary Sector Quarterly, 39*(4), 588–610.

Lucía, M., Carla, C., & Jesús, G. (2019). The triple bottom line on sustainable product innovation performance in SMES: A mixed methods approach. *Sustainability, 11*(6). doi:10.3390/su11061689

Lüdeke-Freund, F. (2009). *Business model concepts in corporate sustainability contexts; from rhetoric to a generic template for 'business models for sustainability'.* Lueneburg: Centre for Sustainability Management.

Maas, K., & Liket, K. (2011). Social impact measurement: Classification of methods. In R. Burrit, S. Schaltegger, M. Bennett, T. Pohjola, & M. Csutora (Eds.) *Environmental management accounting and supply chain management* (pp. 171–202). Dordrecht: Springer.

MacIndoe, H., & Barman, E. (2013). How organizational stakeholders shape performance measurement in nonprofits: Exploring a multidimensional measure. *Nonprofit and Voluntary Sector Quarterly, 42*(4), 716–738.

Magretta, J. (2002). Why business models matter. *Harvard Business Review, 80,* 86–92.

Mäkinen, S., & Dedehayir, O. (2013). Business ecosystems' evolution – An ecosystem clockspeed perspective. *Advances in Strategic Management, 30,* 99–125.

Mäkinen, S. J., Kanniainen, J., & Peltola, I. (2014). Investigating adoption of free beta applications in a platform-based business ecosystems. *Journal of Product Innovation Management, 31*(3), 451–465.

Maller, C. J., & Strengers, Y. (2011). Housing, heat stress and health in a changing climate: Promoting the adaptive capacity of vulnerable households, a suggested way forward. *Health Promotion International, 26*(1), pp. 100–108.

Mangematin, V., O'Reilly, P., & Cunningham, J. (2014). PIs as boundary spanners, science and market shapers. *The Journal of Technology Transfer, 39*(1), 1–10.

Manzini, E. (2007). Design research for sustainable social innovation. In R. Michel (Ed.) *Design research now* (pp. 233–245). Basel: Birkhäuser.

March, J. G., & Shapira, Z. (1987). Managerial perspectives on risk and risk-taking. *Management Science, 33,* 1404–1418.

280 *References*

Markusson, N. (2001). *Drivers of environmental innovation.* Stockholm: Vinnova.

Marsden, P. V. (2002). Egocentric and sociocentric measures of network centrality. *Social Networks, 24*(4), 407–422.

Martins, L. L., Rindova, V. P., & Greenbaum, B. E. (2015). Unlocking the hidden value of concepts: A cognitive approach to business model innovation. *Strategic Entrepreneurship Journal, 9*(1), 99–117.

Massa, L., Tucci, C. L., & Afuah, A. (2017). A critical assessment of business model research. *Academy of Management Annals, 11*(1), 73–104.

Mayoux, L., & Chambers, R. (2005). Reversing the paradigm: Quantification, participatory methods and pro-poor impact assessment. *Journal of international Development, 17*(2), 271–298.

McCarthy, J. J., Canziani, O. F., Leary, N. A., Dokken, D. J., & White, K. S. (Eds.). (2001). *Climate change 2001: Impacts, adaptation and vulnerability.* Cambridge: Cambridge University Press.

McDermott, C. M., & O'Connor, G. C. (2002). Managing radical innovation: An overview of emergent strategy issues. *Journal of Product Innovation Management: An International Publication of the Product Development & Management Association, 19*(6), 424–438.

McDonald, R. E. (2007). An investigation of innovation in nonprofit organizations: The role of organizational mission. *Nonprofit and Voluntary Sector Quarterly, 36*(2), 256–281.

McGranahan, G., Balk, D., & Anderson, B. (2007). The rising tide: Assessing the risks of climate change and human settlements in low elevation coastal zones. *Environment & Urbanization, 19*(1), 17–37.

McKelvey, M., Alm, H., & Riccaboni, M. (2003). Does co-location matter for formal knowledge collaboration in the Swedish biotechnology-pharmaceutical sector? *Research Policy, 32*(3), 483–501.

McKelvey, M., Zaring, O., & Ljungberg, D. (2015). Creating innovative opportunities through research collaboration: An evolutionary framework and empirical illustration in engineering. *Technovation, 39*, 26–36.

McNamara, K. E., & Buggy, L. (2017). Community-based climate change adaptation: A review of academic literature. *Local Environment, 22*(4), 443–460.

McNamara, K. E., Hemstock, S. L., & Holland, E. A. (2012). Practices of climate change adaptation in the pacific: Survey of implementing agencies (phase II). Final report to the European Union – Global Climate Change Alliance. Suva, Fiji: The University of the South Pacific.

McNamara, K. E., Hemstock, S. L., & Holland, E. A. (2015). *PACE-SD guidebook: Participatory vulnerability and adaptation assessment (Vol. Pacific centre for environment and sustainable development).* Suva, Fiji: The University of the South Pacific.

Ménard, C. (2004). The economics of hybrid organizations. *Journal of Institutional and Theoretical Economics JITE, 160*(3), 345–376.

Menguc, B., Auh, S., & Yannopoulos, P. (2014). Customer and supplier involvement in design: The moderating role of incremental and radical innovation capability. *Journal of Product Innovation Management, 31*(2), 313–328.

Meqdadi, O., Johnsen, T. E., & Johnsen, R. E. (2017). The role of power and trust in spreading sustainability initiatives across supply networks: A case study in the bio-chemical industry. *Industrial Marketing Management, 62*, 61–76.

Meyer, J. W., & Rowan, B. (1977). Institutionalized organizations: Formal structure as myth and ceremony. *American Journal of Sociology, 83*(2), 340–363.

References 281

Michelfelder, I., & Kratzer, J. (2013). Why and how combining strong and weak ties within a single interorganizational R&D collaboration outperforms other collaboration structures. *Journal of Product Innovation Management, 30*(6), 1159–1177.

Miemczyk, J., Johnsen, T., & Macquet, M. (2012). Sustainable purchasing and supply management: A structured literature review of definitions and measures at the dyad, chain and network levels. *Supply Chain Management: An International Journal, 17*(5), 478–496. doi:10.1108/13598541211258564

Miller, D. (1983). The correlates of entrepreneurship in three types of firms. *Management Science, 29*, 770–791.

Miller, D., & Friesen, P. H. (1982). Innovation in conservative and entrepreneurial firms – Two models of strategic momentum. *Strategic Management Journal, 3*, 1–25.

Miller, D. J., & Acs, Z. J. (2017). The campus as entrepreneurial ecosystem: The University of Chicago. *Small Business Economics, 49*, 75–95.

Miller, K., McAdam, R., Moffett, S., Alexander, A., & Puthusserry, P. (2016). Knowledge transfer in university quadruple helix ecosystems: An absorptive capacity perspective. *R&D Management, 46*(2), 383–399.

Mills, J., Schmitz, J., & Frizelle, G. (2004). A strategic review of "supply networks". *International Journal of Operations & Production Management, 24*(10), 1012–1036. doi:10.1108/01443570410558058

Mitchell, D., & Coles, C. (2003). The ultimate competitive advantage of continuing business model innovation. *Journal of Business Strategy, 24*(5), 15–21.

Mitchell, R. K., Agle, B. R., & Wood, D. J. (1997). Toward a theory of stakeholder identification and salience: Defining the principle of who and what really counts. *Academy of Management Review, 22*(4), 853–886.

Mitchell, R. K., Mitchell, J., & Smith, J. B. (2004). Failing to succeed: New venture failure as a moderator of startup experience and startup expertise. *Frontiers of Entrepreneurship Research.*

Moore, J. F. (1993). Predators and prey: A new ecology of competition. *Harvard Business Review, 71*(3), 75–86.

Moore, J. F. (1996). *The death of competition: Leadership & strategy in the age of business ecosystems.* New York: Harper Business.

Morello-Frosch, R., Manuel Jr, P., Porras, C., & Sadd, J. (2002). Environmental justice and regional inequality in Southern California: Implications for future research. *Environmental Health Perspectives, 110*(2), 149–154.

Moser, C., & Satterthwaite, D. (2008). Towards pro-poor adaptation to climate change in the urban centres of low-and middle-income countries. In *Social dimensions of climate change.* London: International Institute for Environment and Development (IIED).

Mossel, A. v., Rijnsoever, F. J. v., & Hekkert, M. P. (2018). Navigators through the storm: A review of organization theories and the behaviour of incumbent firms during transitions. *Environmental Innovation and Societal Transitions, 26*, 44–63.

Muegge, S. (2013). Platforms, communities, and business ecosystems: Lessons learned about technology entrepreneurship in an interconnected world. *Technology Innovation Management Review*, 5–15.

Munasinghe, M., Deraniyagala, Y., Dassanayake, N., & Karunarathna, H. (2017). Economic, social and environmental impacts and overall sustainability of the tea sector in Sri Lanka. *Sustainable Production and Consumption, 12*, 155–169.

Mustaquim, M. M., & Nyström, T. (2014, September). Open sustainability innovation – A pragmatic standpoint of sustainable HCI. In *International conference on business informatics research* (pp. 101–112). Cham: Springer.

282   *References*

Nadkarni, S., & Barr, P. S. (2008). Environmental context, managerial cognition, and strategic action. *Strategic Management Journal, 29,* 1395–1427.

Nagy, D., Schuessler, J., & Dubinsky, A. (2016). Defining and identifying disruptive innovations. *Industrial Marketing Management, 57,* 119–126.

Naidoo, M., & Gasparatos, A. (2018). Corporate environmental sustainability in the retail sector: Drivers, strategies and performance measurement. *Journal of Cleaner Production, 203,* 125–142.

Nakao, B. H. T., & de Andrade Guerra, J. B. S. O. (2019). Creativity, innovation, and sustainable development: Decent work and economic growth. In W. Leal Filho, A. Azul, L. Brandli, P. Özuyar, & T. Wall (Eds.), *Encyclopedia of the UN sustainable development goals.* doi:10.1007/978-3-319-95867-5_55

Narasimhan, R., & Narayanan, S. (2013). Perspectives on supply network-enabled innovations. *Journal of Supply Chain Management, 49*(4), 27–42. doi:10.1111/jscm.12026

Newey, W. K., & Powell, J. L. (2003). Instrumental variable estimation of nonparametric models. *Econometrica, 71*(5), 1565–1578.

Nicholls, R. J., Hanson, S., Herweijer, C., Patmore, N., Hallegatte, S., Corfee-Morlot, J., . . . Muir-Wood, R. (2007). Ranking port cities with high exposure and vulnerability to climate extremes: Exposure estimates. Organisation for Economic Co-operation and Development (OECD). Retrieved from https://www.oecd-ilibrary.org/environment/ranking-port-cities-with-high-exposure-and-vulnerability-to-climate-extremes_011766488208

Nidumolu, R., Prahalad, C., & Rangaswami, M. (2009). Why sustainability is now the key driver of innovation. *Harvard Business Review, 87*(9), 56.

Nunn, P. D., & Mimura, N. (1997). Island states at risk: Global climate change, development and population. *Journal of Coastal Research, 24,* 133–151.

Nyaga, G. N., Whipple, J. M., & Lynch, D. F. (2010). Examining supply chain relationships: Do buyer and supplier perspectives on collaborative relationships differ? *Journal of Operations Management, 28*(2), 101–114. doi:10.1016/j.jom.2009.07.005

O'Brien, K., Eriksen, S., Nygaard, L. P., & Schjolden, A. (2007). Why different interpretations of vulnerability matter in climate change discourses. *Climate Policy, 7*(1), 73–88.

O'Connor, G. C., Paulson, A. S., & DeMartino, R. (2008). Organisational approaches to building a radical innovation dynamic capability. *International Journal of Technology Management, 44*(1–2), 179–204.

O'Neill, M. S., Zanobetti, A., & Schwartz, J. (2005). Disparities by race in heat-related mortality in four US cities: The role of air conditioning prevalence. *Journal of Urban Health, 82*(2), 191–197.

OECD. (2009). Sustainable manufacturing and eco-innovation: Framework, practices and measurement. Synthesis report. OECD, Paris.

Oltra, V., & Saint Jean, M. (2009). Sectoral systems of environmental innovation: An application to the French automotive industry. *Technological Forecasting and Social Change, 76*(4), 567–583.

Ooms, W., Caniëls, M. C., Roijakkers, N., & Cobben, D. (2020). Ecosystems for smart cities: Tracing the evolution of governance structures in a Dutch smart city initiative. *International Entrepreneurship and Management Journal, 16,* 1225–1258.

Oskam, I., Bossink, B., & de Man, A. P. (2018). The interaction between network ties and business modeling: Case studies of sustainability-oriented innovations. *Journal of Cleaner Production, 177,* 555–566.

Osterwalder, A. (2004). *The business model ontology: A proposition in a design science approach* (doctoral dissertation). Lausanne Business School. Retrieved from http://www.hec.unil.ch/aosterwa/PhD/Osterwalder_PhD_BM_Ontology.pdf

Osterwalder, A., & Pigneur, Y. (2010). *Business model generation: A handbook for visionaries, game changers, and challengers.* Hoboken, NJ: John Wiley & Sons.

Osterwalder, A., Pigneur, Y., & Tucci, C. L. (2005). Clarifying business models: Origins, present, and future of the concept. *Communications of the Association for Information Systems, 16*(1), 1.

Oxfam. (2019). *Annual report 2018–2019.* Retrieved from https://oi-files-d8-prod.s3.eu-west-2.amazonaws.com/s3fs-public/2019-12/191219_Oxfam_Annual_Report_2018-19.pdf

Oxfam. (2019a). *Our history.* Retrieved from https://www.oxfam.org/en/our-history.

Oxfam. (2019b). *Tackling the climate crisis.* Retrieved from https://www.oxfam.org/en/what-we-do/issues/tackling-climate-crisis

Oxford Business Group. (2016). Growth prospects for Sri Lanka's tea industry. Retrieved from http://www.oxfordbusinessgroup.com/news/growth-prospects-sri-lanka%E2%80%99s-tea-industry, accessed 30 November 2019

Paech, N. (2012). *Liberation from excess: The road to a post-growth economy.* Munich: Oekom-Verlag.

Papadas, K. -K., Avlonitis, G. J., Carrigan, M., & Piha, L. (2019). The interplay of strategic and internal green marketing orientation on competitive advantage. *Journal of Business Research, 104*(C), 632–643. doi:10.1016/j.jbusres.2018.07.009

Paquin, R. L., & Howard-Grenville, J. (2012). The evolution of facilitated industrial symbiosis. *Journal of Industrial Ecology, 16*(1), 83–93.

Paraschiv, D. M., Nemoianu, E. L., Langă, C. A., & Szabó, T. (2012). Eco-innovation, responsible leadership and organizational change for corporate sustainability. *Amfiteatru Economic Journal, 14*(32), 404–419.

Park, C. C., & Allaby, M. (2014). *A dictionary of environment and conservation.* Oxford: Oxford University Press.

Parnell, S., Simon, D., & Vogel, C. (2007). Global environmental change: Conceptualising the growing challenge for cities in poor countries. *Area, 39*(3), 357–369.

Parsons, T. (1967). *On the concept of political power: Sociological theory and modern society.* London: Free Press.

Patt, A. G., Schröter, D., De La Vega-Leinert, A. C., Klein, R. J. T. (2008). Vulnerability research and assessment to support adaptation and mitigation: Common themes from the diversity of approaches. In A. G. Patt, D. Schröter, R. J. T. Klein, A. C. De La Vega-Leinert (Eds.), *Environmental vulnerability assessment* (pp. 1–25). London: Earthscan.

Pedro Filho, F. D. S., Lima, V. A., Neto, J. M. D. S., Muller, C. A. D. S., & Costa, G. B. D. (2017). Building the capacity for sustainable innovation in the Amazon region. *International Journal of Innovation and Learning, 22*(1), 23–43.

Peiris, M., & Gunarathne, A. D. N. (2020). The changing landscape of the plantation sector in the Central Highlands of Sri Lanka. In U. Schickhoff, R. B. Singh, & S. Mal (Eds.), *Mountain landscapes in transition: Effects of land use and climate change.* Cham: Springer.

Pelling, M. (2003). *The vulnerability of cities: Natural disasters and social resilience.* London: Earthscan Publications.

Perkmann, M., & Walsh, K. (2007). University-industry relationships and open innovation: Towards a research agenda. *International Journal of Management Reviews, 9*(4), 259–280.

284 References

Perkmann, M., & Walsh, K. (2009). The two faces of collaboration: Impacts of university-industry relations on public research. *Industrial and Corporate Change, 18*(6), 1033–1065.

Perl-Vorbach, E., Rauter, R., & Baumgartner, R. J. (2014). Open innovation in the context of sustainable innovation: Findings based on a literature review. In *9th International Symposium on Sustainable Leadership, 2014* (p. 169).

Perry-Smith, J., & Mannucci, P. (2017). From creativity to innovation: The social network drivers of the four phases in the idea journey. *Academy of Management Review, 42*(1), 53–79.

Pesqueira, L., & Glasbergen, P. (2013). Playing the politics of scale: Oxfam's intervention in the Roundtable on Sustainable Palm Oil. *Geoforum, 45*, 296–304.

Petersen, A. S., Hals, H., Rot, B., Bell, J., Miller, I., Parks, J., & Stults, M. (2014). Climate change and the Jamestown S'Klallam tribe: A customized approach to climate vulnerability and adaptation planning. *Michigan Journal of Sustainability, 2*, 9–32.

Petteri, R., & Kaisa, M. (2019). Social innovation for sustainability challenges. *Sustainability, 12*(1), 1–12.

Pfeffer, J., & Salancik, G. R. (2003). *The external control of organizations: A resource dependence perspective*. Stanford, CA: Stanford University Press.

Poister, T. H., Pitts, D. W., & Hamilton Edwards, L. (2010). Strategic management research in the public sector: A review, synthesis, and future directions. *The American Review of Public Administration, 40*(5), 522–545.

Ponomariov, B. L., & Boardman, P. C. (2010). Influencing scientists' collaboration and productivity patterns through new institutions: University research centers and scientific and technical human capital. *Research Policy, 39*(5), 613–624.

Pór, G. (1997). Designing knowledge ecosystems for communities of practice. Paper presented at the Conference on Advancing Organizational Capability via Knowledge Management, Los Angeles, September 29–30.

Porac, J., Ventresca, M., & Mishina, Y., (2002). *Interorganizational cognition and interpretation*. In J. A. C. Baum (Ed.), *The Blackwell companion to organizations* (pp. 579–598). Oxford: Blackwell.

Porter, M. E., & Ketels, C. (2009). Clusters and industrial districts: Common roots, different perspectives. In G. Becattini, M. Bellandi, & L. De Propris (Eds.), *Handbook of industrial districts*. Cheltenham: Edward Elgar Publisher.

Porter, M. E., & Kramer, M. R. (2006). The link between competitive advantage and corporate social responsibility. *Harvard Business Review, 84*(12), 78–92.

Porter, M. E., & Van der Linde, C. (1995). Toward a new conception of the environment-competitiveness relationship. *Journal of Economic Perspectives, 9*(4), 97–118.

Potocnik, J. (2014). *Eco-innovation and circular economy*. European Commission. Presented at the Opening of the 16th European Forum on Eco-Innovation.

Prasad, N., Ranghieri, F., Shah, F., Trohanis, Z., Kessler, E., & Sinha, R. (2009). *Climate resilient cities: A primer on reducing vulnerabilities to disasters*. Washington, DC: The World Bank.

Prinsen, G., & Nijhof, S. (2015). Between logframes and theory of change: Reviewing debates and a practical experience. *Development in Practice, 25*(2), 234–246.

Przychodzen, W., & Przychodzen, J. (2018). Sustainable innovations in the corporate sector – The empirical evidence from IBEX 35 firms. *Journal of Cleaner Production, 172*, 3557–3566.

Pujari, D. (2006). Eco-innovation and new product development: Understanding the influences on market performance. *Technovation, 26*(1), 76–85. doi:10.1016/j.technovation.2004.07.006

References 285

Radnor, Z., & Noke, H. (2002). Innovation compass: A self-audit tool for the new product development process. *Creativity and Innovation Management, 11*(2), 122–132. doi:10.1111/1467-8691.00244

Rajapakse, S., Shivanthan, M. C., & Selvarajah, M. (2016). Chronic kidney disease of unknown etiology in Sri Lanka. *International Journal of Occupational and Environmental Health, 22*(3), 259–264.

Rappert, B., Webster, A., & Charles, D. (1999). Making sense of diversity and reluctance: Academic-industrial relations and intellectual property. *Research Policy, 28*(8), 873–890.

Ratten, V., Pasillas, M., & Lundberg, H. (2019). *Managing sustainable innovation: The driver for global growth* (pp. 1–10). Oxon: Routledge.

Rauf, F., Lelia Voinea, C., Bin Azam Hashmi, H., & Fratostiteanu, C. (2020). Moderating effect of political embeddedness on the relationship between resources base and quality of CSR disclosure in China. *Sustainability, 12*(8), 3323.

Rauter, R., Globocnik, D., Perl-Vorbach, E., & Baumgartner, R. J. (2019). Open innovation and its effects on economic and sustainability innovation performance. *Journal of Innovation and Knowledge, 4*(4), 226–233.

Rauter, R., Perl-Vorbach, E., & Baumgartner, R. J. (2017). Is open innovation supporting sustainable innovation? Findings based on a systematic, explorative analysis of existing literature. *International Journal of Innovation and Sustainable Development, 11*(2/3), 249–270.

Raven. R. (2007). Niche accumulation and hybridization strategies in transition processes towards a sustainable energy system: An assessment of differences and pitfalls. *Energy Policy, 35*(4), 2390–2400.

Raworth, K. (2018). *Doughnut economics: Seven ways to think like a 2st-century economist.* London: Random House Business Books.

Reficco, E., Gutiérrez, R., Jaén, M. H., & Auletta, N. (2018). Collaboration mechanisms for sustainable innovation. *Journal of Cleaner Production, 203*, 1170–1186.

Reficco, E., Layrisse, F., & Barrios, A. (2020, in press). From donation-based NPO to social enterprise: A journey of transformation through business–model innovation. *Journal of Business Research.* doi:10.1016/j.jbusres.2020.01.031

Rennings, K. (2000). Redefining innovation – Eco-innovation research and the contribution from ecological economics. *Ecological Economics, 32*(2), 319–332.

Rennings, K., Ziegler, A., Ankele, K., & Hoffmann, E. (2006). The influence of different characteristics of the EU environmental management and auditing scheme on technical environmental innovations and economic performance. *Ecological Economics, 57*(1), 45–59.

Rennings, K., & Zwick, T. (2003). The German survey. In K. Rennings & T. Zwick (Eds.) *Employment impacts of cleaner production* (pp. 213–228). Heidelberg: Physica.

Resilience Alliance. (2016). Resilience. Retrieved May 8, 2016 from http://www.resalliance.org/resilience

Ringberg, T., Reihlen, M., & Rydén, P. (2019). The technology-mindset interactions: Leading to incremental, radical or revolutionary innovations. *Industrial Marketing Management, 79*, 102–113.

Ringhofer, L., & Kohlweg, K. (2019). Has the theory of change established itself as the better alternative to the logical framework approach in development cooperation programmes? *Progress in Development Studies, 19*(2), 112–122.

Ritala, P., Huotari, P., Bocken, N., Albareda, L., & Puumalainen, K. (2018). Sustainable business model adoption among S&P 500 firms: A longitudinal content analysis study. *Journal of Cleaner Production, 170*, 216–226.

286 References

Rivera-Santos, M., & Rufín, C. (2010). Odd couples: Understanding the governance of firm-NGO alliances. *Journal of Business Ethics, 94*(1), 55–70.

Roaf, S. Crichton, D., & Nicol, F. (2009). *Adapting buildings and cities for climate change: A 21st century survival guide*, 2nd ed. Oxford: Elsevier Architectural Press.

Robertson, P. L., Casali, G. L., & Jacobson, D. (2012). Managing open incremental process innovation: Absorptive capacity and distributed learning. *Research Policy, 41*(5), 822–832.

Roche, C. J. (1999). *Impact assessment for development agencies: Learning to value change.* Oxfam.

Rogers, P. J., & Weiss, C. (2007). Theory-based evaluation: Reflections ten years on. *New Directions for Evaluation, 114*(2), 63–67.

Romero-Lankao, P., & Qin, H. (2011). Conceptualizing urban vulnerability to global climate and environmental change. *Current Opinion in Environmental Sustainability, 3*(3), 142–149.

Romero-Lankao, P., Qin, H., & Dickinson, K. (2012). Urban vulnerability to temperature-related hazards: A meta-analysis and meta-knowledge approach. *Global Environmental Change, 22*(3), 670–683.

Roscoe, S., Cousins, P. D., & Lamming, R. C. (2016). Developing eco-innovations: A three-stage typology of supply networks. *Journal of Cleaner Production, 112(Part 3)*, 1948–1959. doi:10.1016/j.jclepro.2015.06.125

Rosenzweig, C., Solecki, W. D., Parshall, L., Chopping, M., Pope, G., & Goldberg, R. (2011). Characterizing the urban heat island in current and future climates in New Jersey. *Environmental Hazards, 6*(1), 51–62.

Rotmans, J., Kemp, R., & Asselt, M. v. (2001). More evolution than revolution: Transition management in public policy. *Foresight, 3*(1), 15–31.

Rowley, T. J. (2017). The power of and in stakeholder networks. *Stakeholder Management. Series Business and Society, 360*, 101–122.

Russel, M. G., & Smorodinskaya, N. V. (2018). Leveraging complexity for ecosystemic innovation. *Technological Forecasting & Social Change, 136*, 114–131.

Saebi, T. (2015). Evolution, adaptation, or innovation? A contingency framework on business model dynamics. In N. J. Foss & T. Saebi (Eds.), *Business model innovation* (pp. 145–168). Oxford: Oxford University Press.

Sahni, N., Lanzerotti, L., Bliss, A., & Pike, D. (2017). *Is your nonprofit built for sustained innovation?* Retrieved from https://ssir.org/articles/entry/is_your_nonprofit_built_for_sustained_innovation

Sanderse, J., de Langen, F., & Perez Salgado, F. (2020). Proposing a business model framework for nonprofit organizations. *Journal of Applied Economics and Business Research, 10*(1): 34–48.

Santoro, M. D., & Bierly, P. E. (2006). Facilitators of knowledge transfer in university-industry collaborations: A knowledge-based perspective. *IEEE Transactions on Engineering Management, 53*(4), 495–507.

Saunders, M. (1997). *Strategic purchasing and supply chain management*, 2nd ed. London: Pitman.

Schaeffer, V., & Matt, M. (2016). Development of academic entrepreneurship in a non-mature context: The role of the university as a hub organization. *Entrepreneurship and Regional Development, 28*(9–10), 724–745.

Schaltegger, S., Beckmann, M., & Hockerts, K. (2018). Collaborative entrepreneurship for sustainability. Creating solutions in light of the UN sustainable development goals. *International Journal of Entrepreneurial Venturing, 10*(2), 131–152.

Schaltegger, S., Hansen, E. G., & Lüdeke-Freund, F. (2016). Business models for sustainability: Origins, present research, and future avenues. *Organization and Environment, 29*(1), 3–10.

Schaltegger, S., Lüdeke-Freund, F., & Hansen, E. G. (2012). Business cases for sustainability: The role of business model innovation for corporate sustainability. *International Journal of Innovation and Sustainable Development, 6*(2), 95–119.

Schiederig, T., Tietze, F., & Herstatt, C. (2012). Green innovation in technology and innovation management – An exploratory literature review. *R&D Management, 42*(2), 180–192.

Schlange, L. E. (2009). Stakeholder identification in sustainability entrepreneurship. *Greener Management International, 55*, 13–32.

Schmidt, J. B., & Calantone, R. J. (1998). Are really new product development projects harder to shut down? *Journal of Product Innovation Management, 15*(2), 111–123.

Schoenmakers, W., & Duysters, G. (2010). The technological origins of radical inventions. *Research Policy, 39*(8), 1051–1059.

Schot, J., & Steinmueller, E. (2016). Framing innovation policy for transformative change: Innovation policy 3.0. Science Policy Research Unit, University of Sussex.

Schwarzenbach, A. (2011). *Saving the world's wildlife: WWF – The first 50 years.* London: Profile Books Ltd.

Scott, W. R. (2013). *Institutions and organizations: Ideas, interests, and identities.* Thousand Oaks, CA: Sage Publications.

Seebode, D., Jeanrenaud, S., & Bessant, J. (2012). Managing innovation for sustainability. *R&D Management, 42*(3), 195–206.

Seip, M., Castaldi, C., Flikkema, M., & de Man, A. P. (2019). A taxonomy of firm-level IPR application practices to inform policy debates. In *LEM working paper series 2019/3. Institute of Economics.* Scuola Superiore Sant'Anna Pisa.

Sensing Local-Urban Poverty. (2007). Retrieved from https://www.sensinglocal.in/copy-of-urban-vulnerability

Seuring, S. (2004). Industrial ecology, life cycles, supply chains: Differences and interrelations. *Business strategy and the Environment, 13*(5), 306–319.

Shah, K. U., Dulal, H. B., Johnson, C., & Baptiste, A. (2013). Understanding livelihood vulnerability to climate change: Applying the livelihood vulnerability index in Trinidad and Tobago. *Geoforum, 47*, 125–137.

Sharkey, P. (2007). Survival and death in New Orleans: An empirical look at the human impact of Katrina. *Journal of Black Studies, 37*(4), 482–501.

Shepherd, D. A., & Patzelt, H. (2018). *Entrepreneurial cognition: Exploring the mindset of entrepreneurs.* Cham: Palgrave Macmillan.

Sherbinin, A. D., Schiller, A., & Pulsipher, A. (2007). The vulnerability of global cities to climate hazards. *Environment & Urbanization, 19*(1), 39–64.

Shiva, V. (2001). Protect or plunder?: Understanding intellectual property rights. Zed Books.

Siebenhuner, B. & Arnold, M. (2007). Organizational learning to manage sustainable development. *Business Strategy and the Environment, 16*, 339–353.

Siegel, D. S., Wessner, C., Binks, M., & Lockett, A. (2003). Policies promoting innovation in small firms: Evidence from the US and UK. *Small Business Economics, 20*(2), 121–127.

Silvestre, B., & Țîrcă, D. (2019). Innovations for sustainable development: Moving toward a sustainable future. *Journal of Cleaner Production, 208*, 325–332. doi:10.1016/j.jclepro.2018.09.244

288 *References*

Simard, C., & West, J. (2006). Knowledge networks and the geographic locus of innovation. In H. Chesbrough, W. Vanhaverbeke, & J. West (Eds.), *Open innovation: Researching a new paradigm* (pp. 220–240). Oxford: Oxford University Press.

Simpson, M., Taylor, N., & Barker, K. (2004). Environmental responsibility in SMEs: Does it deliver competitive advantage? *Business Strategy and the Environment, 13*(3), 156–171.

Sirmon, D. G., Hitt, M. A., Ireland, R. D., & Gilbert, B. A. (2011). Resource orchestration to create competitive advantage: Breadth, depth, and life cycle effects. *Journal of Management, 37*(5), 1390–1412.

Slavtchev, V. (2013). Proximity and the transfer of academic knowledge: Evidence from the spatial pattern of industry collaborations of East German professors. *Regional Studies, 47*(5), 686–702.

Slotegraaf, R. J. (2012). Keep the door open: Innovating toward a more sustainable future. *Journal of Product Innovation Management, 29*(3), 349–351.

Small, D. A., Loewenstein, G., & Slovic, P. (2007). Sympathy and callousness: The impact of deliberative thought on donations to identifiable and statistical victims. *Organizational Behavior and Human Decision Processes, 102*(2), 143–153.

Smink, M. M., Hekkert, M. P., & Negro, S. O. (2015). Keeping sustainable innovation on a leash? Exploring incumbents' institutional strategies. *Business Strategy and the Environment, 24*, 86–101.

Smol, M., Kulczycka, J., & Avdiushchenko, A. (2017). Circular economy indicators in relation to eco-innovation in European regions. *Clean Technologies and Environmental Policy, 19*(3), 669–678. doi:10.1007/s10098-016-1323-8

Sobrero, M., & Roberts, E. B. (2002). Strategic management of supplier-manufacturer relations in new product development. *Research Policy, 31*(1), 159–182.

Sociaal Economische Raad. (2001). *Corporate social responsibility.* Assen: Koninklijke Van Gorcum.

Soltanifar, M. (2016). Corporate entrepreneurship and triple helix. In R. Segers (Ed.), *Multinational management* (pp. 275–299). Cham: Springer. doi:10.1007/978-3-319-23012-2_15

Song, M., & Di Benedetto, C. A. (2008). Supplier's involvement and success of radical new product development in new ventures. *Journal of Operations Management, 26*(1), 1–22. doi:10.1016/j.jom.2007.06.001

Soosay, C. A., Hyland, P. W., & Ferrer, M. (2008). Supply chain collaboration: Capabilities for continuous innovation. *Supply Chain Management: An International Journal, 13*(2), 160–169. doi:10.1108/13598540810860994

Sparviero, S. (2019). The case for a socially orientated business model canvas: The social enterprise model canvas. *Journal of Social Entrepreneurship, 10*(2), 232–251.

Speckbacher, G., Bischof, J., & Pfeiffer, T. (2003). A descriptive analysis on the implementation of balanced scorecards in German-speaking countries. *Management Accounting Research, 14*(4), 361–388.

Spieth, P., Schneckenberg, D., & Matzler, K. (2016). Exploring the linkage between business model (&) innovation and the strategy of the firm. *R&D Management, 46*(3), 403–413.

Spieth, P., Schneckenberg, D., & Ricart, J. E. (2014). Business model innovation–state of the art and future challenges for the field. *R&d Management, 44*(3), 237–247.

Spigel, B. (2015). The relational organization of entrepreneurial ecosystems. *Entrepreneurship Theory and Practice, 41*(1), 49–72.

References 289

Spigel, B., & Harrison, R. (2017). Toward a process theory of entrepreneurial ecosystems. *Strategic Entrepreneurship Journal, 12*, 151–168.

Spithoven, A., Clarysse, B., & Knockaert, M. (2011). Building absorptive capacity to organise inbound open innovation in traditional industries. *Technovation, 31*, 10–21.

Spithoven, A., Vanhaverbeke, W., & Roijakkers, N. (2013). Open innovation practices in SMEs and large enterprises. *Small Business Economics, 41*(3), 537–562.

Sri Lanka Tea Board. (2018). *Annual report*. Sri Lanka Tea Board, Colombo.

Stam, E. (2015). Entrepreneurial ecosystems and regional policy: A sympathetic critique. *European Planning Studies, 23*(9), 1759–1769.

Stame, N. (2004). Theory-based evaluation and types of complexity. *Evaluation, 10*(1), 58–76.

Steiber, A., & Alange, S. (2013). A corporate system for continuous innovation: The case of Google Inc. *European Journal of Innovation Management, 16*, 243–264.

Steiner, G. (2008). Supporting sustainable innovation through stakeholder management: A systems view. *International Journal of Innovation and Learning, 5*(6), 595–616.

Steinmo, M. (2015). Collaboration for innovation: A case study on how social capital mitigates collaborative challenges in university-industry research alliances. *Industry and Innovation, 22*, 597–624.

Steinmo, M., & Rasmussen, E. (2016). How firms collaborate with public research organizations: The evolution of proximity dimensions in successful innovation projects. *Journal of Business Research, 69*(3), 1250–1259.

Steinmo, M., & Rasmussen, E. (2018). The interplay of cognitive and relational social capital dimensions in university-industry collaboration: Overcoming the experience barrier. *Research Policy, 47*(10), 1964–1974.

Sterr, H. (2008). Assessment of vulnerability and adaptation to sea-level rise for the coastal zone of Germany. *Journal of Coastal Research, 242*, 380–393.

Stokols, D., Hall, K. L., Taylor, B. K., & Moser, R. P. (2008). The science of team science: Overview of the field and introduction to the supplement. *American Journal of Preventive Medicine, 35*(2), S77–S89.

Stopper, M., Kossik, A., & Gastermann, B. (2016). Development of a sustainability model for manufacturing SMEs based on the innovative doughnut economics framework. In *Proceedings of the International MultiConference of Engineers and Computer Scientists* (Vol. 2, pp. 16–18).

Strauss, A., & Corbin, J. M. (1990). *Basics of qualitative research: Grounded theory procedures and techniques*. Sage Publications, Inc.

Stubbs, W., & Cocklin, C. (2008). Conceptualizing a "sustainability business model". *Organization & Environment, 21*(2), 103–127.

Styhre, A., & Lind, F. (2010). Balancing centripetal and centrifugal forces in the entrepreneurial university: A study of 10 research centres in a technical university. *Technology Analysis & Strategic Management, 22*(8), 909–924.

Szekely, F., & Strebel, H. (2013). Incremental, radical and game-changing: Strategic innovation for sustainability. *Corporate Governance, 13*(5), 467–481.

Tapaninaho, R., & Kujala, J. (2019). Reviewing the stakeholder value creation literature: Towards a sustainability approach. In W. Leal Filho (Eds.), *Social responsibility and sustainability* (pp. 3–36). World Sustainability Series. Cham: Springer.

Teece, D. J. (1986). Profiting from technological innovation: Implications for integration, collaboration, licensing and public policy. *Research Policy, 15*(6), 285–305.

290   References

Teece, D. J. (2010). Business models, business strategy and innovation. *Long Range Planning, 43*(2), 172–194.

Thistlethwaite, D. L., & Campbell, D. T. (1960). Regression-discontinuity analysis: An alternative to the ex post facto experiment. *Journal of Educational Psychology, 51*(6), 309.

Thomas, L. D., & Autio, E. (2019). *Innovation Ecosystems.* Available at SSRN 3476925. Retrieved from https://ssrn.com/abstract=3476925

Paillé, P., & Halilem, N. (2019). Systematic review on environmental innovativeness: A knowledge-based resource view. *Journal of Cleaner Production, 211*, 1088–1099.

Tijssen, R., & Yegros, A. (2017). UK universities and European industry. *Nature, 544*(7648), 35.

Tijssen, R. J. (2018). Anatomy of use-inspired researchers: From Pasteur's Quadrant to Pasteur's Cube model. *Research Policy, 47*(9), 1626–1638.

Tikkanen, H., Lamberg, J. A., Parvinen, P., & Kallunki, J. P. (2005). Managerial cognition, action and the business model of the firm. *Management Decision, 43*(6), 789–809.

Tiwana, A., Konsynski, B., & Bush, A. A. (2010). Platform evolution: Coevolution of platform architecture, governance, and environmental dynamics, *Information Systems Research, 21*, 675–687.

Tripsas, M., & Gavetti, G. (2000). Capabilities, cognition, and inertia: Evidence from digital imaging. *Strategic Management Journal, 21*, 1147–1161.

Tsai, W. (2001). Knowledge transfer in intraorganizational networks: Effects of network position and absorptive capacity on business unit innovation and performance. *Academy of Management Journal, 44*(5), 996–1004.

Turner II, B. L., Kasperson, R. E., Matson, P. A., McCarthy, J. J., Corell, R. W., Christensen, L., . . . Schiller, A. (2003). A framework for vulnerability analysis in sustainability science. *Proceedings of the National Academy of Sciences of the United States of America, 100*(14), 8074–8079.

United Nations. (2015). *Transforming our world: The 2030 agenda for sustainable development, resolution adopted by the General Assembly, 25 September, A/RES/70/1, United Nations, New York.*

United Nations. (2020). *Sustainable development goals.* Retrieved from https://sustainabledevelopment.un.org/sdgs

UNDRR. (2019). Terminology. Retrieved from https://www.unisdr.org/we/inform/terminology

Unruh, G. C. (2000). Understanding carbon lock-in. *Energy Policy, 28*(12), 817–830.

Uzzi, B. (1997). Social structure and competition in interfirm networks: The paradox of embeddedness. *Administrative Science Quarterly, 42*(1), 35–67.

Vachon, S., & Klassen, R. D. (2008). Environmental management and manufacturing performance: The role of collaboration in the supply chain. *International Journal of Production Economics, 111*(2), 299–315.

Valkokari, K. (2015). Business, innovation, and knowledge ecosystems: How they differ and how to survive and thrive within them. *Technology Innovation Management Review, 5*(8), 17–24.

van Bommel, H. W. M. (2011). A conceptual framework for analyzing sustainability strategies in industrial supply networks from an innovation perspective. *Journal of Cleaner Production, 19*(8), 895–904.

van de Vrande, V., De Jong, J. P., Vanhaverbeke, W., & De Rochemont, M. (2009). Open innovation in SMEs: Trends, motives and management challenges. *Technovation, 29*(6–7), 423–437.

References   291

Van der Borgh, M. v. d., Cloodt, M., & Romme, A. G. L. (2012). Value creation by knowledge based ecosystems: Evidence from a field study. *R&D Management, 42*(2), 150–169.

Van der Have, R. P., & Rubalcaba, L. (2016). Social innovation research: An emerging area of innovation studies? *Research Policy, 45*(9), 1923–1935.

van der Heijden, K. (2005). *Scenarios. The art of strategic conversation.* London: Wiley.

van Echtelt, F. E. A., Wynstra, F., van Weele, A. J., & Duysters, G. (2008). Managing supplier involvement in new product development: A multiple-case study★. *Journal of Product Innovation Management, 25*(2), 180–201. doi:10.1111/j.1540–5885.2008.00293

van Gelderen, M., Thurik, R., & Bosma, N. (2005). Success and risk factors in the pre-startup phase. *Small Business Economics, 24*(4), 365–380.

van Hemert, P., Nijkamp, P., & Masurel, E. (2013). From innovation to commercialization through networks and agglomerations: Analysis of sources of innovation, innovation capabilities and performance of Dutch SMEs. *The Annals of Regional Science, 50*(2), 425–452.

van Kleef, J. A., & Roome, N. J. (2007). Developing capabilities and competence for sustainable business management as innovation: A research agenda. *Journal of Cleaner Production, 15*(1), 38–51.

Vankan, A., Frenken, K., & Castaldi, C. (2014). Designing for a living? Income determinants among firm founders in the Dutch design sector. *Industry and Innovation, 21*(2), 117–140.

Varadarajan, R. (2017). Innovating for sustainability: A framework for sustainable innovations and a model of sustainable innovations orientation. *Journal of the Academy of Marketing Science, 45*(1), 14–36.

Verganti, R. (2009). *Design driven innovation: Changing the rules of competition by radically innovating what things mean.* Boston, MA: Harvard Business Press.

Vimalnath, P., Tietze, F., Eppinger, E., & Sternkopf, J. (2019). *Open, semi open or closed? Towards an intellectual property strategy framework.* Presented at the 19th European Academy of Management (EURAM) Conference, Lisbon (Portugal), 26–28 June 2019.

Voinea, C. L., Logger, M., Rauf, F., & Roijakkers, N. (2019). Drivers for sustainable business models in start-ups: Multiple case studies. *Sustainability, 11*(24), 6884.

Von Hippel, E. (2007). Horizontal innovation networks – By and for users. *Industrial and Corporate Change, 16*(2), 293–315.

Vorbach, S., Müller, C., & Poandl, E. (2019). Co-creation of value proposition: Stakeholders co-creating value propositions of goods and services. In *Management for professionals.* Cham: Springer. doi:10.1007/978-3-319-97788-1_5

Vörösmarty, C. J. (2000). Global water resources: Vulnerability from climate change and population growth. *Science, 289*(5477), 284–288.

Waddock, S. A. (1988). Building successful social partnerships. *MIT Sloan Management Review, 29*(4), 17.

Wadin, J., & Ahlgren, K. (2019). Business models for sustainability—Change in dynamic environments. *Journal of Business Models, 7*(1), 13–38.

Wagner, M. (2009). The links of sustainable competitiveness and innovation with openness and user integration: An empirical analysis. *International Journal of Innovation and Sustainable Development, 4*(4), 314–329.

Wagner, S. M. (2010). Supplier traits for better customer firm innovation performance. *Industrial Marketing Management, 39*(7), 1139–1149. doi:10.1016/j.indmarman.2009.12.001

292   References

Walker, S. (2014). *Designing sustainability: Making radical changes in a material world.* Oxon: Routledge.

Waller, M. A., & Fawcett, S. E. (2013). Data science, predictive analytics, and big data: A revolution that will transform supply chain design and management. *Journal of Business Logistics, 34*(2), 77–84. doi:10.1111/jbl.12010

Walrave, B., Talmar, M., Podoynitsyna, K. s., Romme, G. L., & Verbong, G. P. J. (2018). A multi-level perspective on innovation ecosystems for path-breaking innovation. *Technological Forecasting and Social Change, 136*, 103–113.

Walter, A., Ritter, T., & Gemünden, H. (2001). Value creation in Buyer-seller relationships. theoretical considerations and empirical results from a supplier's perspective. *Industrial Marketing Management, 30*(4), 365–377.

Wang, C., & Hu, Q. (2017). Knowledge sharing in supply chain networks: Effects of collaborative innovation activities and capability on innovation performance. *Technovation.* doi:10.1016/j.technovation.2017.12.002

WCED, S. W. S. (1987). World commission on environment and development. *Our Common Future, 17*, 1–91.

Weber, M., Hoogma, R., Lane, B., & Schot, J. (1999). *Experimenting with sustainable transport innovations: A workbook for strategic niche management.* Seville/Enschede: Universiteit Twente.

Weerawardena, J., McDonald, R. E., & Mort, G. S. (2010). Sustainability of nonprofit organizations: An empirical investigation. *Journal of World Business, 45*, 346–356.

Weerawardena, J., & Mort, G. S. (2012). Competitive strategy in socially entrepreneurial nonprofit organizations: Innovation and differentiation. *Journal of Public Policy & Marketing, 31*(1), 91–101.

Weiss, C. H. (1995). Nothing as practical as good theory: Exploring theory-based evaluation for comprehensive community initiatives for children and families. In J. P. Connel (Eds.). *New approaches to evaluating community initiatives: Concepts, methods, and contexts, 1* (pp. 65–92). Queenstown, MD: Aspen Institute.

White, H. (2009). Theory-based impact evaluation: Principles and practice. *Journal of Development Effectiveness, 1*(3), 271–284.

White, H. (2014). Current challenges in impact evaluation. *The European Journal of Development Research, 26*(1), 18–30.

White, H. (2019). The twenty-first century experimenting society: The four waves of the evidence revolution. *Palgrave Communications, 5*(1), 47.

White, M. A. (2013). Sustainability: I know it when I see it. *Ecological Economics, 86*, 213–217.

Whiteman, G., Walker, B., & Perego, P. (2013). Planetary boundaries: Ecological foundations for corporate sustainability. *Journal of Management Studies, 50*(2), 307–336.

Wickramagamage, P. (2017). Role of human agency in the transformation of the biogeography of Sri Lanka. *Ceylon Journal of Science, 46*(5), 19–31.

Wiek, A., Ness, B., Schweizer-Ries, P., Brand, F. S., & Farioli, F. (2012). From complex systems analysis to transformational change: A comparative appraisal of sustainability science projects. *Sustainability Science, 7*(1), 5–24.

Wilbanks, T., Lankao, P. R., Bao, M., Berkhout, F., Cairncross, S., Ceron, J.-P., . . . Zapata-Marti, R. (2007). Industry, settlement and society. Climate Change 2007: Impacts, adaptation and vulnerability. Contribution of Working Group II. In M. L. Parry, O. F. Canziani, J. P. Palutikof, P. J. v. d. Linden, & C. E. Hanson (Eds.),

IPCC Fourth Assessment Report of the Intergovernmental Panel on Climate Change. Cambridge: Cambridge University Press.

Wilby, R. L. (2008). Constructing climate change scenarios of urban heat island intensity and air quality. *Environment and Planning B: Planning and Design, 35*(5), 902–919.

Wilkinson, I. F. (1996). Distribution channel management: Power considerations. *International Journal of Physical Distribution and Logistics Management, 26*(5), 31–41.

WILPF. (2019a). *Annual report 2018.* Retrieved from https://www.wilpf.org/wp-content/uploads/2019/05/WILPF_Annual-Report-2018_web-spreads-1.pdf

WILPF. (2019b). *Our movement.* Retrieved from https://www.wilpf.org/our-movement/

WIPO, (2004). *Intellectual Property Handbook: policy, law and use.* ISBN 978-92-805-1291-5.

Women's International League for Peace and Freedom. (1983). *The women's international league for peace and freedom: Papers 1915–1978.* Sanford, NC: Microfilming Corporation of America.

World Commission on Environment and Development. (1987). *Our common future.* Oxford/New York: Oxford University Press.

Worley, C. G., Feyerherm, A. E., & Knudsen, D. (2010). Building a collaboration capability for sustainability: How Gap Inc. is creating and leveraging a strategic asset. *Organizational Dynamics, 39*(4), 325–334.

Wu, J., Wu, Z., & Si, S. (2016). The influences of Internet-based collaboration and intimate interactions in buyer-supplier relationship on product innovation. *Journal of Business Research, 69*(9), 3780–3787. doi:10.1016/j.jbusres.2015.12.070

WWF. (2019). *Annual review 2018.* Retrieved from https://d2ouvy59p0dg6k.cloudfront.net/downloads/wwfintl_annualreview20182.pdf

WWF. (2020). *Annual review 2029.* Retrieved from https://d2ouvy59p0dg6k.cloudfront.net/downloads/wwfintl_annualreview2019.pdf

Xavier, A. F., Naveiro, R. M., Aoussat, A., & Reyes, T. (2017). Systematic literature review of eco-innovation models: Opportunities and recommendations for future research. *Journal of Cleaner Production, 149*, 1278–1302.

Xu, G., Wu, Y., Minshall, T., & Zhou, Y. (2018). Exploring innovation ecosystems across science, technology, and business: A case of 3D printing in China. *Technological Forecasting & Social Change, 136*, 208–221.

Yamakawa, Y., Yang, H., & Lin, Z. J. (2011). Exploration versus exploitation in alliance portfolio: Performance implications of organizational, strategic, and environmental fit. *Research Policy, 40*(2), 287–296.

Yeniyurt, S., Henke, J. W., & Yalcinkaya, G. (2014). A longitudinal analysis of supplier involvement in buyers' new product development: Working relations, inter-dependence, co-innovation, and performance outcomes. *Journal of the Academy of Marketing Science, 42*(3), 291–308. doi:10.1007/s11747-013-0360-7

Yin, R. K. (2003). *Case study research: Design and methods.* Los Angeles, CA: Sage Publications, Inc., 5, 11.

Yin, R. K. (2009). *Case study research – Design and methods.* Los Angeles, CA: SAGE.

Yin, R. K. (2017). *Case study research and applications: Design and methods.* Los Angeles, CA: Sage Publications.

Yoon, B., Shin, J., & Lee, S. (2016). Open innovation projects in SMEs as an engine for sustainable growth. *Sustainability, 8*(2), 146.

Young, W., & Tilley, F. (2006). Can businesses move beyond efficiency? The shift toward effectiveness and equity in the corporate sustainability debate. *Business Strategy and the Environment, 15*(6), 402–415.

Yukl, G. (2009). *Leadership in organizations.* Englewood Cliffs, NJ: Prentice Hall.

Zhou, K. Z., & Li, C. B. (2012). How knowledge affects radical innovation: Knowledge base, market knowledge acquisition, and internal knowledge sharing. *Strategic Management Journal, 33*(9), 1090–1102.

Zhu, Q., Lowe, E. A., Wei, Y. a., & Barnes, D. (2007). Industrial symbiosis in China: A case study of the guitang group. *Journal of Industrial Ecology, 11*(1), 31–42. doi:10.1162/jiec.2007.929

Ziegler, N., Gassmann, O., & Friesike, S. (2014). Why do firms give away their patents for free? *World Patent Information, 37,* 19–25.

Zolkiewski, J. (2001). *The complexity of power relationships within a network.* Paper presented at the 17th Annual IMP Conference, Oslo.

Zott, C., Amit, R., & Massa, L. (2011). The business model: Recent developments and future research. *Journal of Management, 37*(4), 1019–1042. doi:10.1177/0149206311406265

Index

Note: **Bold** page numbers refer to **tables**; *italic* page numbers refer to *figures* and page numbers followed by "n" denote endnotes.

accountability: charities 201–202; description 201; learning and 199–200
Adams, R. 42, 44, 224
adaptive capacity 187
Adner, R. 98
Aguirre, B. E. 213
Ahuja, G. 127
Albareda, L. 43
Allen, R. 188
Amazon Web Service 155
Ardito, L. 215
Arnold, M. G. 126
Artificial Intelligence (AI) 149, 155
Arvidson, M. 203, 204
Aspara, J. 22
Athreye, S. 235
authenticity 67–68, **69,** 71

Balanced Scorecard (BSC) 202
Banerjee, A. V. 200
Barrios, A. 39
Barr, P. S. 19, 25
Bessant, J. 215, 217, 224
Big Data 149, 155
Bigliardi, B. 9, 118
biological assets, defined 240
Birchall, D. 241
Bloom, P. N. 116
Blün (Agriculture) 59, 61–62
Bocken, N. 43, 57, 66, 73, 75
Bogers, M. 144
Bossink, B. 5
Brass, D. J. 86
Bretschneider, U. 145
Brotsüchtig (Food) 60–61
"Brundtland Report" 3, 55

Buggy, L. 187
building resilience: climate change resilience 185–186; knowledge and innovation 185; traditional (or indigenous) climate knowledge (ICK) 185; vulnerability indicators (*see* vulnerability)
Burkhardt, M. E. 86
business ecosystem 98, 102, 103–104
Business Insider 213–214
business model canvas 42, 72; authenticity 67–68, **69**; Blün 61–62; Brotsüchtig 60–61; business modelling for sustainability 56–57; consciousness 62–63, **69**; defining sustainability 54–55; Die Fairmittlerei 61; framework development 62–68; limitations and suggestions for further research 74–75; meaning 63–64, **69**; methodology 58–62; pioneering role 66–67, **69**; proactive attitude 64–65, **69**; responsibility 65–66, **69**; sample of sustainability startup cases 60; startup success and entrepreneurial cognition 57–58; sustainability and economics 55–56; transparency 68, **69**
business model, definition 56
business model innovation: case selection 24, **24**; credibility shaping 32, 35; data acquisition and analysis 24–25, **26**; identifying the research gap 22–23; limitations and further research 35–36; managerial cognition 21–22; market approach shaping 31, 35; process, defined 20; product and/or service offering shaping 31–32, 35; research

Index

design 23–25; role of manager–stakeholder interaction (*see* manager–stakeholder interaction); shaping processes 28, **29–30**; stakeholder interaction 21; sustainable business model innovation 20–21; three shaping processes and related types of managerial cognition 34–35; value proposition, changes in 24, **24**

Castaldi, C. 235
Ceptureanu, E. G. 41, 42
charismatic leadership *173, 174*
charity sector: data 204–207; evaluation and impact practices 209–210; main findings 207–209; measuring impact 196–204; results 207–210; sample 205–206; survey 204–205, *206, 207*; typology per size and sector 209, **210**
Charter, M. 109
Cheng, C. C. J. 90
Chesbrough, H. 117, 144
Chief Executive Officers (CEOs) 145
"chronic kidney disease of unknown aetiology (CKDu)" 256n3
Cillo, V. 215, 243
circular economy: eco-innovations and 80–81, **81**; effect of buyer-supply network collaboration 90; limitations 92; network theory 84; power and innovation 84–85; power in reference to others 86; spatial-linked collaboration 89–90; strong ties and incremental innovation 87–88; supplier collaboration for innovation 81–82; from supply chains to supply networks 82–83; traditional measures of power in networks 85–86; weak ties and radical innovation *88,* 88–89
circular value chain **81**
Clark, T. 109
climate change resilience 185–186
climate exposure 187
climate vulnerability 186–187, *187*
Cloodt, M. 100
Cloud 149, 155
Cobben, D. 8
coercive isomorphism 202
coherent logic model 204
Colgan, D. 235
collaboration 89, 130; effect of buyer-supply network collaboration 90; network collaboration literature 97, 102, **102**; for radical innovation

130–133; R&D collaboration 131–132; spatial-linked collaboration 89–90; supplier collaboration for innovation 81–82; types and network collaborations **102**
community-based adaptation (CBA) 187
consciousness 62–63, **69,** 71
"contextual vulnerability" 193
Cousins, P. 83
Cradle to Cradle (C2C) standards 82
CSR (Corporate Social Responsibility) 73
cultural values: cultural change for sustainable innovation 168–173, *169*; dialogue strategy 170; leadership for sustainable innovation 173–175; learning strategy 169–170; managing sustainable innovational values 175–181; motivating and development strategies 169; organizational culture and business ideas for innovation 163–168; power strategies 169; rational and planned strategies 169
Customer Service Requests (CSRs) 158

Daub, C. H. 39
'decoupling' process 195
de Jesus, A. 80
de Langen, F. 5
Del Giudice, M. 215
Delmas, M. A. 235
de Man, A. P. 5
Dentchev, N. 40
Denyer, D. 224
design patents 232
design rights: description 232–233; motives to 235–236, **236**; properties of 233
"2030 Development Agenda" 126
D-Grade case **26,** 27–28
Die Fairmittlerei (Social service provider/NGO) 59, 61
differences-in-differences (DD) approach 199
DiMaggio, P. J. 202
Di Minin, A. 142, 145
discontinuous or breakthrough innovation 217
Dommerholt, E. 214, 218, 222
Dosi, G. 224
Doughnut Economy 42
Drabe, V. 82
Dubinsky, A. 217
Duflo, E. 200
Duysters, G. 134

Ebrahim, A. 202
eco-effectiveness 80
eco-efficiency 4, 80, 129
eco-innovations 90, *91,* 126; and circular economy 80–81, **81**; defined 241; environmental impact of innovation 3; environmental innovations 80; green innovations 80; network effects 8; outputs, conceptual model *91*; sustainability-oriented innovations 80
ecological ceiling 42
Ecology of Business Models Experimentation Map 57
economics, definition of 71
economic sustainability 71
Economy for the Common Good 56
eco-product innovations 81
ecosystems: business ecosystem 98, 102, 103–104; customer value creation 103; entrepreneurial ecosystem 100–101, 102, 105; immunity 245; incumbent actors 105–106; innovation ecosystem 98–99, 102, 104; knowledge ecosystem 100, 102; network collaboration literature 97, 102, **102**; open innovation (OI) 93, 97–101; strategic, tactical, and operational activities 104–105; in sustainability transitions 103–106
Effective giving or *What Works Movement* 199
efficiency innovation 111
elimination innovation 111
enablers of firms, in research centers: forwarding enablers *134,* 139–140; knowledge-transfer enablers *134,* 137–139; steering enablers 133–137, *134*
entrepreneurial ecosystem 100–101, 102, 105
entrepreneurial leadership *173,* 174
entrepreneurship 58

Fassio, C. 235
Forest Stewardship Council (FSC) 47
forwarding enablers: end phase *134*; spin-off projects 139–140
Fourth Industrial Revolution (Industry 4.0) 149
Franco, M. A. 82, 85, 87
Frankl, V. E. 63
Frattini, F. 142
Freeman, R. E. 21, 118

Galati, F. 9, 118
Gavetti, G. 25
Geels, F. W. 222, 224
Geissdoerfer, M. 39
geographical proximity, defined 89
Ghisetti, C. 235
Ginsberg, J. M. 116
Global Alliance for Banking on Values (GABV) 162; business idea and guiding principles 164, *165;* choosing and combining change strategies *171;* communities of practice **172**; cultural change and leadership 162–163; dialogue, learning, and development 170–173; GABV Leadership Academy 175; leadership and innovation 174–175; meaning 164–165; MSIV *177,* 178; positioning 167–168; sustainable innovation 162; uniqueness 165–166; Value-based Strategy Map 177–181; values and guiding principles *166,* 166–167
'The Golden Standard' 199
Goldstein, D. B. 116
Gomes, L. A. d. V. 102
Gomez-Mejia, L. R. 250
Granovetter, M. S. 87
green growth terminology 194
Greenwashing or superficial CSR 67
greenwashing practices 235
Gunarathne, N. 243

Hailey, J. 41
Heaton, S. 144
Herstatt, C. 82
Hinkel, J. 193
Hockerts, K. 126
homophily 87
Huber, M. 145
Huff, A. S. 19
Hulme, D. 196
Huotari, P. 43
Hu, Q. 90

idea suggestion platform (ISP) 149; bottom-up innovation program 149–151; build consensus for innovation *151,* 151–152; case firm, introduction of **148,** 148–149; challenges of 159–160; change agent 146, 147, 156–157; consensus of sustainable innovation 154–155; current status 157; evaluation of ideas *151,* 152–153; evaluation

298 *Index*

results 159–160; firm A's innovation manager 153–154; idea proposal *151,* 152, 156; implementation of ideas *151,* 153; innovation training program 154; innovators for sustainable innovation 158–159; NIH syndrome 159; opportunity of new business 158; process of 151–153; reigniting innovation 149, *150*; systematic knowledge management: 145–146; thinking about continuing ideas 160; work process improvement 157

impact perspective **12–14,** 14–15; in building resilience 185–194; holistic perspective on *15*; innovations' environmental or social impact 12; intellectual property rights 229–238; measurement challenge 11–12; measuring sustainable innovations performance, challenges in 239–256; on organizational performance 213–227; strategic or symbolic 195–211

incremental innovation 125, 216–217; "carbon lock-in" 129; defined 127; knowledge and skills 131; and radical innovation, distinction between **128**

Industrial symbiosis (IS) 89

Information Technology (IT) 145

inherent urban vulnerability 190–192

innovation collaboration: breadth of 131; defined 125; depth 131

innovation ecosystem 98–99, 102, 104

innovation-oriented supply network partnership 79

Innovations for Poverty Action (IPA) 199

innovativeness, defined 44

institutional theory 195

intellectual property rights (IPR) 229–230, 238n1; applicable to sustainable innovation 232–233; archetypes of sustainable innovation 231, **233**; design rights, motives to 235–236, **236**; patent innovation, motives to 234, **236**; research avenues 237–238; towards a research agenda 236–238; trademarks, motives to 234–235, **236**

intergenerational environmental strategies 221

intergenerational social strategies 221

International Union for the Conservation of Nature (IUCN) 46

Internet of Things (IoT) 149

intragenerational environmental strategies 221

intragenerational social strategies 221

inventions, defined 232

Isenberg, D. 100

'I-TOGETHER' 152, 155, 158

Jaskyte, K. 50

Jeanrenaud, S. 224

Joyce, A. 226

Kaplan, R. S. 242

Kennedy, S. 8

Kiefer, C. P. 250

knowledge ecosystem 100, 102

knowledge-transfer enablers: goal alignment and clarification of expectations 137–138; high levels of firm involvement 138–139; mutual understanding and trust through social embeddedness 138; performance phase *134,* 137, 141

Krcmar, H. 145

Kremer, M. 200

Lamming, R. 83

Lane, E. L. 235

Lankao, P. 188, 192

Layrisse, F. 39

leadership for sustainable innovation: charismatic leadership *173,* 174; entrepreneurial leadership *173,* 174; GABV 174–175; participative leadership *173,* 173–174; perspectives on *173*; transforming leadership *173, 173*

Leimeister, J. M. 145

Liket, K. 196

Logger, M. 5

Logical Framework Approach (LFA) or Logframes 197

Lyon, F. 203, 204

Maas, K. 196

managerial cognition 20, 21–22; boundary beliefs 22, 23, 34; industry or corporate recipe 22, 23, 34; manager-stakeholder interaction 32–34; product ontologies 22, 23, 34; reputational rankings 22, 23, 34–35

manager–stakeholder interaction: archival data sources 24, 25, **26**; axial coding 25; in enabling managerial cognitive change 32–34; latent stakeholders 34;

open coding 25; outside-in perspective 33; selective coding 25; semi-structured interviews 24–25, **26**; stakeholder-induced managerial cognitive change 26–28; stakeholder types 33

managing sustainable innovational values (MSIV): cultural values and innovation 175–177; GABV *177, 178*; Value-based Strategy Map 177–181

Marine Stewardship Council (MSC) 47

Martins, L. L. 25

McDonald, R. E. 44, 50

McNamara, K. E. 187

meaning 63–64, **69**

Mendonca, S. 80

Meyer, J. W. 202

Microsoft's Azure Cloud 155

Mimura, N. 186

Mishina, Y. 22

mission innovation 50

Mitchell, R. K. 21, 33

Montresor, S. 235

Moore, J. F. 98

Morris Lampert, C. 127

Mort, G. S. 39, 44

multifarious sustainability issues 4

Multi-Level Perspective (MLP) 94

Munasinghe, M. 244

mutatis mutandis 226

Nagy, D. 217

Narasimhan, R. 82

Narayanan, S. 82

Natural Plastics (NP) case **26,** 27

Netherlands Fundraising Regulator (CBF) 204

network centrality 85; betweenness centrality 85, 86; closeness centrality 85–86; degree centrality 85

network perspective 4, 7–9, **8–9**; eco-innovations in circular economy 79–92; holistic perspective on *15*; open innovation and sustainability 93–107; sustainable innovation 109–122

network theory perspective 80, 84

new product development (NPD) process 215–216

niches 220

Nidumolu, R. 219

NIH (Not-Invented-Here) syndrome 160

Noke, H. 216

nonprofit organizations (NPOs): business model framework 43, *43,* 51–52; comparing perspectives

on sustainability **41**; defined 41; documentary research 45; 'financial' customers 43; findings and research propositions 49–51; literature review 44–45; long-term existence 45; materials on innovations 45; methodology 44–45; multiple income streams *43*; Oxfam (case study) 48–49; programmatic and operational framework 43; sustainable business model **41,** 41–44; sustainable innovation 44; Women's International League for Peace and Freedom (WILPF) (case study) 47–48; World Wide Fund for Nature (WWF) (case study) 46–47

Norton, D. P. 242

Not-Invented-Here (NIH) syndrome 120

Nunn, P. D. 186

open innovation (OI): absorptive capacity 144; actors of collaboration 117; adoption 142; advantages of 93; barriers 118; bi-directional relationship 119; definition of 142, 143, 144; depth 143; dimensions of ecosystems 102; ecosystem types and characteristics 93, 97–101; entrepreneurial, financial and innovation reasons 118; external networks, use of 109; knowledge and partnership 130; knowledge management platforms 142–143; policy makers and firms 107; in sustainability transition (*see* sustainability transitions); sustainable innovation using 143–144; types and network collaborations **102**

open sustainable innovation (OSI): barriers 120, 121; creation of 119; defined 118; direct and indirect stakeholders 119; framework *121*; Not-Invented-Here (NIH) syndrome 120; stakeholders, direct and indirect 119

'operational optimization' level 224

organizational culture: and business ideas for innovation 163, *164*; clear identity 163; GABV (*see* Global Alliance for Banking on Values (GABV)); image of future 163

organizational decoupling, process of 202

organizational learning 200–201

organizational performance: defining sustainable innovation 215–218;

300 *Index*

incremental and radical innovation *216,* 216–217; innovation compass and innovation spaces 215–216; proposed definition of sustainable innovation 217–218; sustainability performance construct 218–222, *219*; sustainable innovation analysis framework (SIAF) 222–227

organizational SI 111

Osterwalder, A. 42, 56

Overy, P. 224

Oxfam (case study) 48–49

'PACE-SD Methodology' 187

Pacific Centre of Environment and Sustainable Development (PACE-SD) 187

Paquin, R. L. 226

participative leadership *173,* 173–174

patent: description 232; innovation, motives to 234, **236**; properties of 233

Perez Salgado, F. 5

Perkmann, M. 131

Perl-Vorbach, E. 116

Petersen, A. S. 186, 187

Petruzzelli, A. M. 215

Phaal, R. 102

Piccaluga, A. 142

Pigneur, Y. 42, 56

pioneering role 65, 66–67, **69,** 71

plantation agriculture sector: annual and perennial crops 256n1; challenges 240–241, **243**; herbicide-free integrated weed management (HFIWM) 245–246, **246, 247**; strip-spreading of tea bushes (SSTB) 245, **246, 247**; tea industry in Sri Lanka 244–245

Porac, J. 22

Post-Growth Economy 56

Powell, W. W. 202

power: definition of 84; existence of strong ties 87–88; and innovation 84–85; in networks, traditional measures 85–86; "outside perspectives" 88; "overembeddedness," notion of 88; position in network 87; in reference to others 86

3P – "people, planet, profits" 55

Prahalad, C. 219

proactive attitude 64–65, **69,** 71

Probert, D. R. 102

process perspective 4–5, 9–10, **10–11**; cultural values 162–182; firms'

innovativeness and competitiveness 9; holistic perspective on *15*; making innovation sustainable 142–161; organizations' culture and mindset 10; role of research centers 125–141; social and environmental value 9

process SI 111, 231

product SI 111, 231

profiting from technological innovation (PFI) framework 229

Przychodzen, J. 241

Przychodzen, W. 241

Pujari, D. 81

Puumalainen, K. 43

Qin, H. 188, 192

radical innovation 217; collaboration for 130–133; defined 127; organizational performance *216,* 216–217; R&D collaboration for 131–132; role of research centers (*see* research centers); sustainability transitions 129; weak ties and *88,* 88–89, 92

Radnor, Z. 216

randomized control trial 199

Rangaswami, M. 219

Rauf, F. 5

Rauter, R. 241, 243

Raworth, K. 42

Reficco, E. 39

regime 94, 224

regression discontinuity (RD) design 212n2

Rennings, K. 255

research and development projects (R&D) 80

research centers: "blue-sky" innovation 133; collaboration for radical innovation, role of 130–133; defined 132; enablers of firms 133–140; firms' innovation activities 125; incremental and radical innovation, role of 127–129, **128**; radical innovation, knowledge development 129–130; R&D partners 132; role in radical innovation 132–133; sustainability-oriented innovation 126–127; university-based research units 132–133

responsibility 65–66, **69,** 71

Ritala, P. 43

Robotic Process Automation (RPA) 158

Roijakkers, N. 5
Romme, A. G. L. 100
Rowan, B. 202
Rowley, T. J. 118

Saebi, T. 22
Salerno, M. S. 102
Sanderse, J. 5
Schaltegger, S. 41
Scherrer, Y. M. 39
Schlange, L. E. 21, 34
Schoenmakers, W. 134
Schuessler, J. 217
Seebode, D. 215
Seip, M. 236
sensitivity 187
service innovation 231
shaping processes: credibility shaping
30, 32; managerial cognitive change
28; market approach shaping 28, **29,**
31; product and/or service offering
shaping 28, **29–30,** 31–32
Sheu, C. 90
Shin, J. 120
Silvestre, B. 248
Simard, C. 87
Si, S. 90
Small Island Developing States (SIDS)
192–194
Social Enterprise Model Canvas 43
social impact, defining 196–199
social impact measurement 195;
accountability 201–202; coherent
logic model 204; defining impact
196–199; evaluation 198–199;
institutional pressure 202–203;
learning and accountability 199–200;
learning organization 204; long-term
results and logic models 197–198;
organizational learning 200–201;
symbolic logic model 203–204
social innovation 3, 220
social safety nets (SSN) 185, *191,* 192
social SI 111–112
spatial proximity 90
stakeholder-induced managerial cognitive
change 26–28; D-Grade case 27–28;
NP case 27; WeGo case 28
stakeholder interaction 19, 20, 21
Steady State Economy 56
steering enablers: "application-oriented"
researchers 135, 136; contractual
provisions 136–137; coordination

and internal firm management
of involvement 134; "crossover"
researchers 135–136, 140; establishing
phase *134,* 140; identifying the
crossover researchers 135–136;
influencing research activities 134–135;
knowledge-creation process 137;
"science-oriented" researchers 135;
"user-oriented" researchers 135, 136
Stimpert, J. L. 19
Stopper, M. 42
strategic niche management (SNM)
95–97
strategy perspective 4, 5, **6–7,** 7; beyond
business model canvas 53–75; business
model innovation for sustainability
19–36; coding scheme 37–38;
holistic perspective on *15;* nonprofit
organizations 39–52
"strong sustainability" 55
substitution innovation 111
success, definition of 58, 63
supply chain management (SCM) 82–83;
chain of suppliers 83; dyadic linkages
83; supply network 83
supply network (SN) perspective 79,
83, *83*
sustainability, defined 109
sustainability oriented innovation:
definition of 126–127; knowledge
sharing 129–130; role of incremental
and radical innovation 127–129, **128**
sustainability performance construct *219;*
business models 221–222; context
219–220; organizational culture 220;
regime orientation 219; strategies
220–221; transition orientation
219–220; values 220
sustainability start-ups 60; success and
entrepreneurial cognition 57–58
sustainability transitions 95–97;
dealignment and re-alignment
96; multi-level perspective (MLP)
95, 96; reconfiguration 96; role
of ecosystems 93–95, 103–106;
strategic niche management (SNM)
95, 96; technological substitution
96; transformation 96; transition
management (TM) 95, 96
sustainable business model (SBM) 231;
environmental and social 42–43;
factors 56–57; in general 40–41; with
multiple income streams *43;* nonprofit

302 *Index*

organizations (NPOs) **41,** 41–44; "soft success factors" 59, 74; sustainable innovation and 44
sustainable business model innovation 20–21
sustainable development: definition of 39; ecological principle 221; economic principle 221; social principle 220–221
sustainable development goals (SDGs) 39, 239
sustainable impact *see* impact perspective
sustainable innovation (SI) 241–242; in building resilience 185–194; for business model of nonprofit organizations 39–52; change agents as facilitators 146; classifications 114–116; data collection 147–148; definitions of 109, **112–114,** 116, 218; discussion of findings and implications for theory and practice 120–122; efficiency innovation 111; elimination innovation 111; environmental orientation 112; holistic perspective on *15*; institutional theory 117; and intellectual property rights 229–238; interview participants **147**; ISP (*see* idea suggestion platform (ISP)); multifarious perspective 3–5; open sustainable innovation 118–120; organizational 111; performance and measurement 242–243; in plantation agriculture sector (*see* plantation agriculture sector); process 111; product 111; research method 147–148; social 111–112; social benefits 114; strong leadership for change 144–145; substitution innovation 111; systematic knowledge management 145–146; technological 111; traditional innovation 116; two-level taxonomy of **115**; using open innovation 143–144
sustainable innovation analysis framework (SIAF) *223*; business model innovation 226–227; multiple value creation–regime-oriented strategies 225; multiple value creation–transition-oriented strategies 225; single value creation–regime-oriented strategies 224–225; single value creation–transition-oriented strategies 225
sustainable innovation measurement: under different dimensions 249, 252; dimension of sustainability

performance 248; establishment of accurate measurement methods 249, 252; solutions **254**; system boundary, determination of 249–250, 252–253; time horizon, determination of 250, 253; variability in sustainability performance 250–251, 253
sustainable open innovation, definition 143–144
sustainable strategies: intergenerational environmental strategies 221; intergenerational social strategies 221; intragenerational environmental strategies 221; intragenerational social strategies 221
symbolic logic model 203–204
system-level impacts of innovation 3

technological SI 111
Theory of Chance (ToC) 198
Tikkanen, H. 22
Țircă, D. 248
trademarks: description 232; motives to 234–235, **236**; properties of 233
trajectories 224
transforming leadership 173, *173*
transition management (TM) 95–97
transition-oriented businesses, defined 222
transparency 68, **69**
triple bottom line framework 4, 55, 126
triple layered business model (TLBM) 57, 226
Tripsas, M. 25

Uber moment 142
urban vulnerability: climate change scenarios 189; as impact 188–189, *189*; inherent 190–192; urban resilience 188

Valkokari, K. 102
value(s): defined 220; long-term relationships with clients 167; long-term, self-sustaining, and resilient 167; managing cultural values and innovation 175–177; principles embedded in culture 167; real economy 166–167; transparent and inclusive governance 167; triple-bottom-line approach 166; values-based strategy map 177–181
Value-based Strategy Map *178*; to attract more members to the movement

178; business development 177–178; to help members and strengthen networking 180; measuring impact and providing capital solutions 181; network and service development 180; overall development 180; partnership development 179; Partnerships and the #BankingOnValues movement 179; profile development 178; to raise visibility through advocacy and communication 179; results 181
value capture mechanisms 20, 221
value creation 221; financial value creation 223; multiple value creation 222, 223; single value creation 222–223; social, ecological and economic 49, 223
value delivery 221
Value Mapping Tool 57
value proposition 49, 221
Van den Ende, J. 8
Van der Borgh, M. v. d. 100
Varadarajan, R. 117
variability of sustainability performance: on innovation process 251, 253; on nature of biological assets 250–251, 253; on uncontrollable factors 251, 253
Ventresca, M. 22
Verkuil, A. H. 39
Voinea, C. L. 5
Vresh (Fashion) 59, 60
vulnerability *190,* 194n1; building resilience 186–192; climate

vulnerability 186–187, *187;* conceptual framework 186–188; defined 186, 188, 193; indicators, challenges 192–193; inherent urban vulnerability 190–192; reducing in urban centers and cities 188; social safety nets *191;* urban vulnerability 188–189, *189*

Walsh, K. 131
Wang, C. 90
"weak sustainability" 55
Weerawardena, J. 39, 44
WeGo case **26,** 28
West, J. 87
Whiteman, G. 8
Women's International League for Peace and Freedom (WILPF) (case study) 47–48
World Commission on Environment and Development (WCED) 213
World Economic Forum 174
World Wide Fund for Nature (WWF) (case study) 46–47
Wu, J. 90
Wu, Z. 90

Xu, G. 102

Yang, C.-l. 90
Yegros, A. 135
Yin, R. K. 147
Yoon, B. 120

Printed in the United States
By Bookmasters